Also by Alain Silver

David Lean and His Films
The Vampire Film
The Samurai Film
Film Noir: An Encyclopedic Reference to the
American Style, Editor
Robert Aldrich: a guide to references and resources
The Film Director's Team
Raymond Chandler's Los Angeles
More Things Than Are Dreamt Of

Also by James Ursini

David Lean and His Films
The Life and Times of Preston Sturges, An American Dreamer
The Vampire Film
Film Noir: An Encyclopedic Reference to the
American Style, Editor, 3rd Edition
More Things Than Are Dreamt Of

A Directors Guild of America Publication

Alain Silver and James Ursini

What Ever Happened to
Robert Aldrich?
His Life and His Films

Foreword by
Burt Lancaster

Special Research
Elizabeth Ward

Limelight Editions
New York

First Limelight Edition, July 1995

Copyright © 1995 by Alain Silver and James Ursini

All rights reserved under International and Pan-American Copyright Conventions. Published in the United States by Proscenium Publishers, Inc., New York.

Library of Congress Cataloging-in-Publication Data

Silver, Alain, 1947-
What ever happened to Robert Aldrich? : his life and his films / Alain Silver and James Ursini ; foreword by Burt Lancaster ; special research Elizabeth Ward. — 1st Limelight ed.
    p.   cm.
"A Directors Guild of America publication."
Includes bibliographical references and index.
ISBN 0-87910-185-7 (cloth)
   1. Aldrich, Robert, 1918-1983.   I. Ursini, James. II. Title.
PN1998.3.A44S56 1995
791.43'0233'092—dc20

                      95-9172
                      CIP

Contents

Acknowledgements

Thanks must go, first of all, to Robert Aldrich for making the films. Thanks to him also for providing prints and scripts back in the 1970s and bequeathing his extensive archives to the Directors Guild.

Much of the current volume is derived from two other works: the 1973 UCLA Master's thesis of Alain Silver, which was updated and expanded by Silver and Elizabeth Ward for the book <u>Robert Aldrich: a guide to references and resources</u> published by G.K. Hall in 1979. The Special Research credit on this volume reflects the extensive work done by Elizabeth Ward on that book, substantial portions of which are wholly reproduced in the filmography of this volume. Even fifteen years later, her original notes and research files were of immeasurable value in writing this book.

Portions of the original thesis have appeared in diverse forms elsewhere and the history of those materials is part of this chronological acknowledgement process. The interview with Robert Aldrich was commissioned by *Film Comment*, and thanks for assistance on that go to Howard Suber at UCLA; Jerry Pam, William Aldrich, and Joan Bennett at Associates and Aldrich; and, at *Film Comment*, Austin Lamont, Melinda Ward, Richard Corliss, and Sayre Maxfield. *Film Comment* also published a piece on *Kiss Me Deadly,* which was based on a similar, stylistic analysis of *World of Ransom* developed in conjunction with Janey Place. A review of *Kiss Me Deadly* was originally published in the UCLA *Daily Bruin Intro* edited by Stan Berkowitz and Evelyn Renold.

The 1973 Masters thesis was reviewed by a UCLA Theater Arts Department Committee composed of Elyseo Taylor, Hugh Grauel, and Howard Suber and first published by University Microfilms, Ann Arbor, Michigan. Portions of the thesis chapter on *Attack!* were later published as an entry in Magill's Survey of Cinema, edited by Stephen L. and Patricia King Hanson. Portions of other thesis chapters were the basis for entries in Film Noir: An Encyclopedic Reference to the American Style, commissioned by Peter Mayer and originally edited by Mark Gompertz. Variants of the biographical information in the thesis were used in both the G.K. Hall book—where thanks go to Ronald Gottesman, Elizabeth Kubik, Barbara Garrey, Ronald M. Wright, and Ara Salibian—and as an entry on Aldrich co-written with Elizabeth Ward for the Dictionary of Literary Biography, published by the Gale Research Tower and edited by Randall Clark of BC Research.

In the original research Richard Symington and the Film Screening Cooperative at UCLA provided screening facilities for various prints. David Bradley, Blake Lucas, Lowell Peterson, and James Ursini helped with reference materials on other titles. Ian Cameron kindly provided a photo copy of René Micha's monograph.

Many more persons assisted with the research for the G.K. Hall volume, most of which was conducted at the Margaret Herrick Library of the Academy of Motion Picture Arts and Sciences in Beverly Hills with the help of Bonnie Baty, Terry Roach, Bonnie Rothbart, Stacy Endres, Carol Cullem, Mary Olivarez, Cheryl Behnke, and Sam Gill. Additional research help came from Anne Schlosser and Debra Bergman. Pierre Sauvage provided a pre-publication transcript of his interview. Pattie Zimmerman at Lorimar and Susan Pile at Warner Bros. helped with pre- release information on *The Choirboys* and *The Frisco Kid* respectively. Elmer and Christiane Silver and Paul and Roberta Ward helped proofread the manuscript.

For the current volume we are most indebted for the support of the Directors Guild of America, particularly from Selise Eiseman, the DGA Special Projects Officer, and Adele Field, who is in charge of DGA publications and assisted with the manuscript printing. The entire Special Projects Committee endorsed this project and lent the staff support of Samantha Williams, the Special Projects assistant, and others at the Guild. This is, after The Vampire Film and More Things Than Are Dreamt Of, our third book in as many years with Mel Zerman at Limelight Editions, which speaks most eloquently of our appreciation. It is also, along with the autobiographies of Norman Lloyd and Sheldon Leonard, the third volume of books produced through the DGA publications program that Limelight has published.

The material bequeathed to the DGA by Aldrich included his personal film prints and career production files, which the Guild houses at the UCLA Film and Television Archive and at the American Film Institute respectively. The DGA loaned scripts and illustrative materials from its collection and screened prints at its theater in Hollywood.

Adell Aldrich also reviewed drafts of the book, provided several key illustrations including the *film noir* photo, and offered her suggestions and support.

Many DGA members and others who knew and/or worked with Aldrich at various stages of his career shared their reminiscences, including (in chronological order) Robert Justman, Daisy Gerber, Buck Houghton, Bernard Tabakin, Cheryl Downey, George Schaffer, Paul Stanley, Norman Lloyd, Abraham Polonsky, Jerry Pam, and Robert Wise. We are also very grateful to Mr. Lancaster's business manager, Jack Ostrow, and secretary, Cindy, for helping coordinate his Foreword, which was completed less than a month before his death.

For the most recent research assistance, we thank Alan Braun, Gladys Irvis, Corinna Chaney, and Jeanne Reed of the Louis B. Mayer Library of the American Film Institute in the basement of which Aldrich's files and memorabilia are kept. Aldrich's director's chair and hand megaphone are displayed in the library itself. Howard Prouty, now at the Academy of Motion Picture Arts and Sciences Library, produced the catalogue of the extensive array of materials which was an invaluable research aid. Other research was done at the A.M.P.A.S. library in Beverly Hills; and Carl Thiede provided information on the television work. Of the illustrations not taken from the Aldrich collection or provided by Adell Aldrich, some were lent by David Chierichetti and the remainder are from the authors' personal collections. Most of the illustrations were the work of the set photographers. They are infrequently credited in books; but much as we would like to rectify fully that common omission, despite the resources of the Aldrich archives, we can only credit: Bernard Abramson (*The Killing of Sister George* [U.S.]); Jack Albin (*What Ever Happened to Aunt Alice*; other candids); Ted Allan (*4 for Texas*); Yani Begakis (Cinématheque Française award); Kenneth Bell (*The Legend of Lylah Clare; The Grissom Gang*); John Bryson (*Too Late the Hero*); Don Christie (*Vera Cruz; What Ever Happened to Baby Jane?; Hush...Hush, Sweet Charlotte*); S.W. "Marty" Crail (*Apache; Kiss Me Deadly*); Jack Gereghty (*Hustle*); Durward "Bud" Graybill (*The Flight of the Phoenix*); Norman Gryspeerdt (*The Dirty Dozen*); Enzo Papi and Giovanni Poletto (*Sodom and Gomorrah*); John Miehle (*The Big Street*); Ivan Nagy (*The Greatest Mother of 'Em All*); Al St. Hilaire (*Attack!; 4 for Texas*); Jack Shannon (*The Frisco Kid*); Ricky Smith (*The Angry Hills*); Phil Stern (*The Flight of the Phoenix*; various other candids); Orlando Suero (*Emperor of the North Pole; The Choirboys*); James and Linda Swarbrick (*The Killing of Sister George* [U.K.]); Michel Szabo (Aldrich Studios); Frank Tanner (*The Big Knife*); Anthony Ugrin (*Kiss Me Deadly*); Karl Heinz Vogelmann (*Twilight's Last Gleaming*); Steve Wever (*The Longest Yard*); and numerous others whose names could not be determined. The stills are reproduced courtesy of Associates and Aldrich, Allied Artists, Columbia

Pictures, Metro-Goldwyn-Mayer, 20th Century-Fox, United Artists, Universal, and Warner Bros.

Prints of the *Four Star Playhouse* episodes directed by Aldrich were screened at the U.C.L.A. Television Archive. Jessica Rosner at Kino International and Richard Peña of the Film Society of Lincoln Center helped stimulate interest in the early stages of this project by promoting the career retrospective of Aldrich's work in March, 1994. Later in the year Jean-Pierre Garcia and Michael Wilson did likewise in preparing for another career retrospective in November in Amiens and Paris, France.

Glenn Erickson helped with the plot summaries and proofread the final draft of the book. James Paris assisted with updating our production software. As always Linda Brookover also read portions of the manuscript and provided moral support throughout.

The analysis of *Kiss Me Deadly* which originally in *Film Comment* has been substantially edited. Details of the changes in the Interview with Aldrich are given in the Appendix. Although they are both revised, substantial amounts of material are from:

Preface

The beginnings of this book go back to our days as undergraduates in the film department at U.C.L.A. In putting together the bits and pieces that had already been written and variously published into one comprehensive volume, we had to confront again the same problem that all who have written studies of film directors and their work have faced: the subject of the book as a working professional and the subject as an *auteur*.

We use the French term for two reasons: the want of a better word in English and as a segue to discuss our critical approach. Since its inception, auteurism has been at once incontrovertibly valid and unavoidably polemical. Auteurism was born of an era when both the seventh art and its observers were not universally regarded as serious. In some quarters that is still true. Out of the struggle both to defy and to create convention came such outrageous pronouncements as the legendary "Nicholas Ray is the cinema!" from the auteur critics at *Cahiers du Cinema*. For many of those writers and their English counterparts at *Movie*, the work of "le gros Bob" Aldrich was as worthy of admiration as Nicholas Ray's. The difficulty for us, writing in the auteurist tradition long after the need for shock tactics had passed, was to resolve the issues of critical analysis and critical advocacy.

Many prominent critics have argued that criticism is by definition about evaluation. In the shorthand ratings devised by *Cahiers* that ranged from the four-starred *chef d'oeuvre* to the contemptuous black dot and in the epithets that described Andrew Sarris' hierarchies in <u>The American Cinema</u>, early auteurism was certainly grounded in evaluation. On the other hand, the details of film criticism, whatever the methodology, need not—and here we resist saying "should not"—be about value judgments. Clearly our interest in Robert

Aldrich and his films over more than twenty years has not been sustained because we thought his work was mediocre. If the reader wants to know, "Do we think that Robert Aldrich is a great director?" the simple answer is yes. Otherwise why would we have written this book? But the complex answer is that, as we did in our previous director study on David Lean, we must make a distinction between Robert Aldrich the person and Robert Aldrich the persona.

What makes a "great" directorial persona are not just some films which could be called "masterpieces" by the writers at *Cahiers* or anywhere else but a body of work with a consistency of theme and style, the classic auteurist "world view." On the other hand, a director is a person whose creative and practical responsibilities are part of the very complicated and costly process of making a motion picture. That process from casting to editing and its significant constraints such as budget or the MPAA ratings system are what the director as a person works through. The repetition of that process is what defines the director as a person. The finished product alone is what defines the director as persona.

This book has presented different challenges than the one on David Lean, whose work is not highly regarded by traditional auteurists or most critical writers in other methodologies. Still, the average filmgoer is likelier to know the name of the director of *Lawrence of Arabia* or *Doctor Zhivago* than of *The Dirty Dozen* or *The Longest Yard*. Both men, it seems to us, like most other "great" directors, did make a number of masterworks and did have an easily discernible world view. Like Aldrich, Lean wrote a few articles and expressed his opinions about filmmaking in interviews. Both men worked in subordinate capacities in the industry for more than a decade and gained reputations for being among the best at those jobs, Lean as an editor and Aldrich as an assistant director. After becoming directors both men were also the effective if not nominal producers of most of their films and the uncredited co-writers of many, which gave them a greater degree of control over their final pictures than many other directors. Working in another country and within a somewhat different system than Lean, Aldrich made the similar discovery that it was necessary to be involved as a producer and/or writer to protect one's vision. Unlike Lean, Aldrich was quite vocal about the time he spent fighting "the enemy," the studios and distributors who wanted to influence his decisions from casting to editing and who controlled his budgets. Both men lost time and money on projects that were never made or taken from them and given to others. But whereas Lean did not air many of his grievances publicly, Aldrich was an outspoken advocate of directors and a thoughtful adversary of what he deemed an imperfect system throughout his career. Aldrich's family, friends, and professional associates are of one voice in remembering that his outspoken behavior, beginning as a young filmmaker and up through his terms as president of the Directors Guild, alienated many in positions of power and cost him professionally in terms of lost projects and opportunities.

As a consequence, we decided that this book would be structured differently from our earlier director study of Lean and most other director studies. We begin with a lengthy biographical chapter that details Aldrich's career and, hopefully, creates a comprehensive portrait for the reader of Aldrich's multifaceted professional experiences primarily as director and producer. Having done this, we abandon the questions of production history and move to the finished films, which define Aldrich the directorial persona. Here several choices for the order in which the films were grouped and discussed were possible. Our choice was a compromise between the chronological and the generic. Rather than attempt to discuss each film exhaustively, the thematic groupings allow us to illustrate selectively how the filmmaker creates and modifies meaning. This process may be as much in evidence in the mediocre or "bad" pictures as in the "great" ones. But, while the amount of words which we devote to any one picture should not be taken as an indication of our personal value judgments or "favorites," it will be obvious that we have not devoted as much space to the films which we consider to be failures.

Our natural assumption about those who read the pages on Aldrich's films is that he or she has seen some or all of the pictures made by Robert Aldrich. If we, as critical writers, have any underlying belief, it must be that to understand the world view of Aldrich or any director, there is no substitute here or anywhere else for actually seeing the pictures. We have summarized or recapitulated portions of the films only when it is necessary to the critical discussion. For those who have not seen all the movies, plot summaries are included in the Filmography.

While this book has been extensively researched in Robert Aldrich's archives and elsewhere, on many occasions, particularly with filmographic data, different sources disagreed on factual points. In one or two instances, we have noted such discrepancies; but otherwise we have gone with the information from the source we considered more reliable. As always, we welcome any reader's comments, particularly with regard to errors or omissions. Two final notes: (1) So that the reader may quickly distinguish between films, plays, and books with the same title, we have italicized the film (and film project) names, underlined books, and put plays in quotes. (2) In quoted excerpts, we have reproduced the punctuation used in the original, so that film titles may appear in all caps or underlined; the reader will be readily able to distinguish them as the names of films or projects from the context.

Foreword

I've said it before and Bob Aldrich himself would probably have called it an "overused expression" in this business, but he was a sweetheart. He was a candid, no-nonsense man of conviction, who would stand up not only for what he believed but also for those individuals he valued. I first worked with Bob when Harold Hecht and I started up our production company. Hecht knew of Aldrich as a first assistant director who had a great reputation for bringing in difficult shows. In 1950 we hired him to be a production supervisor. He watched the money on two pictures, and he did an excellent job for us. But he wanted to move up to director, and we couldn't take a chance on a first-time director. Bob did start directing a couple of years later in television and he made a feature using the cast and crew from the *China Smith* series. He invited Harold Hecht and me to a screening, and we were quite impressed with how big a look he got with what we assumed was very little money. That's how we decided to offer him the directing job on *Apache*.

I've spoken of the disagreements we had on that picture before and how Bob and I both wanted to use the original ending that United Artists pressured us into changing. From the beginning of his directing career, a Bob Aldrich picture had to be a Bob Aldrich picture. He wasn't just being stubborn. When he thought he had found the way to shoot a scene or stage some action, he was impossible to dissuade until he at least got to try it his way. Bob not only brought *Apache* in on time and on budget, he made a good picture. And it did well at the box office. So we moved right on to *Vera Cruz* which had three times the budget, a much bigger risk for Hecht-Lancaster and a heavier responsibility for Bob. Despite some technical and location problems, Bob turned out an extraordinary action picture. It made a lot of money for us, and it gave Bob the chance to make his own deal with United Artists and start his own company.

We didn't work together again until *Ulzana's Raid* in 1971. That picture and *Twilight's Last Gleaming* a few years later are the kinds of project that I am proudest of making, because they had something to say about this country, its past, present, and future. That was one thing Bob and I always agreed on. I've explained before how I felt that some people have despaired about democracy in the United States. Some people took *Ulzana's Raid* and *Twilight* as entertainment, others saw an underlying truth about the good and bad in America. We all want the world to change for the better, and filmmakers have the unique opportunity to portray the possibilities for change in a moving and dramatic way.

Bob and I shared the disappointment in that there were good possibilities in *Twilight* that weren't brought out, and audiences didn't take to the picture. Bob had particularly high aspirations for it. Even though he made a few more pictures after *Twilight*, I don't think he ever got as fired up over a project again. Like many of his friends and associates, I went to see Bob just before he died. He wanted to talk about what good things had come to him in his life, not about his problems; but you knew that he didn't want to stick around any longer.

For all the fame those of us in this business may attain, we're all forgotten sooner or later. But not the films. I'd like to believe that in the future new generations will look at the work we did, look at all these pictures, and be moved by them. That's all the memorial we should need or hope for.

Burt Lancaster,
Century City, California

What Ever Happened To
Robert Aldrich?

Above, Aldrich directs Jack Palance and Ida Lupino in *The Big Knife* in early 1955, the first production of the Associates and Aldrich.

Biography

I...became fascinated with show business. I said to myself this is more fun than working in a bank or working in a newspaper. And I was a film nut...everybody was a film buff in those days when...the most fascinating and interesting part of show business was film. Ergo, my decision to go to California.[1]

"What Ever Happened to Robert Aldrich?" I got disgusted and came home but am scheduled to be back in New York by the end of this week.
Okay?...Okay![2]

Robert Burgess Aldrich was born in Cranston, Rhode Island, on August 9, 1918, the son of Edward and Lora Lawson Aldrich. His family was prominent in both banking and politics. A grandfather, Nelson W. Aldrich, was a four-term United States Senator. His Aunt Abby, who married John D. Rockefeller, Jr., was one of the founders of the Museum of Modern Art and the mother of his politically prominent cousins, including Nelson Aldrich Rockefeller, the longtime governor of New York and later U.S. Vice-President. One uncle, Richard, was a member of Congress, and another, Winthrop, was Ambassador to Great Britain in the Eisenhower administration.

Aldrich's mother died while he was still quite young, and his relationship with his father, whom he remembered as a "man of considerable means and reasonably intelligent; but very old school,"[3] was never close. Aldrich often did recall one particular life lesson: "My father once told me that anything really worth having is worth asking for, no matter how difficult it is to I've always

3

been convinced he was right."[4] What Aldrich remembered most fondly about his education was his participation in athletics, especially football. He played tackle at the Moses Brown School of Providence and was on the football and track varsity teams for three years at the University of Virginia. Aldrich was an economics major at Virginia's Wilson School and was ostensibly preparing to use his family connections to pursue a career in banking or in journalism with his father's publishing company. Although he attended college for four years, Aldrich failed to earn a bachelor's degree. In his final year at Virginia, Aldrich headed the dance society and booked such major orchestras as the Dorsey Brothers and Glenn Miller to play the campus. Rather than continue at college, Aldrich decided to try a show business career. Through the influence of his uncle Winthrop of Chase National, which had a banking relationship to RKO Studios, he secured a job as a production clerk. On May 21, 1941, he married his childhood sweetheart, Harriet Foster of Warwick Neck, Rhode Island, in Greensboro, North Carolina, and left for Hollywood.

On July 28, 1941 Aldrich began six months as a Production Clerk or Third Assistant Director at $25.00 for a six-day week. He was a self-described "gofer, you get coffee and you keep the time cards of the actors and the production reports."[5] Before and after the shooting day, Aldrich could also be pressed into service as a cut-rate chauffeur: "Once I had to pick up Ginny Simms in a 1930 Ford to take her to surprise birthday party that Kay Kaiser was throwing for her on the set of a musical. She wasn't too happy about me and the Ford."[6] While

working on the same picture, *Playmates*, Aldrich not only got a different perspective on big bands than he had as a college booker but was also quickly exposed to the less savory side of the glamourous entertainment business. He was the one most often assigned to roust a dissipated and dying John Barrymore, acting in his last film, from his fetid dressing room.

In early 1942, shortly after the United States entered World War II, Aldrich was promoted from "the lowest human animal on the production scale, the lowest form of life on the set"[7] to Second Assistant Director on *Joan of Paris*, starring Michele Morgan in her American debut and directed by Robert Stevenson. For the next two years, working at RKO on films directed by Irving Reis, Richard Wallace, Edward Dmytryk, and others, Aldrich quickly learned that the director is the "creative hub of what makes a picture work, and if you have any ambition, and you don't want to be a producer or a writer, then you want to be a director."[8] Although not many had risen from the ranks of assistant director to creative positions, Aldrich had unlimited aspirations to produce, write, *and* direct. He was drafted, but Aldrich "got a real break. I was thrown out of the Air Corps after a day and a half because of an old football injury."[9] Back on the set, the lack of manpower in the studios made a young, energetic, and eager assistant like Aldrich stand out.

When he graduated to Second Assistant Director in 1942, Aldrich became a member of the Screen Directors Guild, an organization of which he would become President thirty three years later. Before that, Aldrich would serve as Vice-President of the Guild while still an assistant director in 1946 and 1951 and would preside over its Assistant Directors Council in 1947-48. In 1960 after a merger of film and television directors, the organization became the Directors Guild of America, and Aldrich was Vice-President again in 1973-74. As then DGA President Gilbert Cates remarked about Aldrich's early career at his memorial service, "He must have been a phenomenal 'second' for his star shot upward and he quickly became first assistant to many of the great talents and mavericks of filmmaking: Jean Renoir, Charles Chaplin, Abraham Polonsky, Bill Wellman, Joseph Losey..."[10] Aldrich was, in fact, promoted to first assistant on a series of RKO shorts and then took the chance of leaving the security of a staff position at a studio to seek feature assignments. At Enterprise Studios, a small stage in East Hollywood often used by United Artists, Aldrich found feature work and more. From late 1945 to 1948, under contract to Enterprise, Aldrich worked as an assistant director, studio manager, and occasional writer. By 1949 Aldrich had established a reputation as a topnotch feature film first assistant director and worked on a freelance or project-by-project basis. He had also graduated to a better car in which he might chauffeur luminaries like William Faulkner back and forth to the studio.[11]

Opposite page, Aldrich in 1942 on the set on *The Big Street*, one of his first Second Assistant Director assignments. Stars Lucille Ball and Henry Fonda are at right on the stairway. Aldrich stands at bottom left by the crane with his right hand in his back pocket and First A.D. Albert van Schmus (in white hat) to his immediate left.

By the end of four more years, he had worked as a first assistant director on productions for all the major studios except Warners. In later interviews, he usually credited director Losey for showing him how to work with actors; Wellman for how to control the pace of the set; and Renoir for attention to authenticity and detail. Aldrich found Chaplin "a great artist but a terrible director. He couldn't communicate ideas to a performer; he could only show them how he would do it."[12] Chaplin, whom Aldrich did consider "an enormous contributor to the film as art and as a business," did teach him about "the impossibility of defeat. No matter what happens, he had enough energy and enthusiasm and confidence to overcome any disaster"[13] On the business side, Aldrich noticed that Robert Rossen made the most of the opportunities that came his way, and John Cromwell wore down the opposition with "infinite, endless patience,"[14] a directorial trait that Aldrich always admired but never fully acquired. Perhaps the greatest influence on Aldrich was director Lewis Milestone who, Aldrich later said, "understood what the game was. The game is power.... Milestone had all the tools, but above all he had the capacity to know when trouble was coming and how to deal with it."[15] Aldrich also discovered that "you learn from the bad directors. I don't mind naming a few of those bums. You learn from Leslie Fenton how not to alienate a crew, so they won't work for you, they'd drop a light on him rather than keep him on schedule."[16] Many of the directors for whom Aldrich worked reciprocated the admiration. "Aldrich was a marvelous man," according to Joseph Losey, "He had such immense energy and such good humour that everybody who worked with him adored him. His discipline, honesty and authority were tremendous. He was the top assistant in Hollywood at the time and...I've seldom had a closer relationship with anybody professionally"[17]

When he first arrived at RKO, Aldrich was still in top physical condition, as a shot of him standing with the crew of *The Big Street* in 1942 reveals. Over the next decade, Aldrich succumbed to the gastronomic excesses of Hollywood. "And when he stopped the rigors of athletic training," according to Losey, "he began to put on weight."[18] Despite his costume for his cameo appearance in Losey's *The Big Night* in 1951, by that time Aldrich claimed that he could no longer button his collars and had adopted the abiding affectation of wearing a tie draped around his neck and clasped to his shirt front. "I put on forty pounds, and I just didn't have the time or the money to get a brand new wardrobe."[19] By 1952, Aldrich and his wife had added four new members to their family, Adell (born 1943), William (1944), Alida (1947) and Kelly (1952). Both of Aldrich's older children would eventually work in the film industry and with him: Adell Aldrich as script supervisor and later director and William Aldrich as studio manager and later producer. Aldrich's younger daughter, Alida, was

Opposite page, Aldrich in 1951 in a bit part in Joe Losey's *The Big Night*, as a fight fan who offers Flanagan (Howland Chamberlin) a swig from his pint. Obviously, for an appearance in front of the camera, Aldrich could still knot his tie.

briefly on the production staff of the Aldrich Company. His younger son, Kelly, became a studio driver and eventually a transportation coordinator.

Throughout his apprenticeship, Aldrich benefited from a number of what he called "lucky breaks." While many budding motion picture careers were interrupted, if not ended, by the war, Aldrich's medical condition had exempted him. "Between '41 and '45 I was fired twice: once by Adolph Zukor for telling his nephew that he didn't know his ass from a hot rock, and once by Louis Mayer because one of his 'important' directors [Clarence Brown] had told him I was a Communist. Zukor was right and Mayer was wrong."[20] After the war more careers were interrupted, if not ended, by the House Un-American Activities Committee and its hearings on Communism in Hollywood. Many of the directors, writers, and producers with whom Aldrich had worked at RKO and elsewhere were blacklisted. Some went into exile, some, in contempt of Congress, even went to jail for refusing to testify before the committee. One of those who left the country, Joseph Losey, affirmed that "Bob Aldrich, as an assistant director, and I, as a director, were very much involved in the whole fight to keep the loyalty oath out of the Screen Directors' Guild."[21] Aldrich himself was "served but nobody ever picked up the subpoena, and I was never called to testify. Just fortunate...I was either too dumb or too young to be a Communist. If I had worked with Ring Lardner or Losey or Rossen or Polonsky or Butler or Trumbo or any of those guys, who were five or ten years older than I was, earlier, a kind of hero worship might have made it necessary for me to be a member of the party. But by the time I got into close contact with them, the heat was already on. They were already in trouble or about to be—the handwriting was on the wall. They weren't looking for recruits."[22]

Left, while working as a First Assistant Director on *Abbott and Costello Meet Captain Kidd* in 1952, Aldrich poses against the wall of a sound stage with celebrated cinematographer Stanley Cortez.

While he was never on either a blacklist or a gray-list, the existence of both did indirectly alter the course of Aldrich's career. Aldrich had come to Hollywood hoping to become a producer. After working with Polonsky and Losey, he tried to develop projects that they would direct and he would produce or vice-versa.[23] A hoped-for film with Losey on the life of Aimee Semple McPherson from a script by Herman Mankiewicz ended with Aldrich lending a blacklisted Losey money to move to England. *The Gamma People*, a script of Aldrich's optioned by producer Irving Allen, was shelved when its would-be star, John Garfield, was gray-listed. After just a short time working on actual sets, Aldrich's ambitions had broadened to include directing. But after almost a dozen years not just as an assistant but also as production manager and assistant to the producer on scores of projects, Aldrich had still not managed to make the move up to either producer or director. His break finally came in late 1952 in a relatively new medium: television. Aldrich's last job as a first assistant director was on Chaplin's *Limelight*. Actor-producer Norman Lloyd, whom Aldrich knew well from their common association with Lewis Milestone, "got him the job" because Chaplin "wanted someone on the set who would be like a cop." Lloyd described Aldrich's style on *Limelight*: "As he was very ambitious to be a director but had not yet found the opportunity, Bob formed the habit of standing behind directors. He stood behind Charlie, snapping his fingers and pounding his palms impatiently."[24] Then Walter Blake, who was to remain an associate of Aldrich throughout his career, met with the New York producers of a television program and stretched the truth slightly: he asserted that because Chaplin had been in front of the cameras for so much of *Limelight*, Aldrich, as first assistant, had called "action" and been a kind of co-director.[25] Whether it was just *Limelight* or the whole of Aldrich's experience in assisting highly-regarded filmmakers that influenced their decision is not certain, but Proctor &

Gamble offered Aldrich the chance to direct one of their weekly, half-hour shows, *The Doctor*, a dramatic anthology which producer Marion Parsonnet believed could be made with more quality for less money in New York. Over the next few months, Aldrich worked on *The Doctor* in New York, while in Hollywood he directed episodes of the syndicated series, *China Smith*. By November 19, 1953, Aldrich had episodes of two different network shows airing the same week. Of course, by that time Aldrich was already directing his third feature film.

Aldrich's first chance to direct a feature came early in 1953. Herbert Baker, a writer, had been impressed by Aldrich's work as first assistant on the production of Baker's script for *So This Is New York*. When MGM decided to film another Baker script, the writer recommended Aldrich to producer Matthew Rapf as "a very bright guy who's done a lot of productions."[26] As a result Aldrich was offered *The Big Leaguer*. A baseball picture shot partly on location in Florida, *The Big Leaguer* was not the most auspicious of feature debuts. As Aldrich noted, "It was a picture about the New York Giants and Metro had the foresight to open it in Brooklyn; so you can't have expected it to do very well."[27]

Aldrich returned to work on the *China Smith* series and, less than two months after completing *The Big Leaguer*, Aldrich proposed to the producer of *China Smith*, Bernard Tabakin, that he could work with the star, crew, and sets of *China Smith* to co-produce and direct a feature during a hiatus in the series work. The result was *World for Ransom*, which was released the following year. The script had originated as a proposed episode of the series by Australian writer Lindsay Hardy. The basic premise, which revolved around a third-world plot to kidnap a nuclear physicist and sell him to the highest bidder, was full of a torturous plot twists in the original screenplay. Aldrich brought in blacklisted scenarist Hugo Butler to adapt the material with him; and the character written for *China Smith* star Dan Duryea acquired a forlorn romanticism that was atypical of the espionage genre in America. To underscore this, Aldrich's visualization began with the motifs of *film noir* and progressed from there. The shadowy, wet streets and back alleys were made all the more ominous by low angles that coincidentally obscured the fact that they were cheap, recycled sets from the series. The low-key interiors were further obscured by dark foreground objects that helped keep the sparse set dressing unnoticed. Long takes were both an efficient method for fast shooting and also created a most appropriate visual tension. When the project ran out of money, Aldrich and the crew made some beer and razor-blade commercials and pooled their earnings to complete the film.[28] Although he claimed to have more trouble with Hollywood's unofficial censors in the Code office over singer Madi Comfort caressing a microphone in *Kiss Me Deadly*, Aldrich's first dispute over controversial content occurred in *World for Ransom*. In the original opening, which was dropped, a shot of a couple embracing pulled back to reveal the female lead kissing another woman. While Lesbianism was never to become a major motif of Aldrich's work, it's portrayal would cause a major problem for Aldrich later when he made *The Killing of Sister George*.

After completing *World for Ransom*, Aldrich went briefly back to television and to direct episodes of the half-hour dramatic anthologies, *Four Star Playhouse* and *Schlitz Playhouse of the Stars*. Two of the *Four Star Playhouse* shows were seriocomic episodes which featured Dick Powell as the wisecracking owner of "Dante's Inferno." For *Schlitz* Aldrich directed his first outright, if improbable, comedy with a Western motif, featuring Joan Blondell as Calamity Jane and a family of ethnically uncertain "coyotes," named Ripplehassian, who smuggle workers across the Mexican border disguised as rocks.

While in New York, Aldrich chanced to meet playwright Clifford Odets, whose Hollywood play, "The Big Knife," appealed to Aldrich as a potential low-budget film. Aldrich put together footage from three episodes of *The Doctor* which had been partially shot on the streets of New York and used this as a

demonstration of his directing ability to persuade Odets to let him develop his play as a movie.[29] Back in Los Angeles, Aldrich/Tabakin Productions, a partnership with the producer of *World for Ransom*, was formed to continue development of this project.[30] In early May of 1953 just after finishing shooting on *World for Ransom*, Aldrich sent Odets an offer to option the play for $500 for a film version with a proposed budget "not to exceed $100,000"[31]

A few years earlier, Aldrich had worked as an assistant to producer Harold Hecht and helped supervise two feature films at Columbia. In partnership with actor Burt Lancaster, Hecht now had a deal with United Artists. Hecht knew of Aldrich's directorial ambitions and that, while working for him on the Western *Ten Tall Men*, Aldrich had wanted to option the novel Bronco Apache by Paul Wellman but failed to negotiate a price which he could afford. Aldrich took the novel to Hecht, who had been reluctant to give Aldrich his first chance to direct. *World for Ransom* and the television work now convinced Hecht-Lancaster that Aldrich could deliver a picture and, perhaps also "because I was young, ambitious, eager, and inexpensive,"[32] he was entrusted with a film based on the Wellman novel.

Apache was another big step for Aldrich: an "A" picture with a name cast to be shot in Technicolor at a cost in excess of $1 million. It was also Aldrich's first experience as a director with the forced compromises of mainstream production. *World for Ransom* may have had risqué scenes deleted under threat of outside censorship; and political realities had made it impossible to credit blacklisted co-writer Hugo Butler. But *Apache* was altered because of, to use the current catch-phrase, the distributor's desire for a "feel-good" ending. As Aldrich recalled in many later interviews, while Lancaster supported "the original ending of *Apache* in which I was killed by Charles Bronson," his partner and the distributors pressured him and ultimately though he hated the idea, he "went along with them."[33] While the version in which Lancaster's character survived a final confrontation with pursuing troopers was shot as an "alternate" ending, it became part of the finished picture; and Aldrich learned that "if you shoot two, they will always use the other one, never yours."[34] Despite this, *Apache* is a good example of Aldrich's nascent film vision. Although the visualization is quite different from *World for Ransom*, the framing, cutting, and camera moves again underscore the central character's perception of the world, which is one of quasi-mythic conflict.

The association with Hecht-Lancaster continued the following year with *Vera Cruz*. For the first time Aldrich had two weeks to rehearse the cast and block his scenes on the studio sets. Aldrich knew from his work as an assistant that many directors who could not or would not have formal rehearsals then had to spend time on basic staging or line-reading problems during production. By devoting time beforehand to rehearsals involving only the director and cast,

Opposite page, Aldrich on the set of *Arch of Triumph* (1948) with director Lewis Milestone (right), star Charles Boyer (second from right), and actor-producer Norman Lloyd, who is peering over Aldrich's shoulder.

Aldrich could work out purely performance problems without taking valuable time on a restricted shooting schedule. "When the scenes are actually being shot," Aldrich later wrote, "the actors will know what is expected of them, so that none can say, as we are about to roll the cameras, he doesn't understand the scene or that the dialogue doesn't fit, etc.... The enormous help that this gives in keeping large production crews from standing idly by at great expense can be appreciated by all of us who make films."[35] Besides the saving of production time, Aldrich valued the rehearsal period for its creative fecundity: "Actors are famous, you'll find, for not being able to articulate whatever disturbs them. But...if you watch my rehearsals carefully...all the nuances are worked out and they exploit each other's performances. It is a mutual aid society."[36] For himself, Aldrich used this period to visualize the scenes before shooting began: "I know that other people don't consider rehearsals helpful but to me it's the difference between what the script says and what the picture says. There is a transition period before you freeze a concept when you still have the latitude to mentally experiment—it doesn't cost anything."[37]

Except for the complicated, split-screen sequences in his later films, Aldrich seldom used storyboards. But on *Vera Cruz* he began working with an informal "worksheet," a list of his action cuts to help him focus on his visual line through the out-of-sequence filming of the script and let him "know where you are, what goes here, why you're there, what you have to get, because no script is ever written like that."[38]

The budget of *Vera Cruz* was fifty per cent greater than that of *Apache* and nearly twenty times greater than that of *World for Ransom*. Despite these and other production values, including use of the *Super*Scope wide-screen process and location shooting in Mexico, Aldrich felt somewhat constrained by the moral restrictions of the story and the lead actors; or as Aldrich later implied he could not make a movie with "balls, energy, and real sex."[39] Although the script anticipates the similar antagonists in *Ten Seconds to Hell*, as its reluctant allies in a revolutionary cause *Vera Cruz* had movie stars Lancaster and Gary Cooper. Consequently, Aldrich was unable to meld the star personas and the characters to achieve the subtle moral shadings of that later film.

Vera Cruz was certainly a commercial success: the first picture in his career to gross more than the $4 million dollars domestically which *Variety* then considered the threshold for its annual list of "blockbusters." This gave Aldrich the first opportunity of his career to choose from several offers for his next project. He settled on *Kiss Me Deadly*, a project with Victor Saville, an executive producer who controlled the film rights to the novels of Mickey Spillane and whose Parklane Productions had already completed *I, the Jury* and *The Long Wait*. While those pictures were straightforward adaptations of Spillane's raw prose and plotting, as he explained it, Aldrich "took the title and threw the book

Right, in late 1953, Aldrich lines up a shot on the set of *Apache*. The cameraman, before his replacement, is Stanley Cortez (center).

away."[40] Then he and writer A.I. Bezzerides created their own "sensational" concept. The explosive and articulate result, *Kiss Me Deadly*, is what critics Raymond Borde and Etienne Chaumeton would call in their study of American *film noir*, "the end of an epoch, the fascinating and shadowy conclusion"[41] of that cycle. English critic Raymond Durgnat dubbed it, with a bit more verve, "The Apotheosis of Va-va-voom." Aldrich's own assessment of the aesthetic merits of *Kiss Me Deadly* vacillated. He was proud of its portrayal of an anti-hero and allusions to the McCarthyism that had ruined so many colleagues. But he did not find it "as profound as many of the French thought it was.... French critics, particularly when Truffaut and Chabrol and all those guys were at *Cahiers*, read many, many things into *Kiss Me Deadly*. I appreciated their enthusiasm, but I just couldn't take a bow for it."[42]

Kiss Me Deadly was also the first of a dozen films on which Aldrich would be credited as sole producer as well as director. Aldrich feelings about producers, from his first hand experience with them as an assistant director and production manager, were mixed. "I say a producer should get the money [for the production] and go home. But a lot of producers won't agree with that"; but, remembering the man who introduced him to Losey, Aldrich admitted that "Sam Spiegel for example makes an enormous contribution to a picture. There's no doubt about it. There are other producers who make no contribution."[43] As a director, Aldrich welcomed the producer role for himself because it meant "you lessen the enemy. Then you only have the distributor to fight."[44] In the course of shooting *Kiss Me Deadly*, however, Aldrich took time to write an angry letter to a local union and complain about having to pay a meal allowance to some electricians who worked late. It was not, Aldrich asserted, a money issue but the fact that, of the entire crew, the electricians had not been team players, had been instead rather slow to the task and quick to complain. On future productions, Aldrich would try to leave such entanglements to the production manager and tried to limit his producer tasks to the more creative areas of script changes and casting.

Kiss Me Deadly was a modest financial success. Hecht-Lancaster had been among the first independent producers to make a distribution arrangement with the revitalized United Artists headed by Arthur Krim. When *Apache* and *Vera Cruz* grossed $6 million and $11 million respectively worldwide, the return on investment for both the production company and the United Artists was substantial. After having directed those two pictures and brought *Kiss Me Deadly* in on budget, Aldrich had demonstrated to U.A. that he could be entrusted with his own project. That was the last step towards the formation of a new company, the Associates and Aldrich, to produce Aldrich's next project, *The Big Knife*. The Associates—which included Aldrich's agent, Ingo Preminger; his attorney, J.H. Prinzmetal; and Walter Blake, whom Aldrich credited for his first directing job—and Aldrich would produce a total of fourteen feature films over the next seventeen years. Although Aldrich and his wife and children controlled 80% of the company, the Associates always got first billing, which reflected Aldrich's attitude about who they really were. "They are all the people with whom I like to make movies," he would say in 1967, "they are Walter Blake or Mike Luciano or Joe Biroc just as much as my children, who are the legal and technical stock holders of Associates and Aldrich."[45]

On *The Big Knife* Aldrich and his scenarist, James Poe, did nothing to mitigate the bitter indictment of the Hollywood system in Odets' play. *The Big Knife* was a true *succes d'éstime*, as it won favorable American reviews and the Silver Lion award at the Venice Film Festival. *The Big Knife* was Aldrich's "first completely independent production, and it lost money. This, in spite of...taking in $1,250,000 with a negative cost of $400,000. The distributor made all the profit."[46] Ironically, writing later that year in the New York *Times*, Odets himself commended Aldrich's adaptation and took the very fact that his play had been filmed as an indication that Hollywood was changing for the better.[47] Even more ironically, it was Harry Cohn, head of Columbia, the studio where Odets had bristled under the Hollywood yoke, and the main inspiration for Stanley Hoff, *The Big Knife*'s caricature of shallow Hollywood producers, who signed Aldrich to a three picture/three year contract.

Aldrich's first assignment for Columbia was "a classy soap opera,"[48] *Autumn Leaves* starring Joan Crawford. Because Aldrich refused to make changes in the script which Crawford wanted, filming began under strained conditions. At the end of the first week, during which time Crawford would not speak to him,

Aldrich's emotional reaction to one of Crawford's scenes convinced her of his sincerity and she became a friend until their dispute over *Hush...Hush, Sweet Charlotte*. Harry Cohn was less convinced of Aldrich's sincerity. *The Big Knife* opened in Los Angeles theaters on the day after completion of principal photography on *Autumn Leaves*. It was only after hiring Aldrich that Cohn had learned he was responsible for adapting *The Big Knife* and retaining its unflattering portrayal of the studio system of which Cohn was a founding father. As Aldrich described it, "I had an across-the-room relationship with Cohn: he wanted me to come there; I didn't want to come there. He had certain projects; I didn't like them."[49]

While waiting for another acceptable assignment from Columbia, Aldrich and James Poe completed the script of another adaptation of a Broadway play, "Fragile Fox." As with *The Big Knife*, the distribution arrangement with United Artists allowed Associates and Aldrich to finance *Attack!*. Also as with *The Big Knife*, the budget was under a half a million dollars, which presented a logistical problem: how to obtain needed assistance in the form of technical advice and, more significantly, free use of equipment from the United States Army. After reviewing the script with its undisguised portrayal of a cowardly Army captain who is "fragged" by his own men, Army officials refused to sanction any aid to the filmmakers. Aldrich had to tighten the budget in every category and cut down the physical requirements of the battle scenes in order to lease the equipment and filming sites which the Army would not provide.

"I wanted a tank to roll over Jack Palance in *Attack!* The effects guys had built a trough out of two by fours. I said, 'Jack, what the hell are you afraid of. You put your arm in the trough, the tank runs over it. You've got nothing to worry about.' He said, 'Ah, come on.' So I said, 'I'll show you.' I laid down there, put my arm in the trough, and they put the dirt on top and the tank ran over it. I thought my damn arm was going to break in half!"[50]

Despite the lack of cooperation from the Army, shooting on *Attack!* was finished less than three months after *Autumn Leaves*. Both films were ready for festival exhibition in the summer of 1956. As with *The Big Knife*, Aldrich again took them to Europe prior to their domestic release. It may well have surprised him that, while *Attack!* was well received in Venice, it was *Autumn Leaves* that won the Silver Bear for Best Direction in Berlin. In the meantime Associates and Aldrich was preparing its next project, a Western entitled *The Ride Back* to be produced by and star William Conrad and directed by Allen Miner. Because of his company's track record with United Artists, the distributor had brought Aldrich onto the project as Executive Producer. He in turn brought Anthony Quinn onto it as the co-star.

In mid-1957, Aldrich had another deal with U.A. which was, according to Arthur Krim, to "produce two pictures—THE SNIPE HUNT and NOW WE KNOW.... Both pictures, of course, will be directed by Bob Aldrich. THE SNIPE HUNT will be for this summer; NOW WE KNOW will be made some time before the end of the year."[51] United Artists budgeted these pictures at $600,000 and $900,000 respectively; but much of that would have been spent on cast. Aldrich's salary on each project would have been collateralized so that "A[ssociates] & A[ldrich]'s interests alone in RIDE BACK and ATTACK will be protection against any loss"[52] for U.A. Had he been able to get the right cast for either project, Aldrich might have put off his commitment to Columbia. For despite Aldrich's second major European award in less than a year, Cohn and his studio flunkies could not regard the man responsible for *The Big Knife* as a prestigious name on their roster of contract directors. Aldrich had been developing a project called *Until Proven Guilty* for Columbia since 1955; and in late 1956 he sold them another script, *3:10 to Yuma*. Aldrich actually sued Columbia in a contract dispute over *Until Proven Guilty* in April. That dispute was settled, and when neither *The Snipe Hunt* nor *Now We Now* could overcome casting obstacles, Aldrich accepted another assignment from Columbia, *The Garment Jungle*.

Shooting began in October at Columbia Studios and in New York for location work. At first, there was a problem with the script's subject matter and a menacing message delivered by a "very polite" criminal type. Aldrich went back the West Coast, and Cohn smoothed out those problems. Lee J. Cobb had never liked the unsympathetic attitude of his character and joined the studio in resisting Aldrich's wish to "harden" the script. Finally, just five days before the scheduled completion of the project, Aldrich got ill and found himself unexpectedly removed from the picture. Less than three months after Executive Producer Aldrich had felt compelled to replace the *The Ride Back*'s original director because he was behind schedule, Director Aldrich suffered a similar fate when *he* fell behind schedule on *The Garment Jungle*. Vincent Sherman, who had been hired for one day when Aldrich became ill, finished the picture and then "reshot eleven days" to replace certain scenes. According to Sherman, "Cohn then said he was putting my name on the film. I told him I thought that was unfair, that Aldrich, if he wished, should certainly share the credit."[53]

In a draft of a written response to the dismissal, Aldrich defended his position with numerous claims: that he had always asserted he needed 42 days to shoot the picture; that he had been promised but not given Glenn Ford to star; that he had suggested the entire production be shelved, the script be changed, and he be relieved as director after the New York filming. What is certain is that, after dropping plans to shoot in CinemaScope, Aldrich was given 9 days of rehearsal but only 32 days for shooting. Columbia refused to permit further script changes or, as producer Harry Kleiner's memo said, "Mr. Cohn does not want *any* changes made in any of the dialogue in the script";[54] and, just three days after filming was scheduled to end on November 28, the company fired Aldrich via telegram. "So far as The Associates and Aldrich are concerned," Aldrich's draft reply rhetorically began, "Robert Aldrich's discharge by Columbia...is without cause or justification and the latest in a lengthy series of efforts by Harry Cohn to embarrass and humiliate Aldrich. That Cohn should go through such maneuvers should come as no surprise to the industry. Historically, as hundreds of other artists in the industry can attest, Harry Cohn's device has been to woo the creative man, the writer, actor, director, producer, and, having won their services and affections, proceed to destroy them in any manner possible."[55]

Left, Aldrich in late 1956 looking hot and tired on the location for *The Ride Back*.

Of course, Columbia just ignored Aldrich's request about the first cut and made the decision for him about removing his name. Aldrich claimed in many subsequent interviews that he had never looked at the finished film and did not know how much of his material remained.[56] Nonetheless, in a letter to the head of the garment worker's union in New York, Aldrich admitted "that I finally gave in to my curiosity and last night went to the a local screening of GARMENT JUNGLE.... In my opinion it is a cheap, evasive, gutless travesty."[57]

The next project Aldrich had hoped to direct at Columbia, *3:10 to Yuma*, was reassigned. On the advice of his associates, Aldrich had decided against aggressively protesting being removed from the picture, and Columbia was obligated to pay his contracted salary; but Aldrich was prevented from working as a director for anyone else in Hollywood without Cohn's permission. Despite what he thought Columbia had done to his work, Aldrich first attempted to break the impasse by swallowing his pride and asking Cohn for a meeting through an intermediary. When that failed Aldrich wrote Cohn a confidential letter: "I never thought the dawn would break on a day that I would write you a letter of apology.... I have a strange premonition that although we may be different in many ways, we are similar in some. Among the similarities are rebellion, self-reliance and, above all, pride. As such a man you must understand how difficult it was for me to write such a letter."[58] Cohn's immediate reply was curt but not rude: "...since you feel we have similar characteristics, you will understand why I feel this way. And, you will also understand that under ordinary circumstances with what has occurred, except for not wishing to hurt any man's pride, I would have allowed my [verbal] answer to remain as the final word."[59] What infuriated Aldrich was not Cohn's written reply, but when he later heard that the studio head was ridiculing to others Aldrich's attempt at a cordial settlement. Aldrich filed his second lawsuit against Columbia and ultimately settled out of court, prompting his ironic announcement to the trade papers that "it cost me $20,000 but it was worth it."[60] Aldrich was exaggerating slightly in later interviews when he claimed to have "sat home for a year and a half"; but as a result of the dispute, 1957 *was* spent without directing a picture. Aldrich did work on developing *Taras Bulba*, with Anthony Quinn in the title role, and other projects. Even after his release from Columbia, there were more jobless months before United Artists, which had a production deal at UFA studios in Berlin, helped him secure a directing assignment in Europe for Hammer–Seven Arts, an adaptation of a novel by Laurence Bachmann entitled The Phoenix.

Aldrich's first European project in 1958 was retitled *Ten Seconds to Hell* and shot in Berlin from a script he co-wrote with Teddi Sherman. As with *Vera Cruz*, the film's characters are in conflict at several levels, as idealist and cynic both pursue the same woman. More significantly, Aldrich underscores the concept of a second chance, something which was to figure often in his later work. After Aldrich finished his cut, which ran 131 minutes, the producers began reworking and shortening the film. Max Youngstein of United Artists wrote candidly to Aldrich that the company had spent much more than they expected on a "picture which none of us like, and which some of us, including myself, consider to be terrible."[61] *Ten Seconds to Hell* was finally released, in truncated form, more than a year after completion of production.

By then Aldrich's next directing assignment, *The Angry Hills*, had already come and gone from U.S. theaters. The experience of making *The Angry Hills*, a drama set in Greece during World War II, was even worse than the last one. Robert Mitchum, with whom assistant director Aldrich had worked on two occasions, was cast in the lead role originally intended for Alan Ladd. Aldrich the director would later admit that he was unable to inspire Mitchum to do anything but walk through the assignment.[62] After his departure, Aldrich's version was again substantially reedited by the film's producer. As he recalled, "Raymond Stross...understood that Metro was buying film by the yard then...so as long as it was an hour and a half with [Robert] Mitchum and some Greek scenery, it would work. Obviously, it didn't."[63]

It was after he returned from these two, mostly unsatisfactory experiences that Aldrich's outlook changed "in terms of what preference to give survival."[64] Aldrich made public his dissatisfaction with aspects of the industry. Rather than merely mention his problems in interviews, he wrote a series of articles tellingly entitled "The High Price of Independence," "My Travails in Europe," and "Learning from My Mistakes."[65] Aldrich's co-workers and friends had always known that he was very direct and freely spoke his opinions. To vent his frustration Aldrich candidly continued to give interviews and write articles throughout the 1960s.

Throughout his career, Aldrich would have difficulty with both his personal and company finances, particularly by spending more and more money to acquire and develop many projects that were never produced. Aldrich's personal tax returns for 1955 and 1956, showed earnings of just over $65,000 and $75,000 respectively, considerable sums for that period. Aldrich's total compensation on *Attack!* was $100,000, but the deals as "director only" at Columbia and on *Ten Seconds to Hell* and *The Angry Hills* averaged only $50,000 per production. That coupled with his tax problems put him on the brink of bankruptcy. Creditors went unpaid and even the Screen Directors Guild was forced to send dunning notices about back dues. After working overseas, Aldrich tried to develop *Taras Bulba* and another project, *The Tsar's Bride*, as European co-productions to be shot in the Soviet Union. With United Artists' backing in early 1959, Aldrich announced that he would make *Taras Bulba* with Anthony Quinn on a $6 million budget in Yugoslavia and England. Then

U.A. withdrew financing. Almost bankrupt and about to lose his house in Hollywood to tax foreclosure, Aldrich first sold his residual interests in *Kiss Me Deadly, The Big Knife,* and *Attack!* back to United Artists for $20,000. Then, to save his house, he gave up *Taras Bulba.*[66]

To make money to support his wife and four children, Aldrich was forced to return to television directing; but, at least, it was on "pilots which pay more money."[67] Other than this work on *Hotel de Paree* and *Adventures in Paradise* in the spring of 1959, it was another year of inactivity as a director. In 1960, Aldrich, whose work producer Edward Lewis admired, was hired by Kirk Douglas' Bryna Productions to direct the Western, *The Last Sunset.* According to Douglas, who did not know of Aldrich's financial problems, the director campaigned vigorously for the assignment by writing that "I am completely dedicated to the hope that somehow, some way, you will decide it is in our collective best interests that I direct [your picture]...I have to do your picture, and I have to do it better than any picture you have ever made before."[68] Douglas' appreciation of Aldrich's enthusiasm waned considerably when he discovered Aldrich had brought writers to location to work with him on other projects in off moments.

Despite major disagreements with Douglas and some difficult locations in Mexico, *The Last Sunset* was completed on schedule; but problems in post-production would delay its release for almost a year. In the meantime, Aldrich had again returned to Europe as a hired director to fulfill a commitment to Joseph E. Levine for the Biblical epic *Sodom and Gomorrah.* Given that the average running time of features released today normally ranges between 90 and 105 minutes, it is remarkable that exactly half of Aldrich's thirty pictures are two or more hours in length. Several others are only one or two minutes short of 120; and a total of twenty-three are over 100 minutes long. Of all these, *Sodom and Gomorrah* was to remain the longest in terms of both shooting schedule and final length. After several months of pre-production, Aldrich worked for nearly six months shooting on six-day weeks, much of it on location in Morocco.

Aldrich had mixed feelings about *Sodom and Gomorrah* and could, in almost the same breath, call it a "bad film" and "a marvellous experience."[69] Spanning as it did the midpoint of what was to be Aldrich's forty-two year career, *Sodom and Gomorrah* was a turning point in many other respects.

> I hope to go on making pictures—but...you're talking about the *auteur,* the guy who makes the movie, and he's got to run out of gas sooner than the guy sitting under the umbrella, drinking lemonade. A director is the first guy there, and the last guy home. He works harder and longer and, physically,

more is taken out of him. Now that's what a director who *is* a director is![70]

Below, in Morocco on location for *Sodom and Gomorrah*, Aldrich with star Stewart Granger (right) and "a guy under an umbrella."

Whether or not Aldrich was thinking about some cast or crew member on *Sodom and Gomorrah* sitting under an umbrella drinking lemonade is not certain. "Sergio Leone was second unit director on *Sodom and Gomorrah*, and he was loafing."[71] Aldrich paid a surreptitious visit to the second unit on his day off and waited for something to be shot. "Four hours and still nothing happened. I called him and I said, 'Get your ticket and go back to Rome. You're through.'"[72]

Sodom and Gomorrah was Aldrich's first extended use of multi-camera shooting; and "ever since then I've had as part of my contract, a two-camera system. It's strange that an outrageous picture like *Sodom and Gomorrah* turned around the whole way that I shot pictures."[73] As he was preparing to shoot what would be his last feature in 1981, Aldrich was still using the experience in Morocco to psych himself up: "Unless I believe in a picture, I can't make it. I'm the guy, remember, who spent two years making *Sodom and Gomorrah*. You've got to be an idiot to pretend to yourself that a film like that is worthwhile. But I did."[74]

When the producers of *Sodom and Gomorrah* started to re-cut his final version, Aldrich sued. "What was I thinking of—arguing in an Italian court for the cutting rights?... I had to be a jerk."[75] Much to his surprise, Aldrich actually won an injunction, when a judge found that re-cutting the director's version violated Italian copyright law and forfeited the right to a government subsidy: "It was ludicrous to have had that fight over an Italian sex-and-sand epic. It's the court's decision that is interesting."[76]

Aldrich would later characterize the results of his efforts from 1958 to 1962 as "four bad films and the dissolution of a marriage. It can't be much more disastrous than that."[77] After years of long hours and months at a time working outside of Los Angeles, Aldrich's marriage to Harriet Foster officially ended in June of 1965, because Aldrich had "stayed away from home on numerous occasions and showed no interest or affection."[78] He had openly been in a relationship with Sibylle Siegfried, a German former fashion model, since shortly after they first met in Berlin while he worked on *Ten Seconds to Hell*. The year following his divorce, Aldrich married her.

In 1962, emotionally and physically exhausted by the rigors of the desert location and the grueling schedule, Aldrich left Europe determined to find a project that was worth his effort, a project he could see through to final cut, a project that would reestablish a reputation still tarnished by his dispute with Columbia and unredeemed by his journeyman work since.

The project he chose was his second "Hollywood" movie. But instead of accentuating the melodrama as in *The Big Knife*, Aldrich concentrated on black comedy and gothic touches in *What Ever Happened to Baby Jane?*. Aldrich wrote a detailed account of the development of the project in an article for the

Opposite page, Aldrich at a Cannes Film Festival press luncheon with *Baby Jane* co-star Bette Davis (left) and actress Anita Ekberg (right) who would soon co-star in *4 for Texas*.

New York Times. In it, he explained how he found out about the original novel, while it was still under option to someone else, from Geraldine Hersey, a woman who had been his secretary on his first European projects and "a better judge of what will make a good movie than are several major 'experts' on the subject."[79] First partnered with producer Joseph E. Levine to acquire the property in 1961, Aldrich attached aging stars Joan Crawford and Bette Davis to the project. Aldrich had used his ongoing cordial relationship to sign Crawford. For Davis, Aldrich recounted to more than one interviewer how he sent the script to her with a note announcing that if it was not the best script she had ever read, there was no need to reply. Davis apparently thought it the second best she had ever read but replied anyway. Unfortunately by the time Aldrich bought out Levine, the story price had grown from $10,000 to $85,000 and no one seemed interested. At one point Aldrich thought that "*Baby Jane* is now so prohibitive, it doesn't make sense."[80] A greater problem was that major studios and distributors were turning the project down because they did not believe Davis and Crawford, even together, could still draw audiences. Then, Aldrich related, "Eliot Hyman at Seven Arts read the script, studied the budget. and told me candidly: 'I think it will make a fabulous movie, but I'm going to make very tough terms because it's a high risk venture.'"[81]

Just as he had won over Crawford during *Autumn Leaves*, Aldrich's faith in the project made Davis an enthusiastic participant. She took on the rather unattractive role of "Baby" Jane Hudson with a fervor that matched Aldrich's, even devising the chalk-faced make-up that the pathetic Jane puts on to launch her "comeback." The end result was Aldrich's first box-office smash since *Vera Cruz*, and the first he had developed and packaged himself. *What Ever Happened to Baby Jane?* grossed $4 million in the U.S. and Canada and worldwide nearly twelve times its reported negative cost of $1,025,000. Although Warner Bros. received a 25% share of profits for undertaking the domestic dis-

tribution and Aldrich had to give substantial shares to Crawford (15%) and Davis (10%), the remaining monies permitted a complete financial revitalization of Associates and Aldrich.[82] Despite the prizes Aldrich had received from European film festivals, *Baby Jane* was also the first Aldrich picture to be nominated for an Academy Award. There were five nominations in all, most notably for actors Davis and Victor Buono, and one win for costume designer Norma Koch.

Undismayed by the lack of critical enthusiasm over *Baby Jane*, Aldrich next packaged *4 for Texas*, a Western action comedy, which he had co-written from his own story, and began filming less than six months after *Baby Jane*'s release. The resulting motion picture was, by Aldrich's own reckoning, a failure on all counts. A major problem was the behavior of Frank Sinatra, whose Essex Productions was partnered with Associates and Aldrich and co-star Dean Martin in the SAM (Sinatra/Aldrich/Martin) Company to produce the movie. At one point, Aldrich considered legal action against Sinatra for failing to complete his assigned work and exacerbating tension on the set by "negative and derogatory remarks by Sinatra (but never to me) about the uselessness of two shots being made and that the crew was unpardonably slow...(we only made 82 setups in 2 2/3 days...SLOW???)."[83] Aldrich also had Sinatra's time on the set compiled, revealing a total of only 80 hours of work spread over 37 days.

Despite the distracting squabbles with Sinatra and not wanting to lose the impetus of *Baby Jane*, Associates and Aldrich had, as usual, numerous properties in active development.[84] Aldrich moved on quickly to *Hush...Hush, Sweet Charlotte*, which was to re-team Bette Davis and Joan Crawford. Filming began less than six months after the release of *4 for Texas* in mid-1964 but was suspended several times. One problem was a third-party lawsuit involving Paramount Pictures and Davis' commitment to added scenes on *Where Love Has Gone*. Much more significant was Crawford's real or imaginary illness.

Reputedly, Crawford was still incensed by Davis' attitude on *Baby Jane* and did not want to be upstaged again, as Davis' nomination for Best Actress convinced her she had been. Crawford worked only four days in all of July. Because she had told others that she was feigning illness to get out of the movie entirely, Aldrich was in an even worse position than he had been with a merely disgruntled Frank Sinatra. Desperate to resolve the situation, "Aldrich hired a private detective to record her [Crawford's] movements."[85] When shooting was suspended indefinitely on August 4, the production insurance company insisted that either Crawford be replaced or the production cancelled.

Having ruled out or been turned down by Vivien Leigh, Loretta Young, and Barbara Stanwyck, Aldrich flew to a remote resort in Switzerland and somehow cajoled Olivia de Havilland, the last acceptable actress, into taking over the part: "I spent four terribly difficult days with all the persuasion I could com-

Above, pre-production on *Hush...Hush, Sweet Charlotte*: Joan Crawford meets with Aldrich and costume designer Norma Koch, who won an Oscar for her work on *Baby Jane*.

mand.... I don't believe half of the things I said myself; but I knew there was no other place to go. If I came back without de Havilland, we wouldn't have a picture, because we had gone through all the other people that Fox would live with."[86] It's not surprising that Aldrich himself was briefly hospitalized for exhaustion after shooting was over.

The film was based on a story by Henry Farrell, the author of the novel <u>Whatever Happened to Baby Jane?</u> He had replaced Aldrich's frequent collaborator, Lukas Heller, as screenwriter in fall, 1963, when *What Ever Happened to Cousin Charlotte?* was the project's title. When finally released, by any other name, *Charlotte* was not as sweet at the box office as *Baby Jane* and cost more than twice as much to make.[87] Nonetheless, even a picture that just broke even would help to maintain the burgeoning overhead of literary rights owned by Associates and Aldrich.

His experiences in Europe and an instinct for survival defined Aldrich's new strategy as a producer—towards "safe" pictures, that is, projects that would not lose money and would allow Associates and Aldrich at least to tread water while waiting for the next moderate financial success. At the same time, Aldrich the director had wider aspirations: "I must create and I can't always create what I want artistically and culturally under present methods of financing.... I'd like to make one such [art] film just to prove that we can make artistic and cultural films right here in Hollywood as well as they can abroad."[88] In early 1965,

Aldrich was "not figuring on more like *Jane* and *Charlotte*.... Having no desire to become 'a middle-aged Alfred Hitchcock' [with] any more suspense melo-dramas."[89] Later that year, Aldrich again went beyond the trade papers and wrestled with the issue of art versus commercial films in a first-person article for the *New York Herald-Tribune*. Using an extended analogy of French farmers who went on strike and spilled their milk rather that let merchants make excess profits, Aldrich asked "what about American filmmakers? How sick is their mar-keting system?"[90] While he understood that studios needed "safe" projects be-cause "it is not really fair to ask any businessman to lose money.... But what of the new pictures? The idea pictures? The controversial pictures that would at-tack much in our way of life that some feel needs to change?"[91] Ironically, the more Aldrich as a producer and not just director-for-hire tried to assert his inde-pendence and take control of his own projects, the more he was dependent on their financial success. "If I weren't wearing both hats, I'd like to make a picture that would free Angela Davis. But I don't want the producer part of me to lose so much money that he can't make the next one."[92]

Despite a cast of veteran actors, headed by James Stewart, Associates and Aldrich's second picture for 20th Century-Fox, *The Flight of the Phoenix*, was not even a moderate success. Like *Ten Seconds to Hell* and *Attack!*, *Flight of the Phoenix* focused on a group of men fighting long odds against their sur-vival. Although disheartened by the death of stunt pilot Paul Mantz during pro-duction, Aldrich brought a long and difficult location shoot in on schedule. Then despite a costly advertising campaign culminating in Los Angeles and London premieres, *The Flight of the Phoenix* proved a box-office failure.

Before the completion of *The Flight of the Phoenix*, Aldrich had been ap-proached by Kenneth Hyman, who had brought *Baby Jane* to Warner Bros. and was now an independent producer, to direct a script by Nunnally Johnson based on the novel, <u>The Dirty Dozen</u>. Unable to get a deal from Richard Zanuck at Fox for a project called *...All the Way to the Bank*, Aldrich accepted *The Dirty Dozen*

On the surface, this project seemed quite similar to *The Flight of the Phoe-nix*, with a narrative focused on a small, exclusively-male group. This context, whether it featured a sports team or a bomb disposal unit, had already been explored several times in *The Big Leaguer, Attack!* and *Ten Seconds to Hell*. But not even the mercenaries of *Vera Cruz* were as outcast from society as the condemned men who become a "suicide squad" in *The Dirty Dozen*. MGM, the distributor, wanted the lead role offered to John Wayne, whom Aldrich himself had courted just a few weeks earlier for *...All the Way to the Bank*.[93] For *The Dirty Dozen*, Aldrich wanted a less idealized hero, the actor who had portrayed the unprincipled colonel in *Attack!*, Lee Marvin. With Marvin's name

Opposite, extended rehearsals on a sound stage were part of Aldrich's preparation for every picture, here with the cast of *The Flight of the Phoenix* (which included son Bill, top left) in the taped outline of the plane.

value suddenly greatly enhanced by his Academy Award for *Cat Ballou*, MGM relented.

The Dirty Dozen was to become a second turning point in Aldrich's career. On a creative level, the cynicism about personal survival which Aldrich acquired during his "travails in Europe" colored the outlook of his outlaw/idealist characters from *The Dirty Dozen* to *The Longest Yard* and *Twilight's Last Gleaming*. Aldrich and his scenarist, Lukas Heller, restructured Johnson's script to reflect this sensibility and to match Lee Marvin's rougher screen persona in the role of Major Reisman.

On a business level, the domestic earnings of *The Dirty Dozen* in its initial release were enormous. $19.5 million may not seem like much by current standards, but in 1967 that made *The Dirty Dozen* the 15th highest grossing picture of all time. Its popularity set a standard for action pictures and images of male bonding that was first emulated, then parodied, and still persists. (When the 40ish, male characters in *Sleepless in Seattle* must wax nostalgic about their *macho* movie alternative to *An Affair to Remember*, the picture they talk about is *The Dirty Dozen*.) The millions of moviegoers who saw *The Dirty Dozen* worldwide coupled with Aldrich's profit participation finally gave him the fiscal leverage he had wanted to become a genuinely independent filmmaker.

In many ways, Aldrich was still a child of the original studio system. His experiences first at RKO and Enterprise and then with Associates and Aldrich had led him to the belief that the ideal method of making movies was with a crew of "regular," efficient technicians using his own compact set of location vehicles and/or in his own equally compact studio. Enterprise Studios, in particular, Aldrich often asserted later, had been a model of well-run operations and high

morale. As early as 1956, Aldrich had written "I sincerely hope to be able to remain in independent production. Mike Luciano (my editor) and Frank de Vol
[sic] (my composer) are still with me. On FOX [*Attack!*] I used Joe Biroc as
Cameraman (he did WORLD FOR RANSOM and the CHINA SMITH series for
me.) You might also be interested in knowing that through all these pictures I
have used the same production staff...(Jack Berne, Robert Justman, Nate
Slott)...the same Property Master, John Orlando; the same Grip, John Lively.
It would seem, the longer the association, the better the teamwork."[94]

Like many producers and directors, Aldrich preferred working with the same
group of people and considered these writers, crew members, and actors as
part of his extended family. Aldrich's loyalty to someone such as Hugo Butler
meant not only giving him and his wife, Jean Rouverol, work writing treatments
and scripts, but sometimes paying a living allowance in between projects. In
lean times, Aldrich had often put off paying his own obligations to insure that
someone like Butler got what he needed. Aldrich's list of "deal points" whenever he worked as a hired director always included approvals over all key and
many secondary technical personnel.

Several events in 1967 permitted Aldrich to contemplate some sort of permanent production facility for Associates and Aldrich. As already noted, the first
was that, as Aldrich had hoped, *The Dirty Dozen* was "enormous at the box office."[95] Even before *The Dirty Dozen* was released, Aldrich had a deal with
MGM for two more pictures, *The Legend of Lylah Clare* and *Angry Odyssey*.
After *The Dirty Dozen*, a second potential deal materialized. By August 15, after *Lylah Clare*, Associates and Aldrich had pulled out of the remainder of the
MGM commitment and negotiated a broader agreement with the new production arm of the American Broadcasting Company, Palomar Pictures, for an
even larger slate: *Too Late the Hero, The Killing of Sister George, What Ever
Happened to Aunt Alice?*, and *The Greatest Mother of 'Em All*. The "Aldrich
pact" was, according to the trade periodicals, "ABC's biggest feature deal to
date, and it offers proof that the net...intends to be a major factor in the film industry."[96] Five weeks later, on September 21, Aldrich sold his 15% share of net
profits in *The Dirty Dozen* back to MGM for $1,150,000 to be paid out over ten
years. As a result of these events, at the beginning of 1968 *Daily Variety* trum-
peted "Bob Aldrich's 'Dream' Deal."[97] Leading off with Aldrich quoting Clifford Odets that "Everybody's entitled to a Dream," the trade article revealed
that Aldrich used $300,000 of the proceeds from the sale of *The Dirty Dozen* to
buy his own studio. Aldrich cited the Enterprise model to the writer of the article, who prophetically added that Enterprise was the "indie which eventually
went bust."

The purchase of the Sutherland stage, a small facility in East Hollywood
originally constructed by Famous Players-Lasky, was only part of the plan to

give Associates and Aldrich a firm foundation that could not be eroded by one or two unprofitable pictures. The only problem was that, as he had done in selling residual interests in the United Artists pictures back to them and in selling *What Ever Happened to Baby Jane?* to Warner Bros., Aldrich had no library of pictures. Given the vagaries of Hollywood bookkeeping, it is uncertain whether the 15% share of *The Dirty Dozen* would ultimately have yielded more or less than $1,150,000. In any case, Aldrich was now banking more than just his reputation as a director on the ABC-Palomar deal.

1967 had been the most successful year in Aldrich's career both as a filmmaker and a film industry entrepreneur. Aldrich had taken the $200,000 from Warner Bros. for selling back future profits on *Baby Jane*, bought 5,000 shares of MGM stock, and, after leaving MGM for ABC, sold the shares for an $80,000 profit. 1967 ended with honors from both the National Association of Theatre Owners as "Director of the Year" and a retrospective at the prestigious San Francisco Film Festival on his 25th Anniversary. It was, of course, actually Aldrich's 26th year in the industry. Still, that was a remarkably short amount of time to progress from merely filling out the time cards to assuming the responsibility of paying them. Even a small studio creates a considerable overhead burden and Associates and Aldrich needed more than just the ABC-Palomar deal to carry it. Clearly he was aware of this challenge: "Aldrich, who always can be counted on for refreshingly candid opinions anent production overhead and distribution accounting (to producers), noted that 'average' overhead, in his ideal thinking, is about 'seven percent.' He thinks he can make it work in practice at his studio."[98]

Aldrich's disenchantment with "distribution accounting" and a system where "the ground rules are: you don't get yours, they get theirs,"[99] had already often led him to announce alternative plans. In 1963, after the success of *Baby Jane*, he had announced four pictures and plans for limited self-distribution.[100] In late 1964, Aldrich raised the ante in the trade papers to eight projects at a total cost of $14 million and claimed a quarter of million dollars was invested in *Lylah Clare, The Sheik of Araby*, and *The Greatest Mother of 'Em All*.[101] By 1967, the trade paper headline was: "Associates and Aldrich Co. Hopes To Make 4-6 Pictures Per Year."[102]

As he completed work on *The Dirty Dozen*, Aldrich's personal finances had been in worse condition than ever. In a detailed memorandum, his accountant reported more than $60,000 in current and back taxes owed and over $150,000 borrowed from Associates and Aldrich that needed to be repaid.[103] The memo went to on to explain that "this financial dilemma arose through a progression of events: [most notably] the expenditure of $474,300 in story development costs [from 1955 to 1966] which have either been abandoned or have not as yet been committed for production." *The Dirty Dozen* had bailed

Aldrich out. Now the terms of the ABC deal seemed to guarantee him considerable personal income and creative freedom. The fee for producing was to be 7 1/2% of each picture's budget but no less than $75,000 or more than $150,000. For directing, Aldrich was to receive $350,000 per project. While ABC retained final cut, Aldrich was guaranteed two previews of his director's version, and he knew that "since *Sodom and Gomorrah* nobody has ever changed the picture after the second preview."[104] Aldrich also knew that if he were dealing with the likes of Raymond Stross then "those people are going to cut the picture anyway, regardless of whether you have a contract. And your job really is to be so expert at what you do that there can be no quarrel, and that everyone says, 'Yeah, that's right.'"[105]

By the time the Aldrich Studios formally opened in August, 1968, Aldrich's newest "five-year" plan was for eight to sixteen productions. The commitment to MGM for *The Legend of Lylah Clare* had long been completed and shooting on the first ABC project, *The Killing of Sister George*, was already well underway. Aldrich had hoped that *Lylah Clare* would be another successful "meta-movie," a film that like *Baby Jane* was about filmmaking. When *Lylah Clare* failed to perform up to *Baby Jane*-sized expectations, opening to poor reviews and minimal grosses, Aldrich's disappointment was more aesthetic than fiscal. At one time, Aldrich blamed the editing: "On *The Legend of Lylah Clare* I knew it wasn't a good picture. Mike [Luciano] lost that picture."[106] Kim Novak had been paid $250,000 for the dual roles of Lylah and Elsa. *Lylah Clare* was Novak's first picture after nearly two years off following a riding accident and career indecision. Her portrayal of the German-accented Lylah had not been up to Aldrich's expectations, so at other times he would blame *her*. Ultimately he realized "that would be pretty unfair.... To make this picture work, to make *Lylah* work, you had to be carried along into that myth. And we didn't accomplish that. Now, you know, you can blame it on a lot of things. but I'm the producer and I'm the director. I'm responsible for not communicating to that audience. *I* just didn't do it"[107] Aldrich could afford to be philosophical about *Lylah Clare*. If he were to experience a conflict like those depicted in *Lylah Clare* between *prima donna* director, Lewis Zarkan, and the brusque studio head, Barney Sheean, Aldrich would have to be arguing with himself. Producer Aldrich had an office like Sheean's on his own lot with a picture of Kim Novak as Lylah behind his desk.

Director Aldrich was on time and on budget for his first ABC picture. The second, *What Ever Happened to Aunt Alice?*, was in pre-production and a few weeks from filming. The ABC deal was about to be restructured to include four more projects—*Rebellion; The Angry Odyssey; Coffee, Tea, or Me; and No Orchids for Miss Blandish*, which became *The Grissom Gang*—and a $200,000

Opposite, creating the "myth" of Lylah Clare, Aldrich stages a Hollywood meeting at the Brown Derby restaurant with actors Ernest Borgnine (bottom left), Kim Novak, Peter Finch, and Michael Murphy.

line of credit. Finally, initial plans were being made for a public offering that could turn the Aldrich company into a mini-major.

The first misstep along that path came before year's end when the completed *Sister George* received an "X" rating from the Motion Picture Association of America. While *Sister George* may hardly seem like "X" or "NC-17" material by today's standards, for a picture made in 1968 and dealing openly with Lesbian relationships, such a rating could not have been entirely unexpected. Nonetheless, the result was that not only did many theaters refuse to exhibit the film but also many newspapers and broadcasters, as policy, would not permit advertising of this "X"-rated movie. Aldrich "didn't know who to fight."[108] ABC released Aldrich's cut of the picture, but would not support his lawsuit against the *Los Angeles Times* or his petition to the Federal Communications Commission to revoke the licenses of Los Angeles radio/TV stations KMPC and KTLA for refusing to accept advertisements. Aldrich even threatened to sue the MPAA unless they joined his denunciation of censorship. The mediocre box office performance of *Sister George* soon made all these actions moot. "Two years have gone by," Aldrich noted ruefully in 1970, "and you find [MPAA President Jack] Valenti battling the press up in San Francisco and paraphrasing word for word our indictment about censorship of movies, which is a little ludicrous."[109]

In his second experience as a producer only on *What Ever Happened to Aunt Alice?*, Aldrich had again replaced the director more than halfway through shooting. At almost the same time, he also had a dispute with his long time collaborator composer Frank DeVol over *Sister George*. Despite these various problems, the most serious of which was the "X" rating, ABC still agreed to extend the deal with Associates and Aldrich to a total of eight pictures, which was officially announced in January, 1969.[110] Because "ABC

wanted another *Dirty Dozen*,"[111] two weeks earlier Aldrich had began shooting in the Philippines on a project he hoped would satisfy them, *Too Late the Hero*.

Before the shooting of *Sister George* was finished, ABC proposed cuts of $232,700 in the submitted budget of $6,449,374 on *Too Late the Hero*.[112] Either number was certainly less than MGM had thought feasible: "At Metro they wanted a budget of nine million seven [hundred thousand] to make it, which was too high."[113] The $3 million plus difference in cost meant $7.5 to $10 million less was needed in gross receipts to break even. Aldrich wrestled briefly with ABC over casting. They made the argument which Aldrich himself had used with MGM regarding Lee Marvin in *The Dirty Dozen* and insisted on signing recent Academy Award winner, Cliff Robertson. Aldrich wanted "Anybody but Cliff Robertson. You, me, anybody";[114] but eventually he relented, accepted the actor who had co-starred in *Autumn Leaves*, and began work. Despite a heavy publicity campaign by ABC and special roadshow engagements of 70mm prints with six-track stereo sound, *Too Late the Hero* did not gross the amount of money needed to recover its cost. In fact, it grossed less than $1 million.

ABC's experience with Aldrich and other producers would seldom result in profit. The headline trade paper postmortem on ABC-Palomar succinctly told all: "ABC Films Result: 30 of 36 in Red: Total Loss $47 Mil."[115] When total costs including prints and advertising and interest were compared to total revenues both foreign and domestic, the final ABC balance sheet showed that they

Below, Aldrich in the Philippines on the set of *Too Late the Hero* with co-stars Michael Caine (left) and "anybody but" Cliff Robertson.

lost money on all four Aldrich projects: $750,000 on *Sister George*; $860,000 on *What Ever Happened to Aunt Alice?*; $3,670,000 on *The Grissom Gang*; and a staggering $6,765,000 on *Too Late the Hero*. That loss of nearly $7 million on one film was only good enough for second best, or second worst, on ABC's list of 30 losers. Nonetheless, Aldrich's four productions, which represented 1/9th of ABC's total output, disproportionately accounted for nearly $16 million or 1/4th of ABC's total loss.

Even before *Too Late the Hero* was released, ABC was having major misgivings about its commitment, particularly about *Rebellion* which Aldrich publicly indicated was "not quite in the $20 million class" but the costliest production he had ever planned.[116] In fact, the budget for *Rebellion* as an ABC-Palomar project was *only* $7 million; but even when Associates and Aldrich offered to cut it to $5.5 million, ABC refused to proceed. This led to "lawyers hollering at each other"[117] because, in Aldrich's view, "They approved the project. They had a major commitment; and we came up with a budget of seven million dollars. Now, I don't blame them for not wanting to make the picture for seven million. I do blame them for not honoring their contracts for not trying to find a way out, a compromise solution."[118] In May of 1969, ABC had also rejected *The Greatest Mother of 'Em All* because "it would be impossible, based upon said proposed screenplay for MOTHER, to produce a first-class feature motion picture which would qualify for the MPAA seal and which would be of such entertainment value as to qualify for exhibition."[119] Before the end of year, "lawyers hollering" had become lawyers filing suit for breach of contract.

While matters with ABC were unresolved in 1969, Aldrich came up with what he "thought was an ingenious piece of showmanship"[120] and a way to keep the studio and production personnel occupied. He produced a promotional film of selected scenes from *The Greatest Mother of 'Em All*, a script by A.I. Bezzerides and Leon Griffiths loosely based on starlet Beverly Aadland's celebrated affair with Errol Flynn and her mother's attempt to cash in on it. Whether or not, as Aldrich believed, "a year before that picture would have sold like hot cakes,"[121] in 1969 it didn't sell to ABC or any other company.

Like many of his other lawsuits, Aldrich versus ABC was quickly settled in less than a month. In brief, Associates and Aldrich got to keep all the money ABC had invested in acquiring and developing properties which now went into "turnaround" and, except for *The Grissom Gang*, ABC got out from under their remaining four picture commitment.

A few months after the ABC settlement, the public offering of Geneve Productions was filed with the Securities and Exchange Commission. In a complex partnership with Sierra Enterprises, formed by Starwood, a venture capital firm, and an East Coast retailer, Aldrich's new company, Aldrich Films Inc., would receive $44 million in production funds to produce and distribute 16 to 24 pictures. As the offering explained "the movie industry is highly competitive and the Geneve-Aldrich joint venture will be competing with many companies with greater resources...in recent years a significant number of motion pictures have earned no profits."[122] As with most offerings, there was a floor or minimum investment required for closing, and it was never reached.

The Grissom Gang was shot in the second part of 1970 and released the following Spring. Some reviewers admired the performances of Scott Wilson as a romantic psychopath and Robert Lansing as a world-weary private detective, but the response of critics and audiences alike was largely negative.

While The Grissom Gang was in production, Aldrich's associates, his son William, development head Peter Nelson, and company attorney Ronald Sunderland, were exploring the possibility of productions for ABC television. The William Morris Agency, as packagers, convinced Aldrich to consider ABC network head Barry Diller's interest in a What Ever Happened to... series, as well as "some sort of deal whereby they would supply several films to ABC in the Gothic, suspense, melodrama area where they feel that they do better than anybody else."[123] A formal proposal was made in early 1971, but ABC-TV did not come to terms.

Aldrich spent much of 1971 working on The Plaza, originally a concept for an anthology television drama. After purchasing a nonfiction book on the celebrated New York hotel, Aldrich had devised a melodramatic story-line dealing with the employees and guests of the hotel, including a pre-Die Hard subplot about a militant group taking guests hostage to force release of political prisoners. Aldrich wrote a draft script himself; then he hired Gore Vidal to do a rewrite. The negotiations with Vidal's agents, CMA, led to a packaging arrangement with them. But as both Aldrich and the agency discovered when the round of studio submissions were made, a large, star-driven cast and a nearly $7 million budget were no longer very enticing. As Richard Zanuck wrote in classic studio-speak, "the cost factor plus, in all candor, not a total sense of enthusiasm for the project itself makes it necessary for me to reply to you in the negative."[124] In other words, "No." At one point, when an agent failed to arrange a promised meeting with a possible lead woman for The Plaza and Aldrich made a long trip for nothing, his exasperation boiled over: "There is really only one rewarding thing about being involved in the motion picture industry. If one can avoid getting hit in the ass by a taxi, or somehow escape a coronary, the merry-go-round never fails to come back to its starting point. And when it does, dear Peter, I will be waiting for you. How I will be waiting for you."[125]. The 1971 merry-go-round ended as it had in 1957 and 1959, on another year in which Aldrich did not direct a feature film. Since the enforced idleness after being fired by Cohn, this had always been troubling for Aldrich. "I can't believe that you become a better director by not directing. Now there are

Opposite, Aldrich rehearses a dinner scene with the Grissom gang portrayed by actors (from right) Ralph Waite, Tony Musante, Joey Faye, Irene Dailey, and Don Keefer.

some people who...wait four, five, six years between pictures, the David Lean-George Stevens theory. But I can't believe that they wouldn't be better directors doing a film a year."[126]

More significant than the idleness, without the income from the multi-picture ABC deal or funding from the Sierra-Geneve offering, Aldrich realized that he could not maintain the overhead of the studio, and it was soon put up for sale.

Aldrich did, however, make a deal to direct a feature in October, 1971. After his long association with agent Ingo Preminger, Aldrich had been represented by the General Artists Corporation. His agent there, Marty Baum, had left to "join the enemy" and become president of ABC pictures. Aldrich now signed with CMA for representation as a director for hire. Under the settlement terms with ABC, Aldrich's salary on *The Grissom Gang* was "reduced" to $550,000. The deal which CMA negotiated with Universal Pictures to direct *Ulzana's Raid* was for just $150,000, plus ten points or 10% of net profits. That salary was less than 7 1/2% of *Ulzana*'s $2,016,000 budget compared to the nearly 13% Aldrich had made on *Baby Jane* ten years earlier. Aldrich knew that Universal had engaged him in the expectation that he would bring Burt Lancaster into the project, and he made a side deal with Lancaster whereby $50,000 of the amount allocated for the actor's salary was kicked back to Aldrich.

Even before production began on *Ulzana's Raid* in early 1972, Fox announced *Emperor of the North*, a project "re-teaming the same filmmakers who brought *The Dirty Dozen* to the screen,"[127] Aldrich, Kenneth Hyman, and Lee Marvin. Aldrich again received a $150,000 fee, plus 10 points and a deferment, which depended on the film being profitable and thus ultimately

amounted to zero. Aldrich had signed on to the project in late 1971, after director Sam Peckinpah and Hyman had dissolved their association and the producer got the script back from Paramount. "I have been deeply involved in *The Emperor of the North Pole* for the last few years," Peckinpah wrote to Aldrich. "I cannot say that I am happy about not doing it but I can say that I'm very happy that you are in charge. I have been a devoted fan of your pictures over the years and I feel that my adopted baby is in very good hands."[128] Aldrich no doubt thought it was in better hands: "I think Peckinpah's a fine director. I don't think he's as good as I am, but I think he's sensational."[129] Although *Ulzana's Raid* went several days over schedule and several hundred thousand dollars over budget, Universal was pleased with the results, and they signed Aldrich to direct and produce *Kill the Dutchman*. While Leon Griffiths worked on the script for *Dutchman* and he went into pre-production on *Emperor of the North*, Aldrich tried to interest MGM, which owned the story rights, or any other studio, in *Film of Memory*, and proposed a co-production with Carlo Ponti and Sophia Loren. As Aldrich was completing post-production work on the retitled *The Emperor of the North Pole* in early 1973, lack of studio interest forced him to abandon *Film of Memory*. While waiting for a commitment from George C. Scott for the title role in *Kill the Dutchman* and for *Emperor* to be released,

Aldrich signed with Warner Bros. to co-produce and direct *The Yakuza*. Warners had given writer Paul Schrader certain approval rights over the director, and Aldrich was a compromise selection.[130] "It was a *terrible* script, I thought, but a *sensational* idea.... Still, it might have happened my way if Lee Marvin had been cast in the lead"[131] When Marvin failed to come to terms with Warners, the role was offered to Robert Mitchum, who had director approval. Aldrich met and reminisced for six hours with Mitchum at the Beverly Hills Hotel and "never talked about the movie one minute."[132] On Monday, Aldrich was off the picture.

After a mediocre New York opening, *The Emperor of the North Pole* became again *Emperor of the North*, so that viewers disinterested in snowy vistas and sled dogs would not be misled by the title into staying away. They stayed away nonetheless. The week before *Emperor* opened in Los Angeles, Aldrich re-

Left, megaphone at the ready Aldrich and two cameras ride the train in *The Emperor of the North Pole*.

counted his experiences on *The Yakuza* in *Daily Variety* under the headline "Aldrich Philosophizes On Biz Where You're 'Only As Good As You Last Pic'."[133] The title of the piece when it was reprinted in weekly *Variety* was equally appropriate, "Bob Aldrich: Candid Maverick." After revealing his opinions on the script of *The Yakuza* and Mitchum's disapproval of him, Aldrich opined that "if *Emperor of the North Pole* had taken off at its New York opening, I'd have dropped him, he wouldn't have dropped me."[134] The immediate result was a phone call from Mike Medavoy to Aldrich "with the news that Warners wanted no further professional relationship with Aldrich because of what had appeared in a Variety article."[135] Aldrich's reply was typical. "The re-mote possibility exists that I may not be the world's greatest director but I am terribly practical and...I am neither sorry nor embarrassed by anything I did in our entire 'YAKUZA' relationship."[136]

On the first of July a Sunday supplement piece in a Los Angeles newspaper described Aldrich as the "Emperor of an Empty Studio."[137] Two days later, the sale of the Aldrich Studios to Video Cassette Industries was quietly announced.[138] In talking about the failure to maintain the studio, Aldrich returned repeatedly to the same analogy: "We built a better mousetrap, and the mice went out of business. What in the hell is the difference if you can make a picture 35% cheaper and better and no one wants to make the picture."[139] It was also effectively the end of the road for the Associates and Aldrich, which had merely functioned as the company that loaned out Aldrich's services on *Emperor*. Aldrich already had the Aldrich Company and now formed the Cheshire County Company, Inc., nominally headed by his son William, for future loan-outs.

Aldrich did not mention *Kill the Dutchman* in the *Variety* piece, and it also fell through shortly thereafter because of an actor's disapproval. George C. Scott wanted "to produce as well as star and I was even willing to let him produce except that he wanted to take that literally. In other words, he wanted to control who I wanted to use as cameraman, cutter, assistant ad infinitum. Figuring that heart attacks are easy enough to come by without seeking them out, I declined to go forward under those conditions."[140]

By the time *The Dutchman* was finally laid to rest, Aldrich was already in pre-production

Right, more amicable times: actor Robert Mitchum at Aldrich's 40th birthday party.

on *The Longest Yard*. "I'm a football nut," Aldrich would always readily admit, "It has nothing to do with reasonableness."[141] "I'm not kidding myself I was the first guy to be asked to do this picture," Aldrich later told an interviewer, but he added that his enthusiasm over the story in treatment stage convinced producer Al Ruddy that "it took someone who has played football—is freaked out about it—to do that kind of movie."[142] For a self-avowed "football nut," *The Longest Yard* had to be an exciting assignment, the opportunity to combine the melodramatic suspense elements of *The Dirty Dozen* with the reality-based suspense of a sporting contest. Aldrich believed he could make the climactic guards-versus-convicts game as compelling as the real thing; and both producer Ruddy and star Burt Reynolds shared Aldrich's passion for the game and the project. The result more than lived up to Aldrich's expectations. While critics may have found it simplistic, Aldrich extracted the same thematic statement from the prison milieu as he had from other contexts as diverse as renegade Indians, crashed planes, and World War II. More significantly, for the first time since *The Dirty Dozen*, audiences responded to Aldrich's point of view by paying to share it at the box office, and *The Longest Yard* was a bona fide hit. In fact, the domestic grosses ultimately exceeded $22 million or more than *The Dirty Dozen*. Aldrich's up-front fee as director had increased only slightly to $175,000; but this time his points would be worth some money.

In early 1974 the working experience on *The Longest Yard* led to a new partnership with Burt Reynolds, first called B and B Productions and later RoBurt Productions, Aldrich's first actor partnership since the SAM Company. Aldrich had already tried to get funding on another project with Reynolds that was to co-star Brigitte Bardot, *Time Off*, about free-spirited blue-collar guys who pick up a Frenchwoman while en route to Mexico. When that failed to attract backing despite repackaging it to co-star Robert Redford, RoBurt got a deal on a project, *City of the Angels,* which Reynolds had with Paramount, the distributors of *The Longest Yard*. While in pre-production and a few months after the release of *The Longest Yard*, Reynolds got publicity for RoBurt by arranging for an episode of Merv Griffin's syndicated prime time talk show to be dedicated to Aldrich. The program on which Aldrich appeared with Reynolds, Ernest Borgnine, and Connie Stevens aired on October 9, 1974.

After again trying vainly to get Bardot to co-star in *City of the Angels*, which would be released as *Hustle*, RoBurt settled on Catherine Deneuve. Aldrich got $250,000 to produce and direct and more than offset his fee increase for the partnership when he brought the picture in $75,000 under budget. In some respects, Reynolds' character, police Lt. Phil Gaines, is Mike Hammer twenty years later. While Gaines' disaffection and cynicism are verbalized more frequently than Hammer's, the character himself is trapped in the same violent

Opposite, Aldrich directs Catherine Deneuve and
Burt Reynolds in *Hustle*.

underworld as Hammer. While not as popular with filmgoers as *The Longest Yard*, *Hustle* did earn over $10 million domestically and returned a profit.

After *Hustle* was released, Reynolds had to honor other acting commitments. "The problem with a recently arrived superstar is to find periods that are mutually agreeable to both parties. The demands on his time are extraordinary, and I don't elect to be in a position of waiting around to make a picture with Burt."[143] Aldrich attached his son, Reynolds, and RoBurt to *Stand On It* but after two years had still not struck a deal. Disagreement over other projects and the course RoBurt should follow, exacerbated by inactivity, built up over time. The partnership made no more pictures.

The success of *The Longest Yard* and *Hustle* had restored Aldrich's marketability as a director, and he agreed to what became a multi-picture deal with Lorimar, a successful, independent television company which, like ABC had, wanted to break into feature production. The basis of Aldrich's deal on his first project at Lorimar, *Twilight's Last Gleaming*, was again the actor who had anchored his first major features and *Ulzana's Raid*, Burt Lancaster. "Lorimar," as Aldrich explained it, "had had this project for a long time and they couldn't get it financed.... So I told Lorimar that I would only do it if I could turn the story upside down. And if Lancaster would agree to do it."[144] Early on Aldrich lobbied vigorously for both a major rewrite and no restrictions on the length of the final picture which he won. But as the time spent on the project stretched out and Lorimar's attitude was not properly appreciative, Aldrich became quite upset about his $350,000 total salary. Because he could "see a multitude of advantages...if we can keep the Lorimar relationship alive," Aldrich weighed carefully whether to "undertake 'the Battle of Lorimar'."[145] In a lengthy inter-

nal memo Aldrich noted that "because a deal is a deal is a deal"[146] he had only asked for more money twice before when projects took much longer than expected and received generous bonuses on both. The reasons for pressing the issue were many and varied: because he still did not have a signed contract; because he had been *de facto* producer; because writers, actors, and others had received bonuses; because he had brought the picture in on the scheduled 65 days when the executive producers expected to shoot for 75 and to spend another $500,000; because he had signed for 26 weeks which became nine months then 18 months; because he had lost the opportunity to make *Seven Day Soldiers*. *Twilight's Last Gleaming* had consumed as much time as Joseph Levine wanted from Aldrich as would-be director on *A Bridge Too Far*, for which Aldrich turned down a million dollar fee and 10 points. Aldrich did not mince his last words: "I 'understand' more than any of you will ever realize that in Aldrich you are representing a neurotic nut whose life revolves around not getting fucked regardless of the eventual price. But in [Lorimar chief Merv] Adelson, you are dealing with a psychotic who has dedicated his life—and successfully—to <u>always</u> getting the edge."[147]

At the same time that he contacted his lawyer, Aldrich was equally blunt in expressing his frustration to agent George Chasin:

> An area that sometimes deeply disturbs me is when an agent is reluctant to <u>REALLY</u> do battle with an employer in behalf of his client, knowing that he (the agent) could very well win the battle but lose the war; meaning that that client could prevail but the agent would never be able to merchandise any of his "other" clients with that employer again.
>
> It seems to me that the one difference between most creators—and certainly directors—and an agent, is that the Director is <u>always</u> in the pits. What he does or fails to do is scored every day, every week, every picture. So that the Director is always held accountable for every picture that fails, and should a picture succeed the Director only shares that dubious distinction. However, the bottom line is the Director is in the trenches "every day." The agent, however, in almost every instance, is back at the Command Post, safe, secure and out of the battle zone. There are rare, rare exceptions when the agent is called upon to enter and to compete in this terribly tricky, treacherous and vulnerable domain.[148]

In the pits, in the trenches, with someone keeping score—the analogies to sports and to war are telling. What was it that Lewis Milestone had understood? That the game was power; but he "had the capacity to know when trouble was

Opposite, Aldrich sits in the President's chair on the set of Twilight's Last Gleaming

coming and how to deal with it." Throughout his career Aldrich tried for the same understanding and the same capacity. No matter how many times he rationally decided to put survival in the industry first, Aldrich's could not quell his sense of outrage when confronted with betrayal and inequity or his stubborn refusal to be taken advantage of. No wonder Merv Adelson felt that "every time he turns around, Aldrich is threatening him!"[149] What he probably felt was the same moral outrage that Capt. Cooney sensed from Lt. Costa in *Attack!*. Or, more aptly, perhaps it was same seething idealism that drove Gen. Dell to action in *Twilight's Last Gleaming*.

In the end, Aldrich relented, perhaps as much because he thought too much of *Twilight* and did not want to jeopardize his control of it as to preserve future projects with Lorimar: "I was more involved in it and I think prouder of it than any [picture] I'd ever done. I felt it had something to say; I thought it was desperately important."[150] Despite a distinguished cast and ambitious script, *Twilight's Last Gleaming* became one of Aldrich's most bitter disappointments. A Cold War melodrama of high-level cover-ups and nuclear blackmail, Aldrich sustained considerable suspense over the 143 minute running time he fought to have. Despite this and compelling performances by Burt Lancaster and the other stars, the film was poorly received at the box office. On *Emperor*, *The Longest Yard*, and *Hustle*, Aldrich had not hesitated to question and criticize the advertising campaign and distribution efforts of Fox and Paramount. Aldrich believed that halfhearted and misguided distribution schemes had cost him thousands of profit-participation dollars in the past. On the strength of that conviction, he excoriated Al Ruddy about not being consulted and not reaching black moviegoers on *The Longest Yard*: "I suggested send[ing] three of our black actors to those cities [Philadelphia and Chicago] to make the potential black audiences aware that this is something other than a Burt Reynolds-jockstrap-romance picture...you told me Charlie Glenn [of Paramount distribution]

didn't want to spend the $5,000 involved to get these three actors [there]...and that is bullshit! For this picture to do what it did at the United Artists theatre in the loop in one week is fucking lunacy! Thousands of dollars have been pissed away trying to promote this project...but to fail to reach black audiences...is a costly, inexcusable and unforgivable mistake."[151]

Because it was "the campaign for Lorimar's first theatrical motion picture," the distributor of *Twilight's Last Gleaming*, Allied Artists, had pledged $3.5 million which, as the trade papers noted, was "more than was spent to hype *Papillon* and more than was allocated to beat the drums for *Cabaret*."[152] Domestically, *Twilight's Last Gleaming* grossed $4.5 million, which even *Variety* would have to admit was no longer a truly blockbuster amount but not a dismal total either. Eventually, Aldrich realized that after the foreign sales, including a lucrative Italian deal which he had helped to put in place, Lorimar broke even on the picture.[153] At the time, however, Aldrich saw the project as a complete failure: "It died; it was a disaster. It wasn't the critics, wasn't the campaign. It just plain died because nobody damned well wanted to know. They just didn't want to know."[154]

The Choirboys, based on a best-selling novel by Joseph Wambaugh, unexpectedly stirred up more controversy than *Twilight's Last Gleaming*. Production problems ranged from the death of one of the featured actors to the need to reconstruct a Los Angeles park on a sound stage because the actual location was too unsafe for night photography. After several changes were made by Aldrich and Lorimar, Wambaugh sued the production company and Aldrich for violating his screenwriting contract. Aldrich had thought that "Wambaugh's anger...will be lessened by the reception of the picture";[155] but the novelist had already taken out trade advertisements denouncing the filmmakers and initiated an arbitration through the Writers Guild to have his name removed from the picture. As it happens, Aldrich had only recently vigorously supported the removal of first draft writer Tom Mankiewicz's name from the screen credits of *Twilight's Last Gleaming* and had expressed his position to the trade papers: "Aldrich identified himself as the shadow third and supervisory writer.... 'The Writers Guild in arbitration gave none of the previous writers credit,' he noted, 'so I've got to presume they believe the contribution of the new ideas erases the contribution of the old ideas.'"[156] Aldrich did not feel the same way about Wambaugh's work on *The Choirboys*: "We changed his script a maximum of 1 to 3 percent...to make the revisions the producers and I thought necessary."[157] Despite this Lorimar lost the arbitration and Aldrich later rationalized Wambaugh's victory, "[Writer Christopher] Knopf changed the intent of the work, and that's why they allowed Wambaugh to take his name off...he wrote a dirty, tasteless, vulgar book, which I think I've managed to capture. But he would like to have you think that we changed the thrust of those scenes."[158] Besides re-shooting Wambaugh's ending because "it's nonsense," Aldrich was forced by running time restraints to cut "marvellous scenes" as well.[159] As disheartening as these events may have been to Aldrich, the previews were worse. *The Choirboys* opened to small audiences and scathing reviews.

After having been the West Coast DGA Vice-President under Robert Wise and chairing the most recent contract negotiating committee, Aldrich had been elected President of the Directors Guild of America in mid-1975. Ironically, one of his first actions in this position involved confronting the Writers Guild, of which Aldrich had also become a member in 1970 for the script of *Too Late the Hero*. "The Directors Guild is going to take a firmer, tougher stand than it has in the past," Aldrich announced immediately after his election by acclamation: "There are some collision warning signs with the writers that are going to have to be resolved."[160] As the WGA negotiated its new contract, the Directors Guild membership was drawn into the issues of possessory credits and the right of directors to make script revisions during production that would be restricted by a WGA demand that all changes be made by their members. Aldrich even filed a personal grievance with the National Labor Relations Board accusing the WGA of unfair practices in refusing to let him resign from the organization prior to a threatened strike. Ultimately the Writers Guild modified or dropped their demands.

Aldrich was reelected DGA president in 1977, so that concurrent with the post-production on *The Choirboys*, he was actively involved in negotiating a new contract between the Directors Guild and producers. Aldrich had said that he "accepted a second term only because he had assurances the membership was prepared to strike—for higher wage guarantees 'and particularly for assistant directors'."[161] Aldrich oversaw what the DGA itself describes as "the most difficult film negotiations in its history, working to address economic inequities and obtain artistic rights."[162] To get those guarantees in creative rights and increases in basic wages, Aldrich brought in a team of professional negotiators to support the DGA committee. The result, after a strike threat, was the most extensive increase in compensation and benefits in the history of the film industry or, as the DGA calls it, simply "its most significant contract." Besides almost doubling the minimum salaries of its assistant director and production manager members, the 1978 Basic Agreement between the DGA and the producers began a new era in the rights of feature film directors that would ultimately include: at least ten weeks cutting time and unhindered supervision of all aspects of post-production; a strengthened "pay-or-play" position to avoid capricious firing by producers; payment for consulting on script development; and, something Aldrich had been extracting from producers since *Sodom and Gomorrah*, two guaranteed previews for the director of his or her cut.

The association between the Aldrich Company and Lorimar ended after *Who Is Killing the Great Chefs of Europe?*, produced by William Aldrich on behalf the Aldrich Company but without Aldrich *père* who was "doing *The Choirboys* for them. That's the way it happens."[163] Despite the financial failure of *Twilight's Last Gleaming* and *The Choirboys*, Aldrich, perhaps recalling how *The Dirty Dozen* engendered a deal on *Too Late the Hero*, was working with producer Mace Neufeld to spin another football picture off of *The Longest Yard*, this one entitled *Sudden Death* for Warner Bros. In addition to not agreeing on casting—Aldrich wanted Jeff Bridges, Warners wanted Ryan O'Neal—the studio was having trouble making arrangements with an NFL team and stadium to be featured in the picture. Since its option on the project was about to expire, Warners asked Aldrich to replace Dick Richards on another Neufeld picture, *No Knife*.

1979 was to be a disturbing year for Aldrich; it began propitiously but ended on quite the opposite note. Aldrich the director began the year shooting a movie on which he had replaced someone else. Shortly thereafter, Aldrich lost *Sudden Death*, the second project at Warners; and in December he was fired from *Arctic Rampage*. As Guild president, Aldrich ended his term by pushing through plans for a new national headquarters building, to which he hoped the DGA might eventually attract other guilds and unions as co-tenants. The infighting over the need for and cost of a new structure left a lot of hard feelings, and at the midyear DGA elections Aldrich was "devastated at not even being elected to the [National] Board after his terms as President."[164] Aldrich believed he had alienated many potential employers by his vigorous efforts during contract negotiations and was stung when his colleagues repudiated him at the end of his second term. "He laid down his life for this guild," recalled longtime DGA executive Joe Youngerman, "and he's not even elected [to the board] after being president. And his nose was really out of joint. They voted against him. Everything he did, they voted against him. That's what killed him."[165]

It was in August, 1978, that Aldrich was offered *No Knife* by Warner Bros. Aldrich agreed to start work immediately on this Western adventure-comedy, to star Gene Wilder, and even abdicated his usual prerogatives on key personnel, as many of the crew were already at work when he took over as director. The budget on this project had vacillated considerably between 8 and 10 million dollars. Aldrich asked for about $200,000 in increases. Then Harrison Ford was brought in to co-star, and reality hit in the below-the-line categories, sending the total to $9.9 million. In the end, Aldrich brought the picture in for $700,000 less than that. As for the creative result, Aldrich would later observe that he could make a picture "better, faster and cheaper than anybody alive, but I need tools, professional help, a revised, workable, believable, funny script, and ac-

Opposite, Aldrich on location for *The Frisco Kid* with stars Harrison Ford and Gene Wilder (far right).

tors. <u>Not stars</u>; actors. Anything else would be like buying a ticket on the Titanic."[166]

Warners had hopes of recreating the success of *Blazing Saddles*. But despite the casting of Ford fresh from the success of *Star Wars*, the film—released as *The Frisco Kid*—was closer to *4 for Texas* than *Blazing Saddles*. Its $4.7 million gross was slightly more than the amount taken in by *Twilight's Last Gleaming* and certainly better than *The Choirboys*, but *The Frisco Kid* also cost a lot more to make than either of the Lorimar pictures. A more telling comparison came when Warners reissued *Blazing Saddles* and it grossed $8 million in re-release. To Aldrich's great surprise, six weeks before *The Frisco Kid* was released, Warners decided not to use him on *Sudden Death*. "To give you an actual quote," Aldrich's agent informed him, "the people at Warner Brothers thought 'there should be some air' between pictures before you do another one for them."[167] Aldrich had been paid $475,000 plus 15% of net profits to direct *The Frisco Kid*, the same as his proposed deal on *Sudden Death*. As he had in the Lorimar dispute and so many times before, Aldrich wrote another letter to another attorney about another possible lawsuit. Aldrich was particularly incensed because in anticipation of his being tied up on *Sudden Death*, his agency had turned down three other possible features. While still deciding whether or not to sue, Aldrich accepted a directing assignment he had twice before turned down. When *Longest Yard* producer Al Ruddy offered Aldrich $700,000 to direct *Arctic Rampage*, the loss of *Sudden Death* became moot.

According to Aldrich he eventually accepted the job on *Arctic Rampage* not only because Ruddy increased the directing fee but also because Ruddy had

signed *Dirty Dozen* stars Charles Bronson and Lee Marvin. What Aldrich did
not know when he began work was how seriously underfinanced the project
was. Assuming that the film would cost around $18 million, Aldrich was
astonished to discover that the maximum amount the executive producers
would spend was only $10 million. Even before the budget debacle, Ruddy
seemed to be making end runs around Aldrich's contractual approvals on re-
writes and cast, which confused and exasperated Aldrich: "If Ruddy knew what
my deal was, he wouldn't have told me that he had made a deal with Telly
Savalas, which made it necessary for me to inform Ruddy that I didn't approve
of Telly Savalas...to contemplate making a movie as difficult as *Arctic Rampage*, should it prove necessary to pull out my contract every day and a half
seems ludicrous."[168]

It was not until he finally saw the budget that Aldrich understood how "ludicrous" it really was. The basic problem, which Aldrich felt he had been suck-
ered into having to fix, was that after deducting all the producer, director, and
star salaries, "we have only four million dollars left to make the picture...I didn't
have to go to Canada to know that Rampage cannot be made for four million."[169] Holding firm to this position led Aldrich to be fired for the second time
in his career on December 14, 1979. The long and complicated grievance pro-
cedure, initiated by Aldrich and the Directors Guild, only extended and intensified Aldrich's frustration. In the end "after considering 22 witnesses, 100
exhibits and 2500 pages of testimony,"[170] the arbitrator awarded Aldrich
$25,000 or $675,000 less than the lost salary. Aldrich appealed, and part of
Ruddy's reply was to file his own $1.2 million lawsuit which was not dropped
until a year later. By that time Aldrich had spent much more than the $25,000
award on his own legal fees and appeals. For Aldrich, who had "joked many
times about my cynicism re lawyers (and agents),"[171] it was to be a final re-
sounding example that "the ground rules are: you don't get yours, they get
theirs."

In the end, Aldrich reasoned that "there just isn't enough time to get mad at
everybody. So you've got to figure out who it is you really want to get mad at.
Otherwise there'd be no time to make movies."[172] So he began work on what
would he his last picture, *...All the Marbles*. For the last time, Aldrich would
claim in an interview, as he had about *The Longest Yard* and other earlier projects, that he had "used the Abe Polonsky screenplay for *Body and Soul* as the
basis for this film."[173] At least, in the context of a ring sport, the allusion to a
figure's "fall from grace" seemed less of a stretch. Perhaps it was because he
had reached an age when many think of retirement that Aldrich waxed nostalgic by invoking so many examples from past work when he spoke about *...All
the Marbles*.

Opposite, Aldrich might be indicating "Onward and Upward" to
actor Peter Falk on location for *...All the Marbles*.

Aldrich had been in ill-health before production began but rebounded to tackle the project with great enthusiasm. MGM shared Aldrich's enthusiasm and had gone so far as to begin planning a sequel. As usual he detailed the progress of the movie with memos, many of them to studio chief David Begelman. During post-production, Aldrich recapped his thoughts on how the box-office might be improved through previews and special marketing. For all this, ...*All the Marbles*, an unusual comedy about a promoter and two female wrestlers, fell very far short of expectations. The final match, which Aldrich had hoped would equal the excitement of the end of *The Longest Yard*, did not seem that way to most viewers. Plans for a sequel were promptly cancelled.

Aldrich had never been one to play it safe in choosing his projects; he chose them based on personal enthusiasm, sometimes against the advice of those around him. "Not a single person likes our screenplay except me," he said about *Coffee, Tea, and Me*; "I respect these other opinions and start thinking, 'Jesus Christ, I must be wrong.' Then I take it home and read it again and I laugh myself to death, I think it's hysterical."[174] As Aldrich said many times, he might have to "be an idiot" on occasion to do so, but he had to believe in a picture in order to make it.

He might have lost a step or two at the end of his career but, no matter how much he talked about survival, he had never lost the inclination he shared with so many of his characters. from Mike Callahan onward, to "take a chance" on something he believed in. After the failure of The Aldrich Studios, he seemed content to be, on some occasions, in charge of projects he had developed and, on other occasions, merely a director for hire. Aldrich conceded after ...*All the Marbles,* that "For every picture I've wanted to do and finally made, there've

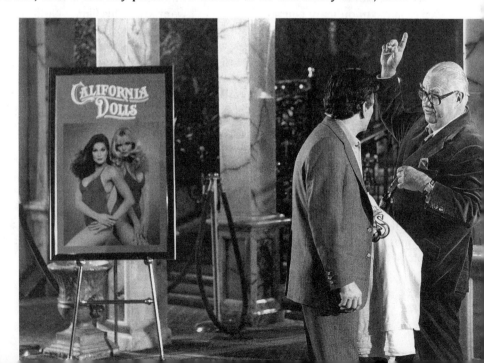

been three or four that nobody wanted to hear about much less finance.... the truth is the directors that are working all the time are the ones that don't make waves. This isn't to say they're good or bad directors, they're just not trouble-makers."[175]

None of Aldrich's last four pictures were successful, either in critical or box-office terms; and yet Aldrich seemed less concerned than ever with attracting moviegoers for purely fiscal reasons. The social consciousness he had first evidenced in *Attack!* and *The Big Knife* had evolved considerably by the time of *The Longest Yard, Hustle,* and *Twilight's Last Gleaming*; but it remained for Aldrich a significant consideration in any project which he undertook. While his films had always contained personal statements, Aldrich was more dedicated than before to finding an audience that could respond to these statements. His attitude was still, as he wrote in countless letters and memoranda, "Onward and Upward."

"Aldrich Wants to Make Dream Film" was the headline of an article written in 1963. As if anticipating a scene from *Lylah Clare* at a press lunch in the Brown Derby restaurant, Aldrich talked about an unnamed "film that I have in mind [which] won't be in any manner but my own. It will be original and different."[176] Twenty years later at a retrospective of his work at the La Rochelle Festival in France, a report on what would be Aldrich's last press conference was titled, "Aldrich's long-term dream project."[177]

In La Rochelle, Aldrich did talk about *Kinderspiel*, a project that was almost forty years old and that he would never make. He also returned to his theme of how a "Czar beats a Committee": "In the days of the Cohns, the Mayers, Warners, Zanucks, of course, it was corrupt and evil, but those particularly people had extraordinary courage. You said, 'I want to do this film, with these actors,' they would think about it, not for weeks or months, but if they liked the idea, the answer would come back within hours."[178] It was not just nostalgia that made Aldrich talk about how the system was when he broke in, it was that "the big problem of all us independent producers is finding out who to talk to at the studios; who has the power to say yes as well as no. I can talk to David Begelman direct. But he's the only one. Who do I talk to at the other studios? I don't know. I really don't."[179]

Part of this final dilemma may indeed have been that the people and the system Aldrich remembered were gone. Whether it was a Czar or a committee, whether it was Merv Adelson at Lorimar or a roomful of anonymous Germans for whom Aldrich "auditioned" before *Twilight's Last Gleaming*, part of it may have just been an old veteran's fatigue over fighting the same fight year after year. Movies are a new art, just a century old, and its first artists, men and women like Aldrich, were not always comfortable with the concept of art. In that sense his statement in the American Room of the Brown Derby in 1963

Above, Aldrich poses with one of the last of the "Czars": Bette Davis and Joan Crawford flank Jack Warner before beginning work on *What Ever Happened to Baby Jane?*

was all the more extraordinary: "I must create and I can't always create what I want artistically and culturally under present methods." The studio committees, Aldrich lamented, "they're no longer in the movie business, they're in the money business."[180]

What greater irony could there be for Robert Burgess Aldrich, the progeny of banking and publishing fortunes, to struggle all his life in a field where money and art embraced so uncomfortably. There is no question that movies were Aldrich's life. "I relax by working," Aldrich often said, and "since I have no hobbies such as girls, horses, cards, etc., etc., my principal preoccupation other than pictures is politics."[181] As a child, Aldrich's daughter Adell remembers always having to be quiet when her father was home on weekdays because he was always working, preparing his shot lists or something else needed for the next day.[182] She also remembers the times when the family was short of money because her father had spent the savings on a script option. As an adult Adell Aldrich worked on many Associates and Aldrich productions where she learned first hand not just of her father's loyalty to those with whom he worked but also of his commitment to his liberal beliefs. That was manifest not just in the hours he spent involved with the Directors Guild, the "union" of directors and their production team, but in the production jobs he offered to women and minorities long before it was fashionable. Aldrich's loyalty extended both to the creative or "above-the-line" talents and to the technicians or below-the-line personnel with whom he worked. Sometimes he acted out of motivations that were both political and personal. After Hugo Butler's death in 1968, Aldrich helped his widow, Jean Rouverol. As he revealed when soliciting a donation from Joseph Losey, who still owed Aldrich money from more than a dozen years earlier, "at present [Dalton] Trumbo, [Albert] Maltz, Ingo Preminger, and I are continuing monthly sustenance contributions."[183] At other times when, as William Aldrich noted, his father "carried and carried and carried these people forever when there was nothing to do," it was because "he felt an obligation to these fellows. It was a family kind of thing. It was an extended family of people who liked to make movies."[184]

What greater secondary irony could there be for Aldrich, which was the middle-name of a Republican Vice-President, than to "think [that] anybody with any brains in 1936 to '40 would have been a Communist. There's no doubt about it.... I can't imagine how people, certainly working people, can be Republicans. It amazes me."[185] While Aldrich contributed to an occasional Democratic candidate and to Common Cause, he never forced a political viewpoint into the dramatic structure of his films. "Is Aldrich a leftist?" asked Raymond Borde in an early career article entitled "A Non-conformist Filmmaker" for Jean-Paul Sartre's Marxist-Existentialist magazine, *Les Temps Modernes*. "We've been discouraged so often that we are wary of American liberals," Borde continued. "Like most left of center Americans Aldrich can evidently deceive us from one day to the next."[186] Aldrich, who felt his cousin Nelson Rockefeller's liberal credentials "went out the door the day of Attica,"[187] never

Below, Aldrich as his own mogul, posing with an artist's rendition of the Aldrich Studios in 1968.

waivered from the convictions he brought with him to Hollywood in 1941. Quite unlike Ronald Reagan, a better-known former head of a Hollywood guild, Aldrich always felt he should "be described as moderately left of the Democratic position. Not radical, but certainly more extreme than whatever the Democratic platform is, which is nonexistent."[188]

Aldrich's celebrated impatience with those less dedicated is typical of an obsessive workaholic, typical of an artist who got into buying studios and film industry politics as possible ways to defend his creative rights. "Sometime between the age of 45 and 55, you come to a decision about yourself," an ostensibly mellower Aldrich told an interviewer after his last film. "You realize that as a director, you're either going to be discovered in your lifetime, after you're dead, or not at all. And if you conclude it might be 'not at all' or 'after you're dead,' than you start to relax and just concentrate on how you're doing, on how well you've done the job"[189] How well did he do the job? In the final analysis, one must look to the results, to Aldrich's body of work, for the answer.

Aldrich was still developing *Kinderspiel* and several other projects before his death. Although he had commitments for part of the budget on *Kinderspiel*, he feared that the controversial subject—children and students "striking" to compel world peace—might hamper him in securing full funding. While waiting for that or something else to develop, Aldrich underwent two surgeries in 1983 that resulted in kidney failure. After several months on dialysis, Aldrich decided to suspend treatment. Realizing that he would not recover, Aldrich planned one final production. He outlined a detailed scenario for the conduct of his memorial service at the Directors Guild. He died on December 5, 1983.

> If you're going to spend 25 years as a filmmaker, as I have, you have to make films to please yourself. Whatever I've thought of them later, and whatever the critics and the public thought of them, the way I've made my movies has seemed right....
> If you blow one, that can't be the end; you pick up the pieces and go on. If you're a filmmaker you can't disappear into a bottle of whiskey or anywhere else.
> But you've given a year or two of your life to a film. And if it fails, you have no idea how emotionally painful it can be. Still, win or lose, you put yourself back together and move on, because that's all you want to do.[190]

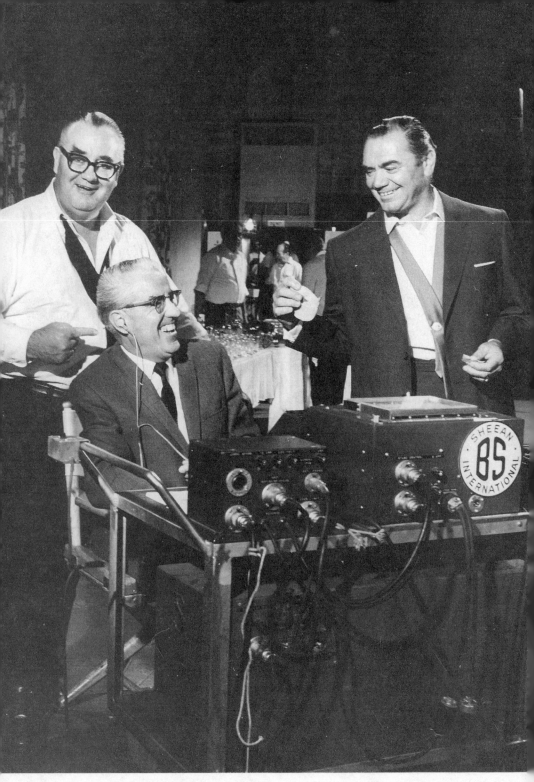

Above, Aldrich poses with Ernest Borgnine, who portrays studio mogul Barney Sheean in *The Legend of Lylah Clare*. Sheean wears his tie in the Aldrich style.

An Introduction to the Films

A better director than most people think I am. A less commercial
director than they think I am...but in this town, you are the sort
of director they think you are, not the sort of director you think
you are.[1]

There's no winning the critical game. If you're half-smart, you
abandon that elusive hope. You make the picture that you find
attractive or interesting, and you make it as well as you can. If
the critics like it, great. If they don't, forget them.[2]

The critical reputation of Robert Aldrich, scion of the Eastern establishment
and graduate of the best finishing schools in Hollywood, burst out of Europe
with *La Politique des Auteurs*. As early as 1957, Aldrich became No. 7 of "Les
Grands Créateurs du Cinéma" in a series published by the Belgian Club du
Livre du Cinéma, which followed earlier monographs on Robert Bresson,
John Huston, Jean Renoir, Vittorio De Sica, Luis Buñuel, and Marcel Carné.
This was certainly heady company for a new American director, not yet forty
years old; but as René Micha explained in his monograph, "At a single sitting,
one could see six films. By some chance Europe received in three months,
three years of Aldrich's work. It was soon clear that...Aldrich was an auteur—a
quality which *Cahiers du Cinéma, Positif, Bianco e Nero* valued above all."[3]
Micha may have properly attributed the European critical esteem for Aldrich
to good timing. Certainly, in the 1950s, for a director with less than three
years of feature work to be winning prizes at major festivals was somewhat
unusual. In preparing an article on Aldrich for Jean-Paul Sartre's review, *Les
Temps Modernes*, another French critic, Raymond Borde, wrote to Aldrich in
February, 1956, that "in the eyes of French critics, film directors play a leading

part in all productions, much more so than movie-stars who we hardly mention, and this is the reason why the year 1955 of American motion pictures has been named by us 'the Aldrich year.' We saw successively *World for Ransom, Apache, Vera Cruz, Kiss Me Deadly, The Big Knife* in the course of a few months. These films seemed as different from the usual Hollywood productions, as bearing the stamp of an original, engaging personality."[4]

The critical adulation, and the attendant festival prizes, came early in Aldrich's directorial career, but it never crossed the Atlantic and took root in his own country. There are many critical studies of American directors in English, more than one on such contemporaries of Aldrich as Nicholas Ray, Samuel Fuller, and Joseph Losey, but little has been written on the man whom the French critics admired as "le gros Bob." Now, more than ten years after his death, a likely response to an expression of admiration for the work on Robert Aldrich is still a puzzled look and perhaps the query, "Don't you mean Robert Altman?" In fact, in an article about him entitled "Aldrich's Safari in Mogul Country" published in 1974, the first mention of Aldrich's name in the text is an uncorrected typo which identifies him as "Bob Altman."[5]

In just the second year of what was to be a 28-year career as a director, Aldrich made *Kiss Me Deadly*. With that picture, according to Borde and Étienne Chaumeton, the critics who popularized the term *film noir*, "Robert Aldrich brought the *noir* cycle to a dark and fascinating close." Since Paul Schrader called *Kiss Me Deadly*, "the great masterpiece of *film noir*"[6] in 1972, it has been analyzed in depth in a score of other books and articles and remains, forty years after its release, an entirely remarkable movie. Yet its director is still confused with the very different auteur who made *Nashville*.

François Truffaut, Jacques Rivette, Claude Chabrol, Marcel Ophuls, and Bertrand Tavernier, the critics of *Cahiers du Cinéma* who dogged Aldrich's trail at film festivals across Europe in the mid-1950s, went on to their own careers and acclaim as filmmakers. While a new generation of French critics conducted interviews, wrote essays and even two full-length books on Aldrich, both published shortly after his death, other than on *Kiss Me Deadly*, little appeared in English. In 1973, when the first draft of this study was written, auteurism was still new to America. It was only five years before that Andrew Sarris had placed Aldrich, along with Ray, Fuller, and Losey, in the second tier of his hierarchy in <u>The American Cinema</u>, and proclaimed him "one of the most strikingly personal directors of the past two decades."[7] Ironically, there was nowhere for Aldrich's critical reputation to go except into stasis or downward. By the time of *...All the Marbles*' release, Sarris had gone from applauding Aldrich as an "underrated genre stylist" to finding that "what once seemed broad and heavy-handed in his approach now seems, in these deliberately mindless times, intelligently forceful by default."[8] Others were far more negative.

It is one thing for someone writing a biography of Joan Crawford or Burt Lancaster to accuse Aldrich of having a "sledgehammer style," however glib or imperceptive that might be. It is quite another thing for a critic such as Robin Wood, in comparing *Kiss Me Deadly* with Fritz Lang's *The Big Heat*, to invoke the same image in saying that "the sledgehammer sensibility that is both the strength and weakness of *Kiss Me Deadly* prohibits any nuance."[9] Even Sarris' early assessment suggests an uncontrolled atmosphere: "Aldrich's direction of his players generally creates a subtle frenzy on the screen, and his visual style suggests an unstable world full of awkward angles and harsh transitions."[10]

From his earliest work, Aldrich often addressed the questions of violence and brutality, even outside of the context of the war film, with an uncommon directness. *The Longest Yard* unflinchingly depicts the savagery of prison life and football with equal grimness; but how does this lead to the offhanded remark about Aldrich's attitude from a Lancaster biographer that "if it's worth killing, it's worth killing as violently as the censor will permit."[11] The "censor," represented first by the Hays Office and then the ratings board of the MPAA, seemed more concerned with the sexual content of Aldrich films from *World for Ransom* and *Kiss Me Deadly* to *The Killing of Sister George*. The final fight in *The Emperor of the North Pole* is as graphically violent as any sequence in Aldrich's work, but no more so than sequences in, for instance, Hitchcock's contemporary *Frenzy* (1972).

Yet Aldrich's critical reputation seems more one-dimensional today than while he was still at work. Sarris concedes that he was "intelligently forceful *by default*." Wood quotes Leonard Maltin ("an indispensable barometer of contemporary taste") about *Kiss Me Deadly*'s "major influence on French New Wave directors" but holds that, compared to Fritz Lang, who "is among the cinema's subtlest and most subversive moralists; Aldrich's moral sense does not lend itself to the finer discriminations."[12]

In one sense, Wood's recent critique reflects the same ambivalence that Raymond Borde had when he questioned Aldrich's political beliefs in 1956. Whether Aldrich is a moralist or a leftist outside of the context of the films themselves seems less of a concern for Wood, who forthrightly deems Aldrich an "interesting director" and Lang a "great" one. Since Wood's article, like Sarris' entire book, is about evaluation, such a judgment is not unexpected. But all of these judgments by Borde, Sarris, or Wood involve certain *pre*-judgments and/or comparisons that may be neither appropriate not accurate. Borde speaks openly of being "deceived" before by "American liberals"; yet writing in the addendum to <u>Panorama du Film Noir Américain</u>, Borde clearly shares Schrader's assessment of *Kiss Me Deadly* as a masterwork. In 1968 Sarris also believed that *Kiss Me Deadly* was a "most perplexing and revealing work.... a testament to Aldrich's anarchic spirit."[13] By 1981, there is a hint of condescension from Sarris. How could a filmmaker as direct and uninhibited as Aldrich be intelligent except by default? How could a sledgehammer be used to make fine discriminations?

In fairness, Wood, at least, does consider the issue of how a merely interesting director can make "the more 'satisfying' (i.e., coherent)" film and concludes that "the extraordinary, irresistible force of Aldrich's film is achieved at a certain cost: the elimination of all complexity of attitude."[14] In the particular instance of The Big Heat and Kiss Me Deadly Wood seems to equate complexity with a "tragic," i.e., flawed, hero. Obviously, a critic of Wood's stature must and should be permitted his beliefs not just about creativity and authorship but even such digressions as rescuing Yasujiro Ozu "from the clutches of neo-formalism."[15] At the same time, Aldrich's reputation needs to be rescued from the constraints of a neoclassical preference for a flawed hero or whatever other critical bias Wood, Sarris, Borde et al. might harbor.

Perhaps if Wood compared The Big Heat to World for Ransom in the contexts of film noir and the interaction of male and female characters, Aldrich's sensibilities would appear to be more refined. As for Kiss Me Deadly, it typifies those rare films which transcend critical modalities. Borde and Chaumeton, Schrader, Durgnat, Sarris, Wood, and scores of other critical writers all agree on the merits of the film. Structuralist, formalist, feminist, auteurist, and Marxist critics alike have all found something to admire in it. A quarter of century apart, Borde and Wood both remark on how Aldrich transformed Spillane's solipsistic and reactionary novel into something remarkable. Whether or not Kiss Me Deadly does anticipate the freeform narratives of the New Wave or, it

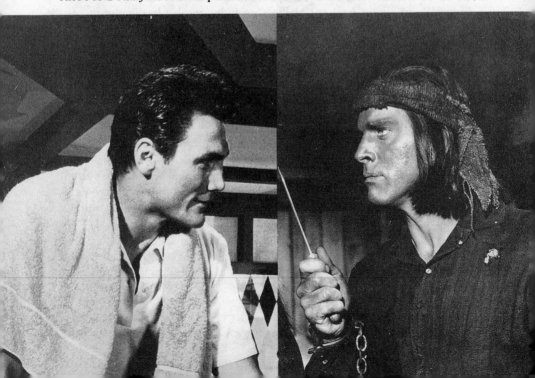

could be argued, the self-conscious stylistic de-constructions of later Godard, it is undeniably multi-faceted and complex in attitude.

For many observers the mixture of *film noir*, McCarthyism, and "va-va-voom" has, to use Sarris' celebrated analogy from <u>The American Cinema</u>, caused a confusion between the forest and the trees. Borde sensed it when he wrote that "on the extreme right, certain imbeciles have identified this *thriller* as the quest for the Grail."[16] Obviously, *Kiss Me Deadly* is a quest for the Grail, not as a reactionary archetype but in the sense that social historian Mike Davis describes as "that great anti-myth usually known as *noir*."[17] Hammer is indeed an "anti-Galahad" in search of his "great whatsit," a colloquialism that stands in for and parodies the fabled concept of a Grail. Wood calls Christina's perception of Hammer's narcissism at the beginning of *Kiss Me Deadly* "abrupt and rhetorical." But in an anti-mythic structure, a classic invocation of the epic hero, such as "Of arms and the man I sing" must be transformed into something like: "You're the kind of person that has only one true love: you." This tension between myth and anti-myth, between hero and antihero, is one key to Aldrich's films and the root of the complexity which Wood finds lacking. Hammer is a radically different character than many who preceded and followed him in Aldrich's work, equally unlike the defiant warrior Massai in *Apache* and the tormented Charlie Castle in *The Big Knife*. "I guess you have a weakness for a certain kind of character," Aldrich readily admitted; "It's the same character in a number of pictures that keeps reappearing, characters that are bigger than life, that find their own integrity in doing what they do the way they do it, even if it causes their own deaths."[23] Although they are culturally quite different, both Massai and Charlie Castle appealed to Aldrich because of their idealistic struggle. As supporting characters remark, Massai cannot give up his fight and Charlie cannot sustain his; both are fatally imperiled by "doing what they do the way they do it." For Aldrich, who often spoke of turning concepts on their heads, Hammer is the consummate anti-idealist.

Perhaps the clearest example in Aldrich's work of the conflict between myth and anti-myth, between pragmatism and idealism on several levels, is *The Legend of Lylah Clare*. Like John Ford's much more celebrated *The Man Who Shot Liberty Valance*, myth and fact are confounded; but in Aldrich's picture that happens not only in the narrative reality but also in the minds of its principal characters. From this restricted point of view Aldrich's picture has a complexity of attitude that is certainly not "by default" and is arguably greater than Ford's. Are these examples indicative of Aldrich's and Ford's relative positions as filmmakers? Do certain similarities between *The Big Heat* and *Kiss Me Deadly* validate career comparisons of Lang and Aldrich? If so, how indicative are comparisons between the superficially similar narratives of *The Woman in the Window* and *Lylah Clare*, *You Only Live Once* and *The Gris-*

Opposite page, square-jawed Aldrich idealists: Charlie Castle (Jack Palance, left) in *The Big Knife* and Massai (Burt Lancaster) in *Apache*.

som Gang, The Return of Frank James and Apache, Secret Beyond the Door and Autumn Leaves, While the City Sleeps and Hustle, or even American Guerilla in the Philippines and Too Late the Hero?

Polemics are part of criticism, and it is understandable that even a rabidly auteurist viewpoint which valorized Aldrich early in his career might concur that he is merely "interesting" now. As the facts of Aldrich's professional life and the body of his work attest, he made many different types of films. If Aldrich's critical identity was constantly in flux, the generic breadth of his work and his stated opinions as a filmmaker did little to resolve it. In 1970, two years after buying his studio and making The Legend of Lylah Clare, Aldrich still could not choose between his own characters, between the dilettante director, Lewis Zarkan, and the crass studio head, Barney Sheean. In an April press release, in which his own publicists called him "The Last of Hollywood's Moguls," Aldrich complained in an unpublished article that "it has never been realistic for management to control artistic and/or creative decisions."[19] For a November survey piece in Look Magazine, Aldrich sounded like Zarkan decrying the "ludicrous setup" of the major studios while he looked like Sheean posed before a wide-angle lens atop a platform from his mobile production van parked in front of the Aldrich Studios.[20]

Which one was Aldrich? Both, obviously. These characters personify the Hollywood dichotomy that both frustrated and sustained Aldrich's work. The cynicism of Sheean and the idealism of Zarkan combined from the earliest in other Aldrich characters to create violent, angst-ridden outbursts of existential

despair. Little wonder that such a thematic outlook should give Aldrich a cutting edge status with European observers.

One of Aldrich's favorite homilies was the concept of "staying at the table." In interviews and panel discussions and memoranda, the phrase and the image of one "who sits at the table long enough and lets the dice get hot in my hand" is often invoked. As a businessman and producer, Aldrich often was "like a gambler" taking chances to keep his options open, balancing commercial and aesthetic impulses to survive, to stay at the table. As a filmmaker, Aldrich always came straight on, usually with more visual style than Ray, more raw energy than Fuller, and more social consciousness than Losey. Still many American critics were likelier to know such films as *Ten Seconds to Hell* or *The Last Sunset* from their posters seen in the background of Jean-Luc Godard's *Breathless* or Bernardo Bertolucci's *The Spider's Stratagem*. In other words, to say that the bulk of Aldrich's work was ignored in his own country would be an understatement.

As already observed, despite his record as an individual and union leader fighting for a director's rights, Aldrich was, like most American filmmakers of his own and earlier generations, never entirely comfortable with the thought of being an artist. "I don't give a shit what critics think, have thought or will think about my work," Aldrich wrote to Vincent Canby of the New York *Times* in 1974; "I have a totally trustworthy, interior thought mechanism that allows me to recognize...when I have done a good job, a mediocre job or a bad job."[21] Did Aldrich truly not care or was he protesting too much? Whatever he may have thought of his own work, Aldrich was never self-conscious about it. How else could he, as noted earlier, write facetiously to a studio executive about "the remote [underlining this] possibility exists that I may not be the world's greatest director..."? To whom then was he speaking when he said, "I'm a better director that most people think I am"? To producers? To critics? To filmgoers? To all of the above?

II

> The struggle for self-determination, the struggle for what a character wants his life to be...I look for characters who feel strongly enough about something not to be concerned with the prevailing odds, but to struggle against those odds.[22]

Robert Aldrich's films concentrate on the most basic situation: man attempting to survive in a hostile universe. Like most filmmakers, Aldrich uses and reuses such general devices as narrative tension between subjective and objective viewpoints and frustration or fulfillment of the audience's genre expectations. There is nothing unusual or distinctive in this process as such. Generally

Opposite page, which one was Aldrich? Zarkan (Peter Finch) the artist mirrors Aldrich's pose on the set of *The Legend of Lylah Clare*.

speaking, all films can be classed by genre and narrative mode. What isolates Aldrich, like any author, is his choice of narrative elements, which might also be called his thematic preoccupations or world view, and the organizing structure or style which he imposes upon them.

In order to survive, certain Aldrich heroes can be more consistently vicious, self-centered and cynical than any villain. The accusation leveled at Hammer by Christina in *Kiss Me Deadly* is echoed by Zarkan's admission in *The Legend of Lylah Clare*: "I'm not sick, I'm in love...with me." Others like Massai in *Apache*, Joe Costa in *Attack!*, and Phil Gaines in *Hustle* are driven by an irreducible and essentially idealistic personal code. In following it, their behavior becomes even more extreme than either Hammer's or Zarkan's. Characters who are in narrative terms basically antagonists, like Joe Erin in *Vera Cruz* and Wirtz in *Ten Seconds to Hell*, both reflect on and try to explain their compulsive destructiveness by telling essentially the same story. They each recount learning from and eventually murdering a father figure who had taught them to look out for number one.

In films such as these, the presence of a ruthless pragmatism in one of the two principals would normally promise a clear-cut alignment into hero and villain, into Erin versus Ben Trane, Karl Wirtz versus Eric Koertner, black versus white. The actual result is ambiguous. Each film is less than absolute in its definition of a moral man yet *is* absolute in its definition of morality. In *Vera Cruz* and *Ten Seconds to Hell*, the protagonist does finally defeat the antagonist; but the triumph is more societal than personal. In *The Flight of the Phoenix* and *Too Late the Hero*, the moral distinctions among the members of a group are so finely drawn that the chance or haphazard manner deciding which of them live and which die constitutes the pervasive irony of the films. As Major Reisman counsels the prisoner Wladislaw early in *The Dirty Dozen*, innocence or guilt, reward or condemnation, are purely matters of circum-

stance. "You only made one mistake," he says, pausing by the cell door and grinning back at the man sentenced to death, "you let somebody see you do it."

In this sense, Aldrich is a rigorous determinist. His fables about bands of outsiders remain remarkably consistent across generic lines. *Attack!, Ten Seconds to Hell, The Flight of the Phoenix, The Dirty Dozen, Too Late the Hero, Ulzana's Raid, The Longest Yard,* and *Twilight's Last Gleaming,* adventure films, war films, and Westerns—all isolate a group of men in a specific, self-contained and threatening universe. The core plots are diverse: soldiers behind enemy lines; a bomb disposal unit in post-World War II Berlin; passengers on a plane down in the Sahara; inmates of a prison; ex-convicts in a missile silo. Yet in each situation, the characters undergo the same, inexorable moral reduction. And often both the idealists and the cynics—the social extremists—perish.

Usually, these conflicts are between men and nature and between men and other men. All three war films as well as *The Flight of the Phoenix* and *Ulzana's Raid* effectively have no women characters at all. In *The Longest Yard* and *The Choirboys,* the restricted perspective of convicts and cops reduces women to objects, and unattractive ones at that. In the few films that do focus entirely on them, *The Killing of Sister George, What Ever Happened To Baby Jane?* or *Hush...Hush, Sweet Charlotte,* many of the women are deviate or psychotic. Notably, Baby Jane and Sister George are performers, personas behind which some women retreat in a male-dominated society. Even more notably, Frennessey in *World for Ransom* and the title character in *The Legend of Lylah Clare* are also performers *and* bisexuals. For both, Lesbianism is an alternative to the men who love them obsessively and want desperately to control their behavior. The societal assumptions which make relationships between men and women so difficult are most clearly addressed and left unresolved in *Hustle.* The man is too alienated to make a commitment; the woman is forced to separate sex from love by working as a prostitute.

For Aldrich, the gender of his protagonists was less important than their struggle: a film is only "'masculine' in the sense that it was done by a majority of masculine players. In theory, it was supposed to be metaphorical. In practice, it wasn't that important."[23] Beyond Westerns and war films, Aldrich's films have a generic breadth matched by few other filmmakers. Aldrich's work ranges widely from the self-described "classy soap opera" *Autumn Leaves* to the "sex and sand epic" *Sodom and Gomorrah* to the "desperately important" political thriller *Twilight's Last Gleaming.* In between, there are a few comedies and several *noir* films, as well as the occasional psychological melodrama and the neo-Gothic. There are prison pictures, cop pictures, sports pictures, and pictures about people who make pictures.

Opposite page, other Aldrich figures, sneering egomaniacs and cool blondes: Hammer (Ralph Meeker) with Friday (Marian Carr) in *Kiss Me Deadly* (left) and Zarkan (Peter Finch) with Elsa/Lylah (Kim Novak) in *The Legend of Lylah Clare.*

A comparison of Aldrich's first and last films, *The Big Leaguer* and *...All The Marbles*, is instructive on many levels, as they mirror the simultaneous evolution of his work as a filmmaker as well as a change in studio movies and social mores over a thirty-year span. Both are sports dramas, where survival is an issue but not a literal matter of life and death. Both are MGM releases; but one is programmer, developed and marketed by the studio as a "B" picture. The other is an independent package, put together by Aldrich. Both star well known character actors, Edward G. Robinson as Hans Lobert, the coach of a major league farm team, and Peter Falk as Harry Sears, a down-at-the-heels wrestling promoter. Both characters believe that their careers hang in the balance, and that their professional survival will depend on the performance of the athletes in their charge. The milieus are quite disparate; and more separates major league baseball from women's wrestling than just the gender of the participants. But the fundamental outlook of the athletes, the young men at the tryout camp and the two women on the road with Harry, is the same. They strive to succeed, first for the sense of accomplishment in the contest itself and then for the monetary rewards that winning may bring. In *The Big Leaguer* the immigrant father of one of the hopefuls disapproves of baseball as an endeavor that his work ethic considers lacking in seriousness. In *...All the Marbles* wrestling itself is an exhibition sport with little social validation.

As different as the narratives of two films may be, the conflicts, the characterizations, and the staging of the games and matches all create an expressive concordance between them. This interior consistency of theme and style in Aldrich's films resists classification according to genre. Erin and Wirtz recount their twisted, nearly identical histories in the context of an adventure Western and a return-from-the-war melodrama respectively. Zarkan is a retired film director, Hammer is a private detective: yet their self-love, their egocentric disdain for the lives and feelings of others, and their inability to rectify this attitude even when presented with second chances are traits which mark them as sibling personalities from radically different genre backgrounds.

Aldrich's visualization also transcends the conventions of genre. Strong side lighting, angles of unusual height or lowness, foreground clutter, and staging in depth appear as frequently in his Westerns, war pictures, neo-Gothic thrillers, even in Aldrich's television work, not just where they might be expected in a 50s *film noir* like *Kiss Me Deadly* or the richly colored frames of a Hollywood melodrama like *The Legend of Lylah Clare*.

Transmuting and expressing in sensory terms the physical and emotional make-up of the situation, of the characters caught in these frames, remains the basic dynamic of an Aldrich picture regardless of genre. More often from a disturbingly high or low angle than from a natural eye level, Aldrich's camera will capture a figure crouching behind a lamp, which is Charlie Castle's favorite re-

Opposite, bands of outsiders posed in their hostile environments: the squad in *Attack!* (left) and the crash survivors in *The Flight of the Phoenix*.

treat in *The Big Knife*, or lurking at the edge of a pool of light, like Lily Carver in *Kiss Me Deadly*. Grimacing faces or dark objects will suddenly intrude into the foreground of medium long shots, disturbing previously flaccid compositions, possibly in anticipation of a violent turn in plot events. Recurring high angle medium shots peer down from behind ceiling ventilators in every type of film, *World for Ransom*, *The Angry Hills*, *Hush...Hush*, *Sweet Charlotte*, and *Too Late The Hero*, so that the dark blades slowly rotating above the characters' heads become an ominous shorthand for the tension whirring incessantly inside them. Conversely, the hissing sound of man's life leaking out in *Kiss Me Deadly* or a postmortem burst of gunfire in *Attack!* become objective correlatives to the dissipation of the audience's tension. In a subjective manner, the characters sometimes "choose" to situate themselves within the frame. For the guilt-ridden Charles Castle, the lamps about the room have a symbolic value which unconsciously draws him back to them again and again. Or characters may be placed objectively: Lily Carver at the edge of the light is simultaneously in a figurative darkness appropriate to her mental state.

The overhead ventilators are variable metaphors: in *World for Ransom* the fan in the room where Mike Callahan is interrogated by an underworld figure is not only a distracting influence at the frame's center but casts multiple shadows on the surrounding walls. This de-focuses the reading of the shot away from the human figures to create a visual confusion appropriate to Callahan's emotions. In *The Angry Hills*, a crane down to eye level from an opening position behind a similar fan diminishes the object's importance as a distraction and suggests an unwinding, an impending detente rather than a knotting up of plot events. In both these pictures, Aldrich adapts the photographic styles of *film noir* to make specific visual statements about characters and events. In Callahan's initial movements through the somber streets, alleys, and stairwells of Singapore, angle and editing shift the wedges of light and the dim bounda-

ries of narrow passageways as if he were travelling through a dark maze, anticipating for the audience the uncertainty of his actual, emotional condition. From early films as narratively diverse as *Attack!*, *Autumn Leaves* and *The Angry Hills*, Aldrich's characteristic low light and side light cast long shadows on interior walls and floors and form rectangular blocks to give the frame a severe, constricting geometry which can symbolize the director's moral determinism.

While Aldrich's definition of milieu may be superficially realist—must be so, in fact, as the overall context of the films themselves is superficially realist—selection of detail is the most readily applicable method by which figurative meaning may be injected. In *The Legend of Lylah Clare*, the contrast between Barney Sheean's office and Lewis Zarkan's home, between autographed black and white photos of various stars on the walls and lustrous oil paintings of Lylah, between evenly distributed fluorescent light on flat white surfaces and candelabras glistening off the broken texture of wood paneling—all this is not merely a contrast of setting, but of sensibility as well. Both are established within a stylized conception of "producer's office" and "director's home" that is ambivalent, being both serious and satirical, descriptive and analytical. Subject/object versions of reality, genre preconceptions, and sensory input are all in play. Decor and camera angle inform character, character affects angle and decor; and the recognition of type reconciles or estranges the audience to the aptness or inaptness of these interactions.

If there is an indisputable cynicism in Aldrich's presentation of figures like Zarkan and Sheean, it is bifocal, acting as both directorial opinion and directorial conjecture of what the world's opinion of such men might be. If there is any vulgarity in the way they are presented, it is less a formal deficiency than an appropriate reflection of the lifestyle in which they are trapped. Ultimately, characterization and caricature, like all of Aldrich's thematic and stylistic components, refocus on the basic question: survival.

In *Hustle*, Lt. Phil Gaines' partner remarks as the two watch pornographic home movies featuring a suicide victim that her action was rash because "her survival wasn't threatened." Gaines's reply is, "It depends on how you define survival." Because survival is the key term for Aldrich, there is no overriding morality in his work, no sense of good and evil to which all must conform to be sanctioned. There are, however, personal codes and personal moralities. "He didn't divide the world up into good and evil," Abraham Polonsky said of Aldrich, "he didn't see it that simply. He found himself as someone who knew that *his* idea of himself was why he existed; and that his self-esteem and respect for himself could never be jeopardized by any compromise that involved that deep portion of himself."[24]

Opposite, decor informs character: Bart Langner (Milton Selzer, left), Rosella (Rosella Falk), and Lewis Zarkan (Peter Finch) in Zarkan's dining room in *The Legend of Lylah Clare*.

Reflecting this personal belief, Aldrich's judgment of Ben Trane or Eric Koertner, of Zarkan or Joe Costa is more severe than the judgment he passes on
characters less idealistic or with less sense of honor. The former are foolish
enough to place their faith in societal institutions, which collapse around them
or betray them. They repress personal values for the vaguely postulated good
of society at large; their disillusionment and sometimes fatal alienation is the
price that must be paid. Not that the "mealy-mouthed" compromisers from
the self-immolating Charlie Castle to the craven Erskine Cooney fare any better. Aldrich and most of his heroes are caught in that almost Manichaean perception of the world as a dichotomy between natural and artificial, between
chaotic and ordered, between instinctual and institutionalized conduct that impels the unaware or unprepared into indecision and that can short-circuit a
saving or creative act into an impotent and deadly vacillation.

The ending of *Ten Seconds to Hell* is a montage of the introductory close-
ups of the men of the unit intercut with shots of the rebuilt city. A quick reading might be that those who died did so meaningfully, for a reconstructive
purpose. The conclusion of *Ten Seconds to Hell* is echoed in *The Dirty Dozen*
which uses similar shots of the commando unit at the dinner celebration before the mission that will kill most of them. The same reiteration of the "male
unit" takes place in the end credits of *The Choirboys*. In the context of what
has gone before, all these endings recapitulate the fact that many have miscal-
culated and some have perished. To use a sports analogy from *The Big
Leaguer*, the sequences remember the "teams" from opening day and underscore those who did not make the cut.

"What really gets you is the idea that maybe you're wrong" is the accusation aimed at Frank Towns in *The Flight of the Phoenix*. It could be hurled at
many other Aldrich heroes as well. Trane and Koertner, Towns and Lt. De-
Buin in *Ulzana's Raid* survive their mistakes and misjudgments. For others, the

rectification of error comes too late. For none is it easily accomplished. Being wrong is not a moral deficiency in Aldrich's work. It neither mitigates nor insures salvation. What it does is make the "offenders" into outsiders, because, as Reisman tells Wladislaw, it is getting caught, not being wrong, that creates the violation of acceptable social conduct. When circumstances put the protagonist in an untenable situation, any solution is permitted. What separates the amoral Hammer from the self-righteous Costa are not just personal codes of conduct. Each protagonist also has an experiential notion of how society will react to his behavior, whether it will validate or condemn it. That is what separates Reisman from Wladislaw.

"Pilot error" is what Frank Towns ultimately enters into his log as the cause of the crash in *Flight of the Phoenix*. Most of Aldrich's film, in their own genre contexts and particular plots, are explorations of the infrastructure of error. What each makes progressively clearer is the conditional limitations of attributing blame. A frustrated Towns takes solace in his bitter and defensive accusations of Moran: "If you hadn't made a career of being a drunk, if you hadn't stayed in your bunk to have that last bottle, you might have checked that engineer's report and we might not be here." Blaming another gives way gradually to the resignation of Fenner in *The Grissom Gang*, McIntosh in *Ulzana's Raid*, or Crewe in *The Longest Yard*. Some early characters like Koertner anticipate the grim assessment of McIntosh in *Ulzana's Raid*: "Ain't no sense hating the Apaches for killing, Lieutenant. That'd be like hating the desert 'cause there ain't no water on it." This is a conscious expression of the capricious causality at work in Aldrich's pictures. For the reasons for the crash in the Sahara in *The Flight of the Phoenix* are as arbitrary, as free of pure causality, as the military assignments in *Too Late the Hero* or *Ulzana's Raid*.

In these later films particularly, characters begin to regard the organizing structures that compel their actions with a degree of sardonic humor. *The Flight of the Phoenix*: "I got a story for the *Daily Mirror* when I get back: How I Stopped Smoking in Three Days." *Ulzana's Raid*: "You put a hell of a lot of trust in a man who can't tell an inside curve from a three-legged horse!" Moreover, they begin to question explicitly the manifestations of inversion which seem to control their destinies: "The army don't take kindly to sergeants shooting their horses" (*Ulzana's Raid*) or "You behave as if stupidity were a virtue. Why is that?" (*The Flight of the Phoenix*). There are a limited number of resolutions to such situations: escape, death. or perhaps madness, the latter being the option "chosen" by Trucker Cobb in *Phoenix* and Mrs. Riordan in *Ulzana's Raid*. For the escapees, like Koertner, Towns, or Hearne in *Too Late the Hero*, there is a necessary expiation and reintegration. For the dead, there is only, time and circumstances permitting, a burial. Only the dying, such as McIntosh, seem to have any choice in that matter; but when offered the possibility of interment. he disdains it. Neither the artificiality of a cemetery ("Being

Opposite, two uniformed antiheroes pose inside a prison: Major Reisman (Lee Marvin, left) in *The Dirty Dozen* and Paul Crewe (Burt Reynolds) in *The Longest Yard*.

another one of them little markers back at the fort don't appeal to me") nor the naturalness of the open country ("I don't fancy sitting around passing the time of day with no gravediggers") are preferable to waiting for the vultures. Presented with a conventional moral value when Lt. DeBuin remarks that "it's not Christian," he makes the only reply than an outsider can: "That's right, Lieutenant. It's not."

From Mike Callahan's rejection by the perverse and aptly named Frennessey in *World for Ransom* through the fatalistic freeze-frames at the end of *The Legend of Lylah Clare* and *The Grissom Gang* to Gaines's offhanded death in *Hustle*, the one constant in Aldrich's work is that ultimately no one is untouched by the savagery of the surrounding world. For those who expose the more visceral layers of their psyche to it, the risk is intensified. It is not merely annihilation but also, what may be worse, a descent into an unfulfilled, insensate existence. If, in the final analysis, Aldrich's sympathy resides most with individuals who are anti-authoritarian, with antiheroes like Reisman in *The Dirty Dozen* or Crewe in *The Longest Yard*, it resides there because these are persons who survive. They survive by resolving all the conflicting impulses of nature and society, of real and ideal, of right and wrong, in and through action.

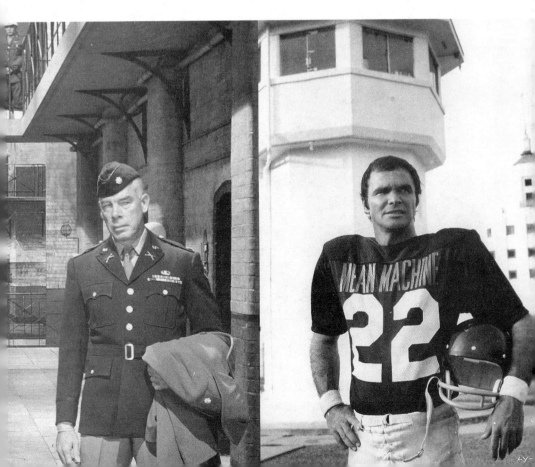

Above, Aldrich directs Anouk Aimee (left) and Pier Angeli in *Sodom and Gomorrah*.

Chapter One:
The Foreign Adventure

Resolution through action is a basic postulate in the mathematics of survival, a coded response common to a number of genres which might all be grouped within the informal class of "adventure film." Mike Callahan in *World for Ransom*, Trane and Erin in *Vera Cruz*, and Mike Morrison in *The Angry Hills* operate within this context and under the added condition of a foreign setting. Superficially, all four men could be typed as "soldiers of fortune." What separates them more than any specifics of milieu (the Far East in the 50s; Mexico under Maximilian; and Greece under the Gestapo respectively) is the question of motivation—the lost romanticism of Callahan, the lost cause of Trane, the lure of gold for Erin, and elements of all three in Morrison—and the dynamic of action through which these motives are clarified.

World for Ransom

"You shouldn't play Galahad. You're way out of character."

Callahan is the first of Aldrich's feature heroes and in some ways the most dependent on stereotypification.[1] While the "Galahad" remark may economically "place" the character by direct reference to myth or define him by implying something about his present mental state or the idea of playing a role, it also evinces a subject/object tension between this conception of Callahan by another character, Julian March, the antagonist who makes the observation, and the stereotyped picture of him presented to the audience up to that point. *World for Ransom* is something of a "film noir maudit," using the visual and character conventions of the movement but in a foreign locale which is atypical. From the perspective of *film noir* or from genre typing, the details of Callahan's life are not unusual or unexpected: private detective; war veteran; frustrated Irish revolutionary; loser in a love affair and sexually fixated as a result. This image of a loner insulated from both his physical surroundings and an oppressive emotional situation by a cynical veneer is not an original one. It derives as much from those expectations built on genre as from direct character exposition. Thus Callahan the character is read from type.

Having formed and accepted this image, the audience can quickly bracket and define Mike Callahan for itself and, subsequently, can appreciate the "inaccuracy" of March's assessment. For, in saying that he is not, March ironically confirms that Callahan is precisely the "Galahad" type—disillusioned idealist turned hard-boiled in the tradition of 30s pulp fiction and *film noir*— and makes clear that such a role is not at all "out of character." This apprehension of Callahan is additionally colored by the element of locale. The very word "Singapore" stenciled over the first black-and-white frame triggers associations with mystery and exoticism: with opium rings and knife-wielding assassins bringing sudden death, with all the clichés of the inscrutable and perilous Orient. From this background of sleazy bars and wet shiny streets, the thin, white-suited figure of Mike Callahan will detach itself. The opening conflict contained within this first sequence, within this first frame in fact, is a profoundly archetypal one: east (milieu) versus west (hero), Galahad (white-suited purity) versus the forces of darkness (the shadowy, low-key aspect of the city).

It is through essentially generic perceptions—the audience having been primarily conditioned to respond to setting, to wet streets and low-key lighting by previous films of this type—that the viewer both anticipates and experiences the course of *World for Ransom*'s narrative. Like most of the alienated heroes of genre fiction and most of Aldrich's later feature heroes, Callahan is caught in a struggle to survive, emotionally facing the peril of insanity and physically facing the peril of death. His awareness of a threat to his survival may key two responses, evasion and disguise (playing a role; not Galahad but a broader generic role) or counteraction. These basic concepts form the non-specific core of the plot and motivate an expressive exploration of the forces which threaten the hero. They reveal the confining structures—the "trap"—and the compelling factors which cause the entrapment. The initial discovery which derives from such an exploration in *World for Ransom* is Aldrich's underlying determinism. From the establishing long shot of the street banked with flashing neon the cut in is to a medium close shot of a woman selling fortunes. Callahan enters the rear ground of the frame and moves forward quickly, almost bumping into her—they identify each other to the audience:

WOMAN
And you. Good evening, Mr. Callahan.

Reverse Medium Close Shot over Callahan's shoulder

WOMAN (continued)
You are the luck of your father and mother.
Your luck is here. Take a chance?

Medium Close Shot Callahan over the Woman

CALLAHAN
Thanks, Mai Ling. Not now. Maybe tomorrow.

The tout is to "take a chance"; but the talk of inherited luck, of an hereditary
fate, seems to contradict the notion of chance. Realistically, the ambiguity of
the fortuneteller's line is a necessity, a formula of rote words chosen for their
come-on value. They also have a surface figurative value—his future (fortune)
is in the past ("father and mother") and the present ("here")—which Callahan
is not conscious of, in narrative or character terms. Subject/object split over
this realization makes clear to the viewer that "taking a chance," that acting, is
unavoidable, that "luck" is not a question of buying and selling, but something

Below, sleazy bars and wet streets, Singapore on a sound stage in *World for Ransom.*

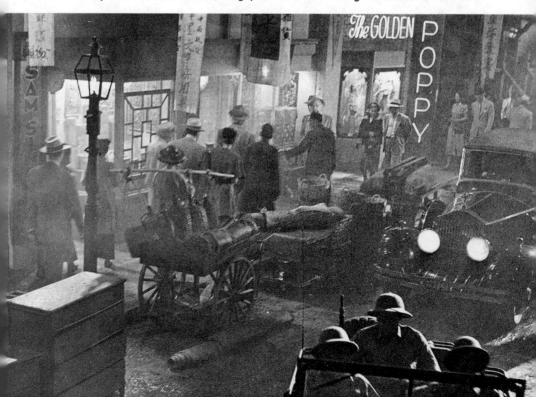

to be tested and defined in generic action, action which Callahan in his obvious haste may already be taking. In this light his "Maybe tomorrow" can be interpreted as either an unconscious wish or an ironic afterthought but not as a real possibility. The viewer can appreciate, even from this inconspicuous beginning, that the preoccupied Mr. Callahan must and will "take a chance."

Aldrich elaborates on the figurative values of *World for Ransom* with both dialogue and visual elements. To this point the audience's understanding of Callahan's position remains non-specific. They sense that some conflict is present, in progress, but do not know the narrative details. The opening dialogue suggests a causality without reference to effect; genre expectation is, so far, the only defining factor. A clarifying medium shot follows, isolating Callahan against a dark building as he turns up an alleyway. Visually, the conflict has now been fully stated, high angle of the entire street (milieu), emergence of a figure from a background (hero), and finally situation of the hero (white) in graphic opposition (contrast) to milieu (black).

Callahan moves up the alley, goes through a doorway, and starts to climb a flight of stairs. The camera, as if under the power of a predestined pull, travels in behind him. It might be argued that this reading of the travelling shot is only one of many equally possible and plausible interpretations but this reading is

Below, *film noir* style on a budget: strong side light and dark shadows in the background, while Callhan (Dan Duryea) ponders a cache of grenades.

not a generalization about the "deterministic" nature of all travelling shots. Rather the "ideal" viewer appreciates from past experience several possible meanings, such as moving to close-up for a reaction or revealing detail, simulating the point of view of someone walking, or dramatically underscoring or anticipating a physical event. The particular circumstances of this camera movement reveal none of the usual meanings. The camera "follows" Callahan; it does not go into his face for a reaction but comes up behind him; it has no point of view and hence must be taken as impersonal; it is not drawn in to underscore or anticipate any physical event; and it discloses no detail not visible from the wider angle. The notion of predestination derives from the viewer's objective response, from the unconscious sensation or conscious reasoning that something unseen and unknown, in short something fateful, impels the camera inward. As the angle narrows, two wedges of light on either side of the doorway disappear from the frame. The blank diagonal walls at the side of the the stairwell focus the converging lines of perspective on a corridor at the top of the stairs. A figure steps out into the vanishing point. For a moment, the points of view of Callahan and the viewer merge as they share the sudden perception of a dark form at the top of the steps. A reverse angle looking down at Callahan reveals another figure blocking the doorway to the alley. A trap has literally closed on him, a trap which the components of the shot imply holds him in its grasp halfway between top and bottom, between polarities. How central this physical image of the corridor is to the entire film is uncertain. The corridor is in actuality the movie's first image appearing in a static composition under the titles. Nor is it clear how fully the subject/object split is bridged by having the viewer co-experience "being caught" with Callahan. It would seem reasonable to conclude, though, that some sort of identification has been established by this sequence of only seven shots and that through the non-literal expressiveness of those shots the hero has been designated, the conflict abstracted, and the figurative concept of the trap communicated.

Generally, *World for Ransom* employs a third-person narrative technique, i.e., many character points of view, developing plot elements in isolation. At the same time, what Callahan does or does not know of these events is relatively unimportant. Callahan's interaction with other characters includes both subjective and objective information for the viewer. In many ways Callahan's acts are non-referential—anticipating Hammer's search for the "great whatsit" in *Kiss Me Deadly*. If there is an indicator of the psychology of his acts, it is rooted in the idea of a second chance. As he says to Frennessey: "I can always tell myself that I've got some second chance with you someday." This is colored by Mai Ling's uncertain prediction. Uncertainty is, in fact, the only constant, and generically it serves to liberate Callahan from the bonds of conventional behavior, becoming both an impetus and a rationale for action that is, by societal standards, illegal. Much of this delineation and liberation of Callahan is, of course, still within the traditional conception of the "private eye." The character's own words reveal his mocking self-appraisal ("Mike Callahan... [shaking his head] private eye!") and his insistent idealization of Frennessey March, the woman who rejects him ("You were the only one that was way out there on that hill...the only one that was straight from beginning to end") are not without irony or precedent. What gives dimension to Callahan the character and to the film as a developing dynamic line are the five scenes with Frennessey, two in her dressing room, three in her apartment. In these settings she provides an ostensible refuge from a hostile outer world within the enclosure of her private life. She is seen only once outside of them, at the Golden Poppy nightclub, a markedly artificial environment where she performs in a tuxedo. The scenes in Frennessey's rooms can be taken as a pause in the development of the exterior narrative, a "breather," so to speak, for both Callahan and the audience.

It is in the use of sustained camera, particularly in a sequence shot—that is, when an entire sequence is staged in one take without a cut—in Frennessey's dressing room which reveals Callahan at ease for the first time. Unlike the meetings with Chan and Julian March which preceded, Callahan is alone at the outset and, as the placement of objects in the frame and angle suggest, in a "superior" position for the first time. He is momentarily and by default the

Below, Frennessey (Marian Carr) and Callahan (Dan Duryea) in her dressing room.

visual center. In the discussion with Chan and his henchman, which follows the encounter on the stairs, the master shot is a high angle and medium long, nearly centered on Callahan. However, not only is his size "inferior" in relation to the frame's overall width and to Chan in the foreground but also the motion of an overhead fan above the image's center casts multiple shadows on the surrounding walls and de-focuses the reading of the shot away from his figure. Only Chan receives an isolated medium close shot, at a low angle which suggests dominance over the intervening material, over the scene itself.

The second interview begins with a shot of an office door which has March's name painted on a glass panel. Callahan opens it to reveal March over his shoulder. Again, he is not the visual center. Both men are full lit, but March receives the only close-ups, tending as it did with Chan to infer his dominance or control of the scene and other characters. When Callahan is framed in medium close shot, the right foreground focus is carried on March, standing behind him in the left background and fanning himself with his Panama hat, again distracting viewer attention away from Callahan in much the same way as the multiple shadows and the fan in the previous confrontation did. In contrast, the initial view of Callahan in Frennessey's dressing room is at eye level, middle ground, with unlit clutter in front and back forming a sort of natural iris around him. The dynamic of this shot enhances rather than contests his bid for audience attention.[2]

This does not necessarily mean a diminished subject/object tension between Callahan's being at ease in the room or visual superiority over it, which is the subject attitude, and the viewer's apprehension, which is the object attitude. Such a diminution depends primarily on individual identification with Callahan. This may be impeded by the viewer's lack of "familiarity" with the dressing room; but the effect of the sequence shot is twofold.

First, by withholding the cut, which is contrary to the audience's normal expectation, an underlying tension is created. The expectation here is not generic but a broader, conditioned reaction. Experience suggests to the audience that one camera angle is "normally" sustained for ten to forty seconds only. Consequently it expects or anticipates, on some level of perception, that a cut will be made within that time. Sustaining the take—not necessarily the shot, which may vary with travelling, panning, zooming, etc.— both frustrates and heightens that expectation, creating tension between the sense that a cut must be imminent and the continued delay in making one. This tension can only resolve itself in a substantive shift of expectation, stemming from a growing subconscious awareness in the viewer that the shot is being manipulated. In other words, the use of a sequence shot compels a pause between reading the shot (anticipation and reflection) and rereading (clarification and meaning). The audience is "tensed" and, depending upon how thoughtful its response is, becomes aware of the "fact of tension" created by delaying the cut and by the stylistic "unusualness" which precipitates the tension. On a narrative level, these sensations are then linked to Frennessey's entry and continuing presence in the scene.

Second, within the sustained camera effect there is an increased possibility for a continuity of physical interaction between characters, a continuity demanded by the absence of the cut. A blow or fall, for example, cannot be cheated in the editing; a miscue cannot be removed. Consequently the physical interaction between the actors both seems and is "more real" than in an edited sequence. Like March fanning the hat, Frennessey's movement from foreground to background as she changes clothes draws attention away from Callahan and towards her. At one point she turns and literally casts a shadow over him. Eventually Callahan retreats to the background and adopts March's action of fanning himself which restores a semblance of visual equilibrium. The final camera movement is forward, into a medium close two shot favoring Callahan as he grips Frennessey by the arms. This dominant posture is roughly timed to the audience's revised expectation, i.e., some dissipation of tension; but the angle which is still eye-level does not reinforce the dominance as a low angle of Callahan over her might, and her shadow still falls partially over his body. The shot is held for a kiss, but only a brief one on the forehead, and then dissolves to a darkly lit, night exterior. The cut, which is essentially dynamic, has been superseded by the long take, which is essentially static. The kiss dissolves not to light, which could imply energy, goodness, orgasm, the specific symbology is not relevant, but to dark. On a sensory level, it is more difficult to peer into darkness; by association, it is foreboding or depressing. Callahan is basically satisfied with Frennessey; the viewer is left with sentiments of frustration, disquiet, even suspicion. Because the cumulative effect of this sequence is ambiguous, the difference between Frennessey's relation to Callahan (subject) and the film (object) cannot be precisely stated as yet.

The next scene, in her apartment, provides little if any clarification. A side-travelling on the opening medium shot moves the camera behind the wrought-iron headboard of Frennessey's bed. This sudden restriction of the foreground undercuts the viewer's initial orientation to the scene and compels a rereading. A composition in depth, where Callahan and Frennessey are visible and may be relocated through the foreground clutter, is followed by a close two shot photographed with a longer focal-length lens, as if the camera (viewer) were still behind the bed. This spatial "endistancing" leaves the subject/object split between Callahan and the audience in regards to Frennessey undiminished. In other words, the identification factors which propel the audience in towards Callahan's point of view are controverted or at least neutralized by the staging.

The sequence-shot encounter between Callahan and Frennessey on the eve of the pursuit and combat in the jungle provides a final illustration of this effect. A low angle captures Callahan reclining on a divan with a small table fan behind to his right in frame center, a possible extension of the earlier fan motifs, which can serve as metaphor for turmoil at the emotional center of the film itself. Frennessey is again "frenetic," walking nervously back and forth on the left, an action which continues as they discuss the coming day's endeavors. As she tries to bring Callahan around to her way of thinking, the camera cranes up, coming in close behind her and tilting down at him, aligning itself with her attempt at dominance. The scene ends in much the same way as the earlier sequence in her dressing room. Callahan stands and the pent-up energy of the sustained take is concentrated into a close two shot. With Frennessey's visual dominance reduced and Callahan's delivery of the line about her being "way up there on that hill," the viewer may expect the tension built up in the staging to be released in a kiss; and this time it is. Depending on how wary of Frennessey the viewer is, the dissolve-away-from-kiss that follows represents not just a time-lapse to imply an unseen completion of their sexual encounter but also a final, possibly fatal enmeshment (entrapment) epitomized by the visual overlay. Objectively, all these scenes with Frennessey have been sufficiently "abnormal" in their execution to cause the surface reality or, more particularly, the genuineness of her emotions to be suspect; but Callahan's subjective faith in her remains obviously undiminished throughout. The ultimate irony or tragedy of *World for Ransom*, then, derives from the narrative revelation that Frennessey has indeed been lying, that a blind side in Callahan has prevented him from seeing her as the real peril to his survival.

Callahan survives the real world or specifically the combat in the jungle by physically defeating March and his associates through action; but that fails to insulate him, when he is cursed and viciously slapped by Frennessey, against emotional destruction. This world view, that injury can only come from those we love and trust, is superficially a rather cynical one. Subjectively, Callahan suffers a loss; objectively, the viewer must conclude that he is better off for it. Callahan's attitude all along has been verbalized as "I wouldn't be making a good hero"; Frennessey's slap in the face is, for him, a bitter confirmation. How well he survives is an unanswered question tinged with the fallen idealism that was misplaced somewhere in the past. All that Callahan is offered by way of consolation are Mai Ling's closing words: "Take a chance, Mr. Callahan. Love is a white bird, yet you cannot buy her."

Vera Cruz

A title appears before the credits alluding to the incursion of soldiers of fortune into Mexico after the American Civil War. The actual wording is fairly prosaic; but under the credits the images (groups of men riding southward) and sound (a rapid, fully orchestrated Spanish melody) combine with the title to immediately evoke the genre indicators of action and adventure. At this point, such an anticipation is real but non-specific, that is, no particular characters, situations, or actions have been indicated. "And some came alone," the title concludes, over a shot of a solitary figure in a panoramic *SuperScope* long shot.

It is clear from the fact of his isolation and the separate title devoted to his introduction that this lone man on horseback is not just another "soldier of fortune." Abstractly, such an image also suggests alienation, much as the visual contrasts in *World for Ransom* initiated a conflict with the milieu. However, this shot of a lonely rider dwarfed by the surrounding terrain requires a longer reading time. It is faceless and hence not easy for the viewer to identify with it. The form is not just faceless but totally undistinguished, except in an alienated sense, a concept which defines two relationships: of the figure to the landscape, which is a dwarfed vertical arrayed against an expansive horizontal, and of the audience to the figure, which is literally and figuratively endistanced. In this instance the title acts as the final generic qualifier. It does not imply that the alienation is a one-sided effect in which an ostracized character is struggling to reenter society. Through the rhetorical directness and simplicity of the words, "and some came alone," and through the visual itself, the implication is that the character has voluntarily detached himself. More significantly, it focuses the generic apprehension of the viewer and designates the lone rider as the likely hero. Despite the use of an expository title, the information about character and situation communicated in the introduction of Ben Trane, like that of Callahan, depends primarily on the expressive value of the images. The immediate visual contrast here is provided by a human antagonist, Joe Erin, as well as by the milieu. When Trane meets Erin, the sequence is intercut using medium close-ups over the shoulder at slight high angles with balanced framing in the two shots to establish a visual equality or equilibrium between the two men. This, in turn, reinforces the delicate balance that exists between them in the narrative. The use of low angles and opposing close shots underscores the fact that such a standoff is a tenuous one, constantly threatening to deteriorate into violent confrontation.

In this case the use of a low angle does not necessarily suggest dominance or exaggerate stature but rather creates disequilibrium. Since both men are framed low, often in successive shots, neither can really be said to dominate or "tower over" the other; but there are radical changes in perspective from a

Above, Gary Cooper (left) as Ben Trane and Burt Lancaster as Joe Erin in *Vera Cruz*.

few feet above the figures to nearly ground level. This, rather than a consistent use of normal or conventional shots at eye-level, disorients the viewer. The disjunctive effect of this type of editing can be taken as an externalization of the inner emotions of the characters. In other words, Trane and Erin and the viewer in his or her generic consciousness realize that, no matter what temporary alliances the characters may strike up, combat between them is inevitable. After this realization of generic antagonism, the sensory distortions of framing and editing dynamically reaffirm it and cause the viewer to experience it with them.

This narrative/visual clash both initiates and defines the dramatic center. Erin's presence provides the character conflict which is the core of the dramatic development. To sustain this conflict, Erin's character needs equal weight to balance Trane's. Erin becomes an alternate visual center. For example, there is an elaborate craning and panning shot that reveals the Juaristas who surround Trane and Erin and their men. It begins on a close shot of Erin and holds him in its foreground. This does not necessarily diminish viewer identification with Trane. However, Erin is in other ways the more accessible of the two figures. Despite his cynical observations on Trane, such as "I don't trust him. He likes people and you can never count on a man like that," the portrayal by Burt Lancaster evinces the archetype of a likeable rogue. The viewer understands from genre typing that this actor is normally cast as a heroic character. While Erin's beliefs are obviously not heroic, the grinning, glibly self-confident interpretation of the character by Lancaster diminishes viewer apprehension. Humorous vignettes such as Erin's morning ablutions— a hand brushed through the hair and a quick wipe of the teeth—reinforce Erin's insouciance which is often easier to relate to than the stiff and silent lost idealism of Gary Cooper's defeated Confederate, Trane. The amorality of Erin is capsulized in his anecdote about Ace Hannah: "He lived thirty seconds after I shot him. Ace lived long enough to know he was right." The naturalness and spontaneity of Erin's behavior mitigates his amoral outlook. "Why are you telling me all this?" asks Trane. "Why not?" Erin replies; "You're the first friend I ever had!"

Erin's competition with the protagonist for viewer sympathy is somewhat unconventional, but less so in the context of the Western genre. As will be discussed further below, Aldrich's visual usage and character development rely heavily on the shorthand of genre indicators and the viewer's expectations. The frontier context of the Western permits a rough-hewn mercenary to be accepted as a "normal" person. However, the competition between characters in *Vera Cruz* is never fully developed. It is not that the narrative or genre requirements of either the Western or an adventure film prevent or subsume the development of such a conflict. The genre indicators clearly establish that conflict

Above, shooting from holster level: a low angle of the reluctant partners Erin
(Burt Lancaster) and Trane (Gary Cooper).

from the first chance encounter of Trane and Erin. But the informing values in
Vera Cruz are not concentrated towards probing that conflict.

The final travelling shot which follows Trane during the last battle separates
him physically and dynamically from the conflict with Erin just before their climactic confrontations. This effectively supersedes the dramatic impact of the
"showdown," the act which will dispel Trane's sense of alienation, since in siding with the Juaristas he has already rediscovered social values and made a
new commitment. But genre expectation tells the viewer that Erin, the "villain," must perish at the film's conclusion. So Trane becomes the mechanistic
implement of that required retribution. Meanwhile the narrative confirms what
the visuals have already implied, that emotionally Trane has no need for revenge.

Survival, physically or spiritually, is not really at stake for the protagonist in the ending of *Vera Cruz*. Insofar as survival is a fairly constant issue in Aldrich's films, Trane's position at the end of this picture is vastly more secure than Callahan's in *World for Ransom* or any number of later Aldrich figures from Mike Hammer, Lt. Woodruff in *Attack!*, Morrison in *The Angry Hills* to Zarkan or even Barbara Blandish in *The Grissom Gang*. Still the fact of Erin's death must affect the audience response to this ostensibly happy ending. Erin's role has not been that of a simple foil who is expendable once the conflicts are resolved. It is Erin, in fact, who has helped to change Trane's relationship to his environment. Erin has been one of the most important, if not the principal, factors in relocating Trane from the alienated posture of the opening images to that "reunion" with a cause. At the end, Trane is visually integrated with the Juaristas in a sustained travelling shot through the battle because of Erin.

How consciously Trane allows Erin to influence his decisions is uncertain; but there are scenes in which both are present where Trane allows the other man to speak or act for him. In the meeting with Maximilian, for instance, Erin does most of the talking while Trane stands by silently watching. Ultimately, Erin becomes Trane's figurative bridge back to the real world, a bridge which, extending the metaphor, must be allowed to burn after being crossed. The passive mode is the key here. It explains the lack of emotion or sense of dramatic climax in Trane's killing of Erin. In the same way that Koertner would merely allow Wirtz to perish at the end of *Ten Seconds to Hell*, Trane's action is passive because it lacks personal malice. Since the reabsorption of Trane into society has already taken place, all that must be affirmed in Erin's death is a detached generic need to punish his antisocial behavior.

A final note should be made on visual usage and "tone" of *Vera Cruz*. Even within the action context, the fist fights, gun battles, and chases are staged and edited with a particular emphasis on their kinetic quality. There are numerous, fast-moving tracking shots past fixed vertical objects intercut with short running inserts of wheels, hooves, sweaty faces, etc. In dialogue and other nonaction scenes, the use of extreme high or low angles, foreground clutter, or depth of focus does much to sustain the dynamism of more violent or active moments. As there is no fixed point of view, subject/object tension between the characters' and the viewer's apprehension of scenes is constantly in play. When the face of one of Erin's men suddenly intrudes into the foreground of a medium shot of Trane, focus is held on both, so that two distinct objects compete for attention within the frame. The tension is most manifest and operates most powerfully as a constant suggestion of impending violence between these visually contesting forces.

The Angry Hills

While Aldrich always disparaged his work on *The Angry Hills* (1959), there are particular applications of the "adventure" context which merit a brief discussion. In character and narrative terms, the parallels with *World for Ransom* or *Vera Cruz* are readily discerned. Morrison's occupation (foreign correspondent), situation (wartime Greece), and attitude (colorful cynicisms: "Not for me, it gives me a nose ache") roughly equate him with characters in the earlier films. Again "luck" or "taking a chance" is a motivating or driving factor. "You're luckier than I am," he is told; "you have some choice." Again exterior forces work as ironic or deterministic influences: "Here I am, right back where I started—a big circle." Morrison's course through the narrative is cyclical, but only to a point. Ultimately, it is neither as progressive—i.e., reintegrating—as Trane's nor as retrograde—i.e., alienating—as Callahan's.

Imagistically *The Angry Hills* is closer to the *film noir* style of *World for Ransom*. Low light and side light cast long shadows on interior walls and floors. Rectangular blocks of light frequently give the frame a severe geometry, which derives from opposing shapes and structures and creates tension between black and white within a depth of field. For example, in the brutal interrogation of Stavros, Heisler's position as non-participant is in question. He sits foreground with his back to the camera while Tassos administers the beating in the background, so his expression is not seen. But his detachment is questioned by the composition. Lines of texture enmesh him, require his "participation" to complete the overall pattern of the shot and will not allow him to be a mere spectator. Many aspects of the staging cannot help but recall *World for Ransom*. Most obvious is the low angle medium long shot which reveals the fleeing Morrison at the top of the stairs or the high angle down through the overhead fan.

There is also emotional tension added through the long take in the last meeting between Morrison and Lisa; and there is emotional isolation through editing in the medium close shot of Oberg intercut with three shots of Tassos, Heisler, and Maria. There are other formal devices used, although the specific applications vary. A crane down to eye-level from behind the fan diminishes its importance as a distraction and could suggest an unwinding, an impending detente rather than a knotting up of plot events. Unlike *World for Ransom* this image of the ventilator occurs near the end of *The Angry Hills*. There is also a stairway shot, which is one of many that are held while Morrison moves from background to foreground and into a low angle medium close shot. After the introductory scene with Mai Ling, Callahan's figure was almost never permitted this kind of movement through the frame, being directed instead across it from left to right or right to left. The figurative distinction—particularly considering the implications of dominant power or control, even in the midst of flight, in the low angle of Morrison—is between the flat, horizontal movement of Callahan and the dynamic, approaching movement of Morrison. This visually underscores the fact that Callahan's actions will eventually prove ineffectual—he remains alienated—while Morrison's will not. This does not mean that *The Angry Hills* is a more optimistic film, since Morrison's success is purely physical in that he escapes; and, since he does rescue the scientist, Callahan's failure is purely emotional. While he may be secure from material peril in a way Ben Trane is not, Morrison's position at the end of *The Angry Hills* is inferior to Trane's. Whether or not he has embraced the partisan cause, Morrison is now separated from it and from Lisa, the woman who gave him love and support. The final shot of the city is a neutral one, objectively detached and drawing no absolute conclusions.

Below, a reluctant hero: Robert Mitchum as Mike Morrison and Gia Scala as Eleftheria in *The Angry Hills*.

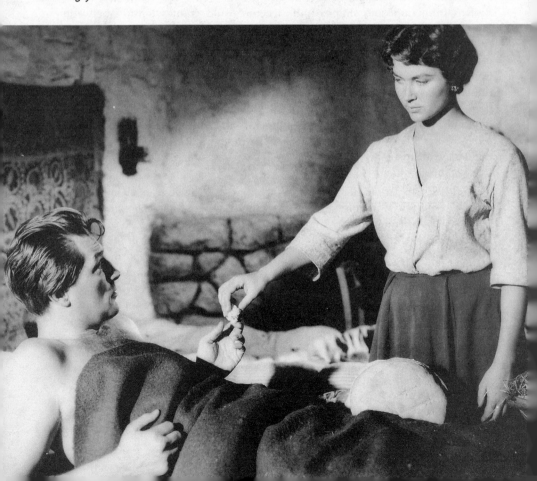

Flight of the Phoenix

Many of Aldrich's films are concerned with group dynamics, namely how does a set of individuals—usually men, as in this film—with different personalities, objectives, and ideologies unite around one purpose in order to survive. This theme runs through all his war films, *Attack!, The Dirty Dozen,* and *Too Late the Hero;* the Westerns, particularly, *Apache,* and *Ulzana's Raid;* and his only prison film, *The Longest Yard.* In all genre contexts, survival remains the central issue.

More than with most other American directors, the elements of existentialism inform the work of Robert Aldrich. His characters are adrift in a world both alienating and at times absurd, a world fraught with danger and conflict. As Jean-Paul Sartre, the chief exponent of modern existentialism, phrased it: "We are alone without excuses. This is what I mean when I say that man is condemned to be free." Whether it is the violent absurdity of war; the perfidious complexities of espionage and detection in *World for Ransom, Kiss Me Deadly,* or *Hustle;* or the spontaneous dilemmas of the adventure films, Aldrich's characters share a desperate need to maintain their identity and dignity in an ever-shifting landscape. "I am against the idea of tragic destiny," Aldrich told François Truffaut. "Each man must fight even if he is broken. My characters have that suicidal attitude because the voluntary sacrifice of their lives is the height of their moral integrity. Suicide is a gesture of revolt."[3] Like any existentialist, Aldrich envisions one sure answer to these dilemmas—action. If that action is within the limits set by an inherently absurd existence, it conforms to Sartre's viewpoint of existentialism which "tells him that hope lies only in action, and that the only thing that allows a man to live is action." The battle in war, the search in *film noir,* the frontier conflict in the Western, the struggle against long odds in the adventure films—all these emphasize the same underlying dynamic. Because it synthesizes much of that dynamic, football was an important metaphor for Aldrich. Whether it is merely present by analogy as in *Hustle,* or as the central event of the film as in *The Longest Yard,* the stress on teamwork, on violent, brutal action, and on survival within a limited period of time, all condense the elements of existential life into a single trope.

The Flight of the Phoenix confronts the issues of existentialism in their purest form, much as Sartre's own classic play, "No Exit" ("Huis Clos"). Aldrich deposits a group of plane crash victims onto a burning desert hundreds of miles from any settlement. In order to survive, this very diverse group of men must form a cohesive unit and formulate a plan of action upon which they all agree. Like the characters in Sartre's play, this random assortment of individuals end up battling each other more than the hellish environment around them. For as one of the characters in "No Exit" notes, "Hell is other people."

To create an initial feeling of comfortable normality, Aldrich establishes the initial compatibility of these characters. As the film begins and the plane carrying the men is in flight, a panning shot of the aircraft is followed by an overhead shot of the shadow of the plane on the desert sand. The scene then shifts to the interior where the crew, pilot Frank Towns and copilot Lew Moran, and the passengers are introduced as an amiable and diverse social group. Their common link is the oil company for which they work. A Greek passenger plays a song while passing around a bottle of ouzo. Most engage in friendly banter, as Towns allows a timid Moran to take the controls of the plane for a few minutes. Absent are any of the sociopathic symptoms immediately apparent in other of Aldrich's male groups from *Attack!* to the *The Longest Yard*. But when the plane begins to sputter and fall, Aldrich freezes on the terrified expressions of the individual passengers, presaging the ordeal to follow and isolating them before the critical moment.

As the days pass and the men's hopes for rescue diminish, each of the surviving passengers is stripped to his psychological core. Gone are the distractions and illusions of civilization. Each individual is now "free," as Sartre used the word, to face the reality and absurdity of life. The pilot, Towns, retreats into morbid guilt, visually underscored in the second half of the narrative by his forlorn glances at the crosses on the hill, which mark the graves of the dead. His need to take responsibility for all that happened is what drives him to action, what sustains him. At the grave site of those killed in the crash, Standish, one of the passengers, asks him to say a few words. His clipped response is, "Like what? Sorry?" When Cobb, the emotionally unstable oil worker, wanders away to die in the desert, Towns not only laments that it is "my fault. I should've watched him," but actually goes after him. Like the analogous sequence in *Lawrence of Arabia* when Lawrence recrosses the most forbidding part of the desert for a lost man, Town also tracks down his man, but Cobb is dead.

The other men retreat into self, their actions and reactions conditioned by their normal occupations. The military officer, Captain Harris, falls back on his military training and "goes by the book." He begins a futile march into the desert to reach a settlement, which no one is sure even exists. His aide, Sgt. Watson, cravenly feigns injury to avoid following his superior into the desert. When Capt. Harris returns after walking in circles, Watson hides in his bed, refusing to report Harris' return or face his own cowardice. Dorfmann, the "airplane designer," tries to control his environment by organizing the activities of the men in his effort to rebuild the plane.

Only Moran, the stuttering, timid copilot, manages to retain his equilibrium. Moran is the one, in fact, who goads the depressed Towns into following Dorfmann's example, into working cooperatively and putting aside his guilt. He tells Towns that he represents "the past" while Dorfmann represents "the future." "Little men with slide rules and computers will inherit the earth" is Towns' plaintive response. And when they discover that Dorfmann has never really designed a full-size airplane, only toy models, Moran delivers a "guffaw" shared by many of Aldrich's characters in a moment of similar discovery, a vulgar laugh which indicates their bemusement at the absurdity of life.

Below, Towns (James Stewart) searches for Trucker Cobb.

The existential solution to their problem is, of course, action, and in this case, cohesive action. While in *Dirty Dozen* and *The Longest Yard* the dramatic arc is a straightforward movement from disunity to unity, *The Flight of the Phoenix* is, in many ways, a more complete circle. The group starts out as sociable companions. Once the disaster occurs, their superficial camaraderie comes apart at the seams. Finally, the remainder of the film details how they put the pieces of this broken unit back together again.

The catalyst for this reactive behavior is not whom the viewer might expect. Rather than from the iconic James Stewart as Towns, who by billing and star status would seem the anticipated hero or "action-taker" of the drama, Aldrich plays against expectations. He makes the monomaniacal and egocentric Dorfmann the one who leads this band out of the wilderness. Initially Dorfmann is the butt of jokes—because of his aloofness, his Germanic fastidiousness, and his social ineptness. But to the surprise of all, he is the one who comes up with viable plans to save them. He devises an efficient method for rationing water, including distillation of the much-needed liquid from a supply of antifreeze. His designs for a new plane, a "Phoenix" from the ashes of the old one, also proves effective. Towns may pronounce him "crazy," but Dorfmann is right.

When the newly built, single-prop aircraft is pulled by the surviving men in harness across the dunes of the desert, the camera frames them in heroic low

Below, "little men with slide rules and computers": Dorfmann (Hardy Kruger, left) tries to convince Towns (James Stewart) and Moran (Richard Attenborough) of his figures.

Above, the Phoenix prepares to take off. Below, teamwork for survival: Crow (Ian Bannen, left), Bellamy (George Kennedy), and Standish (Dan Duryea) are harnessed to the wing.

angles. This fractious group, or what is left of it, has become a functioning unit. When the dramatic music rises and the plane. with the men strapped to its wings, takes off, it vindicates Dorfmann's "crazy" ideas.

Dorfmann and Towns are typical of the male antagonists whose personal conflicts dominate Aldrich's films. Dorfmann calls Towns a "Romantic," a criticism which Moran reiterates later when he accuses Towns of "living in the past." Even though Dorfmann himself may seem to live in the fantasy world of his model airplanes, he is at core a realist. It is Dorfmann who berates Towns for deserting his responsibility to the unit in order to search for Cobb who has wandered into the desert. Towns is immobilized by his guilt and his ties to the past. Aldrich's characterization of such types of men is akin to novelist Joseph Conrad's in works like <u>Almayer's Folly</u>, <u>Heart of Darkness</u>, or <u>Lord Jim.</u> Immobility permits death and dissolution. Action is redemptive.

Like Conrad, Aldrich refuses to sentimentalize his characters. Although the viewer may be more sympathetic to Towns, who is more traditionally heroic in his concern for others, the plain fact is that Dorfmann is right and Towns is wrong. It is not until the film's conclusion that Towns realizes why admitting guilt was emotionally difficult for him. No matter that he may have written "pilot error" in his log; it was, as Moran told him, admitting that he was wrong that was almost impossible.

Above, Towns (James Stewart) discovers that, before dying, "Trucker" Cobb (Ernest Borgnine) has written his name in the sand.

For Aldrich, conflicts such as these, conflicts which stood conventional plots and expectations "on their heads," were more interesting. He reverses the resolution which a more traditional filmmaker might have depicted not because he wants to be daring or different. Rather those existential reversals are central to his outlook as a dramatist.

The visual style of *The Flight of the Phoenix* encompasses both unusually grim and unusually striking images, especially when conveying the hallucinatory quality of the desert. In those scenes, Aldrich shifts from an objective perspective to a subjective one and compels the audience to enter the mind of the characters. One series of hallucinatory shots is set up in a typical manner. There is only one spectator and the image of a native dancing girl turns out to be a mirage. The identification of the audience with the spectator in this instance, however, remains detached. There are visual keys to the nature of the apparition in the way that the actual shots of the dancer are superimposed over the desert. There is as well the narrative key in that the audience knows that the characters are alone and likely to be in a stressed or hallucinatory state of mind.

Another subjective staging occurs when the men spot what looks to be an Arab caravan moving through the desert. There are cuts between long lens shots of the caravan from the men's point of view with the image distorted by the heat from the dunes to objective reaction shots of the men, which create an initial confusion. The audience, like the men, must wonder about the reality of this mirage-like sighting. The ultimate reality is an entirely ironic one. The bedouins in the caravan are real, but they offer death rather than salvation. The following morning, looking down at the bodies of Harris and the doctor lying with their throats cut, the others still cannot discern what is real. Because a camel has been left behind, they think that the two men may just be resting, waiting for the bedouins to return. When they finally discover the truth, the hope they harbored is what exacerbates their existential despair.

In all of these "adventure" films, Aldrich used the character's perception of surface appearances to create tension and irony. Whether it is the real nature of Frennessey's motives, of a revolution in Mexico, or of recycling an airplane, the persons, places, and things create the context that both character and viewer struggle to understand. The truth is in the real world. The conflict or the dramatic dichotomy is in the characters working through individual biases to discover that truth.

The Period Adventure: *Sodom and Gomorrah*

Aldrich's fictionalization of *Sodom and Gomorrah* is drawn from the Book of Genesis, which might seem unusual for a filmmaker whose disparagement of social institutions often included organized religion. In fact, both the Biblical story of Sodom and Gomorrah and the plot which Aldrich develops in the film have little to do with organized religion and contain many themes that echo other examples of "foreign adventure" in his work.

Based on a relatively minor incident in the original, Aldrich and his screen-writers elevate a secondary character, Lot, and in the process give him the moral attributes of Abraham, the Biblical protagonist. In Genesis it is Abraham who initiates the separation from Lot, his nephew, because of a conflict be-tween their bands. Abraham is the one who defeats Sodom and Gomorrah's enemies and who appeals to the Lord to spare the cities if only ten just men can be found there. In fact, the Lot in Genesis is somewhat weak-willed. He is captured by King Chedorlaomen and must be rescued by Abraham. Lot fur-ther demonstrates his weakness by offering his two daughters to the Sodo-mites, so that they will not sexually assault his sons-in-law. At the end, he must literally be led by the hand out of Sodom to avoid a fiery death. In order to re-focus the story, Aldrich eliminated Abraham entirely and transferred his strength of character to Lot. He also begins the tale after Lot's separation from his uncle, as he crosses the plains of the Jordan River, on the edge of which the great cities of Sodom and Gomorrah are perched. Finally, he fleshes out the rest of the story by introducing new characters among the inhabitants of Sodom and Gomorrah, who are but shadowy implications in Genesis.

In the opening shot of the film, which begins under the titles, Aldrich thrusts the audience *in media res* with characteristic impatience. The camera pans across a mass of intertwined bodies, spent from a night of revelry. As the queen's brother, Astaroth, gives the nod, a young woman, Tamar, runs from the palace and out of the walls of the city. As she exits the camera pans across more half-naked bodies. These, however, are slaves who have been used up by the denizens of the city and are now being callously piled onto carts des-tined for obliteration.

With this opening series of shots, Aldrich embodies the conflicting forces in Genesis. On one side are the intrigues, orgies, and sadomasochism of Queen Bera and her brother, Astaroth. The evil which Yahweh, the Hebrew god, can no longer abide in Genesis is here made palpable. Tamar, who is a messenger from Astaroth to the Helamites, his allies against his sister, is captured by the Queen's forces. In a torture chamber worthy of Poe, she is placed in a cage with a blind man whose suit of armor is studded with nails. The sadism of the scene is unrestrained as shots of Tamar being forced into the arms of the blind man are intercut with her two sisters being brutally stabbed, all while Astaroth, her supposed protector, gazes on impassively and Queen Bera smiles content-edly. While the inhabitants of these damned cities, led by their Queen, relish their sadistic excesses, the slaves of the city are treated with an inhumanity consistent with the Queen's other actions. They are put to work in the salt

Right, Tamar (Scilla Gabel) dies in a cage with a blind man.

quarries and, having served their purpose, dumped on the banks of the Jordan River, like so much refuse. In a markedly ironic sequence, Aldrich intercuts the Hebrews, bathing joyfully in the Jordan, with the slaves' bodies baking in the sun, a little farther up the river.

There are no overt religious issues in such films as *The Flight of the Phoenix, Vera Cruz, The Angry Hills,* and *World for Ransom.* While there are moral conflicts, the individuals who chose sides of an issue do not invoke "god's law" or any similar concept. In the period context of *Sodom and Gomorrah,* God's law *is* the central issue. Certainly the dissipations of the Sodomites are extreme, and the scripting and staging underscore that. But the protagonists are extremists also. They are filled with self-righteousness and a sense of moral superiority. Like the historical Hebrews, these are conquerors, rolling over the native inhabitants of the Middle East with an invincible sense of "manifest destiny." They are the original imperialists. They conquer the Helamites in an elaborately staged battle which begins with the enemy horsemen immolated by walls of flame ignited by the Hebrews and ends with the Helamite soldiers drowning in a wave of water released by Lot from a dam. The Hebrews wield the elements of fire and water with an impersonal savagery that rivals the bombardiers and gunners hidden inside the planes and tanks of modern warfare.

Aldrich's depiction of the angels of destruction and the final holocaust also expresses his disaffection with the self-righteous. The angels appear to Lot in his prison cell. They are mirror images of each other, actually double exposures, who speak in the stentorian and unforgiving tone of the Old Testament God, calling for the total destruction of all in the cities of Sodom and Gomorrah, the innocent along with the guilty. Only after some begging by Lot do the angels agree to call off this annihilation, if he can find ten innocent men. The destruction is, of course, inexorable. As Lot and his people leave the cities, forbidden to look back, an explosion goes off in the background and a mushroom cloud rises from the rubble. As in *Kiss Me Deadly* and *Twilight's Last Gleaming,* Aldrich plays out the fear of an apocalyptic event in this period context.

The character of Lot fits neatly into the schematic of other Aldrich "leaders of men." He is the pompous idealist who, like General Dell in *Twilight's Last Gleaming,* Lt. De Buin in *Ulzana's Raid,* or Dorfmann in *The Flight of the Phoenix,* can only see the world through his own limited ideological bias. As his concubine Ildith, given to him as a gift by Queen Bera, tells him: "You're more of a slave to your beliefs than any slave in Sodom."

Lot's relationship with his two daughters seems to support Ildith's criticism. Lot rules his daughters like the Old Testament patriarch that he is. When Ildith tries to adorn the roughly clad daughters with silks and jewels, Lot rebukes her, although he allows himself to surrender to the carnal comforts of his concubine. He issues proclamations and judgments on all matters great and small: Ildith's way of life, his daughters' appearance, the squabbles among his tribe. All this pontificating enhances the irony when Lot himself is finally assimilated into the comfortable life of a Sodomite. Convincing himself that he is doing what is best for his people, Lot becomes a judge in the kingdom of Sodom and Gomorrah, allowing the Hebrews to settle within the gates of the cities. His complete acculturation is visualized by means of costuming and decor. Lot exchanges his "dull and grey" animal hides for red, flowing robes. His tent is replaced by a lavish palace, replete with erotic reliefs on the walls.

Aldrich's portrayal of Lot's hypocrisy does not end there. When Lot finds out that Astaroth has seduced both his daughters, he kills him in rage and violates his own laws. "You are a true Sodomite," Queen Bera now tells him; "You feed your own vanity!" Having lost the love of his daughters and the respect of his people, Lot can only submit to the punishment of God. When he leads the Hebrews out of the doomed cities, Ildith, who cannot believe in Yahweh's injunction not to look back, turns to see her home. She is transformed into a pillar of salt before Lot's eyes. With his daughters at his side, Lot collapses in tears. The punishment for his classic *hubris,* like the existential anguish of his modern counterparts, is the price of social reintegration. For characters in other Aldrich films, for true existential outsiders, there is no such solution.

Opposite, Queen Bera (Anouk Aimee) holds court while Ildith (Pier Angeli) and her husband, Lot (Stewart Granger), stand in the background.

Above, Aldrich directs Kim Darby in *The Grissom Gang.*

Chapter Two:

The Outsiders

Because there can be no social reintegration for true existential outsiders, many of Aldrich's characters are doomed from the first. In fact, in more than half of his films one of the major protagonists dies. But surviving or perishing does not strictly parallel winning or losing. "Winning is terribly, terribly important; but you can be a winner if you lose better than the guy that won." Accordingly Aldrich concluded that even "Jack Palance wins when he commits suicide [in *The Big Knife*]."[1]

Ten Seconds to Hell

A whistle emits a shrill blast of steam. A low angle medium shot reveals a passenger car, and the first of several men climbs off the train. There is a travelling close shot with each of them, as they move sullenly down the platform, while on the soundtrack a dispassionate voice reveals biographical details about them: they are all former German soldiers returning to the ruins of Berlin.

This semi-documentary opening sequence for *Ten Seconds to Hell* sets the detached tone for one of Aldrich's many films concerning a cluster of misfits or outsiders. *Vera Cruz, Attack!, The Flight of the Phoenix, The Dirty Dozen, Too Late the Hero, Ulzana's Raid,* and *Ten Seconds to Hell*—all these might be grouped here for one reason or another. They focus in common on groups of men and, through them, deal with isolation, survival, and the determinant faculty of moral values.

In the early films, the opposing figures are clear cut: Erin and Trane, Cooney and Costa, Wirtz and Koertner. In *The Flight of the Phoenix, The Dirty Dozen, Too Late the Hero,* and *Ulzana's Raid*, the focus gradually shifts away from a single internecine struggle towards a confrontation with hostile exterior forces: the desert, the Germans, the Japanese, and the Indians respectively. *Ten Seconds to Hell* is a pivotal film in this continuum. Several parallels between this film and *Vera Cruz* have already been drawn; but, while a sharp, one-on-one opposition of protagonist and antagonist is still in play, *Ten Seconds to Hell* in may ways subordinates the personal conflict to the larger issue of survival against poor odds.

In the most basic terms, the plot, which centers on the pact of a bomb disposal unit to set aside money for the last man left alive, makes the "odds" the chief antagonist of *Ten Seconds to Hell*. The Wirtz-Koertner conflict is visually undercut from their first meeting with the British major. Theoretically, they are co-leaders of the unit, and Wirtz is clearly more assertive than the brooding Koertner. The actors' iconic value reinforces this. Jeff Chandler brings a longer history of sympathetic portrayals to his character, Wirtz, than Jack Palance does to Koertner. The editing pattern, however, as the men are variously framed over and around the major, allots Koertner the foreground close shots

More reluctant allies: Wirtz (Jeff Chandler, left) and Koertner (Jack Palance) together in the bomb pit.

but only permits medium close shots on Wirtz and those are from a diminishing high angle. Moments later outside, Wirtz is allowed some aggressive verbal taunts, as he tries to reestablish his equality and asserts that: "I'll last as long as you will, Koertner!" Koertner just turns and glares at him from atop a heap of rubble in a low angle medium shot that dominates the sequence. In short, Wirtz's opening attempts to assert himself are visually controverted, and nothing of the equilibrium between the two principals of *Vera Cruz* is established.

The narrative line of *Ten Seconds to Hell* is slightly truncated—as already noted, the picture was re-cut by the producers after Aldrich completed it—so it is possible that Koertner was not originally afforded such a dominant portion of screen time. As it stands, his presence and his disillusioned introspection are, much more than they were with Trane in *Vera Cruz*, what holds the film together. There are two ways for Koertner to view his position: "A battle of survival between the Karls of the world and the mes of the world." In his own words this is how he initially perceives it; but he can also regard it as a battle of survival between himself and the impersonal world. The second viewpoint aligns with Wirtz's pose of fatalistic bravado. His favorite expression is "Kismet!" Part of the interplay between the two men involves an active transference of these perceptions.

Visually Aldrich makes few explicit figurative statements on the men's relationship. Outside of the context of genre, as in *Vera Cruz* or later in *The Last Sunset*, where every time two men face off it may be a prelude to a gun fight, the confrontations in *Ten Seconds to Hell* are linked with the ritual of bomb disposal. In the pit with an unexploded bomb, the common interest is much more compelling than the ones which forge temporary alliances between Trane and Erin in *Vera Cruz* or Stribling and O'Malley in *The Last Sunset*. In the pit, antagonists either work together or die together. The metaphor is simple, as well, as simple as the fatefully tight close-up of a flywheel slowly turning, which opens the three-shot scene of Loeffler's death.

Koertner's difficult resolution of his lost idealism, unlike Trane's, is also more accessible to the viewer. While both are veterans of lost wars, Trane, the former Southern aristocrat, is an archetypal stranger in strange land; Koertner, the former architect, is on his home ground. He philosophizes to Margot about the reasons men went to war, "Some political, some private, some personal," while they are sitting amid the debris of a bombed-out building which he had designed. He even brushes the dirt off an inscribed cornerstone before sitting down. This context, stressing the mental anguish of a man who must defuse the bombs which demolished his life's work, creates an explicit irony in *Ten Seconds to Hell* and invests Koertner with a kind of post-War malaise that could only be hinted at in *Vera Cruz*. As Koertner comes to realize that Wirtz is not a personal nemesis but only a particular manifestation of the exterior forces with which everyone must contend, he begins to lose his rancor and re-

adjust to society. Conversely Wirtz, no longer confident in his "good luck" or
the benefits of "Kismet," tries to interfere with the mechanisms of chance. He
tries to murder his last opponent in the most literal game of survival. Again
like Trane, Koertner's response is passive. He abandons Wirtz—it is Wirtz's
bomb; his turn in the rotation—in the shallow pit. An extra long shot shows
him walking away. Another angle frames him in the foreground, as the bomb
goes off behind him. Then a travelling shot keeps Koertner in close-up as he
strides through a tunnel with his footsteps reverberating as the smoke from the
blast catches up to him. He emerges from the tunnel out of deadly smoke to
look up at the sky. The images combine to suggest a completion of the ordeal:
there is a safe exit from the violent arena of nature embodied in the blast and
the smoke. There is at least a partial rediscovery of idealism in the skyward
glance and also a reintegration with the man-made structures of society in the
passage through the tunnel. Finally there is the reaffirmation of personal identity subtly manifested in the sound of his footsteps.

As discussed in the introduction, Aldrich's equation of "offenders" with outsiders relies on the judgment of society. The men of the bomb disposal unit in
Ten Seconds to Hell are defeated. They are literally so, as soldiers on a losing
side. They are figuratively so as well, for when they return to Berlin at the beginning of the film, they are carrying that defeat as an emotional burden.
Whatever their occupations, from adventurers to cops to combat troops, the
outsiders are like specks of grit that might abrade the societal machine. Some
are ground up in the mechanism. Some destroy themselves. A few survive.
The endings of *Ten Seconds to Hell* or *The Dirty Dozen* recapitulate how few
rather than how many are left.

Below, the bomb squad: Koertner (Jack Palance), Wirtz (Jeff Chandler), Sulke (Wesley Addy),
Tillig (Dave Willock), Loeffler (Robert Cornthwaite), and Globke (Jimmy Goodwin). Only one will
survive.

The Emperor of the North Pole

A white on black title card reads: "1933. The height of the Great Depression." The soundtrack of *The Emperor of the North Pole* opens with a song by Hal David and Frank DeVol entitled "A Man and a Train." Over helicopter shots of a steam locomotive rolling through the Northwest, the lyrics of the song succinctly summarize the deceivingly simple plot of the film: a man on the run and a train. But on the run from what? For the next two hours the audience experiences a minimalist exploration of Aldrich's now familiar themes: the outsider, survival in a hostile universe, life as a game, all of which can make a man run from responsibility and commitment. By definition bums, 'bos, or bindlestiffs, whatever one chooses to call them, are outsiders, homeless drifters squatting momentarily on the edges of cities and towns.

In *Emperor* Aldrich reduces his stylistic and thematic equations to their lowest common denominators. The film takes place almost entirely along the railroad line leading through the Oregon woodlands. Aldrich severely limits the space in several of his movies: in *Baby Jane, Hush...Hush, Sweet Charlotte,* and *The Big Knife* to a house; in *The Longest Yard,* a prison; in *Twilight's Last Gleaming,* a missile silo and the Presidential cabinet room. The existential and psychological limitations of life are reified in the physical surroundings. Although the landscape in *The Emperor of the North Pole* is ostensibly as vast as the forests, it is emotionally confined to the few feet between the rails. Unlike the constricted figures in the earlier films, the action of *The Emperor of the North Pole* takes place in such a circumscribed and monotonous terrain, namely, the train, the train yards, the tracks, and their respective environs, that the viewer rarely has a feeling of moving forward towards an objective. Like the three main characters, "A No.1," "Shack," and "Cigaret," the viewer is caught between the rails, an appropriate metaphor for the psychological stasis of the three men.

Aldrich has certainly made this figurative statement before. Charlie Castle in *The Big Knife* is frozen in indecision about his career and life. Baby Jane Hudson and her sister are frozen in a scenario which took place three decades before, as is Charlotte in *Hush...Hush*. Paul Crewe in *The Longest Yard* finds himself unable to live normally after a football scandal that immediately colors how others perceive him, even in prison. If Aldrich recalls Conrad in regarding immobility as the greatest transgression and if salvation lies in action, this entire interaction is dependent on a crisis to set it in motion. A crisis is what the self-conscious allegory of *The Emperor of the North Pole* is lacking.

Certainly, as the opening title suggests, the economic upheaval of the Depression which put so many men and women on the road is a crisis. Its last

Above, figures compressed by a long focal length lens: A No. 1 (Lee Marvin, left) comes up behind Shack (Ernest Borgnine) as he corners Cigaret (Keith Carradine).

words underscore the importance of "their only source of survival—the trains"; but none of the protagonists in *The Emperor of the North Pole* make this conscious association or seem motivated by it. In the war films, the Westerns, and adventure films like *The Flight of the Phoenix*, even in the sports films, there is something riding on the outcome. In *The Emperor of the North Pole* the entire fabric of society and its rules is distilled down to a conductor who won't have hobos on his train and two men determined to ride it. The men share one overwhelming emotion: pride. Shack lives for *his* No. 19 train. It has become, in fact, an extension of himself. He guards it like a jealous lover, punishing brutally any other man who tries to "mount" his "beloved." "Shack would rather kill a man," one of the rail yard regulars notes without exaggeration, "than give him a free ride."

In the first few minutes of the movie the camera moves with Shack as he compulsively examines both train and tracks, his eyes darting from side to side to detect any hobos hiding in the bushes. When one brave 'bo tries to climb aboard, Shack is on him immediately, looming above in a low angle, steel hammer in hand, pounding at the victim who hangs desperately from the couplers of the moving train. As the 'bo falls and the train rolls on, the camera looks back briefly for a shot of the man's battered body. This is all the plot there ever will be: a tough conductor and the two down-and-outers, the wizened old-timer and the greenhorn, who will hop a freight just to prove a point. Except for pride, motivations are subsumed by the action, being true to the underlying sense of transience. Why A No.1 came from Portland or why he is going back does not matter—just that he is doing it.

The very names "Shack," "A No.1," "Cigaret" represent the figures' minimalist personas and make them seem more like ciphers than traditional characters. "A No.1" is the "king of the hobos...the Emperor of the North Pole...the top of the heap." His status is tied to being king of the road as well, able to ride anyone's train, even Shack's. He's a professional hobo, with no observable ambition and no discernible past. The only motive he needs is the social reality that "this country's gone to hell." A No.1 proclaims as much, flashing a smile of green teeth in a face filthy and sunburned.

In fact, A No. 1 has so little ambition that he ignores the hobos' suggestion that he beat Shack at his own game and ride the No. 19 to Portland. He only changes his mind when Cigaret, another male from the "tribe" of tramps, claims to have ridden No. 19. Although both men know the truth is that A No.1 saved Cigaret's life by helping him escape from Shack's clutches, Cigaret's boast is like a primal challenge; and the rules of A No.1's society require him to meet it. Cigaret is just a callow, brash newcomer to the tracks who struts before the male onlookers like a herd animal vying for leadership. But by taking credit for riding Shack's train and setting fire to the boxcar when in fact it was A No.1 who had been responsible for it and their resulting escape, Cigaret creates the crisis that the narrative was lacking.

Although *The Emperor of the North Pole* is largely devoid of more positive emotions, being focused entirely on male pride and anger, there is a potentially positive interaction between Cigaret and A No.1, no matter how brief or how ultimately disastrous for both. As Cigaret and A No.1 mount Shack's train to ride it to Portland, A No.1's initial antipathy turns to pity after they are both forcibly ejected from the train. Sullenly and almost silently, A No.1 begins the arduous process of teaching Cigaret "the ropes." In a series of shots virtually without dialogue, he demonstrates how the perplexed Cigaret should find discarded grease buckets and use their residue on the tracks. In response to Cigaret's query as to what he is doing, A No.1 explains the obvious: "Teaching you." When Cigaret asks, "Why?" all he can answer is "I'm still working on that."

This potential surrogate father-son relationship remains the only really positive emotional moment in a film filled with challenges, brutality, pranks, and an underlying rage embodied in the final fight. Of course in Aldrich's universe, sentiment is out of place in the existential struggle to survive. By the final scenes of the movie, Cigaret has returned A No.1's kindness with malicious recklessness, which endangers the life of his would-be mentor and causes serious injury to the trainmen.

In the final scene A No.1 once again and for the last time saves Cigaret's life, battling with Shack aboard a moving train. But by this time A No.1 has had enough. After A No.1 has pushed Shack from the speeding train, Cigaret thinks of his grand plans for *their* future. Without warning A No.1 throws Cigaret off the train and into the river below: "Kid, you've got no class." As Cigaret bobs up and down in the water, the camera lingers on an extra long shot of the receding train and the voice of A No.1 victorious and screaming back at Cigaret for his shortsightedness.

If Cigaret could have "been somebody," where does that leave the actual "Emperor of the North Pole"? His shouts echoing over the desolate terrain give the scene a grimly ironic tone. Could a victory be more hollow? He has indeed become "the emperor" by conquering both Shack and Cigaret. He has fulfilled the demands of male pride. But ultimately he is alone, without a past, without a future, without companions no matter how fickle. The father-son bond has been ruptured to be replaced by the emptiness of the Northwestern landscape.

As implied by the opening song of the movie, the railroad is the key metaphor. The train moves on through space and time to a given destination and then returns to repeat the same trip over and over again. With the train on its journey are its crew and the attendant hobos who try to conquer it. If these challenges to the authority of Shack are constructed like a sporting event, they lack the clarity of the contests in *The Longest Yard* or even ...*All the Marbles*. What defines this game is not the rules as much as the spectators. The setup of the game and A No.1's attempt to ride the No. 19 to Portland takes place in a series of cross cuts between the gathering of railroad workers and a congregation of hobos. Like any office pool betting on the Super Bowl, the money flies fast and furious as both groups bet on their respective favorite.

A No.1 suffers several setbacks and almost derails No. 19 in order to mount it as Shack highballs out of the yard. As the contest goes back and forth, Cigaret realizes the truth of it all. When he confronts A No. 1 with his discovery, the "Emperor" denies it: "This ain't no game" "The hell it ain't," asserts Cigaret, who, for all his arrogance and inexperience, can grasp the obvious. This is the "game" that crowns the kings of the road and earns the railroad men their gold watches. A No.1's only card is his sneer and his look of disapproval, just as Shack's wild-eyed expressions reveal his monomania. When the two men square off on the flat car, the viewer may expect something like a wrestling match from its chest-beating participants. In this sense, the graphic brutality of the combat is most disquieting, both for its images and for its revelation that the game is far deadlier that the players let on.

Visually, Aldrich eschews his typical high and low angles in *The Emperor of the North Pole*. Instead there are the naturally tilted and cramped perspectives of men wedged into undercarriages and leaning out of cabs. The overt manipulations, like the antiquated iris effect which opens the film or the wipes and lap dissolves for transitions, reinforce the period and the sense of the film as a set piece. One of the film's most complex shots is a slow, point-of-view zoom when Cigaret slowly picks the figure of A No.1 out from amidst the heap of camouflaging debris of the dump in which he sits. In that shot the viewer shares Cigaret's discovery of how A No.1 survives by passively blending with the environment.

As A No.1 rides off at the end, the music sounds the refrain. Like Camus' reading of Sisyphus, eternally rolling his stone up the mountain only to have it fall and then to be forced to roll it up again, or any fated figure, these men and trains go back and forth repeating the ritual. "If you ever let go," the song says, "she'll throw you under." It is all part of a dangerous, repetitive, and ultimately pointless scenario of survival of the fittest.

Left, A No. 1 (Lee Marvin) blends in with the scrap heap.

Above, after taking over the missile silo, Garvas (Burt Young, left), Powell (Paul Winfield) and Dell (Burt Lancaster) in *Twilight's Last Gleaming*.

Twilight's Last Gleaming

The context of *Twilight's Last Gleaming* is as significant as any in Aldrich's work. Whether or not *Twilight's Last Gleaming* is an "important" or a radical motion picture from either the filmmaker's or audience's point of view, it depends on the sociopolitical perceptions of the time it was made. Much as *Kiss Me Deadly* reflected the McCarthyism of its time, *Twilight's Last Gleaming* mirrors not just America's anxiety over nuclear war but also a basic distrust of its leadership, particularly in the late 1960s and 1970s. *Twilight's Last Gleaming* is born of what has been called "post-Vietnam/Watergate syndrome." The revelations through the Pentagon Papers that the U.S. government was lying to the American public about the methods and objectives of the Vietnam War, the resignation of Nixon over his illegal activities surrounding the Watergate break-in, and the ignominious withdrawal from Vietnam created the atmosphere of distrust and malaise in America that underlies the film.

An early scene in *Twilight's Last Gleaming* exploits this perception. The fictional President Stevens is meeting with his former Professor, James Forrest, who is appealing for the life of a political prisoner who assassinated an African country's repressive dictator. The President, as portrayed by Charles Durning, is warm, jovial, and lacking in pretensions; but he smoothly refuses to grant the request of Professor Forrest because the U.S. cannot give "sanctuary" to an assassin. After the crestfallen Forrest leaves, the President and his adjutant reveal the real reason: they have traded the revolutionary for U.S. air bases in that same African country's territory. The audience has no difficulty in accepting the depiction of a deceitful and pragmatic chief executive. And *Twilight's Last Gleaming* will rely on these disillusioned perceptions to sustain identification with its protagonists, a trio of men who take over a missile silo.

The group's leader, former General Dell, is an idealist, determined to force the U.S. to come clean about its deception of the American public. The cabinet meetings which are called to discuss "the terrorists'" demands are sophisticated examples of Orwellian "double talk." Framed about a round table, the heads of the various departments express no other priority than maintaining the veil of secrecy surrounding the government. They readily admit "railroading" General Dell for threatening to blow the lid off the "Vietnam lie." They are unaffected by the existence of National Security Council documents, fictional stand-ins for the Pentagon Papers, which Dell presents as evidence of the complicity of the President and his advisors in a plot to deceive the American public. Even the dignified, aging, Ivy-league Defense Secretary Zachariah Guthrie, a clear analog for such actual presidential advisors as Robert McNamara, hesitates at Stevens' assertions about the American people that "we have an obligation to trust them." There is no one in this "distinguished"

group with a personal moral code, no one passionate about putting the Con-
stitution over political self-interest.

The group's ultimate betrayal is of their own "chief." In order to "trust the
people" and prevent Dell from launching the nine nuclear missiles against the
Soviet Union, the President agrees to his demands: he provides money, Air
Force One, himself as a hostage, and promises publication of NSC Document
9759. He makes Guthrie his liaison. As the two remaining "terrorists," Dell
and Powell, escort the President to the plane, using him as a shield, Aldrich intercuts contrasting images: black-and-white shots on SAC monitors of the men
spinning to avoid the sharpshooters they know are awaiting them and color
long shots from those sharpshooters' points of view. On command they fire,
hitting all three men. The film cuts to horrified close-ups of those watching at
SAC headquarters as the president slowly falls, like a wounded ballet dancer,
to the ground. His last words to Guthrie are whispered, "Will you tell the people?" Guthrie's only response is to lower his eyes.

While the filmmakers' sympathies are clearly not with the government, the
"terrorists" are not untarnished idealists either. Dell behaves like a para-
noid/schizophrenic. If he has good reason to suspect conspiracies, he is also
willing to kill countless millions to make his point. Aldrich establishes this for
both the audience and the President in an early sequence. Dell discovers that
a counter-terrorist team has planted a bomb in the silo, and he initiates the
launch sequence. Aldrich uses a four-way split screen and rapid cutting between each one: the missiles rising in their silos; the LED displays counting
down the seconds; General MacKenzie asking permission of his President to
fire the device they have planted; the President immobilized by indecision;
Dell counting down orally. When the President caves in to Dell's threat and
the sequence is aborted, neither the characters nor the audience have any further doubts about Dell's seriousness.

As in *The Longest Yard* Aldrich adopts the split screen technique for several
of the action sequences of this film. Besides the near-launch of the missiles by
Dell, the other notable exploitation of the technique is the sequence in which
General Mackenzie's team plants a nuclear device in the silo to destroy Dell
and his cohorts. The sequence is heavily layered with concurrent action divided into two, three, and four parts within the same frame and with video images in black and white. Shots of Dell and Powell carefully studying the
monitors of the surveillance cameras are intercut with tanks, acting as decoys,
rolling up to the silo and an expert military team entering the facility with a
nuclear device in hand. It is a tense sequence, with a powerful release when
an alarm is activated which alerts Dell to the presence of the intruders.

Besides actually pushing the button, Dell permits the torture of his former
comrade-in-arms, Captain Towne, who has the combination to the safe con-

Above, Secretary Guthrie (Melvyn Douglas, left) and the President (Charles Durning).

taining the keys to the missile control panel. Like any terrorist, Dell is fixated with the goal and is, at heart, a fanatic, Like Lieutenant DeBuin in *Ulzana's Raid,* who is convinced that he is right, Dell does "intend to hold up the truth to the world." Like DeBuin, his ideology refuses to admit that morality can be ambiguous or, like Towns in *The Flight of the Phoenix*, that he may be consummately wrong in his methods, if not in his objectives.

Dell's fellow escapee and partner in the enterprise, Powell, is the pragmatic counterweight to Dell's idealism. Powell joined with Dell not for altruistic reasons but for purely selfish ones: a ransom and freedom. While Dell maintains a childlike faith in President Stevens, a man whom the audience has already seen lying to his former professor, Powell tries to jolt Dell out of his "fantasy world." Trying to dissuade him from launching the missiles, he tells Dell simply, "Nobody honors nothin' No reason to blow up the world." As for Dell's

Below, Dell (Burt Lancaster) and Powell (Paul Winfield) attempt to leave using the President (Charles Durning) as a shield.

conviction that the President will reveal the contents of NSC document 9759 to the American public as he promised, Powell predicts, rather accurately, "They'll kill us all before they let him read that speech."

Dell and Powell's faces when the President arrives to negotiate with them wordlessly underscore their attitudes. As they both watch the action on their monitors in the control room, Aldrich contrasts a close-up of Dell's ecstatic face with Powell's skeptical expression. As they both are viewing the same images but reacting in opposing ways, there is a necessary split of viewer identification away from Dell and towards Powell. On its own, Dell's faith in the system is contradictory. He has already been betrayed by men without honor; yet he now relies on the honor of others. Stevens' earlier prevarication confirms for the audience that Powell's contempt for the system comes out of the system's own behavior.

The threat of nuclear devastation has figured in Aldrich's work from the earliest films, with the kidnapped scientist in *World for Ransom* and the "Pandora's box" of *Kiss Me Deadly*. But the nine missiles ready to be launched at the Soviet Union in this film make an implacably direct statement. Had Aldrich made *Kinderspiel*, his last utterance on the issue of disarmament might have been different. Since that project never came to fruition, *Twilight's Last Gleaming* is the final statement; and that statement is, as the ironic choice of title suggests, a very dark one. Other films end with a near apocalyptic destruction from the nuclear explosion on the beach in *Kiss Me Deadly*, through the field of bodies in the final battle in *Vera Cruz*, to the mushroom cloud over the devastated cities in *Sodom and Gomorrah*. In those films the audience watches as violent characters push each other to the edge of the maelstrom wherein they may consider the probity of their actions. In *Twilight's Last Gleaming* the world is "saved" but at what cost?

The Grissom Gang and The Choirboys

Both of these pictures are difficult to classify in Aldrich's work. Superficially, they could be called gangster and cop films respectively. Aldrich made no pure "gangster film" and, other than *Kiss Me Deadly* and *The Garment Jungle*, no other pictures in which gangsters figure at all. His other cop picture, *Hustle*, is more akin to *film noir* than the ensemble melodrama of *The Choirboys*. Ironically, the Depression-era misfits of Ma Grissom's gang and the 70s beat cops in *The Choirboys* have much in common. The Midwest milieu of *The Grissom Gang* and the Hollywood of *The Choirboys* contain the same type of cheap criminals and violent cops. If anything, Ma Grissom's dinner for her extended family and the collective, off-duty antics or "choir practice" of the cops have the same sardonic humor.

What distinguishes *The Grissom Gang* is its uneasy mixture of offhanded violence and ill-fated romanticism. Slim Grissom's murder of his cohort, Eddie Hagen, is arguably the most purely violent of any scene in Aldrich's films. And yet the reason the simpleminded Slim stabs Eddie so savagely and repeatedly is for love. On the one hand, Slim resembles *The Dirty Dozen*'s deadliest psychopath, Maggot. On the other, there is no character in any Aldrich film whose devotion to a woman is more powerful and uninhibited. Part of this, of course, has to do with the kind of male characters which Aldrich chose to portray. The others who suffer for love, such as Callahan in *World for Ransom* or Gaines in *Hustle*, are also involved in twisted relationships. In fact, Callahan's devotion to the bisexual manipulator, Frennessey, and Gaines' long-term affair with a high-priced prostitute are, in their own ways, as perverse as Slim's.

The Grissom Gang is about crime: kidnapping, murder, and assorted lesser felonies. Ma Grissom's motley group of miscreants do constitute a gang. But Ma herself is as much a caricature as a character, a machine-gun wielding variant on the title figure in the aborted *Greatest Mother of 'Em All*. Her devotion to her retarded son, Slim, is neither touching nor selfless. Slim is, after all, her enforcer, the one whom even his fellow gang members fear, the loose cannon that keeps her in control.

Below, Irene Dailey as Ma Grissom.

"Slim's a good boy," Ma asserts, "always does what his mother tells him." Ma's print dresses, grimy aprons, and unkempt hair suggest half of "American Gothic" gone psycho. And the twang in her voice when she warns Barbara Blandish that "we ain't the kind of people who fool around. Get it, Dearie." makes her all the more menacing. Ma's demise, cackling like a demented Lucy Ricardo, as the police close in and her tommy gun jams, is closer to Captain Cooney's in *Attack!*, two-stepping in a hail of bullets, than to the grisly gang-related deaths in *Kiss Me Deadly* or *The Garment Jungle*. In fact, most of the criminals in *The Grissom Gang* verge on parody, from Joey Fay's pudgy Woppy to Ralph Waite's hayseed, Mace, to Tony Musante's Eddie with his slicked-back hair and white-toothed grin. They are full-color, 70s versions of the gangster movie stereotypes from the 30s.

There are other expressions of this sardonic undertone in *The Grissom Gang*, mostly in the music, full of banjos and up-tempo chase cues, so that the careening period cars recall the Keystone cops as much as *Little Caesar* or *Public Enemy*. There are also the black-and-white freeze frames in the title sequence, that simulate still photographs and are part homage to and part parody of a similar montage of stills in *Bonnie and Clyde.*

Much like *Bonnie and Clyde*, many of the incidents in *The Grissom Gang* are part of a de-construction of the traditional Hollywood gangster film. Like the reenactment of the killing of the real Bonnie and Clyde at the end of Arthur Penn's film, the destruction of all the Grissom gang except Slim is effected in a series of scenes in which the title characters are riddled with bullets. The detail adds a layer a savage satire: Ma's death dance; the art deco panels shattering to reveal armor plate beneath; the colored light that keeps flashing as Woppy expires. Slim learns of the massacre through a radio report in which the scene is jokingly described as "more bullets flying around than ticks on a cow's back."

The slow-witted Slim Grissom is clearly a child of his unwholesome environment. When he and his gang take Barbara from her original abductors, Slim behaves as if his mother were watching. "Like Ma says," Slim notes approvingly to Eddie, who has just pumped a man full of lead, "they's real punks." Slim has no compunctions about anyone's violent behavior, least of all his own. He grins, sticks out his tongue, and wipes his knife blade on his victim's lapels after killing a man himself. For Slim, only the sweaty, traumatized Barbara in her soiled, satiny evening gown, a disheveled vision of loveliness, merits a second glance or a second thought.

The most significant music cue which opens and closes *The Grissom Gang* is Rudy Vallee singing "I Can't Give You Anything But Love, Baby." For Slim, at the picture's beginning, romantic love is an unlikely prospect. So while the others see dollar signs over the Blandish girl's head, Slim sees a halo. The transformation of his captive from angel to sex slave is a hesitant one for Slim, partly because he is unfamiliar with the process, partly because his childlike outlook makes no necessary distinction between the two. What is unusual in the film's narrative is the transformation of Barbara Blandish. To her Slim is the most repellent of the gang, a "cretinous half-wit" or a "creepy crawly slimy slug." His very naivete makes him all the more repugnant.

Since Slim knows he is her sole protector, Barbara's behavior is puzzling to him. When he complains to Ma that "she's saying bad things," Barbara gets beaten but starts guzzling more gin. "Ladies ain't supposed to drink," Slim tells her, "not hard liquor." When she realizes that the gang means to collect the ransom and kill her, Barbara knows that Slim is her only hope for survival, and she actually seduces him. The early scenes with Slim and Barbara are in the dingy upstairs room where she is kept. Shot with little fill light so that dark wedges cut across walls and floors, Aldrich also uses over-the-shoulder shots and travels in from medium close to close to constrict the frame even more and to externalize Barbara's sense of being caged. After their first sexual interlude, Barbara looks at herself in a clouded mirror and Slims comes up behind her. Surrounded by Slim and his reflection and facing the empty liquor bottles arrayed on the dressing table before her, Barbara confronts a grotesque mutation of her previous life. It is in this context, as Slim professes his love, that the emotional transference between them begins.

Below, Kim Darby as Barbara and Scott Wilson as Slim.

Ultimately after the gang buys a night club with the ransom money, Slim takes her to a secret love nest. It is a kaleidoscopic maze of primary colors and diamond shapes complete with a "gold leaf flush toilet" and a kitchen. "I don't cook" is all that Barbara can think to say. Although Slim does seem to become smarter as the narrative progresses, his understanding of how things are is always instinctive rather than intellectual. For Barbara, the rich sophisticate, the reverse is true. The brutalization she endures is also part of the transference in which she comes to understand the insights of someone like Slim.

Slim's devotion is mirrored in Anna Borg, a night club singer and the girlfriend of one of the original kidnappers killed by the Grissoms, who takes up with Eddie Hagen. When Fenner, the private detective hired by Barbara's father to pay the ransom and find his daughter, tricks Anna, she realizes that Eddie killed "her Franky." When she pulls a gun, Eddie shoots her first and notes with disgust that she was "dumb, Anna, you were really dumb." It is this scorn of Eddie, the smart guy and pseudo-sophisticate, both for Anna and for Slim, which mirrors Barbara's feelings at the film's beginning. It is only after Eddie attempts to rape her and Slim violently intervenes that Barbara grasps the nature of the primal emotion which drives people like Anna and Slim. Barbara screams and shudders with each thrust of Slim's knife into Eddie. After this mock orgasm, it remains only for Barbara to reciprocate the love of her valiant defender, Slim, to complete the transference.

Below, Slim (Scott WIlson) repeatedly stabs Eddie (Tony Musante), who has planned to rape and then kill Barbara (Kim Darby) on Ma's orders.

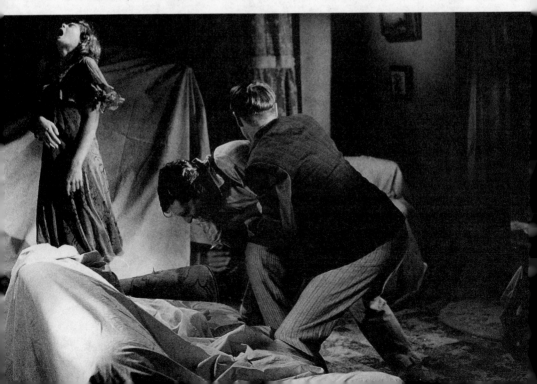

Above, Barbara (Kim Darby) kneels beside the bullet-riddled body of Slim (Scott Wilson).

As the police close in on her and Slim hiding in a barn, Barbara does reciprocate that love. While it may only be with a nod of her head when Slim asks her if she would really care if he died, Barbara's affirmation both liberates and condemns her. Slim dies a grisly Grissom death in a hail of bullets. Barbara's father vilifies her for crying over Slim's body; and the press crowds around. As with Zarkan at the end of *The Legend of Lylah Clare*, Barbara's own personality has been subsumed into the idealized Slim whom she helped to create. Like Zarkan, she is lost without that object. Over a freeze frame of her despairing glance backwards as Fenner drives her away, Rudy Vallee croons on the soundtrack.

As with the hobos and train men in *The Emperor of the North Pole*, the milieu and period of *The Grissom Gang* lend themselves towards the characterization of outsiders. Barbara and her father are the only ostensibly normal persons in the film; but their rupture at the conclusion is indicative of the existential vagaries of Aldrich's world view. Fenner, the bridge between the world of the Grissoms and that of Mr. Blandish, is a shadowy, alienated figure from the first. His social situation and the dialogue with the police chief suggest a dark past, but it is never revealed. He is at his most animated when playing a role, posing as a theatrical agent to extract information from Anna Borg. He wears dark suits which cause him to blend into the shadowy background and is often photographed with sharp side light. The staging of his conversation with Mr. Blandish in the night club love nest after the police raid uses matching close-ups in which a silhouette of each restricts the other's screen space as if expressing the narrowness of their respective outlooks. Fenner is the only one who seems to understand Barbara's pain at Slim's death. Yet he drives her away to an uncertainty which he also understands may be a worse fate than Slim's.[2]

There is a similar character dynamic in *The Choirboys*. The sardonic tone is set from the title sequence. A fugue accompanies a panning down from a brick face to a cheap stained-glass window which features a stylized police officer's head and shoulders. A male chorus begins a paraphrase of various songs, such as "I've Been Working on the Railroad," as the Gothic letters of the main titles continue. At the end a black fist comes through the window, which warps the letters of the main title. That image is held in a freeze frame.

The icons say it all. As a concept, the term "choirboys" is a purposeful irony, a name the off-duty cops give themselves because they are anything but choirboys. As a film, *The Choirboys* is about the vulgarization of society, epitomized by the antisocial behavior of both the cops and the criminals, the classic movie good and bad guys. As one of the cops observes "in those Jesuit boarding schools, there's an absolute good and an absolute evil." On the street, there are no absolutes, except perhaps that everything and everyone is tainted.

In the course of the narrative, Aldrich unabashedly recruits any stereotype which reinforces the vulgarity. When the "choirboys" handcuff the most bigoted of the police brethren, Roscoe, with his pants pulled down to a tree, the pedestrian who happens upon him is a gay man with a pink poodle on a leash. This man, for whom the encounter with a bare-bottomed, trussed-up Roscoe is a "salacious fantasy," is more than a mere stereotype. He is, in more current jargon, Roscoe's "worst nightmare." While the intended effect of using such stereotypes may be to mock them and the people like Roscoe who put stock in them, the humorlessness of the portrayals work against that effect. The encounter between Roscoe and the vice cop, Zoony, in a men's room also hinges on the former's homophobia. Zoony's reply when Roscoe calls him "a faggot" is "you wouldn't poke fun at a cripple, would you?" This subtly reveals Zoony's own prejudice in equating homosexuality with a disability.

Ironically only Sgt. Scuzzi, the least cop-like of all the police portrayed in *The Choirboys*, has any shred of tolerance. The teenager whom Zoony arrests in the park tells Scuzzi that his parents don't know of his sexual orientation, that "I don't know why I'm gay. I just am." Scuzzi tells him to get counseling and lets him go. Occasionally, Aldrich will underscore the point with a particular visual usage. For instance, when Officer Bloomguard reports for his night shift assignment to the vice squad, he mistakes Scuzzi for a janitor. While the sergeant does not take offense, the shot of Scuzzi through the cubbyholes of his desk is a fairly explicit expression of the fact that Bloomguard's white, middle-class attitude caused him to judge Scuzzi by his appearance.

Above, Whalen (Charles Durning) is restrained by Motts (Louis Gosset, Jr.) in *The Choirboys*.

For the most part *The Choirboys* consists of episodes that alternate between low humor and pathos. The low point is when Roscoe's manic insensitivity turns a quarrel between a Latino man and an African-American into an assault on him and his partner. As the two cops are pummeled, they bounce off a slapstick set of bedsprings leaning against a wall.

The violence has a very different connotation in *The Choirboys* than in *The Grissom Gang* or *The Emperor of the North Pole*. It is the police, in fact, who are the most drunken and unruly characters in *The Choirboys*. Even in the overall ironic context of the film, the portrayal of the police is not merely as outsiders but as social misfits. That Lyles' Vietnam flashback leads him to kill an innocent man is a deplorable event. That the others conspire to cover it up is criminal. When Whalen, allowed to retire for informing on his fellow officers, and Motts confront Deputy Chief Riggs at the film's conclusion, it is the fact that so many police are guilty of criminal behavior that permits them to blackmail Riggs into reinstating all the others.

Aldrich repeatedly uses the fate of characters such as Barbara Blandish to suggest the inflexibility of social attitudes. The ending of *The Choirboys* also uses a recap of the characters' laughing, like the endings *Ten Seconds to Hell* and *The Dirty Dozen*. Unlike other outsiders, most of title characters in *The Choirboys* survive. If the freeze frame at the end of *The Grissom Gang* epitomizes the intolerance to which an innocent victim may be subjected, what does the ending of *The Choirboys*, a freeze frame of Whalen and Potts slapping hands after beating the system, suggest? For Aldrich, whether he fully conveyed that meaning or not, the likeliest answer would be that it suggests the pervasiveness of corruption and how thoroughly it can taint those who must deal with it.

Above, Aldrich and Cinematographer Joe Biroc check the sun while on location for *Too Late the Hero*. In the background, left to right, are actors Cliff Robertson, Ronald Fraser, and Michael Caine.

Chapter Three:
The Battle and the Game

The traditions of the adventure film or the Western depend to a considerable extent on imperiled protagonists; but for filmmaker and viewer alike, genres such as the war film and the sports films provide the clearest line: on one side of it you win, on the other you lose. When the game becomes combat, on one side you live, on the other you die. There is an explicit sequence in *Too Late the Hero* and another in *Attack!*, when the men sprint down a hill to the edge of town and later retreat dodging artillery shells, where the staging resembles a broken field run in a football game. Like a sporting event, the winners and losers, survivors and victims, should be clearly delineated. There are no ties, there are no standoffs. For Aldrich the battle and the game share a core assumption. To a certain extent, the mettle of the participants will decide the outcome. And in war, the sporting term "sudden death" acquires an exact meaning.[1]

Attack!

Attack! begins with a literal explosion as an artillery shell lands in an open field with a burst of shrapnel and black smoke. A title is superimposed in letters of the stencil-type used on military vehicles. It reads, "Europe, 1944." This single shot, including the lettering style of its straightforward expository title, evokes the war-film genre with maximum impact and economy. A cutaway shot provides the first glimpse of human combatants as a gaunt, unshaven lieutenant scans the area below with field glasses while two of his men stand

119

by. A helmet covered with tattered camouflage netting rolls clumsily down a grassy slope, its thumping against the ground is eerily audible over the reverberation of the shell blast. Finally it comes to a stop on a flat stretch of ground next to a single flower. The image is held as the main titles begin, accompanied by the clattering, martial music of the film's score by Frank DeVol.

After this opening fire fight—which is never seen in its entirety but is instead depicted through such details as the shell burst, the rolling helmet, and a line officer with his back to the action helplessly waving his hand over his head—the film picks up the line of its source play, "Fragile Fox," in a series of expository confrontations. Lieutenants Costa and Woodruff are aware that their company commander, Capt. Cooney, is a coward. As Costa works a blacksmith's forge to relieve his fury, Cooney talks to the regimental commander, Col. Bartlett, whose political aspirations and hope for sponsorship from Cooney's father make him the craven captain's protector. Aldrich surrounds and amplifies these scenes with telling details.

The aftermath of the assault on the pillbox begins with a huge close-up of a loudspeaker blaring out a popular song. Only after the camera has been pulled back and craned down is the geography of the scene made clear. Costa's platoon is in a rear area, recuperating and speculating on what their lieutenant will do about their nineteen dead comrades. The next sequence also begins with an extreme close shot: a hand vigorously working the lever of a bellows. A cut back reveals Costa at the forge. When the action ultimately

Below, Woodruff (William Smithers) talks with Costa (Jack Palance) at the forge.

moves inside to Cooney's makeshift headquarters, the locus of the play is ree-
stablished. Aldrich uses his customary but otherwise unusual high and low
camera angles, foreground clutter, and wedges of light to add a sense of constriction to the interior sequences. When Bartlett convinces the three other officers to sit down together at a card game, opposing medium two shots
underscore the unspoken antagonism as Bartlett and Cooney are framed on
one side of the table against Costa and Woodruff on the other. Later in the
scene, as the tensions between Costa and Cooney build to a breaking point,
Aldrich subtly reinforces that by framing them at opposite sides of a two shot
and delaying a cut for several seconds.

Attack!, even more than the play from which it is taken, draws its major
themes with broad and violent strokes. Part of that is through the isolated
emotions of its principals: Costa's rage is as inappropriate to a field officer as is
Cooney's terror, and the manner in which they both perish tends to confirm
this. Part of it is the simple context of a war film, the issues of alienation and
simple survival are part of the viewer's genre expectations. As the tag line to
the film's advertising art reads: "It rips open the hot hell behind the glory."

The hostile environment means that the characters need not be typified as
outsiders or adventurers. That much comes, quite literally, with the territory;
and the problem of staying alive in an environment full of stray bullets and
mortar shells needs scant reinforcement. Unlike the group of crash survivors in
The Flight of the Phoenix or even the bomb disposal squad in *Ten Seconds to*

Below, during a card game Woodruff (William Smithers, right) restrains Costa (Jack Palance)
from assaulting Cooney (Eddie Albert) while Col. Bartlett (Lee Marvin, foreground) looks on.

Hell, there is no moment in the film when any of the characters in *Attack!* first realize that they may possibly die. All that has taken place before the narrative even begins and is synthesized for the viewer in the generic shorthand of the title sequence.

For Aldrich in war as in sports, it is those who lose control, no matter how righteously, who are likeliest to perish. The character of Joe Costa is one of the strongest examples of this system of moral determinism in Aldrich's work. The casting of Jack Palance quickly combines with the genre context. In the title sequence and then at the forge, Palance's afflicted visage, familiar from previous films including Aldrich's own *The Big Knife*, immediately conveys to the viewer the past anguish Costa has suffered under Cooney's command. When Costa does lose control, when he grabs Cooney, accuses him of behaving like a "gutless wonder," and threatens to ram a grenade down his throat and pull out the pin if he does it again, the viewer's emotional identification with the underling is certainly not diminished. But on a rational level, Cooney would never fear Costa more than the enemy. If anything, Costa's menacing behavior would inspire Cooney to abandon him again, to let Costa die. And that is exactly what he does.

Above, Costa (Jack Palance, right) threatens Cooney (Eddie Albert) about another "gutless wonder."

In the course of the film, Aldrich continues to exploit this generic and emotive shorthand. When Costa escapes from the advance position only to discover that the soldier he has carried away is dead, a low angle shot frames him from below against a sky filled with black smoke, and his sunken eyes stare cadaverously at the horizon in graphic affirmation of his spiritual death. When Costa destroys a tank, and its momentum pins him against a wall and runs over his arm, his screams connote both the character's physical pain and the anguish of being prevented from finding his real enemy, Cooney. By the time Costa does confront Cooney, his arm is a bloody pulp. He stands at the top of the cellar stairs, a demonic vision drained of life, sustained only by the will to get revenge but ultimately unable to exact it.

Critic Raymond Durgnat calls *Attack!* a *film noir.*[2] Certainly, coming as it does in close proximity to more traditional examples in *Kiss Me Deadly* and *The Garment Jungle*, the visual style of *Attack!* incorporates many motifs used in Aldrich's *noir* films. But the metaphorical or dramatic implications can also be considered in terms of the immediate context independent of film type. After Bartlett has told Costa and Woodruff that "we all have our troubles," there is a long shot which tightens when the camera cranes down under some wires and moves in. Its graphic suggestion of enclosure and enmeshment have a fateful connotation tied to the situation, not to the genre. There is also a long take of the squad assembled prior to being sent back to the front lines that begins with Costa's entry into the scene. The dramatic tension in the story at that moment is heightened by the long period without a cut *and* keyed to Costa, who is still torn between following orders and confronting his irresolute commander.

As in many war films, the personal sacrifice of the combatants is underscored with religious imagery. There are explicit instances, such as the icon of the Sacred Heart on a wall, Abramowitz's recital of the "Hail, Mary," or the panning shot that gives a glimpse of Woodruff through a hole in a stained glass window. There are also Messianic implications in Costa's "death" and resurrection. Even the beam that drops on Bernstein resembles a stem of a cross when his comrades cluster around and pose like a mock pieta. In addition, Costa is linked to Bernstein by a jump cut from one to the other and by their screams of pain.

The final scenes in the cellar are certainly the most visually manipulated in *Attack!* The house where Costa's squad was pinned down earlier had wood beams, stucco walls, and many right angles. The cellar has stone steps, arches,

Left, Costa's men, trapped in the farmhouse with their lieutenant: Bernstein (Robert Strauss, left bottom), Snowden (Richard Jaeckel, left), Tolliver (Buddy Ebsen, center), and Costa (Jack Palance).

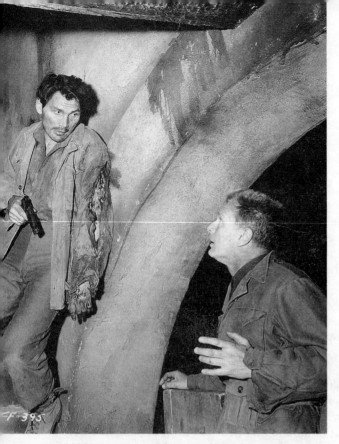

and a more Gothic feel. Sharp shadows add another layer of contour. Light coming from barred windows above spreads across the floor and walls and ripples over bodies and faces at odd angles and in uneven widths. In some medium close shots of Costa, wedges of light isolate his face and hands, one bleeding as if stigmatized, the other holding a gun. Cooney's death, in contrast to Costa's pained expiration, is almost a parody. After prying the gun from Costa's dead fingers and chortles, Cooney is shot going up the steps. He half smiles as he turns, dances down the stairs, and falls face down with a

Above, a mortally-wounded Costa (Jack Palance) confronts Cooney (Eddie Albert) on the cellar steps.

thump that raises dust.

In the ritualization of war, not only is Costa a fallen competitor but the men of his squad, his team, are extensions of his struggle. While it is Lt. Woodruff who fires the fatal shot, the men understand that they should be collectively responsible for Cooney's death. The ritual in which each takes a turn firing a round from his own weapon into Cooney's lifeless body emphatically confirms the sense of killing as a team effort. Woodruff refuses to accept Col. Bartlett's deal to ignore the incident if it can be reported that Cooney died heroically in combat. Woodruff and the viewer's last sight of Costa is on the back of a truck, his body ironically lying next to Cooney's, his face contorted in a grisly death mask. Aldrich's deterministic schematic often equates antagonists in some visual manner. Dead, both men are equal. The differing circumstance of their death, Costa's tortured demise and Cooney's death dance, may be echoed in their faces, Costa's grim rictus and Cooney's sleep-like pose. But both are dead; and the final irony is that for Costa and Cooney both, what Bartlett or Woodruff chose to do is no longer of consequence.

Below, Lt. Woodruff (William Smithers) stands by the bodies of Lt. Costa (Jack Palance) and Capt. Cooney (Eddie Albert, foreground), lying together in death.

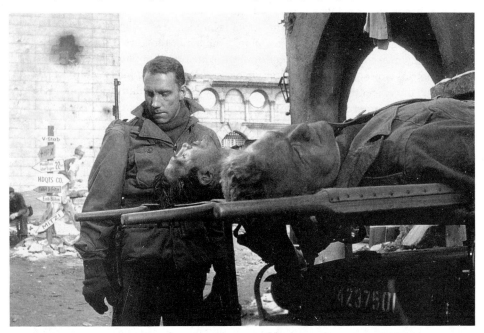

The Dirty Dozen

By 1967, the year of *The Dirty Dozen,* social consciousness had realigned considerably. Aldrich's anti-authoritarian bias manifest eleven years earlier in *Attack!* was no longer an uncommon outlook. The Civil Rights movement, the assassination of Kennedy, the escalating Vietnam War, all contributed to a growing mood of disaffection in the country, especially among the "baby boom" generation, raised in the affluent, conservative 1950s but coming of age in the turbulent 60s.

As he did in *Attack!* and would do again in *Too Late the Hero,* Aldrich made a war film which followed very few of the rules of the genre. Only in his emphasis on "a mission" and his multiethnic mix of characters does Aldrich conform to some traditions. As it was in *Attack!*, the chain of command in *The Dirty Dozen* is neither equitable nor effective. At best the command structure is a brutal method for the empowered few to control the many, a necessity of war that sacrifices individuals to the greater need. At worst it is an oppressive mechanism that flies in the face of the democratic and judicial traditions of fair play which it is meant to defend.

Unlike the contemporary involvement in Vietnam, few viewers of *The Dirty Dozen* would be likely to question the need for World War II. It was a consensus "good war," a war to defeat the evils of Fascism with few of the ambiguities and controversies which plagued the Vietnam and Korean conflicts. Yet the opening sequence of *The Dirty Dozen* is indicative of a slightly different attitude. It begins with a military execution. The camera follows a prisoner as he is led down a corridor flanked by inmates who are chanting in his support. The riotous noise creates a tension which is visible on the faces of those witnessing the execution. As the hysterical prisoner is hooded and summarily hanged, the camera cuts to a jarring low angle shot of short duration, the body dropping like an anchor through the trap door.

This exercise of military discipline is followed by the introduction of the protagonist. In the office of General Worden, Major Reisman, a man described as being "very short on discipline," is compelled to accept a mission which even the General describes as a "maniac's" enterprise. Reisman can submit or face an uncertain but probably worse fate. The casting of Lee Marvin as Reisman creates an immediate typing. As Jack Palance brought an anguished screen persona to Costa, Marvin brings a cynical and willful screen presence to Reisman. Marvin's portrayal of the opportunistic Col. Bartlett in *Attack!* is part of this genre typing. Bartlett bends the rules for personal advancement; Reisman bends them for personal survival. Both bend them, and neither character has a moral dilemma over that fact. Neither would applaud the behavior of either Costa or Woodruff. Bartlett's position is clear from his behavior in *Attack!*. Reisman reveals his outlook when he speaks to Wladislaw, who like

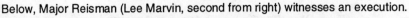

Below, Major Reisman (Lee Marvin, second from right) witnesses an execution.

Costa/Woodruff killed a craven officer: the "mistake" was not in the act itself but in getting caught.

The character who most neatly reifies Aldrich's contempt for authority is Colonel Breed. While the parallels with Cooney in *Attack!* or Captain Hornsby in *Too Late the Hero* are not exact, like them Breed is a martinet. As an officer who "follows the book," a term also used to describe Captain Harris in *The Flight of the Phoenix*, Breed is not contemptible as much as vainglorious. He criticizes the "dirty dozen" more for their slovenly appearance and lack of respect than any deficiency in military ability. This is the character who is the object of the "dozen's" laughter when they capture him during the war games. They humiliate him not because he is their opponent but because his priggishness is symbolic of the attitude which condemned them all.

The plot of *The Dirty Dozen* contains two contests: the war games and the actual mission. This parallel structure represents Aldrich's most explicit equation of the battle and the game. *The Dirty Dozen* is also among the most deterministic of Aldrich's films. Obviously fate is an issue in *Attack!* and *Too Late the Hero* and in many other Aldrich pictures without war as the background. But the opening of *Attack!* with the symbolic helmet representing an unknown casualty and even the ending of *Too Late the Hero*, where one faceless protagonist dies and the other lives, are single events. The introduction of the dozen criminals chosen to go on this "maniacal mission" establishes numerous characters caught in the same deterministic trap. With drum rolls on the soundtrack each man is presented as his sentence is read out by an M.P., as if

Below, Gen. Worden (Ernest Borgnine) tells Reisman (Lee Marvin) his mission.

Above, Reisman (Lee Marvin) taunts Posey (Clint Walker) into attacking him with a knife.

he were no more than an abstraction. In fact, the viewer learns very little else about these characters' backgrounds during the film *except* their crimes. The core concept is an experiment by the unseen military equivalent of a Pavlov or B.F. Skinner. None of the back stories matter when characters become raw material to be conditioned by means of negative and positive reinforcements. Once Reisman has accepted his mission he shows himself to be an unparalleled master of operant conditioning. First, he breaks down the dozen through a routine of grueling training and psychological terror. He beats up Franko, the most rebellious of the recruits. He turns the other prisoners loose on the racist Maggott. He taunts Posey, the simpleminded country boy, until the latter cracks and attacks him. Only after he has broken their will and left them in a state of physical exhaustion, does Reisman proceed to rebuild them.

The Dirty Dozen is, like *The Flight of the Phoenix, Attack!*, and *Too Late*, another of Aldrich's parables of survival, a group of men caught in an existentially absurd or dangerous situation who must act collectively into order to survive. Unlike the other films, this group of men lacks that collective impulse, at least in the first part of the film. For Reisman, the key to his individual survival is the survival of the group. To assure that his "dirty dozen" have a fighting chance, Reisman must mold these men in his image: creating smart, deadly fighters who "go by the book" only when they have to. The "dirty dozen's" performance during the war games epitomizes Reisman's philosophy in action. They violate every rule—changing the colors of their arm bands, deserting their "umpires," masquerading as superiors—but they do win.

As a reward for their ability to act as cohesive unit, Reisman, like any good behaviorist, doles out some positive reinforcement to his trainees. On the night before the mission is to begin, Reisman brings liquor and women in for the "entertainment" of his men. On one side of the barracks a line of tawdry hookers are arrayed while on the other side the bedraggled "dozen" stare in disbelief. The camera pans across the faces of both groups, intercutting their expressions. Slowly the men's looks change from shock to desire, and the women's, from disgust to coquetry.

The first half of *The Dirty Dozen*, by opposing Breed and the unshaven band of criminals, treats the issue of survival in terms of appearances and conditioned responses. Just as situations may not be as they seem, individuals may not react as expected, and the fittest may not survive. The second half of *The Dirty Dozen* is a more active corollary to Aldrich's existential view of the resolution of conflict in and through action: actual combat.

Not only do realistic action sequences reinforce the primary theme, as members of the squad and others perish, the mechanics of survival are again defined. Particularly revealing is the final destruction of the basement shelter in the chateau where the German officers are housed. The fact that innocent noncombatants, chiefly the women of the officers and the servants, are housed there also does not affect the conscience of the top brass who ordered the mission or those who carry it out. The inhumanity of these actions is latent in every scene of the final attack, from Maggott's murder of a young woman for no reason, which precipitates the violence ahead of schedule, to the apocalyptic incineration of the officers and women hiding in the cellar.

Maggott invokes this apocalyptic theme when he cries: "Judgment Day, sinners!" In the cellar, various angles of the victims, scrambling like caged animals to grab at the hand grenades falling on the grating above them, are intercut with Reisman's soldiers dropping the grenades, pouring in gasoline,

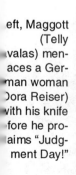

Left, Maggott (Telly Savalas) menaces a German woman (Dora Reiser) with his knife before he proaims "Judgment Day!"

and igniting the mixture. The imagery aptly recalls the Nazi's own gas chambers. More significantly, this "maniac's mission" succeeds in accordance with Reisman's prediction. For, as he says to the psychologist who calls his charges "psychotics," who better to fight and win a war?

Like many of Aldrich's films *The Dirty Dozen* contains other religious allusions beyond Maggott's twisted observations. During the opening execution at the prison, Reisman leaves disdainfully as the chaplain begins his prayers over the dead body of the prisoner. Later the celebration Reisman stages for his men on the eve of the mission is a blatant parody of Da Vinci's "The Last Supper." The dozen are arranged in a row along a table which cuts the screen horizontally. In the middle is Reisman, messiah to these twelve sociopathic apostles.

The most consistent critique of religion is supplied by the character of Maggott, a self-styled fundamentalist preacher who was incarcerated for raping and murdering a young girl. He is a racist who is despised by his fellow inmates. At the pre-mission "orgy,"he stands guard on a platform and, in low angle, rains down curses on the "sinners" below. And, obviously, it is his unnecessary violence in the chateau which precipitates the premature holocaust, as he murders yet another "sinful" young woman.

Of course, Reisman himself is an archetypal Aldrich outsider. From the first he expresses his distaste for the system he serves, criticizing the execution of the prisoner, the mission, even the top brass themselves. He is described, as mentioned earlier, as "very short on discipline." He serves in stark contrast to Breed, the "by the book" officer who carries a grudge against Reisman for his rebelliousness.

When accepting an assignment, however, Reisman evidences his professionalism and survival techniques. He may not follow the rules, but he does survive while achieving his goal. In the final scene of the film, Reisman receives the empty praise of the top brass with an expression of regret and disdain. As if to externalize what Reisman is thinking, Aldrich superimposes the faces of the "dirty dozen," now all dead but one, on the frame of Reisman exercising his arm with a rubber ball.

Too Late the Hero

Too Late the Hero is the finale to Aldrich's men-in-war series and is, in many ways, the most overtly pacifist. While *Attack!* and *Dirty Dozen* clearly make the statement that "war is hell," a brutal and absurd conflict which intermingles personal pettiness with massive demonstrations of naked power, both steadfastly avoid humanizing the enemy. But only in portraying the enemy as other than incarnations of evil, as "devils," can any creative expression break down the mythology of war. An enemy with a human face becomes much more difficult to stereotype and then kill.

From the first shot of the film the humanizing mechanism is in play in *Too Late the Hero*. As the titles progress, the British, American, and Japanese flags are all gradually shredded as if by invisible bullets until they are in tatters. Concurrently the rush of triumphant music which opened the sequence has slowed in tempo to a dirge, visually and aurally foreshadowing the moral and physical disintegration to follow. In concert with this more abstract depiction is the concrete characterization of Major Yamaguchi. Initially Yamaguchi is a disembodied voice in the jungle, an amplified message echoing through the dense underbrush, cajoling the raiders to surrender. When the camera spins dizzyingly in circles it subjectifies the British soldiers' fear and disorientation. When they refuse to give up and continue their flight back to their camp, it is the speakers which carry Yamaguchi's message that are their most palpable pursuers. A montage shows the Japanese soldiers moving the speakers from tree to tree, as they close in on the weary British.

When the audience does finally see Yamaguchi, he appears calm and dignified, definitely not the stereotypical embodiment of the "yellow peril" found

At left:
Pfc. Hearne (Michael Caine) and Lt. Lawson (Cliff Robertson), the last of their squad. Their balanced figures stand at the edge of the "gauntlet," the final obstacle to survival.

in most American war films—even though one of the British is hanging upside down, bleeding to death, in the frame with Yamaguchi. The hanged man is the British raider who had earlier mutilated a Japanese soldier for his jewelry. Yamaguchi explains that he could not control his own men's vindictive emotions. The audience, who have witnessed both the earlier mutilation and the execution of wounded Japanese by the gung-ho Captain Hornsby, know that the British are as guilty as the Japanese. With partisanship, all of the violence becomes part of the same mindless brutality.

But the key scene in this attempt to humanize the enemy is when Yamaguchi apparently threatens to execute three British troopers who have taken Yamaguchi up on his offer of protection for surrender even if the remainder do not do the same. In close-ups, Yamaguchi points his gun at the heads of the individual soldiers and then fires past them. As they open their eyes in relief intermingled with disbelief, he says almost sadly: "Did you really find it so easy to believe I would kill you?" Both sides are so locked into their perception of the enemy that they find it hard to accept any act of humanity. Although Yamaguchi has kept his promise not to kill those who surrendered, he is killed when the two remaining fugitives, Lawson and Hearne, find his location and summarily dispatch him.

The mission given to this band of men in war is as absurd and meaningless as the one in *Dirty Dozen*. As Hearne observes, "None of this will make a damn bit of difference." They are only driven to complete their assignment of disabling a Japanese radio transmitter by the force of authority which the martinet Captain Hornsby holds over them. Hornsby is another "by the book" soldier in the same supercilious mold as Cooney in *Attack!* and Breed in *Dirty Dozen*. This is not his first "suicide" mission. He has, it is later revealed, led several other troops on similar raids. Like Cooney he is despised by his men who talk about "fragging" him. He evidences no devotion to his men, leaving the wounded behind with a peremptory "good luck."

For all his callousness it is Hornsby or, more accurately, Hornsby's image which haunts the American Lieutenant Lawson and drives him to the act of heroism alluded to in the film's title. Lawson is introduced on a beach in long shot. He is dead drunk. He rises unsteadily and belches unceremoniously, a decidedly inelegant first glimpse of a would-be hero. Capt. Nolan, the naval officer who tells Lawson that he is being sent back into combat with a British squad as a Japanese interpreter, also colors the audience's perception of Lawson's character. It is because he believes him to be shirker that he tells Lawson, "I hope they get your Goddamn head shot off."

When he first arrives at the jungle camp, Lawson is greeted by gunfire. His first response is to cower in a lookout platform. It is clear from this behavior that his self-avowed objective is simply to survive so that he can take advan-

Opposite, Capt. Nolan (Henry Fonda, right) disdainfully hands Lt. Lawson (Cliff Robertson) his top secret orders.

tage of the stateside leave he is due. That this outsider should become the "too late hero" of the piece is reminiscent of the ironic death of another American seaman working with British commandos, Shears in *The Bridge on the River Kwai*. In fact, the attack on the Japanese transmitter evokes many of the same character conflicts as the destruction of the bridge in *Kwai*. Lawson refuses to follow Hornsby across the darkened yard. In close-up he looks on in fear as Hornsby is riddled with bullets. Hornsby has managed to blow up the facility, however, and staggers back to fall in close-up directly in front of Lawson. Hornsby's eyes seem to stare unblinkingly at Lawson in recrimination. Or as Hearne puts it, "You let him down. Hornsby's your problem."

From this point on, the guilt which motivates Lawson, like that which haunted Towns in *The Flight of the Phoenix,* is the key emotion. Lawson pushes the remainder of the troop on, threatening the pragmatic Hearne if he tries to desert. Taking on Hornsby's role, Lawson becomes obsessed with returning to camp to inform the British of a hidden Japanese air base; but he does not make it back. In the central irony of *Too Late the Hero* Lawson never even delivers his message, rendering his heroics even more futile. As if to underscore the absurdity of his efforts, Hearne, the only survivor, tells the inquiring officers, "He was a bloody hero, killed fifteen Japs single-handed, thirty if you like."

Private Hearne represents the pragmatic alternative to both Hornsby's pomposity and Lawson's Romantic guilt. He is the one who proposes the idea of "fragging" Hornsby and who tries to convince Lawson to desert. He de-

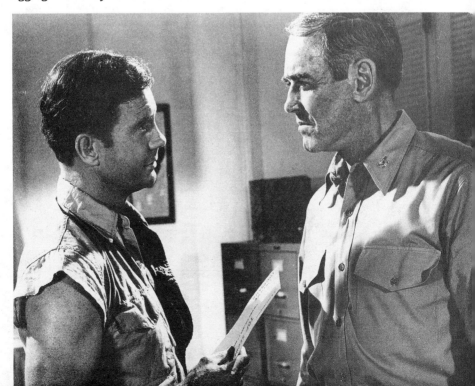

spises the army and all authority, but does demonstrate genuine concern for his fellow soldiers. Hearne's survival instincts extend to his comrades: he objects to leaving his wounded comrades and saves Lawson's life during an ambush in the jungle. Even his final pronouncement, at the end of the film, on Lawson's "heroics" can be read as more than sarcasm. It is his attempt to give Lawson the tribute he would want.

The central metaphor of *Too Late the Hero*, the gauntlet run, is set up by the emotional transference between Lawson and Hearne. On one side of the British camp lies an open field surrounded by the jungle. It is the way in and out of the camp. Its resemblance to a football field is, of course, not accidental. On his arrival at the camp Lawson had watched a detachment of British soldiers race over the field under fire. In the beginning of *Too Late the Hero*, as the British stood at one end cheering their "team" on, Aldrich used high angle long shots of the soldiers, desperately dodging bullets like so many ball carriers in order to reach the goal line, their camp. As previously noted, this is not the only equation of crossing terrain under enemy fire with a broken field run to evade tacklers.

When Lawson and Hearne's troop leaves camp, they walk stealthily through this field littered with the bodies of soldiers the British have been unable to retrieve. When the two men return, they must cross it again. And again Aldrich uses high angle long shots which reduce the men to zigzagging insects in a field of gold. If war is a team effort, does it ultimately matter who has survived? Aldrich begs the question. The pragmatist survives but for no reason other than chance. The cynic who became a team player dies. Like the image of Costa and Cooney lying side by side in death, the capriciousness of war is underscored in the staging of the entire final scene.

The Big Leaguer

Balancing Aldrich's war pictures are three sports films. While there are sports elements in many of Aldrich's films, from the sparring boxers in *The Big Knife* or *Kiss Me Deadly* to the cavalrymen's baseball game in *Ulzana's Raid, The Big Leaguer, The Longest Yard*, and *...All the Marbles* all end with a climactic contest.

As we have noted, the subject matter of his first film was not of Aldrich's choosing. Still his approach to a "programmer" like *The Big Leaguer* demonstrates that, from the first, Aldrich's approach to staging the battle and the game would be both direct and stylized.

The entire narrative of *the Big Leaguer* uses a quasi-documentary framework. A character named Mack, ostensibly a sports writer, introduces the film by speaking directly to the audience and provides voice-over narration throughout. In fact, scenes alternate between a conventional presentation with characters speaking to one another and a third person exposition with the narrating telling the audience what the characters are saying and feeling. On several occasions the dialogue will fade out in the middle of a shot, so that the narrator's comments may be heard.

Also clear in *The Big Leaguer* are the beginnings of Aldrich's equation of sports and combat. The narration evokes the analogy to war in the choice of words. The moment before the tryouts begin is called "zero hour." The first time on the field is "D-Day." The long take at the film's beginning when the bus arrives and the hopefuls descend carrying their bags and walk into the clubhouse anticipates the similar arrival of the squad in *The Dirty Dozen*. Aldrich would often equate lines of men with the concept of a team assembled to accomplish a task.

Aldrich had already experimented with depth of field and high and low angles in his television work. In this first feature, the staging concisely underscores the narrative. The introduction of John "Hans" Lobert, the manager of the camp, is a slight low angle medium close shot. The audience knows simply because the star, Edward G. Robinson, portrays Lobert that he is the central character. Reinforcing this are both the angle of the shot and lines from two banisters which form a v-shape behind his body. Because the ball players are portrayed by little-known actors, Aldrich uses conventional indicators such as the narration to set up their characters. For the most part, the editing scheme is also conventional; but Aldrich inserts an occasional unusual shot. Many of these are centered on Lobert. For example, the low angle medium shot which he enters to yell "What?" when a player apologizes for an error is unexpected and slightly disorienting. In this sense, it captures both the unsettled feeling of the players and Lobert's own surprise at the comment he hears. After a cocky

Opposite, Lawson and Hearne run the gauntlet.

young pitcher throws a ball at his head, Lobert gets up and strides into a tight close shot before shouting, "Were you trying to dust me off?" Lobert's question is rhetorical; and so is the shot that captures it.

If anything, *The Big Leaguer* is a little too big. The narrator's opening and closing remarks about "baseball, the national pastime" and "the names and faces you never heard of" melodramatize very ordinary events. Robinson as Lobert is at times naturalistic and at others bigger than life. Since the script is a straightforward paean to the sport and its seldom heralded "little people," the most effective staging in *The Big Leaguer* is the most subtle. When Christy, Lobert's niece, leads Adam Polachuk out of the clubhouse, a panning shot stops on Julie Davis, the wise guy of the group, and holds for his assertion that "he's gonna marry the boss' daughter." Julie's remark is good-natured and the unbroken shot underscores this emotion. In the first scenes on the playing field, the players are isolated in introductory vignettes which end with a kinetic montage, punctuated as three balls are thrown or hit right at the camera and ending with a surreal image as dozens of balls arc across the sky.

In the actual games, Aldrich uses staging in depth to capture some of the tension. When Davis is at third hoping to score, a single shot includes him in the middle ground at left while Lobert is in the coaches' box at background center, and the opposing third baseman stands in shadow with his gloved raised in the right foreground. The large, dark profile of the opponent taking up most of the space in the frame constricts Davis visually as his presence keeps him from scoring narratively.

While the plot conflicts in *The Big Leaguer* are certainly not earthshaking or even part of a larger momentous event such as World War II, they are clear cut for the characters. Because, as Christy points out, "Baseball is a business," Lobert knows he must have some success or the tryout camp itself may be abandoned. For the players, individually and collectively, the struggle to make the grade is foremost. Because their fates are narratively intertwined, the visuals which link Lobert to the players are more evocative. When Lobert affirms to Mack that everything is riding on the game against the Dodger farm team, that "one game is worth 10,000 words," the camera moves in slightly to tighten the two shot of the men with Lobert in the foreground. While the moment is telling for Lobert, the performance carries the melodrama. The underscoring is unneeded. A more appropriate camera move comes after Lobert reluctantly cuts Bobby, the cocky young pitcher. As he confides to Mack that "I may have just booted one," the camera arcs around Lobert to reveal Bobby walking away in the left background.

The Longest Yard

With *The Longest Yard* Aldrich strips away the gloss from male America's beloved sport and exposes its sadistic core. As we have noted, being a former college football player and lifelong fanatic, Aldrich used the metaphor more than once. *The Longest Yard* is the most extended example. Football's advocates often assert that the game provides a microcosm of the struggle for success. As Warden Hazen in this film puts it: "The game embodies what has made our country great." A goal must be reached within a limited amount of time. And one can only reach this goal through teamwork, strength, ingenuity, and suffering. It is the success/work ethic embodied on the playing field.

In *The Longest Yard* the sport's metaphorical function becomes a plot point. It gives a group of sociopathic prisoners, including the protagonist, ex-football star Paul Crewe, a chance for victory, of cooperative achievement, and a sense of superiority over their cruel guards and sadistic warden within the confines of a prison.

But what becomes clear in this film, particularly during the game and training leading up to it, is that football is also about naked power. It is Warden Hazen who uncharacteristically reveals his true feelings about what the game represents (and who coincidentally echoes Aldrich's assessment of Lewis Milestone) when he links it to "power and who controls it." If the guards lose this practice game against the prisoners, Hazen's whole regime of fear and intimidation will collapse. The prisoners know this, too; and so the "mean machine," as the convicts have dubbed their team, employ every devious method to get an edge. They steal X-rays of the guards' team so they can tar-

Opposite, John "Hans" Lobert (Edward G. Robinson, center) welcomes a couple of prospects, Julie Davis (William Campbell, left) and Chuy Aguilar (Lalo Rios), while sports writer Brian McLennan (Paul Langton, background) listens in.

get weak spots to hit during the game. They fire passes into the guards' genitals. They pile on their opponents, using brass knuckles in the anonymity of this mountain of human bodies. Although *The Longest Yard* actively cultivates the audience's sympathies for the prisoners early on by depicting numerous incidents of inhuman treatment by the guards, these acts of espionage and brutality by the prisoners on the football field should narratively equate the two sides; but they do not.

While the characters may be felons, guilty of all manner of violent crimes, those are unseen past behaviors which do not counterbalance the palpable, institutionalized brutality of the guards. In many screenings when *The Longest Yard* was first released, audiences not only cheered for the convicts as they would a real team but screamed for the guards' blood. The despotic character of Warden Hazen immediately rebuilds whatever sympathy the audience may have lost for the convicts. He is another martinet in the line stretching back to Captain Cooney, also played by actor Eddie Albert. His coercion of Crewe into coaching the convicts' team is merely oppressive; but so much of his pres-

Right, Paul Crewe (Burt Reynolds) threatens his woman friend, Melissa (Anitra Ford).

tige is wrapped up in his prison football team that he is not above threatening Captain Knauer, the coach of the guards, with severe retribution if his prison team does not win the national championship.

In keeping with the seriocomic tone of *The Longest Yard* Eddie Albert plays the warden as a consummately evil figure who becomes hysterical when crossed. Balancing this is the nonchalance which characterizes many of Paul Crewe's actions in the film. Crewe is introduced to the audience after a long pan over the expensive furnishings of a rich woman's mansion. Perfumes, jewels, expensive knickknacks, glamor photos of the owner, all establish this setting as her space. As the woman, Melissa, tries to arouse Crewe, who is more interested in a game on TV, he violently repulses her, which leads to a barrage of insults on the part of Melissa: "Everybody's bought you!...Too expensive to be useless!...Has-been!...Whore!" Crewe manifests very little self-esteem in this scene, never really defending himself against the insults. Instead he responds in the only way he knows—with more violent behavior. He then steals Melissa's car and leads the police on a chase through the city.

In prison he continues this behavior, earning him the disdain of his fellow inmates. They taunt him verbally and physically, but he is too shut down emotionally to respond. To add to his ostracism, the prisoners despise him for "selling out" his teammates and "shaving points" from a game in return for cash. As Caretaker tells him, "You had it all. These boys never had anything. You let your teammates down."

The narrative of Paul Crewe's redemption, elements of which Aldrich took from the earlier sports film *Body and Soul,* is slow and arduous. The scene in the swamps marks the beginning of this *metánoia*. In a sequence of escalating comic violence, reminiscent of a Laurel and Hardy film, Crewe and one of his fellow prisoners gradually load mud into each other's pants and then fall into the swamp in a full-fledged brawl to the delight of the other prisoners. Crewe also begins to enjoy the high jinks to the dismay of Captain Knauer who

Opposite, after beating the guards, a defiant Paul Crewe (Burt Reynolds) displays the game ball to Warden Hazen (Eddie Albert).

rightly sees this laughter as a form of solidarity and rebellion. Under physical duress, Crewe finally acquiesces to the warden's request and agrees to put together a team of convicts to give the guards a tune-up game. For Crewe, this is just part of the greater game of staying alive in prison, not a betrayal of his fellow inmates.

The two events which solidify Crewe's resolve and lead to his redemption are the death of Caretaker and his betrayal at the hands of the warden. Caretaker, Crewe's friend and confidant, is immolated by a booby-trapped light bulb filled with a flammable liquid. The device intended for Crewe subjects Caretaker to a gruesome death, which Aldrich stages in a single take. The second event is when the warden promises to "go easy" on Crewe's team and not to frame him with Caretaker's murder, if he throws the game. Crewe agrees. But when the warden decides to continue to punish the convicts on the field as an object lesson, even though they are losing badly, Crewe is given his second chance. He wins the game by running the "longest yard" to score on the last play. It is an act of single-minded defiance, again in the tradition of existential sports films such as Tony Richardson's *The Loneliness of the Long Distance Runner*. Because it incorporates elements of survival, redemption, moral integrity, teamwork, and a second chance, *The Longest Yard* is a compendium of Aldrich's thematic preoccupations.

The final touch of ambiguity surrounds Crewe's fate. In a tense scene at the end of the film, the warden claims that Crewe is trying to escape from the stadium and so orders Knauer to shoot him in the back. Knauer raises his rifle hesitatingly, as the warden continues to order him to shoot. All the while a long lens, representing the warden's POV, frames Crewe as he strolls leisurely across the field and does what he intended: retrieve the "game ball." He returns to Hazen and flippantly defies his threats. While Knauer has spared him, it is unclear whether Hazen will be able to carry out his threat to frame him for murder and extend his term to a life sentence.

To insure that *The Longest Yard* did not have the connotations of "tragic destiny" which Aldrich disdained, he inserted elements of parody throughout his tale of man's rise from the ashes of humiliation and despair. In a direct take-off of *The Dirty Dozen* Crewe and his adjutant, Caretaker, interview prospective ball players from the pool of convicts. In this case, however, the candidates are comic exaggerations of the original "dirty dozen." His recruits include a hypertrophic muscle man, a baldheaded, five-time murderer, a mental deficient, and a crippled old-timer. Only when he recruits the militant African-American prisoners, some of whom had played ball before and who will only play on their own terms, does Crewe have any semblance of a team.

The recruitment of the African-Americans is typical of how Aldrich uses racial and ethnic issues in his films. Many of his films are multiethnic, *The Dirty*

Above, Hazen (Eddie Albert, right) orders Capt. Knauer (Ed Lauter) to shoot Crewe. He refuses. Below, Crewe (Burt Reynolds, left) is chained to Granville (Harry Caesar).

Dozen, The Flight of the Phoenix, ...All the Marbles, Hustle, et al. Some like *Apache* and *Ulzana's Raid* take prejudice as their main theme. In keeping with his own personal philosophy, Aldrich neither sentimentalizes nor romanticizes the issues. The militant African-American convicts are forthright in their aversion for the whites. They present their position, and it sounds logical and reasonable; but, like combat, the game is designed to cut through these antagonisms in the name of teamwork and victory.

Aldrich exemplified this with two shots. The first occurs when Crewe is handcuffed to Granville, an African-American prisoner, who asks him nonchalantly: "Ever work with a nigger before?" As this happens, Aldrich inserts a short cut of black and white hands joined unwillingly by chains. Later in the film, when Black and White have learned to strive together to achieve the common purpose of winning the game, Aldrich inserts another short shot which matches the earlier one. This time the chains are gone and the men are holding hands in a huddle as an expression of solidarity.[3]

The overall visual style of *The Longest Yard* is very distinctive in its use of the split screen, chiefly in the climactic game, which takes up three-eighths of the film's total running time. This technique allows Aldrich to show simultaneous events rather than follow the linear progression most action sequences are locked into. It also permits the audience to absorb far more of the mise-en-scene within a given period of time, cutting from cheerleaders in drag, to spectators in the stadium, to players from both teams, to the anxious warden, to the reactions from the bench—all within the same shot or time period. Giving the viewer more autonomy with regard to which images he or she may choose to watch creates a tension within the split frame, as those images compete for attention. In this respect, the split screen is an analog for the long takes of some of his 1950s films which, as Andre Bazin has pointed out in writing

Right, Harry Sears (Peter Falk, right) confronts rival promoter Eddie Cisco (Burt Young) in *...All the Marbles*.

about Orson Welles, expand the viewer's freedom to choose, to concentrate on what is of greatest personal interest.

Aldrich also incorporates slow motion into the final seven seconds of the game as the "mean machine" runs its last play for the winning touchdown. He further enhances the tension by dropping out all audio except for the muffled sounds of the players groaning and crunching their way to victory. In a single sequence of extended time he encapsulates both the brutality of the game and the resolve of this disparate band of outsiders.

...All the Marbles

Like *The Longest Yard*, *...All the Marbles*, Aldrich's last film, is a comedy-drama involving sports. It is unique among Aldrich's films in that the athletes are women. Like most light dramas, *...All the Marbles* moves past all narrative obstacles towards a happy ending, where problems are resolved. The lead character of the film is Harry Sears, an opera-loving huckster/female wrestling promoter who has been pushed to the bottom of the circuit by bad luck and powerful enemies. Like most earlier Aldrich protagonists, he is an outsider trying to survive with some kind of dignity and independence.

As much as any of Aldrich's characters, even Barney Sheean and Lewis Zarkan, Harry Sears is a semi-autobiographical creation. Harry's rough integrity and unswerving loyalty is coupled with his pragmatic survival instinct. He refuses to submit to the unreasonable demands of promoter Eddie Cisco; but at the same time he is not averse to booking his female tag team, the " California Dolls," into a humiliating mud wrestling event. On the road he educates his "dolls" on the beauties of opera. While playing Leoncavallo's *Pagliacci,* in one of a series of overhead traveling shots which follow Sears' dilapidated Cadillac throughout the Midwest, Sears draws an analogy between the traveling troupe of the opera and their own situation: they must "put on a good show" no matter what. If that means breaking the kneecaps of two hoods and stealing their money in order to repair his car, Harry will do it. He can lecture Iris about the amorality of sleeping with Eddie so that they can "get a shot" at a championship match in Reno; but he can also seduce a young woman on the road with lies about the important people he knows.

Like Zarkan and other Aldrich "showmen," Harry is not above manipulating an event. In Reno, he plasters cheesecake posters of the "dolls" everywhere and plants ringers in the audience to chant for the "dolls" and sing their theme songs, "Oh, You Beautiful Doll" and "California, Here I Come." He even has trashy new costumes designed for the team which make them look, as one their wrestling opponents points out, like "virgin vampires." In the end, Harry expresses real joy and enthusiasm for his victorious team. He raises their hands in triumph for the final freeze frame of the movie, which leaves them positioned in front of an oversized flag of California, provided courtesy of Harry Sears.

...*All the Marbles* is one of the few opportunities Aldrich had to depict women as three-dimensional characters. The Dolls occupy center stage; but while Iris and Molly are females, they resemble many male characters in Aldrich's films. Iris is the world-weary professional who has survived years on the road as well as a rocky love affair with Harry. She, like Harry, does what is necessary to survive, including having sex with the oily Eddie Cisco in order to assure their position in the championship match in Reno. Like most of Aldrich's pragmatic characters, however, she does have a strong sense of personal dignity. When Harry tricks them into a mud wrestling bout at a county fair, Iris throws mud back at leering men in the audience. After that humiliating exhibition, she takes on Harry, blaming him for exploiting them and finally breaking down in tears: "They laughed at me." Molly, on the other hand, is much more naive and idealistic. She is addicted to pain killers and often turns to Iris for reassurance and mothering.

Laughter is both a liberating and humiliating sound in many Aldrich films. With an actor such as Burt Young in ...*All the Marbles, Twilight's Last Gleaming,* and *The Choirboys,* the hoarse laughter has three different contexts but the same effect of distancing the audience. With Richard Attenborough in *The Flight of the Phoenix* the context is ironic. With Burt Reynolds in *The Longest Yard* and *Hustle* the laughter suggests insecurity. In ...*All the Marbles* Iris may react violently to the laughter of the rural audience during the mud wrestling event; but Harry sees it as part of the game, part of the performance. Like Lobert in *The Big Leaguer* or managers in any sport, Harry knows you have to give the crowd what they paid for. The use of the aria "Vesti la giubba" from *Pagliacci* underlines Harry's position. As Leoncavallo's clown points out, the show must go on, the clown must laugh at his fate even if he feels like crying.

The centerpieces of action in the film are the several tag team wrestling matches. One begins the film and another, the championship match, ends it. All the matches are staged in a very similar manner with minor variations. Whether the setting is the dingy, dimly lit arena in the opening of the film or the tawdry glitter of the MGM Grand Hotel for the final match, Aldrich breaks the action into component parts. The matches generally alternate between shots from the audience's POV, medium to close shots of the wrestlers in motion, and dynamic overhead shots of the ring at climactic moments. Intercut with this mosaic of the physical contest are the reaction shots of the crowd, Harry, and the other sidemen as they respond to the match. By varying the sequence and the length of the shots as the matches reach their respective cli-

Opposite, the California Dolls: Laurene Landon as Molly (left) and Vicki Frederick as Iris pose in their "virgin vampire" costumes.

maxes, Aldrich creates self-contained vignettes. Unlike the games at the end of *The Big Leaguer* and *The Longest Yard*, the contests in *...All the Marbles* have a cumulative impact.

What Aldrich ultimately found most dramatic in any contest, what he admired in *Body and Soul* and actual football games, was the struggle. That struggle can be within the game itself, where the players must overcome superior opponents as in *The Longest Yard*, or against outside forces, as with Polachuk's problem with his father's prejudice in *The Big Leaguer*. In the end, in the battle and in the game, the process itself is the existential affirmation, the arena where "each man must fight even if he is broken." This is what ultimately sustains all of Aldrich's combatants from Joe Costa to the California Dolls—they are true to the process. "Don't worry if you boot one," Lobert tells his charges, "the important thing is to get on with the game."

Above, Burt Lancaster and Aldrich on the set of *Ulzana's Raid*.

Chapter Four:

Ritual Structure and the Western

In the concluding moments of *Too Late the Hero* when the dual protagonists Hearne and Lawson are forced to run the gauntlet across an open field under enemy fire, the elaborate staging of the event stretches it out to approximately ten minutes. This is more than "real" time; and it is photographed variously from helicopters, towers, ground level, and normally mounted cameras equipped with long lenses. It is "denaturalized" in terms of viewpoint and duration to such an extent that it becomes more of a ritual than a reality, a stylized spectacle of survival of the fittest.

Apache

Much, if not most, of *Apache* can be viewed on a similar, ritualistic level. The opening title over an extra long shot of the White Mountains—the "magic" or mystical home mountains of the Apache—sets a distinctly mythic tone: "This is the story of Massai, the last Apache warrior. It has been told and retold, until it became one of the legends of the Southwest. It began in 1886, with the surrender of Geronimo."

As in *Vera Cruz* the expository title economically establishes the historical context. Additionally, in *Apache*, it pre-defines the hero. Massai is identified, his name is given; he is linked to a famous figure, Geronimo; and he is accorded legendary status of his own before any human being appears on the screen. Although it may be somewhat alienating for an audience to have a hero predesignated in this manner, in the sense that their freedom to choose or at least discern him from the generic indicators has been abrogated, the result is not too distancing. What it does do is focus viewer anticipation, in this instance, towards a legendary action. This allows the first sequence to be violent or disruptive without confusion about who will serve as protagonist. The consequence of the title is that when the audience "recognizes" Massai, it does so having already absorbed information. As it happens, the recognition is immediate, deriving as much from Massai's action in initiating the shooting as from his appearance, i.e., since he is played by Burt Lancaster, the star of the film, he must be the hero.

Almost as rapidly the element of ritual is introduced. Cross travelling shots reveal the lines of Indians and whites arrayed at the surrender of Geronimo. The tension is captured in the way the men are arrayed, in their forced placidity, while the camera moves suggest the repressed energy which erupts as Massai bolts from the group. The high angle looking down at Nalinle is doubly subjective. It is a literal point of view of her as she proffers the cartridge belt. But the cheated angle, as if he were somehow above the ground looking down, could only be the point of view of a man whose adrenalin rush makes him feel as if he has been lifted off the ground. As Massai tells Nalinle, his one-man rebellion is a point of honor. "But at least you would be alive, Massai," she argues. His answer is simple: "If an Apache cannot live in his home mountains like his fathers before him, he is already dead." But it is the Army scout, Sieber, who explains the ritual aspect: "To die in battle would be a sweet death, a warrior's death.... But you're not a warrior anymore. You're just a whipped Injun. And nobody sings about handcuffs."

Massai's captivity means not just confinement but humiliation, loss of pride. This fact sets the course of all the subsequent generic action. Within a few minutes of the introductory title, Massai has been cheated of his glory. He must escape, return to his home mountains, and perform the legendary acts which, the viewer has already been told, are his destiny. In this sense, the travelling shot of the Indians boarding the train, the sequence of them posing awkwardly for a humiliating group photograph as captives, and other specifics that fill up the time until Massai's escape are bound by two sets of expectations. First, there are genre particulars of setting and action that are part of the Western. Second, the events that form the detail of Massai's legend are arrayed like the opening lines of an epic poem, as much for expressive as narrative effect.

The bulk of *Apache*'s narrative line must derive from these expectations to conform to generic norm, and it does. Visually, however, the film is more diverse. The intercutting between high and low angles and the depth of field prevalent in *World for Ransom*, *Vera Cruz*, and other early work provide the same interior tension and clarification of character interaction in *Apache*.

Opposite, Burt Lancaster as Massai discovers the marvels
of the white man's world in St. Louis.

Apache is Aldrich's first color film and first period film, and the scheme and decor of the picture are pointedly realistic. The blue and brown of the mountain, which is a key symbol for the entire film and towards which Massai gazes serenely as he boards the train, are the colors of earth and sky, part of the natural order. This contrasts with the civilized, artificial geography of the white men, with the maps they use, and especially with the conventional graphic of the journey into exile which they impose on the Apache and which is superimposed over the train.

While Aldrich uses night-for-night photography and foregoes process screens to maintain an underlying realism, the shot selection and cutting are consistently manipulated for expressive value. When Nalinle visits the fort in her "formal" clothes to speak with Sieber and Col. Beck after Massai's escape, Aldrich uses more than two dozen cuts and repeatedly alters the position of the three characters in the frame. The fracturing of the sequence in this way reflects an awkward interaction between the two cultures and viewpoints. One sustained travelling shot is equally telling in that it is designed to enhance dramatic irony. It follows Massai when he is led away in irons as a result of betrayal by Nalinle's father. His expression makes it clear that he believes she has betrayed him also. It continues moving laterally after he has left the frame and reveals Nalinle bound and gagged out of his sight behind a teepee. The net effect is to carry the viewer in one movement from a strong empathy with Massai and a subjective participation in his sense of betrayal to an objective

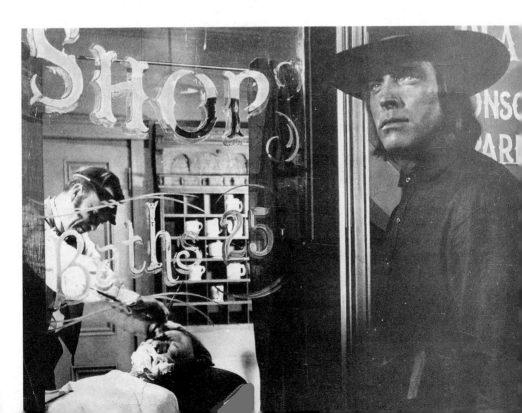

perspective, aware of facts which Massai does not have and an apprehensive identification with Nalinle. This division of interest underlies the lengthy scenes between them which follow.

Such occasional usages are subordinate to the more basic constructs of *Apache*, which most often asks the viewer to share the mythic or heroic figure's point of view. Massai's "odyssey," his long journey back after escaping near St. Louis, is detailed in a way which allows the viewer to co-experience the "marvels" of it with him. Massai's arrival in the city at night is first keyed with a sustained travelling shot that moves with him down a main street. Opening in an objective mode permits the viewer to see the initial causes of his disorientation and his reaction to them in the same frame. Simultaneously Massai's shock and confusion are subjectively conveyed by increasing the noise level of the soundtrack from the banging kettle on the tinker's wagon on which Massai has ridden into town to the clanging bell of the fire engine. But the noises themselves become unnaturally loud over the course of several seconds of a close shot of Massai because these sounds "seem" louder when filtered through his point of view.

After the brush with the fire engine, a low angle, medium close shot of Massai, staring in wonderment as blurred shapes move in the background, focuses attention on his reaction. Then there is a cut to a difficult-to-read view of the street, an overhead wide angle which creates a confusion of vertical and horizontal motion. Some shots of bustles, player pianos, and other "wonders of

the age" are taken through windows from the character's point of view. But his fear of the horse-drawn fire wagon that bolts towards him as the sequence begins is more effectively translated through a ground level, low angle as he dodges out of the way. Aldrich builds an impressionistic sequence both from the natural period details, such as a Chinese laundry, a shoeshine boy, or a doorman in a bright red coat, and from the subtle shifts between objective and subjective visual and aural information.

In a narrative sense, the aspect of Massai most difficult to accept or share is his desire for a noble death. That quest is for what he views as immortality to be "sung about around the campfire"; but what the viewer, who likely has a detached and non-Indian perspective, sees is annihilation. When Massai touches Nalinle's pregnant abdomen, he says, "I can feel the blood." While the viewer can share a momentary perspective with Massai, *Apache* presents no possibility for total identification either with the individual character or the embodiment of an epic hero. The blood Massai feels is of himself, his child, and his entire people, but as one, undivided being.

This split is resolved in *Apache*'s ending. The "magic" corn which Massai was given by the Cherokee farmer—after being discarded scornfully by him and replaced by Nalinle—has become a cornfield. The field is a symbol of both fertility, in that it was furrowed with a homemade, phallic plow by Massai and the pregnant Nalinle, and rebirth, through association with the literal "new life" she is carrying and the figurative one she hopes the corn will pro-vide them. This trope is further reinforced when coupled to the power of the mountain, which is both ancestral or totemic and phallic when seen in the low angle point-of-view shot immediately upon Massai's return. The cornfield is also the ground for Massai's final battle with Sieber and the army, the place where Massai goes out to die. Massai is in the very center of it, fighting with Sieber hand-to-hand among the dry stalks, when he hears the sound of his newborn child crying. When he stands, which, seen from a very low angle, makes him seem to spring ritualistically from the ground, and "calls off the war," it completes a cycle of regeneration with Massai's own psychical rebirth. In fact, the growing of the corn and the birth of a child, both generated by Massai's individual vitality, are more important than whether Massai literally lives or dies.

How fully, if at all, Massai is reintegrated is questionable. If he reenters any social order, it cannot be more than a primal, Edenic one. The high angle, ex-tra long shot which closes the film is ambiguous. On one hand, it diminishes his figure and moves more towards a concealment of it and his identity than an apotheosis. Yet in its abstraction of the image into the coarser texture of a broad landscape, it conforms to a larger ritual. Rendered static and unassail-

Opposite, Massai (Burt Lancaster, right) struggles with Scout Al Sieber (John McIntire) in the cornfield which he has planted.

able, "frozen," Massai remains an archetypal outsider, free as individual but simultaneously reabsorbed into a body of myth.

The Last Sunset

The narrative elements of *The Last Sunset* are atypical. While unquestionably a Western, *The Last Sunset* might be sub-categorized as "offbeat." That description may not suggest purely analytical values; but it is nonetheless an apt one: both in terms of a narrative tone charged with a stylistic fatalism in the acting, staging, and even color scheme and in the use of standard Western motifs. For although many of the latter are present—a revenging brother pursuing a gambler/gunfighter; encounters with Indians and outlaws; a cattle drive, stampede, and singing by the campfire—the central moral question concerns responsibility for the death or psychological scarring of another. In addition, one of the principal sexual relationships is an unknowing, incestuous attachment between a father and daughter. This situation, particularly as developed through Dalton Trumbo's self-consciously "meaningful" genre dialogue, such as "Cowboys aren't very bright...they're always broke, and most of the time they're drunk," infuses *The Last Sunset* with a brooding, quasi-existentialism that deviates markedly from the generic norm.

The point here is that genre characters do not ordinarily pause to comment on their occupation or social standing, which by extension questions the very meaning of their generic existence. The presence of two male figures of fairly equal power—one, flashy, loquacious, cynically amoral; the other quiet, sullen, and somewhat righteous—forms an obvious link with *Vera Cruz* and *Ten Seconds to Hell*. Superficially at least, the introspective victim of postwar alienation typified by Ben Trane and Eric Koertner reappears in *The Last Sunset* as Dana Stribling; and the insouciant, grinning opportunists, Joe Erin and Karl Wirtz, become Brendan O'Malley. But more than in either of these preceding pictures—in which a central premise of the narrative line similarly compels suspension of natural antagonism to further a more immediate project—the notion of a transferent character interaction, through which psychological and moral tendencies are exchanged, is significantly in play.

As in *Vera Cruz*, Aldrich exploits both visual exposition and generic indicators to set up the narrative. The pre-credit sequence of *The Last Sunset* establishes O'Malley on horseback riding in such a way, with backward glances and spurring his animal, as to suggest a pursuer. At this point, while the camera remains at an ambivalent eye-level, the principal reading of the visuals is that of a figure against an expansive landscape. O'Malley emerges from a rocky defile and a panning shot follows him down into a wide valley. This can readily be

Opposite, generic balance: O'Malley (Kirk Douglas, left) and
Stribling (Rock Hudson) face each other on horseback.

associated with an alienated posture, similar to the introduction of Ben Trane in *Vera Cruz*. As he is, initially, the sole figure present, viewer identification is focused on O'Malley if only by default, and sustained through insertive close-ups or, practically speaking, by the revelation to the viewer that Kirk Douglas, a star and hero-type, is playing the role. The reading according to genre type is slightly contradictory: black clothes, black hat, a black kerchief around the throat for a touch of dandyism; a derringer, archetypically associated with the gamblers, in his belt; and the notion of flight. All this faintly suggests villainy, cowardice, etc. The first sight of the pursuer, Dana Stribling, is against the same topographical features. The panning shot mentioned above is repeated, creating a visual equivalency between the two. O'Malley's first "action" will be to smile as he rides past a cockfight in a town street; Stribling's first words will be during an interior scene, which will initially link him with artificial or societal structures rather than the natural, exterior terrain in which O'Malley was first seen. Stribling's apparel is fairly nondescript: blue shirt, white hat, a large, pearl-handled side gun in a cream-colored holster; but with nothing anti-heroic about it. He is seen asking for information about O'Malley and dropping coins into the outstretched hand of a Mexican informant. This action, in itself, is somewhat venal and unsympathetic. Further, Stribling does little to conceal a presumably racist disdain for the Mexican. He gives him a grim regard, which contrasts with O'Malley's gregarious attitude at the cockfight; and he adopts an urgent, menacing tone when he describes O'Malley, who is un-named up to this time: "He has a hole in his chin," he says, forming a cleft in his own chin with a forefinger. "Here." Since Stribling has yet to perform any

"admirable" action, this attitude serves to distance the viewer from him and, by opposition, reinforce sympathy for O'Malley. Much of the viewer's visual interpretation of these expository scenes, in terms of isolating a hero and villain, may prove deceptive later.

There is a natural ambivalence in the audience created by the separate presentation of two male figures. This ambivalence is enhanced by the casting, as both Kirk Douglas as O'Malley and Rock Hudson as Stribling produce expectations of heroic behavior in an otherwise undirected viewer. Aldrich sustains this lack of positive orientation in his framing, using generic indicators which might define either man as "hero" while introducing reservations with regard to each. The one visual point made here and not controverted later is perhaps the most subliminal and detached, the linking of O'Malley with a natural—i.e., impulsive, potentially antisocial—sphere and of Stribling with an artificial one—codified, potentially repressive. The oscillation between these two male figures becomes a visual constant in *The Last Sunset*. As such, it is also an externalization and reinforcement of the emotional position of the main female figure, Belle Breckenridge.

From the beginning, Belle's position in the film is defined by referents that are ontologically rather than materially real. The Breckenridge ranch is a sound stage, a "false" exterior which O'Malley reaches after his flight across a physically genuine landscape. Belle herself is presented in a manner full of unreal, quasi-mythic overtones. A guitar solo on the soundtrack—a deviation from the full score that is conventionally acceptable and unnoticeable in most films—conveys to the viewer in a direct, sensory way the sense of an impending shift to another mode of filmic reality. The physical particulars of setting— dusk, with areas of key light isolated in the frame and dark, silhouetted shapes enveloped in a dense ground fog—and the travelling shot through the mist that gives the first sight of Belle peering apprehensively out from the porch clarify the kind of perceptual rupture that has taken place. Archetypically, a journey through fog connotes passage into another world, in this instance, perhaps, into an underworld which is iconographically typed by a close shot of a dog barking as O'Malley approaches, or a passage through time. Both have some application here. For not only is the setting an apparently otherworldly one as described above; but also the main narrative revelation of their meeting is that Belle and O'Malley have known each other before, have in fact been lovers. Has he "coincidentally" happened upon her home? This is disputable in terms of the overall narrative, since O'Malley suggests later that he rode south searching for Belle; but in the immediacy of the event, coincidence is a possible conclusion. This transmutes the chance encounter into the recapturing of the past for both of them. Finally, the moving camera on Belle is a visual dynamic which compels a subject/object tension between the audi-

Above, O'Malley stays back and strikes a dominant pose as he speaks with Belle (Dorothy Malone). Below, he is closer and more naturally positioned, as he examines a quail's nest with Missy (Carol Lynley).

ence's perception of O'Malley up to that point, which is semi-heroic, and a newer one colored by a newly formed identification with Belle and her inner apprehension, exemplified in her reaction to O'Malley's unseen, ominous whistling as he rides up through the fog. The low angle medium close shot of O'Malley from her point of view is the first visual indication that he is or will become a threatening or disruptive presence.

The introduction of Melissa (Missy), Belle's daughter—and O'Malley's also, but that can be no more than a suspicion for the viewer at this time—inspires the first ironic/visual usage in *The Last Sunset*, namely the film's first three shot, which groups O'Malley, Belle, and Missy into an unconscious "family portrait." But this composition does more than suggest to the viewer something he or she cannot know or add ironic dimension to parts of ensuing dialogue, as in John Breckenridge's remark to O'Malley, "Everything I have is yours." It creates a new narrative/character dynamic in the film and expands the parallel, two-person, and isolated exposition of the opening sequences into mutating, triadic relationships that will continue to be reflected in the framing. For example, the central sexual conflict, which is between Belle and the two men, is embodied in a later three shot. She is seen medium close at its center at a pivot point between Stribling in the left background, and O'Malley in the right background. Similar treatment of groupings of three characters of O'Malley/Stribling/Breckenridge and Stribling/Belle/Missy finally resolves into the two pairs: O'Malley/Missy and Belle/Stribling.

Aldrich stages the direct confrontation of the two men in a slightly different manner. The initial meeting consists almost entirely of close-ups. This disjunctive editing—the physical separation imposed by the shots—can be read as an effect of the characters' antagonism. That is, Stribling's pursuit of O'Malley, whom he holds responsible for the death of his sister, has created too strong a breach to allow them to be framed together for any length of time. It might also be read, from the equal prominence of their respective shots, as a representation of the fact that they are too evenly matched for one to vanquish the other. In fact, when they do fight with their fists sometime later, it ends in a draw. Once it has been decided that both of them will assist Breckenridge in driving his cattle north to Texas, Aldrich directs them into a sustained, following two shot where he withholds the cut until the basic conflict is restated in the dialogue. Stribling threatens, "I'm going to see you hang, O'Malley." O'Malley replies "Hanging's a long term proposition." Even then the cut is to a long shot, slackening rather than tightening the dramatic tension, and they ride off, visually at least, still together.

As the drive continues, Aldrich periodically inserts hints of renewed tension within this two-shot structure. For example, a conversation may begin with O'Malley in close shot, left foreground, and Stribling, medium shot, right background. The staging in depth puts as much space, literally and figuratively, between them as possible. Simultaneously the constriction of the frame—the lack of unused area in its plane aspect—externalizes the sense of "being crowded" that each character feels in the presence of the other. In both the travelling and static compositions, the staging is partially against the dramatic line initiated by the openly hostile dialogue. In a general way such a staging recapitulates the potential violence repressed by the plot device that compels O'Malley and Stribling to cooperate for Belle's sake. Appropriately, after one of O'Malley's sarcastic remarks—"That sister of yours was just a free drink on the house, and nobody went thirsty. I mean nobody."—goads Stribling into fighting, it is Belle, stepping between them with a rifle, whose presence ends the conflict. Eventually, however, the editing must return to the intercut close shots that more directly relate the emotional states of the two men. That visual point is reached and thrust out with particular emphasis near the conclusion of the picture, when the cattle herd is driven across the Rio Grande. Normally, the viewer would expect numerous long shots and wide angle lenses to be used in this type of large-scale action. For purely economic reasons, a conspicuous display of the production values of location work, the cattle herds, and the like would seem in order. Instead Aldrich almost exclusively employs intercut close-ups and uses longer focal-length lenses to throw the background out of focus. For as O'Malley and Stribling ride into Texas, the need for a tem-

porary truce ends, and both revert to their exclusive (being the only figure in a shot), shortsighted (with no depth of field behind), and diametrically opposed views.

Many of the elements in *The Last Sunset*, visual and nonvisual, fulfill a primary rather than subsidiary narrative function. This is obvious in a scene such as the night encampment when the St. Elmo's fire is visible in the sky. As the characters contemplate it, the mythic value of the occurrence becomes an almost direct consideration of the dialogue, somewhat facetiously when O'Malley indulges in "poetic" remarks and more seriously when Belle tells him that "you carry your own storm wherever you go." This line is spoken in a way that not only equates O'Malley with the kinetic phenomenon but metaphorically hints at his residual capac-

Left, "Pretty Little Girl in the Yellow Dress": O'Malley (Kirk Douglas) dances with Missy (Carol Lynley).

ity to excite Belle, to "fire" her imagination as much as the St. Elmo's flames
do. O'Malley's reply—"Only when I travel alone."—reveals another view of
him, his own, in which the loneliness and ostracism of his actual condition
come through. The infrequency of O'Malley's genuine human contact is
linked with the rare manifestations of the St. Elmo's fire. This conception of
O'Malley as a storm recurs in a more understated way when Missy tries to
convince him that their love is possible by saying, "I'm not afraid of clouds."
Both sequences, with Belle and with Missy, are marked by close two shots of
the principals facing each other in profile. There is, in fact, a very clear foreshadowing in the dialogue between O'Malley and Belle early in the film. Belle
asserts that "You loved a sixteen-year-old girl." O'Malley replies, "I stopped
time from touching you."

Even more than the later, "tempestuous" relationship between him and
Missy or all the elements that identify O'Malley with a storm, with a powerfully
or potentially disruptive natural force, perhaps more typical for Aldrich is
O'Malley's brief confrontation with the dog at the ranch house, where meaning is manifested through action rather than a verbal exchange. O'Malley's response to its attack, in clutching the animal by the throat and "staring" it into
submission, has an unsettling quality. On one hand, this implies a Satanic or
mesmeric faculty in him; on the other, it reinforces the aspect of alienation
from all living things. If *The Last Sunset* operates on any consistent figurative
level, it is one involved with death and ritual. The night encampments, for example, are not the usual small, studio exteriors shot predominantly in close.
They provide a contrast to the parched, daylit terrain with expansive, low-key
scenes framed against the crumbling archways of ruined missions or charged
with ritual elements like singing and dancing and the more elaborate St.
Elmo's fire. In the former scenes, in particular, O'Malley's relationship to Missy
is developed through romantic motifs: the song he whistles and then sings for
her while they dance, which reoccurs on the soundtrack during subsequent
meetings, and the exchange of primroses.

In clarifying character interplay or creating a metaphoric line for the film to
follow, a single incongruous shot, such as Belle sitting in the chuck wagon,
framed regally by the high back of a chair and wearing a shawl like a ma-
donna or O'Malley striding through the stockyards like a thin, black spectre,
may prove a more reliable index of figurative meaning than any expository
dialogue. The single element that remains difficult to reconstruct in expressive
terms is the notion of transference between O'Malley and Stribling. Clearly
Stribling's position at the end of the picture is one of succeeding O'Malley as
lover to Belle and, presumably, father to Missy; but the moral questions of that
succession are unresolved. Stribling has doubts about O'Malley's guilt which
inspire his remark that "I was almost hoping he wouldn't cross over [the

Opposite, generic imbalance: O'Malley (Kirk Douglas, left) loses in
the final showdown to Stribling (Rock Hudson) but is the moral victor.

river].” That hope and O'Malley 's apparent choice of suicide invalidate most of the rationalizations about the inevitability of their showdown which Stribling had made before.

The staging of the gunfight itself, which is the generic climax towards which the entire film has been aimed, is ambiguous. The ground level, extra long shot of the approaching O'Malley with railroad tracks looming in the static foreground establishes strongly conflicting lines of force between figure and object, as if to imply again a struggle between the natural (O'Malley) and artificial (steel tracks) but with Stribling removed from the equation. The travelling medium shots, which recede from O'Malley and Stribling as they stride towards each other and are intercut at ever shorter intervals, seem less to oppose the men than to overlay their images: they occupy the same space in the center of their respective frames. In the absence of any screen direction created when they walk directly towards the camera, the figures refer only to each other. It is in this moment of “non-direction” that polarities can shift 180 degrees, and that a transference can take place. In the dynamic of the shot selection and editing, one man shooting the other becomes like firing into a mirror. Reorienting the viewer after such an unusual staging becomes extremely difficult and augments the natural disorientation felt whenever an identifiable principal dies on screen. Accordingly, the ending takes on a suspended, unresolved quality. This is a quality which neither the high angle extreme long shot

Above, Ulzana (Joaquin Martinez, foreground) poses with his band of raiders.

or figures gathered around O'Malley's body, in the manner of *Apache* and *The Big Knife*, nor the end title can de-intensify or dispel.

Ulzana's Raid

Ulzana's Raid mirrors Aldrich's earlier film, *Apache*. This time the story is told from the point of view of the hunter rather than the hunted, but the characters and plot elements are strikingly similar. Ulzana, an Apache warrior, fed up with the reservation and its life of poverty and humiliation, turns terrorist. Like Massai before him in *Apache*, Ulzana wages his own private war on the army and the white settlers who encroached on his native land. As in the earlier film, a grizzled, sullen scout, here called McIntosh, described by his superior as "a willful, opinionated man...[with a] contempt for discipline whether military or moral," is ordered to hunt down the Native American rebel. Also carried over is the character of a Native American scout who helps the hunter track his prey.

This shift in perspective does not accompany any shift in attitude. Aldrich does not romanticize or sentimentalize the Native American, as others before and since him have done in the manner of *Dances with Wolves*. Unlike

Apache and although he is the title figure, Ulzana and his raiders are not the character focus. If anything, they are symbols of the rage of the tribal people on the 19th Century frontier. The conflict, as in *Apache,* is between one culture bent on dominating and another merely trying to survive. Other characters suggest the reasons for Ulzana leaving the reservation: his people are being cheated by the traders, his "spirit" or "power" is shrinking in confinement, and the racism of the whites is unbearable. Burt Lancaster, who starred in both *Apache* and *Ulzana's Raid,* has said that the later film attracted him as much for it inferences that United States' then current involvement in Vietnam was not its first experience with genocide as for its resonances of *Apache.*

Massai was portrayed as a "noble" warrior, fighting out of conviction. Since the story of *Ulzana's Raid* is recounted from the perspective of the white trackers, the raiders here appear cunning and brutal. That is, of course, how Massai was perceived by most of the men fighting him. The cruelty of Ulzana and his band is shot and cut quasi-subjectively to reflect the panic of the settlers. In an initial attack on a soldier escorting a woman and her son to safety, Aldrich breaks up the attack into a series of jarring, short shots: The soldier shoots the woman to prevent her capture and rape; he tries to escape himself; his horse is shot from under him; he rolls over to grab his gun; he puts the gun in his mouth; and in a reverse angle of the previous shot his brains are blown out towards the camera.

Equally brutal is the murder of "the Swede," whose butchered body is found with a dog's tail in his mouth. For Lt. DeBuin, the officer leading the pursuit, such behavior is incomprehensible. McIntosh's explanation of the Apaches' motives is offhanded: "They just find some things funny." When they discover a rancher's wife, crazed after being raped by the Apaches, she acts like a Western Lady Macbeth and tries to scrub the blood from her hands in a pool of water. But not even such self-conscious allusions to classic literature are romanticized.

Ulzana's Raid does end on a different note than that of *Apache.* In one version of the earlier film, Massai was to be shot in the back by Hondo, the Apache scout. In *Ulzana's Raid* the Apache rebel is executed by his own brother-in-law, Ke-ni-tay, the cavalry troop's scout. In a scene which reflects the ritual mood of the earlier film, Ulzana kneels down and begins to chant, accepting his fate, as Ke-ni-tay circles around him. The film cuts away; and the viewer only hears the sound of the shot ringing out in the canyon.

Aldrich's dispassionate depiction of terrorism is unusual in American motion pictures. *Ulzana's Raid* recalls such landmark European films as Gillo Pontecorvo's *The Battle of Algiers* (1966) in that both grapple with the subject of an indigenous people using brutal methods to end colonialism. As in *Apache, Ulzana's Raid* has figures who moralize about the Apache's plight, ponder their behavior, and judge. The narrative itself remains in the ironic mode. While the evangelical Lt. DeBuin questions the motives of the Apaches at every turn, alternating between confusion and hatred, McIntosh takes the detached observer's view when he equates the nature of the Apaches with that of the desert. The Apaches are no more "merciless" in their killing than the desert is "ruthless" in its barrenness. For McIntosh, the equation of the raiders with natural forces is not a disparagement but an acceptance of the Apaches' own belief system. In Aldrich's deterministic view the Apaches, like the whites, do what they think they need to do in order to survive. They act in order to be free within the limits set by an absurd universe. They have no "tragic destiny," only a way of being.

Because *Ulzana's Raid* is a conflict of both men and belief systems, it also express Aldrich's characteristic skepticism of Western religion. Both Lt. De-Buin and the Swede are true believers. The Swede's ranch is attacked by Ulzana in an extended siege which ends with the burning of the his cabin. As the Swede prays frantically, the fire subsides and the sound of the Apaches disappears, as if in answer to his prayers. He walks towards his open door and the smoking exterior, exiting the frame as he raises his voice in thanks: "God, you take all the praise and all the glory." When the audience next sees him, he lies dead with the dog's tail in his mouth.

Lt. DeBuin, the nominal leader of the expedition to destroy Ulzana, is a fundamentalist Christian, the son of an evangelical minister. He wants desperately to understand and convert the Apache; but he is hindered by his own ra-

cism. He distrusts Ke-ni-tay who has done nothing to merit suspicion. DeBuin makes him walk while the others ride and forces him to bury a white man killed by the Apaches. In DeBuin's concept of original sin, Ke-ni-tay's Apache birthright is guilt. Since Ke-ni-tay is at root a savage, DeBuin's underlying attitude towards him is condescension. It is McIntosh who is truly incomprehensible to DeBuin, particularly at the end when the scout asks to be left to die without a funeral, a behavior which DeBuin cannot fathom because "it's not Christian."

Lt. DeBuin and McIntosh are counterparts of the earlier antagonists, Trane and Erin or Wirtz and Koertner. DeBuin is an opinionated, idealistic, "by the book" Army man who is new to the violent milieu of the West. When the film opens and the main titles end, he is revealed in a long panning shot umpiring a baseball game between the men of his troop. To judge by the reaction of his men, DeBuin calls the pitches and plays inaccurately, a process interrupted by a lone horseman who appears on the distant horizon. Photographed with a long lens, the rider slowly approaches the baseball diamond to announce the departure of Ulzana from the reservation, an event the audience had already witnessed in the title sequence. Narratively DeBuin is established as a man of poor judgment, at least when it comes to baseball; visually he is immediately linked to Ulzana. This is the core of a moral dilemma for the evangelical lieutenant which no amount of pontificating will lessen: There are rules of behavior for human beings in life as in a baseball game, but the Apaches refuse to follow them. DeBuin will never discover why. And in a particularly revelatory sequence, the camera pans across a pastoral scene of high grass and reclining troopers to reveal a group of soldiers scalping an Apache. DeBuin is totally aghast at whites acting like Apaches which, as McIntosh says, "kind of confuses the issue."

DeBuin's righteousness and moral indignation is continually being confounded by McIntosh's existential acceptance. McIntosh works for the army but is married to an Apache woman, whom the audience sees as McIntosh and the troop leave the fort. A blanket covers her face. In a powerful close-up, her eyes stare out sadly after her departing husband. McIntosh lives with these divided loyalties. He is accepted neither by his own people nor by those of his wife. He is an archetypal outsider. He is, however, intent on doing his job and surviving. The fact that he does not survive is not due to any deficiency on his part but to the incompetence of DeBuin.

DeBuin and a majority of the troop are left behind while McIntosh draws Ulzana and his men into the canyon. At the assigned moment DeBuin is to ride to the rescue. Unfortunately for McIntosh and the soldiers with him, De-Buin is too late. In a final confrontation, shot in tight close-up, DeBuin apologizes for his mistake. McIntosh responds magnanimously, "Hell, you'll learn."

Opposite, Lt. DeBuin (Bruce Davison, left) and McIntosh (Burt Lancaster).

From this expansive gesture, typical of McIntosh's non-judgmental perspective, the film draws its moral.

In the Western genre with its frontier context, life can clearly be a series of tests and challenges. In the existential concept of "quantity of experiences," the more challenges a person meets, the more a person learns. Life can become endurable if the individual accumulates experiences, both negative and positive. Only in this manner can the individual tolerate the meaninglessness all around. In the final analysis, McIntosh, like most Aldrich protagonists, epitomizes Colin Wilson's classic definition of "the outsider" as delineated in his book of that name: "He is not very concerned with the distinction between body and spirit, or man and nature; these ideas produce theological thinking and philosophy; he rejects both. For him, the only important distinction is between being and nothingness..."

4 for Texas and The Frisco Kid

Like most genre satires, *4 for Texas* is an attempt to deconstruct the Western along the lines of the later, more successful *Blazing Saddles*. The film opens with the narrator, Joe Jarrett, identifying himself as a "good guy" and the stage robbers as "bad guys," as if the genre conventions of men on horses attacking a stagecoach were not sufficient signifiers of who is who.

The rest of the characters also reflect Aldrich's satirical tone. Zack Thomas, Jarrett's sometime ally, sometime antagonist, is a send-up of the smooth, somewhat amoral lady-killer, ogling girls' posteriors while mouthing double entendres. The banker villain, a staple of so many Westerns, here becomes a true grotesque, a sweating, burping, unctuous individual who evicts widow ladies and becomes ecstatic at the sight of a buffet. The gunslinger Matson epitomizes evil Western-style as he murders men, including members of his own gang, for the slightest affront. And when he is shot several times by Jarrett and Thomas, he is carried out on a board screaming revenge, only to return within a short time completely intact, like some immortal demon.

The female characters of the film are like most of Aldrich's females—with the notable exceptions of *Autumn Leaves* and *...All the Marbles*—iconic. They are voluptuous European "sex goddesses," as played by Anita Ekberg and Ursula Andress, who use their sexuality as a way of controlling their men, Zack and Jarrett, respectively. Whether it is by appearing in a transparent negligee or undressing behind a screen, they use their bodies as weapons to attain their goal. Maxine (Andress) gets Jarrett and her river boat renovated, while Elya (Ekberg) becomes Zack's financial as well as connubial partner.

The action scenes are also deconstructed by inserting slapstick into them. Whether it is pratfalls, "witty"patter, or absurdly exaggerated action, the stagecoach attack at the beginning, the several gunfights, and the final brawl at the end are attempts by Aldrich to mock the conventions of action he had so finely honed in his other Westerns.

4 for Texas is arguably Aldrich's weakest film. Aldrich uses comic relief and elements of satire in most of his pictures, but his style never meshed with a traditional Hollywood comedy or even a sustained comic tone. The awkward results are apparent elsewhere in portions of *The Choirboys* and in his only other pure comedy, *The Frisco Kid*. In *4 for Texas* Aldrich falls back too readily on *shtick*. Using such icons of slapstick as The Three Stooges could be considered a weak parody, but leering men spouting tired double entendres are merely tasteless. Typical is Jarrett's comment to Maxine after he has spent the night with her on her river boat: "It was a pleasure being aboard." The film is ultimately most hampered by the performances of Frank Sinatra as Zack and Dean Martin as Jarrett. In many ways they are simply transposing their celebrity personas as "swingers" and leaders of Sinatra's "rat pack." Their characters on the screen become pallid extensions of these public images rather than new personas.

In a sense, the same problem inhibits *The Frisco Kid*. Based on his earlier work for Mel Brooks, Gene Wilder certainly inspired particular audience expectations for his role as a rabbi who is radically out of his element as he crosses the United States in 1850. But as unlikely as the events of *The Frisco Kid* might seem, all of them are depicted realistically. There are no surreal moments when actors step out of character or props defy the laws of nature as in Brooks' films. Viewers who came to *The Frisco Kid* expecting to see *Blazing Saddles* meets *Young Frankenstein* saw something very different. In addition, whatever success co-star Harrison Ford had in the first of the *Star Wars* movies engendered an entirely different expectation from filmgoers. In fact, the re-

Right, out of their element: Frank Sinatra as Zack Thomas (left) and Dean Martin as Joe Jarrett.

lationship between the rabbi and the bank robber, as portrayed respectively by Wilder and Ford, was clearly meant to make statements about tolerance and understanding of other people's ways rather than be a traditional, genre coupling.

But the actual film is a series of otherwise disconnected vignettes held together by the thin, common thread of being new and enlightening experiences for Rabbi Avram Belinski. There is a multicultural self-consciousness that runs through *The Frisco Kid*, but it has no dramatic underpinning. An early joke has the hapless Belinski believing he has found a colony of Orthodox kinsmen in Pennsylvania until he sees the cross on a bible in one of the Amish farmer's pockets. The same gag is repeated after sampling peyote with the Indians, when Belinski regains consciousness, sees a wooden cross dangling over a hooded monk's robe, and wonders if he has gone to a very different heaven than his religion promised him.

Some of the staging in the early scenes is effectively direct. When the Diggs brothers and Mr. Jones set up their scheme to rob Avram, Aldrich uses a long shot. As the unsuspecting rabbi indicates that he has been deceived by saying, "Perhaps I could pay the fifty dollars," the three con men at opposite ends of the frame freeze for an instant and then close in. Minutes later, after they have stripped and beaten Avram and thrown him from the wagon, a ground level shot frames him lying in the dirt road as the wagon drives away in the background. The title sequence follows.

From the encounter with the Amish that follows the titles to the final wedding sequence, *The Frisco Kid* relies more on comic stereotypes and Wilder's mannered acting than on true genre parody or any stylistic manipulations. The sequence with the Indians of an unspecified tribe typifies the narrative and expressive cross-purposes of the movie. Given the social awareness of *Apache* and *Ulzana's Raid*, the essentially "cigar store" Indians of *The Frisco Kid* are surprising. There is a suggestion of a different attitude in Tommy Lillard's reply when Belinski asks why the Indians chased them: "They been shit on by white men so long, they don't ask questions no more." But Chief Gray Cloud, even in the context of a comedy, is a bit too far removed from either Massai or Ulzana. Certainly he ridicules Avram for using pidgin English and Tommy because he "speaks to Indians as if they were children." But where did he learn English or acquire his awareness of these white men's culturally inculcated behavior? The chief is impressed with Avram's religious devotion in risking his life to recover his Torah and asks probing questions about the rabbi's beliefs. But despite his apparent sophistication and being a kind of prairie gnostic, the chief never makes the obvious connection that causes Avram's crisis of faith at the end of the film: that a holy book is still just a book and valueless compared to human life.

Opposite, also out of their element: Gene Wilder as Avram Belinski (left) and Harrison Ford as Tommy Lillard.

For all its good intentions, the vignettes in *The Frisco Kid* more often reinforce rather than question stereotypes. Ironically, Avram's acceptance by the ethnically mixed crew laying track for the railroad or the generosity of the Amish folk and the Catholic monks to a minister of another religion says more about the tolerance of others than of the Jews. For all his good humor, Avram himself is quite inflexible, often to the point of being dangerously foolhardy, imperiling himself and Tommy when he refuses to heed his companion's warnings about bad weather, pursuing posses, and hostile Indians. Avram is both subtly xenophobic and even, as revealed by the bad joke when he and Tommy are caught in the snowstorm and huddle together for warmth—"We are doing this to keep warm, aren't we?"—homophobic.

This is all part of the most ironic sub-text of all in *The Frisco Kid*, its anti-semitism. The loud squabbling council of Polish rabbis in the prologue and their imperious chief, who overrules the vote of his colleagues, are pure stereotypes. So are many of Gene Wilder's line readings as Avram, such as his oft-repeated, wide-eyed, highly inflected response whenever Tommy refuses to go on any farther: "So who's asking you to?" More subtle, less funny, and certainly less excusable are the dynamics of the San Francisco congregation. The jokes about the wandering eye of the leader Bender's elder daughter, who has been promised to Belinski, or the cynical remarks of the resident skeptic are merely humorless. But that character's question when Bender proposes a dinner to celebrate Belinski's arrival—"Who's paying?"—suggests a perception of the congregation that, like other ethnic groups in *The Frisco Kid*, is neither a realistic portrayal nor a parody but more like "cigar store" Jews.

Above, on the set of *Attack!* in 1956, Aldrich poses with a copy of Borde and Chaumeton's book, <u>Panorama du Film Noir Américain</u>.

Chapter Five:

Film Noir

Aldrich began directing as the classic period of American *film noir* was in its closing phase. Aldrich not only made fewer *film noir* than many of his contemporaries but, of the few *noir* films he did make, *World for Ransom* and *The Garment Jungle* were somewhat atypical of the style. So why would the editors of *Film Comment* in 1972 have dubbed Aldrich "Mr. Film Noir"? The answer is simple: *Kiss Me Deadly*.

Kiss Me Deadly

At the core of *Kiss Me Deadly* are speed and violence. The adaptation of Mickey Spillane's novel takes Mike Hammer from New York to Los Angeles, where it situates him in a landscape of somber streets and decaying houses even less inviting than those stalked by Spade and Marlowe in the preceding decades of Depression and War years. Much like Hammer's fast cars, the movie swerves frenziedly through a series of disconnected and cataclysmic scenes. As such, it typifies the frenetic, post-Bomb L.A. of the era with all its malignant undercurrents. It records the degenerative half-life of an unstable universe as it moves towards critical mass. When it reaches the fission point, the graphic threat of machine-gun bullets traced in the door of a house on Laurel Canyon in *The Big Sleep* in the 40s is explosively superseded in the 50s as a beach cottage in Malibu becomes ground zero.

From the beginning, *Kiss Me Deadly* is a true sensory explosion. In the precredit sequence, a woman stumbles out of the pitch darkness, while her

171

breathing fills the soundtrack with amplified, staccato gasps. Blurred metallic shapes flash by without stopping. She positions herself in the center of the roadway, until oncoming headlights blind her with the harsh glare of their high beams. Brakes grab, tires scream across the asphalt, and a Jaguar spins off the highway in a swirl of dust. A close shot reveals Hammer behind the wheel: over the sounds of her panting and a jazz piano on the car radio, the ignition grinds repeatedly as he tries to restart the engine. Finally, he snarls at the woman, "You almost wrecked my car! Well? Get in!"

As in *World For Ransom*, the shot selection and lighting provide immediate keys to the style, to *film noir*. But in *Kiss Me Deadly*, the opening dialogue between Hammer and Christina is the significant component in establishing another sort of hero: one that is sneering, sarcastic, and not really a hero at all.

HAMMER
Can I have my hand back now? (Pause.) So, you're a fugitive from the laughing house.

CHRISTINA
They forced me to go there. They took away my clothes to make me stay.

HAMMER
Who?

CHRISTINA
I wish I could tell you that. I have to tell someone. When people are in trouble, they need to talk. But you know the old saying.

HAMMER
"What I don't know can't hurt me"?

CHRISTINA
You're angry with me aren't you? Sorry I nearly wrecked your pretty little car. I was just thinking how much you can tell about a person from such simple things. Your car, for instance.

HAMMER
Now what kind of message does it send you?

CHRISTINA
You have only one real lasting love.

HAMMER
Now who could that be?

CHRISTINA
You. You're one of those self-indulgent males
who thinks about nothing but his clothes, his
car, himself. Bet you do push-ups every morning just to keep your belly hard.

HAMMER
You against good health or something?

CHRISTINA
I could tolerate flabby muscles in a man, if it'd
make him more friendly. You're the kind of person who never gives in a relationship, who only
takes. (sardonically) Ah, woman, the incom-
plete sex. And what does she need to complete
her? (mockingly dreamy) One man, wonderful
man!

HAMMER
All right, all right. Let it go.

What kind of man is Mike Hammer? *Kiss Me Deadly*'s opening dialogue types
him quickly. Christina's direct accusation of narcissism merely confirms what
the icons suggest about "how much you can tell about the person from such
simple things": the sports car, the trench coat, the curled lip, the jazz on the
radio. Aldrich and writer A.I. Bezzerides use the character of Christina to
explain and reinforce what the images have already suggested, that this is not
a modest or admirable man.

The dialogue also reveals that Hammer knows exactly who he is and the
image he presents: "What kind of message does it send you?" It sends the one
Hammer wants to send, a message which Christina, the "fugitive from the
laughing house," can discuss directly. This is a first hint of what will be something of a role reversal in the way men and women speak. The older male
characters, the Italian house mover and Dr. Soberin, will use figurative images
and make mythical allusions, rather than speak directly about people and ob-

jects. The younger women, Christina, Velda, and even Carver, usually say what is on their minds.

The dark highway of the opening is a kind of narrative limbo: the elements of the plot have not yet been brought into line, let alone focused. Certainly, contemporary viewers brought with them expectations about character and plot both from the underlying novel and from the conventions of *film noir*. The opening selectively underscores aspects of those expectations while withholding detail. Visually, the discussion of the "laughing house" and Hammer's materialism is shot entirely in a medium two shot of Christina and Hammer, either from the front or rear, in the cockpit of his car. The viewer is not distracted from the character interaction, in which Hammer "loses" the verbal sparring: he is effectively "put down" by Christina until he must tell her to "let it go." *Kiss Me Deadly* has no clearly defined landscape at this point to use as a textural reinforcement. The countryside and the rural gas station are all unidentified settings. They are open, shadowy, and, even within the fringes of the station's neon lights, menacing. Generically this last trait primes the viewer for Christina's murder under torture and Hammer's near death.

In terms of subject/object tension, the Aldrich/Bezzerides conception of Hammer is both more objective and "anti-Spillane." Spillane's use of first-person prose is certainly in the hard-boiled tradition.

> All I saw was the dame standing there in the glare of the headlights waving her arms like a huge puppet and the curse I spit out filled the car and my own ears. I wrenched the car over, felt the rear end start to slide, brought it out with a splash of power and almost ran up the side of the cliff as the car fishtailed. The brakes bit in, gouging a furrow in the shoulder, then jumped to the pavement and held. Somehow I had managed a sweeping curve around the babe.

This offhanded objectification of women is in play from the novel's first paragraph. This point of view along with Spillane's lurid sadomasochism and his rabid anti-Communism in the shadow of McCarthy are legendary. From the opening of the novel Aldrich and Bezzerides take the events and little else. Spillane's recurring protagonist, Hammer, provides the predetermined viewpoint of the narratives. Hammer's deprecations and wisecracks in the novel are not detached or objective descriptions of people and events but are part of his "color." Aldrich and Bezzerides abandon most of this also or rather, in Aldrich's preferred method, they "stand it on its head."

Of the opening dialogue only one line—"They forced me...to make me stay."—is from the novel. But much more is changed than just the words. In terms of plot, elements such as the Rossetti poem or the radioactive "great whatsit" are inventions of the filmmakers. Among the characters, Nick the mechanic is wholly original. In terms of attitude, Hammer becomes a grinning predator, the antithesis of Chandler's urban knight and with survival instincts sharper even than Sam Spade's. Even Spillane's Hammer has some glimmer of sympathy for a "damn-fool crazy Viking dame with holes in her head" and follows the trail of those who tried to kill him, out of simpleminded outrage at their misdeeds: "I wouldn't need to look at their faces to know I was killing the right ones. The bastards, the dirty, lousy bastards!" The film Hammer is incorporated into a more sophisticated system that combines the undertone of *film*

Right, the facial expression says it all as Hammer (Ralph Meeker) asks gangster Carl Evello (Paul Stewart) the key question, "What's in it for me?"

Right, Hammer's expression is quite different when someone else has his hand out. The morgue attendant (Percy Helton, left) asks for a pay-off while Lily Carver (Gaby Rodgers) looks on.

noir with Aldrich's moral determinism. While Hammer wants to know "what's in it for me," all around him crime breeds counter-crime, while thieves and murderers fashion the implements of their own destruction.

For Spillane, Hammer's very name revealed all: a hard, heavy, unrelenting object pounding away mindlessly at social outcasts like twopenny nails. The filmmakers refine this archetype slightly: Hammer does think, mostly about how to turn a buck. Christina is arguably the most conventionally "sensitive" of the picture's characters. She reads poetry and, although mockingly, lyricizes her own predicament. It is not without irony that she is the "loony," the one institutionalized by society, yet quickest to penetrate Hammer's tough-guy pose. In that first scene, she helps to reveal that the hero of the film *Kiss Me Deadly* is closer to other characters in Aldrich's work than in Spillane's. He inherits the cynical greed of Joe Erin in *Vera Cruz* and anticipates the transcendent egomania of Zarkan in *The Legend of Lylah Clare*. As Ralph Meeker's interpretation propels Hammer beyond the smugness and self-satisfaction of the novel into a blacker, more sardonic disdain for the world in general, the character becomes a cipher for all the unsavory denizens of the *noir* underworld.

The informal inquiry into Christina's death by the unidentified government agents expositionally establishes that Hammer's professional as well as personal conduct is unscrupulously self-seeking: "Who do you sic on the wives, Mr. Hammer?" Throughout much of the scene, Hammer is framed in the shot's foreground, sullenly staring at a blank wall off camera, ignoring the baiting remarks. His snide retort—"All right. You've got me convinced: I'm a real stinker."—is effectively true. Because the committee members have made more than a few gibes about Hammer, his response does not yet alienate the viewer. But a dichotomy between the audience's and the "hero's" viewpoints is building, creating a subject/object spilt which runs counter to the first person elements of the novel. Hammer first asks, "What's in it for me?" as he speaks to Pat Murphy in the corridor after the inquiry. That utterance completes the character composite: Hammer is certainly not like Callahan, not another selfless "Galahad" as he begins a quest for "something big," for the private eye's grail.

Hammer *is* a quester. He is not an outsider in the *noir* underworld or any equivalent of a mythic "other world." If this is a foreign or alien milieu, Hammer is at home there. For Hammer, the dark streets and ramshackle buildings are a questing ground which is conspicuously detached from the commonplace material world. Deception is the key to this world. Deception not detection is Hammer's trade. His livelihood depends on the divorce frame-up and the generally shady deal. Deception is Lily Carver's game also, from the false name she assumes to the vulnerable pitch of her voice to the pathetic way she brings her hand up against her face like a wing of Christina's dead canary. Failure to deceive is what costs Christina and others their lives.

This deception and uncertainty, as in most *noir* films, lay the groundwork for *Kiss Me Deadly*'s melodramatic tension. The plot-line has all the stability of one of Nick's "Va-va-voom's," so inversion becomes a constant; and subsurface values become central concerns. In this milieu, the first "torpedo" set to go off when a car key is turned necessarily posits a second rigged to explode at a higher speed. From the viewer's objective vantage, the shift from one level of appearances to another is occasionally discernible. An early example is the transformation of the sensual Carver, first framed behind a bed post and swinging a hip up to expose more of her leg through the fold of the terry cloth robe, then becoming shrill and waif-like for Hammer's benefit. Usually, though, the viewer is also deceived.

For those on a quest in the *noir* underworld, instability is the overriding factor and disjunction is the rule. The sensational elements in *Kiss Me Deadly* follow this rule. The craning down and the hiss of the hydraulic jack as the screaming Nick is crushed under the weight of a car; the pillar of fire that consumes Lily Carver; the eerie growl of the black box; even a simple "Pretty pow!" as Nick jams a fist into his open palm—these random acts have no organizing principles. They transcend context to deliver a shock that is purely

Below, a variant on the *femme fatale*: a waif with a gun. Gaby Rodgers as Lily Carver.

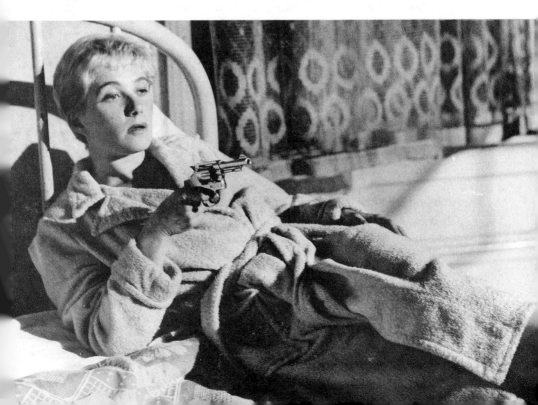

sensory. Still they fit homogeneously into the generic fabric and the subversive whole of the narrative.

Most of *Kiss Me Deadly*'s visual devices are derivations from the generic styles of *World For Ransom* or *Vera Cruz*: high and low angles, depth of field, constriction of the frame through foreground clutter. The long take or sequence shot, however, is used more extensively and more specifically than before. There are four examples of it in *Kiss Me Deadly*, all of which might be classed as interrogation scenes: Pat Murphy's first visit to Hammer's apartment, and Hammer's questionings of Harvey Wallace, Carmen Trivago, and Eddie Yeager. The specifics of the shots vary, from the slow traveling into close shot during the brief discussion with the truck driver, Wallace, to the elaborate tracking and panning in Hammer's apartment, shifting characters front to back and left to right in an uneasy search for equilibrium. In no sequence shot does Hammer get answers to everything he asks; yet each takes him to the brink of some discovery.

More than anything else these shots serve as a sort of punctuation in the narrative line. In the scenes with Trivago and Yeager especially, the sustained camera seems to externalize a reflective pause. Hammer only half listens in these scenes, wandering about and sampling Trivago's wine and spaghetti or with Yeager glancing over at the sparring match. They also create visual pauses at odd intervals. While they diminish tension on the one hand by preserving a level of stasis or consistency, barring the cut and the extreme angle, they reinforce it on the other, playing first with the viewer's expectancy of the cut and then with the interior movements of the camera. As the possibility of a change in angle is removed only for a set period that cannot exceed the length of the sequence, so the pause is a baited one, barely allowing Hammer and/or the audience time to "catch their breath."

As in *World for Ransom*, the trap is a part of *Kiss Me Deadly*'s figurative scheme. Again, its constructs are primarily visual. But the elaborate "capture" of Callahan in the earlier picture is distilled down to single shots in *Kiss Me Deadly*. For example, in the high angle long shot of Hammer outside Lily Carver's room, the dark foreground of stairway and balustrades are arrayed concentrically about Hammer's figure and seem to enclose him. Usages such as this contribute to *Kiss Me Deadly*'s figurative continuity of instability or inversion and the lurking menace, all set up in the opening sequences.

What most distinguishes *Kiss Me Deadly*'s figurative usage from that of earlier and many later Aldrich films is the added dimension of an explicit, aural fabric of allusions and metaphor, the play of myth and anti-myth discussed in the Introduction. The Christina Rossetti poem, "Remember Me," is a recurrent example. Other background sounds are keyed to character. The Caruso recording with which Carmen Trivago sings is the Flotow opera, *Martha*.

More classical music plays on the radio in Christina's room as the manager remarks, "She was always listening to that station." A prize fight is being broadcast in the background when Evello and Sugar Smallhouse are killed.

While these sounds may not be as fully incorporated into the narrative structure as the poem is, all provide immediate textural contrast if not subsidiary meaning. The sibilant tone of Evello's gasp as he is killed echoes the hiss of the car jack in Nick's murder. As tropes both recall in turn the equation of vitality with a "deep breath" made by the old mover. The play of sounds and meaning can create other anomalies. For instance, at one point Velda approaches Mike asking, "But under any other name, would you be as sweet?" and he, not paying attention to her, says, "Kowalski." On one level, all these can be appreciated as textural noise or *non sequiturs*. On another, they are conscious metaphors and puns.

As with Callahan, "chance" is a factor: Hammer says, "If she hadn't gotten in my way, I wouldn't have stopped." Velda's statements about the "great whatsit" and "the nameless ones who kill people" reinforce the sense that the vagaries of chance or destiny, a word which the mythically-minded Dr. Soberin would likely have preferred, are an underlying constant. Soberin himself is one of the most consciously allusive characters in Aldrich's films. He brings up the notion of rising from the dead after Christina expires: "Do you know what that would be? That would be resurrection." He mentions Lazarus again during a conversation with Hammer. The old moving man also speaks of "the house of my body" that can only be left once. These concepts run parallel to Hammer's own search for meaning in the cryptic pentameter of the Rossetti poem: "But when the darkness and corruption leave/A vestige of the thoughts that once we had."

Myth becomes a surface value entirely in the case of the "great whatsit." What Pat Murphy utters—a "few, harmless words...just a bunch of letters scrambled together, but their meaning is very important.... Manhattan project. Los Alamos. Trinity."—are as much words to conjure with as Soberin's pedantic analogies. Soberin's references to Lot's wife and "cerberus barking with all his heads" are too archaic and unfrightening to keep Gabrielle/Lily Carver from opening her own Pandora's box. In the final analysis, the "great whatsit" contains pure phlogiston. The quest for it becomes the quest for the cleansing, combustible element, for the spark of the purifying fire that reduces the nether world of *Kiss Me Deadly* to radioactive ash.

As modern myth, as anti-myth, and/or as *film noir*, *Kiss Me Deadly*'s narrative outlook is equally somber. "A savage lyricism hurls us into a decomposing world ruled by perversity and brutality," wrote Borde and Chaumeton, after which "Aldrich brings to bear the most radical of solutions: nuclear apocalypse."[1] *Kiss Me Deadly* is also a key to the development of Aldrich's visual style. In this "apocalyptic" context, the choices of angle, framing, staging, lighting, and all the other elements which constitute a visual style are all in play in a particularly expressive way.[2]

For example, in the low angle shot from Hammer's point of view on the floor in the sequence when Christina is killed, which shows only her legs and the feet of his captors, the camera placement also functions to withhold critical information—the faces of the men—and to have the viewer co-experience Hammer's mental note-taking of his only clue: the style of Soberin's shoes. Framing works with the choice of angle in that, objectively, both the fact of the viewer empathy with Christina, who the dialogue reveals has just been tortured to death, and the position of her white, lifeless legs in the center of the frame draw attention away from the aspect of the dark shoes in the surrounding foreground.

The shot of Hammer at Soberin's feet is a telling transliteration of the novel which relies on framing, decor or mise-en-scene, and the association of sound and image for its full effect. Spillane wrote. "They had left me on the floor.... Something moved and a pair of shoes shuffled into sight so I knew I wasn't alone." In the film Hammer is unconscious, so the shot is not subjective. Instead of being on the floor he lies on the bare set of bed springs suggestive of a cold, metallic decay. The shoes are on the floor below. While the entire image combines with the sound of Soberin's stentorian voice as he speaks of "resurrection," the springs and bed frame cast a maze of shadows, so that his feet and Hammer's face are enmeshed in the same tangled web.

Such a low angle is "motivated," that is, the camera is placed on the floor to simulate Hammer's semiconscious sprawl. In contrast, the ground level medium shot when Sugar interrupts Hammer's examination of the shoes in Evello's bathhouse represents a director's and not a character's point of view. That angle similarly restricts the visual information which the viewer receives. How Hammer renders Sugar unconscious remains an off-screen mystery, while the tilt upward combines with a shorter focal length lens to distort perspective and exaggerate the magnitude of Sugar's fall.

The tilted angles in the hospital room alternate between directorial and character point of view. As a disembodied voice calls Mike's name, the sequence begins with an optical device used over a shot of Velda and the nurse. A rippling effect through an image from the character's point of view is a convention for awakening from a dream or returning to consciousness (as repeatedly parodied in *Wayne's World*). The tilting off from horizontal approximates the imbalance which Hammer experiences as he comes to; but that tilting is carried over into a shot which includes Hammer. The shift between "first person" and "third person"—the scene ends in the former mode—serves to objectify the unusual angle. As first-person usage and its conventions are undercut, the split between Hammer's viewpoint and that of the narrative is accentuated.

The most frequent use of other than eye-level camera placement in *Kiss Me Deadly* is the slight high and low angles which clarify interpersonal relationships. In certain medium close two shots, the camera aiming down at Nick over Hammer's shoulder implies that he intimidates or controls the other character to some degree. When Velda comes to Mike's apartment, the more extreme angle over him down at her is appropriate to the degree in which he dominates her. Even as he looks away from Velda in her own bedroom, Hammer still dominates. Conversely, the very similar shots aimed upwards at Carver or Pat Murphy reverse that effect to suggest a weaker position on Hammer's part.

Opposite, Dr. Soberin (Albert Dekker) warns Gabrielle/Lily Carver (Gaby Rodgers) after she asks him, "What's in the box?"

The recurrent use of objects and faces in the foreground of various shots, either as indeterminate shapes or held in focus by depth of field, creates a visual tension. These elements both conceal a portion of the rear ground and compete with the more "significant" content for viewer attention, as with Christina's legs, mentioned above. On a connotative level, the foreground clutter of the stairs, banisters, and corridors present in high angle long shots of both Hammer alone and later with Carver occupies a larger portion of the frame relative to the smaller human figures. Rather than forming simple black wedges, they have a textural presence made up of highlights and a confusion of angular shapes. As in *World for Ransom*, characters at frame center thus appear caught in a tangible vortex or enclosed in a trap.

The staging of these elements combines with framing and depth of field to further define Hammer's relationship to his environment and other characters. He has a tendency to stare off towards a point outside the frame. Instances vary from the three shot in the morgue to the interview by federal investigators after the accident or when he awakens Velda after learning of Nick's death. All suggest a high degree of alienation. His inability to look at people at critical times contrasts with his professional but manic interest in examining the fixtures of a strange room, as when he goes to Christina's or interviews Carmen Trivago, pausing in the latter instance to sample wine and sniff spaghetti but seldom glancing at the other person in the shot. Hammer is not only estranged from his environment but alienates others with his deportment.

The choice of setting and the use of real locations reinforce this sense of alienation. The general decay of the city coupled with specific usages such as the flashing street lights and isolated gas station create a tone of lingering menace mentioned earlier. Other usages comment metaphorically on the confusion of identities. The mirrors and panning movement when Hammer visits Velda in her exercise room create a complex of confusing doppelgängers. As the shot opens, the viewer sees two sets of figures as Hammer steps into the room. The pan reveals that neither set was "real" and displaces them with the actual people reflected in still another mirror. Even as Velda elaborates figuratively on the possible consequences of his investigation and speaks of a "thread" leading to a "rope" by which he might well "hang," she spins around on the pole. Her action and the reflections actively undercut the surrounding reality.

Elements of lighting function similarly. The low light on Hammer and Christina conform to a convention of visual expression which associates shadows cast upward of the face with the unnatural and ominous, the ritual opposite of sunlight. The low light when Carver opens the box of radioactive material is, most appropriately at that moment in the film, hellish. Her demonic aspect as she screams anticipates her immolation by Soberin's "brimstone."

Side light is used to reflect character ambivalence. For example, in the low angle medium close shot of Hammer looking down at Nick's body and framed against a night sky, Hammer is both literally and figuratively isolated in surrounding darkness. The half of his face cast in shadow is emblematic of an impulse to abandon the search generated by the sudden death of his friend, an impulse which accounts for the sense of loss and indecision that he manifests in the remainder of the film.

As we noted, even before directing *The Big Leaguer* or *World for Ransom*, Aldrich had experimented with the long take, unusual framing, and foreground objects in his television work. To underscore the pervasive aura of malaise and paranoia in *Kiss Me Deadly*, Aldrich combines many of these elements. For instance with the sequence shot of Hammer's interview with the truck driver, Wallace, the camera moves slowly inwards, reducing the dimensions of the frame around the characters and intensifying its "closure" or constriction even as the duration of the shot adds tension. An even more dynamic usage is the boom down towards Nick as he is crushed by the car, in which the viewer becomes an active participant in his murder, by literally being in the position of the car as he is killed.

Various aspects of the three sequence-shot interviews with Wallace, Eddie Yeager, and Carmen Trivago in the film's chronology have already been mentioned. The withholding of a cut in sequences throughout Aldrich's work introduces a tension between the viewer's expectation of a "normally" occurring cut and its absence. In the scene with Trivago, this tension is accentuated both by the literal violence of the events when Hammer breaks his record to extort information and the frenetic motion of the continuous traveling back and forth in his long, shallow room. Even while the shot is held, the image changes as characters reposition themselves; and clutter such as Trivago's clothes on a line impinges and recedes in the foreground. In the scene with Yeager, the sequence shot binds together a number of "individual" shots linked by traveling and panning and each affected by its respective framing, lighting, depth, etc.

As with duration of shot, montage is primarily a binding mechanism in *Kiss Me Deadly*, joining or opposing other elements of stylistic expression for a compound effect. A simple example that epitomizes the most basic power of montage as posited by Kuleshov is found in two shots from Hammer's "interrogation" of the morgue attendant. As the man reaches down to put the key which he found in Christina's body back into a desk, Hammer slams the drawer shut on his hand. The shot is powerfully violent in itself, even though neither man's head or shoulders is visible. Aldrich cuts to a close-up of Hammer grinning, and in a single shot captures all the sadistic impulses of Spillane's character. To the silent evocation of abstract meaning which Kuleshov defined, Aldrich adds the additional dimension of sound, so that Hammer grins not just at the sight of the morgue attendant's crushed hand but at his screams and whimpers as well.

As many of these examples demonstrate, the interaction of montage and angle, framing and staging, lighting and depth of field create a multiplicity of stylistic expressions whose meanings are colored by the context of *film noir*. Certainly *Kiss Me Deadly* ranks with the most important examples of *film noir* by any director. It has the menace of *Night and the City*, the grim determinism of *Out of the Past*, the cynicism of *Double Indemnity*, the reckless energy of *Gun Crazy*, and the visual flourish of *Touch of Evil*. While it is less about people than *World for Ransom*, both films focus on the underlying sense of nuclear peril that haunted the end of the *noir* period. If *Kiss Me Deadly* also reflects such contemporary issues as McCarthyism and moral decline, those, too, are part of the fabric of *film noir*.

Aldrich's early career coincides with the beginning and end of the classic period of *film noir*; and he would revisit many of the *noir* cycle's themes in later films. But as a symbol of what *film noir* epitomized or of the powerful, malevolent forces lurking in Aldrich's vision of the modern world, nothing would ever loom larger than a mushroom cloud over Malibu.

TV Noir

As already mentioned, Aldrich's earliest directorial work was in television for shows such as *The Doctor, China Smith,* and *Four Star Playhouse.* In those series episodes, Aldrich developed the nascent methods of narrative organization and staging which would mark his later films. The syndicated series, *China Smith*, in particular gave Aldrich some opportunity to explore non-standard angles and lighting, as demonstrated by its informal spin-off, *World for Ransom.*

After directing his first two features Aldrich returned to television for five episodes of *Four Star Playhouse.* Two of them, *The Squeeze* and *The Hard Way*, featured a fast-talking, cynical, hard-bitten gambler named Willy Dante, played by one of *film noir*'s earliest Philip Marlowes, Dick Powell. Although the plots are fairly standard—various quantities of murder, mobsters, cops, blackmail, and politician's children thrown in—the style is notable. With almost all the scenes set at night, the interior photography is low-key and the exteriors are also chiaroscuro. The title sequence has the wet streets reflecting luminous lamp posts typical of *noir*. There is also frequent camera movement with several shots where the camera glides with the characters from one room, through an imaginary wall, and into a second room. This is often combined with staging in depth, so that a two shot will have one character in the foreground and carry focus to a second in the background.

Aldrich's early predilection for long takes is also apparent. In one scene a gangster and his thug grill Dante about some counterfeit money they believe he has foisted on them. The gangster paces back and forth during the long take, at one point completely blocking the camera with his body so that the editor can insert an imperceptible cut, in the technique of Hitchcock's *Rope.* The tension of this slightly counterfeit long take ends with a dynamic close-up of Dante waving the counterfeit money as they decide on a plan of action.

In *The Witness*, where Powell plays a lawyer defending a client accused of murder, long takes are again in evidence. An entire sequence in the lawyer's apartment uses panning and a travelling sideways to sustain a conversation in one shot. Aldrich further anticipates the style of his features using jarring cuts to high or low angles to underline the drama of the moment. When protagonist Donegan visits his client in jail and the tormented victim wrongfully accused of robbery tells his woeful tale, Aldrich cuts to a high angle at the level of the roof which leaves the two men crisscrossed by the shadow of the bars. Later during the trial, Donegan repeatedly objects to the prosecutor's methods. Each objection is framed from a low angle adding physical impact to the ironic humor of the scene.

Opposite, Hammer (Ralph Meeker) interrupts Velda's (Maxine Cooper) workout.

In *The Bad Streak* and *The Gift*, both of which starred Charles Boyer, Aldrich opted for a straightforward, uncluttered staging free of stylistic embellishment to concentrate on theme and characterization. In the former episode, Rennick is a stone-faced, fatalistic gambler. Unlike Dante, Rennick has resigned himself to his up-and-down lifestyle, in which his financial security is nightly at risk in his own club: "The way the cards fall, that's the way you have to play them." He is also a fiercely independent man, like so many of Aldrich's future protagonists, who is being squeezed out by "syndicate" interests. In an early example of the game as a metaphor, Aldrich stresses the elements of survival and tenacity in the face of overwhelming odds.

Even the untimely arrival of his son into the scene when the bad streak has put him on the brink of insolvency—a son who is determined to break his father at the gambling tables in revenge for "deserting him"—does not shake Rennick's existential outlook: "A gambler loses everything. What is one son, more or less?" In an early variant of the quasi-Oedipal conflicts that would key *Autumn Leaves*, *The Garment Jungle*, and *Hush...Hush, Sweet Charlotte*, Rennick's son issues a challenge that cannot be ignored. As a tight two shot holds his father in profile in the left foreground, Rennick's son calls him "a cheap tin horn." "He accused me of being a tin horn," Rennick explains when his girl friend cannot understand why he is risking everything; "I can't have him think me a coward now, can I?" A fateful high angle looks down on the gaming table, as Rennick wins back his casino from his son while teaching him a lesson about the dangers of gambling. His reward for this begrudging act of fatherly care is his son's continued antipathy: "You taught me one thing. I hate gamblers."

In a final act of compassion, Rennick gives back the money he won from his son, breaking himself financially in the process. "It's all over, all over," he says stoically as he leaves the club he once owned. But as with most Aldrich survivors he does not give up. As the episode ends, the viewer finds him back in front of a slot machine, once again "at the table" and risking his future.

The Garment Jungle

Made near the end of the *noir* cycle, *The Garment Jungle* reflects the evolution of the *noir* viewpoint. Although Aldrich was not permitted to "harden" the film or even to finish shooting and assemble the approved script, his visualization is as precise as in *Kiss Me Deadly*. Unlike Mike Hammer, the protagonist of *The Garment Jungle*, Alan Mitchell, is not hard-boiled. Like many characters from the classic period of *film noir*, Mitchell has recently returned from a war and, as he readjusts to society, is an uncertain and ineffective figure. He is bullied in turn by his father, his father's hired thug, and Renata, the union organizer. It is Renata who draws Mitchell from the refuge of Roxton fashions. There sustained shots and full-lit settings create an aura of stability. Renata's is a less privileged, darker universe, which both fascinates and repels Mitchell. As his consciousness of how his father does business is raised, Aldrich alters the visual scheme and uses more low angles with top light and side light that cast irresolute shadows on the protagonists' faces.

The association with Renata also exposes Mitchell to the ire of Artie Ravidge, a cheap strong-arm guy whose white teeth flashing between pock-marked cheeks personify the face of the *noir* underworld. This clichéd, quasi-satirical characterization satisfies the expectations of Mitchell's liberal sensitivities. Ravidge's habit of keeping people at a distance with the tip of a burning cigarette is more the effete gesture of a cheap hood than it is truly menacing.

The conflicting forces at work in the narrative are embodied by a variety of stylistic devices, including Aldrich's favorite metaphor for sub-surface chaos, the ceiling fan. As Ravidge's henchmen close in on a union official, the low angle medium shot reveals a network of twisting shadows thrown by such a fan on all the surrounding walls. As the distracting play of light and severe angles inject instability into the frame, Ravidge's unpredictable violence does the same on a narrative level. The image of the black elevator shaft, down which Walter Mitchell's partner is pitched to his death at the film's beginning, hangs over *The Garment Jungle* and evokes the ever-present threat of annihilation with shuddering simplicity. Like so many *noir* figures, Alan Mitchell discovers that the battlefield can be close to home and that death, which takes Renata and his father, is always at hand.

Left, returning veteran Alan Mitchell (Kerwin Matthews, left) questions the business methods of his father, Walter (Lee J. Cobb).

The final sequence in which Mitchell physically defeats Ravidge is not a resolution of the social problem. When he takes over for his father, Mitchell himself is quickly subsumed by the undertow of business demands. Perhaps, in existential terms, his liberal persona will be annihilated by them just as thoroughly as it might have been by Ravidge. The film ends sardonically on a shot of a Roxton Fashions telephone operator, as she mechanically switches lines and informs callers that "Mr. Mitchell is busy."

Hustle

Phil Gaines represents the prototypical neo-*noir* figure, a contemporaneous character whose "old-fashioned" beliefs are rooted in the classic era of *film noir* from 1940 to 1955. He is, in the manner of many "dark" heroes, fundamentally disillusioned with the course of his life's work and the system that supports it. "Don't you know what country you live in?" Gaines asks; "Can't you smell the bananas? You live in Guatemala with color television."

Below, in the morgue Marty Hollinger (Ben Johnson, left) identifies the body of his daughter for Detectives Belgrave (Paul Winfield, center) and Gaines (Burt Reynolds).

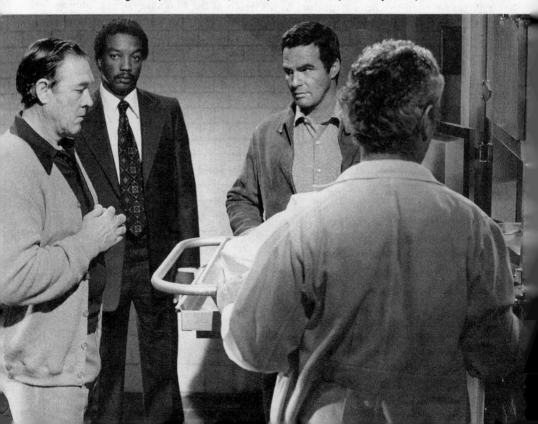

While Gaines' view may seem more introspective and less violent than that of such contemporary fellow cops as "Dirty Harry" Callahan, his painful awareness of the impermanence of both social institutions and personal relationships is characteristic of neo-*noir*. He tries to detach himself emotionally from both his job and his lover, the high-priced call girl, Nicole; but he understands how impossible that is. His jealousy over Nicole's profession and his outrage over the fact that "everybody hustles" are manifestations of a companion neo-existential despair over loss of influence or control.

As much or more than in any of his classic period *noir* films, Aldrich keys the mise-en-scene to the protagonist's alienated point of view. The initial sequence in Gaines and Nicole's home is remarkably diffracted. It begins with an aerial shot that moves in, then there are two cuts which pull back, and finally another cut into a close-up of Nicole's face. The color and details of the setting are attenuated by the high contrast and hard edge in the lighting. The dialogue between the couple is mostly in close shots, which isolate them visually from each other. When two shots are used, they are framed tightly, so constricted that they cut off the foreheads. Gaines' expensive home is made to seem unattractive and claustrophobic, even as he is visually distanced from the woman with whom he lives. The first shots of Gaines' office, after he has been knocked down by the distraught father, Hollinger, in the morgue, reveal an even less appealing locus: dark, grimy cubicles separated by cracked partitions of frosted glass and illuminated by a few traces of filtered sunlight which cannot dispel the pervasive shadows.

Where Harry Callahan takes to the streets in search of confrontation and catharsis, Gaines retreats from oppressive realities into himself. He is openly nostalgic: "I like the 30s, Cole Porter, Dizzy Dean," which suggests the same fallen romanticism of another Callahan in *World for Ransom*. Gaines is not inured to the violence of the world, not even when he administers a coup de grâce to a homicidal mental patient, so that the man will never be allowed to go free again. Gaines adopts metaphors for this violence, his favorite being the movie version of *Moby Dick*. If Gaines does see himself as Ahab, driven mad by his own moral outrage, he must also see himself reflected in the felons and psychopaths, who wage their own war against society and the system. For a street cop in the context of neo-*noir*, there may be an emotional equation between self and other; each action against the social outcasts may reflectively become an action against the underpinnings of his own persona. By the time Nicole comes home to find him watching *Moby Dick* on television and crouched in the shadows like Charlie Castle in *The Big Knife*, the myths have begun to lose their therapeutic value for Gaines. He begins a *noir* transference with the pitiful Marty Hollinger.

Hollinger, the Korean War vet still afflicted by shell shock, has already been identified with Gaines in visual and narrative terms. The balanced framing between the two men as they stand beside the body of Hollinger's daughter in the morgue is carried over into matching shots of the two men, from a low angle with side light, in their respective homes. The memories of an ostensibly happier past for both men are incorporated into the film as brief flashbacks. Gaines' lover routinely "betrays" him with other men, and he knows that Hollinger's wife has betrayed him as well. Finally, both men share a hatred of smooth, syndicate attorney Leo Sellars. Gaines' hatred stems from the belief that Sellars corrupted Nicole. Hollinger holds Sellars responsible for his daughter's involvement in syndicated-controlled pornographic film production, which led to her death. While Hollinger's hatred of Sellars is purely vindictive, Gaines also regards the attorney as a symbol of the "darkness and corruption" in the system itself. When Sellars asks him, "Why single me out?" Gaines replies simply, "I can't get everyone."

Through his surrogate, Hollinger, Gaines does get Sellars; but the death of his antagonist cannot be without moral consequence. After Gaines and his partner make it seem as if Hollinger killed the attorney in self-defense, the transference of responsibility is complete. Gaines carries that into a liquor store where he happens upon a robbery and is gunned down. The anonymity of Gaines' killer is central to the *noir* irony of *Hustle*. Like so many *noir* protagonists from the classic period, Gaines perishes in an existential affirmation of his despair. Unlike Harry Callahan, Gaines cannot dismiss the consequences of his actions. In killing Sellars, he destroys the last vestige of his own faith in the system which employs him to enforce its laws. Whether or not Gaines has a moment of realization before dying about the causes of his destruction is less significant than the event itself. The decisions to cover up Sellars' killing and to confront the armed robber are simultaneously actions which affirm his existence and which cause him to perish.

Opposite top, Lt. Gaines (Burt Reynolds, right) happens upon an armed robber (Robert Englund) when he goes into a liquor store.

Opposite below, Sellars (Eddie Albert) and Nicole (Catherine Deneuve) aboard his yacht.

Chapter Six:

Sociopaths and the Hollywood Morphology

Aldrich's preoccupation with the "Hollywood" film— that is, a motion picture about Hollywood, the business and the filmmaking process—goes back to *The Big Knife*. It marginally encompasses *What Ever Happened to Baby Jane?* and *The Killing of Sister George* and ends with *The Legend of Lylah Clare* and the abortive *The Greatest Mother of 'Em All*. Many of the narrative and figurative patterns of these films are neither repetitive nor redundant; yet taken collectively they give evidence of a consistent cynicism regarding the film industry, particularly its executive and acting personnel. The "Gothic" or hysterical aspects of *What Ever Happened to Baby Jane?* and its attendant commercial success color much of Aldrich's subsequent work. It influenced the styles of both its informal sequel, *Hush...Hush, Sweet Charlotte*, and *The Legend of Lylah Clare*.

Melodramas dealing with the mentally ill are hardly a formal genre. While they share that theme and some actors, the differences within Aldrich's own work between *Autumn Leaves*, *What Ever Happened to Baby Jane?*, and *Hush...Hush, Sweet Charlotte* are considerable. Mental problems figure prominently in other films, through characters such as Maggott in *The Dirty Dozen*, Lyles in *The Choirboys*, Cobb in *The Flight of the Phoenix*, or even, it could be argued, Carver in *Kiss Me Deadly*. Still, Aldrich exploits genre expectations in both the Hollywood films and the melodramas to create larger-than-life characters without engendering viewer disbelief. It is this manipulation—as much as any personal belief Aldrich might have held about the sanity of those who work in the movie business—that tie these diverse films together.

193

Opposite, Aldrich directs Kim
Novak in *The Legend of Lylah Clare*.

I.

Autumn Leaves

Autumn Leaves is Aldrich's earliest foray into the female psyche. While his
"Hollywood morphology" films, *Lylah Clare* and *Baby Jane*, do feature
female protagonists as do *Hush...Hush, Sweet Charlotte* and *Sister George,*
the women are reduced to their iconic components, representing various
deviant behaviors. One need only consider the titles—"Baby Jane," "Sweet
Charlotte," or "Sister George"; one could even add "Aunt Alice"—in which
women are defined by their first names with a controlling adjective which
forms an expectation of how the characters will be portrayed. This is not to
say that men are not also subject to typing in Aldrich's work; certainly *The
Dirty Dozen* and *The Choirboys* suggest negative connotations before the film
even begins. But these are anonymous groups; the closest thing to a man's
name in any Aldrich title is the epithet, "The Frisco Kid." Other men are
celebrated before the fact with anonymous epithets from *The Big Leaguer* to
The Emperor of the North Pole; but only the women have names. As to Lylah
Clare, who is an enigmatic "Other," as the concept is defined in the work of
Julia Kristeva, she may be the most delusional of them all. At its root, *The
Legend of Lylah Clare* is about Pygmalion and a Galatea doppelgänger. What
more tangled combination of movies and madness could there be? Some
might assert that the only "normal" women who star in any Aldrich films are
the worst stereotypes of all, the female wrestlers in *...All the Marbles* and the
dowdy typist in *Autumn Leaves*. But in both instances the "type" is just a
shorthand from which Aldrich develops character and dramatic conflict.

There are no real "lunatics" in *Autumn Leaves*; the female protagonist loves a younger man who is mentally ill. For with the presence of star Joan Crawford and the stress on the anguished nature of her love, *Autumn Leaves* could be classed as "soap opera" or, alternately, a "women's film." In these contexts, Crawford's mere presence creates a particular genre expectation of a long suffering, dignified, matronly figure; but rather than fall back on those stereotypical possibilities, Aldrich searches for the heroic aspects of his middle-aged protagonist, Millicent Wetherby. The result is a subtle one, unlike Aldrich's other films of that period, and filled with contours of shadow and light, literally and figuratively.

The opening of the film sets the mood. It is a slow, lugubrious tracking shot, which glides through shadows into an apartment sign reading "Cedar Courts" and then continues through the Spanish colonial style courtyard towards one of the identical doors. Inside the tiny apartment sits Millicent working industriously at her typewriter. The scene which follows establishes through dialogue and visuals the repressed character of this woman. The scene, which eventually includes her friend Ivy and a customer, is lit in a chiaroscuro style typical of Aldrich's black and white films. Also typical is the deep focus and wide angle lenses, giving Aldrich enough space to array the significant items in his mise-en-scene. In this case, the composition visually reifies the narrow, isolated universe Millicent has constructed for herself. In the foreground of the claustrophobic space is a long table which crosses the frame horizontally. There Millicent sits surrounded by manuscripts and a cumbersome typewriter. By its position in the frame the table seems to trap Millicent behind her machine, adding even more to the claustrophobia of the space.

Like that table which limits her movement forward in the frame, Millicent has foreclosed any forward movement in her life. Through the expository dialogue the audience learns that she has rarely dated men or even gone out with friends. With Millicent apparently buried in her womb-like apartment, the viewers plainly understands Liz's friendly criticism: "Maybe you're just plain scared."

Millicent's outlook is further externalized by the expressionistic staging of a flashback sequence at a concert. It opens on a medium long shot of Millicent in the audience, wistfully staring into space, obviously inspired by the emotional piano concerto being played on stage. As the camera moves in on her, the lights around her fade out, and another scene replaces that of the concert. In it only Millicent's torso and legs are visible moving around a room, but her voice reveals her identity to the audience. The viewer hears her as she breaks off with her fiancé over the telephone in order to take care of her sick father. This caretaker role, which she will assume again with Burt, her eventual lover and husband, puts her in a position of subservience. The flashback ends and

Opposite, Joan Crawford as Millicent Wetherby sits at her neatly arrayed desk pondering her chaotic marriage.

as Millicent exits the concert hall, the camera cranes back to underline her insignificance and loneliness in the crowd of pedestrians.

Her first encounter with Burt further confirms her timidity and isolation. She initially resists his aggressive attempts to "open her up" by bluntly asserting, "You know something? You're lonely." In this exchange, power is securely in the hands of the male, which Aldrich underscores with the shot selection of aggrandizing low angles for him and diminishing high angles for her.

After Millicent finally succumbs to the blandishments of her young lover, Aldrich moves the narrative to the next stage: woman as victim. *Autumn Leaves* is the only film in which Aldrich reflects extensively on the effects of male violence, not on other males, but on women. Burt exercises his patriarchal prerogative immediately after they first meet. He demonstrates his dominance over her by forcing his way into her life even though she objects over and over again. He initiates the male courting ritual very traditionally by bringing her gifts, which he has stolen from the store where he works. He also compliments her somewhat disingenuously on her youthful looks, even though an earlier scene before a mirror in a beach cabana had confirmed Millicent's fears about her spreading, middle-aged figure. When all this fails to win her over, he retreats into the "little boy lost" role and plays upon her sympathies by telling her of the young girls he dated and how they could not measure up to her. Ultimately, of course, he wins. After all, how can a 1950s woman resist this "prince on a white horse," about whom society conditions young girls and older women alike to dream.

This dream, punctuated by an idyllic Mexican honeymoon, becomes a nightmare as Millicent receives a visit from Burt's ex-wife, Virginia. Virginia is pretty, young, glowing, dressed all in white. She sits in the living room across from Millicent, whose face and body are crisscrossed by ominous shadows making her look older than she is, and tells her that her new husband is a liar, a thief, and a neurotic. After Virginia leaves, the camera tracks into Millicent as she looks furtively about the room like a trapped animal, waiting for the return of her sociopathic husband. What Burt has been to ashamed to confide in Millicent is that he divorced Virginia when he discovered her sexual affair with his own father.

Burt's program of psychological manipulation culminates in an act of sadistic, physical violence. Believing Millicent to be involved in a conspiracy with his ex-wife and his father, Burt pushes her to the floor. In shocking close-up he smashes her hand with the tool of her trade, her typewriter. Aldrich's cut to a shot of Burt's smiling face recalls the two shots of the morgue attendant's hand caught in the drawer and a smiling Hammer in *Kiss Me Deadly*. The difference, of course, is that Hammer is ostensibly normal, and Burt is a man who clearly needs help.

Opposite, Millicent (Joan Crawford) gives motherly comfort
to her manic husband, Burt (Cliff Robertson).

As happens in so many cases of battered women, Millicent does not report Burt but tries instead to "mother" him back to mental health. Burt's response is to become more and more withdrawn. One night he awakens in the throes of a recurring nightmare. He falls tearfully into her lap, and they assume the classic pieta pose, reinforcing the mother-child analogy. In current parlance Millicent and Burt have become co-dependents, bound to each other by need.

Both Burt and Millicent's problems reside within the nexus of the Oedipal triangle. Millicent gave up her love life to take care of her father, as underscored in flashback, while Burt is obsessed with the image of his father and wife in bed together. This is an image the audience sees repeated when Burt discovers his father and ex-wife's love nest. As he slumps in the foreground of the shadowy hotel corridor, in deep focus in the background is the quasi-incestuous couple's rumpled bed. Together Millicent and Burt have repeated their original traumatic experiences. She takes care of yet another father-son, he runs to the arms of a surrogate for his absent mother.

In order to find redemption both Millicent and Burt must cut their parental ties. As the psychiatrist tells Millicent, "He has to grow up...I expect you have the necessary strength to act." She does find that strength. While Burt cries like a child in the background, she gathers her courage and grabs the oversized phone in the foreground of this deep focus shot. When two burly men in white arrive to drag Burt away kicking and screaming, Aldrich intercuts Burt bellowing, "You did this. I'll get you" with close-ups of Millicent's conflicted expression.

Adlrich's depiction of the therapeutic process which eventually leads to Burt's recovery is purposely designed to be shocking and uncomfortable for the viewer. In a montage the audience sees assorted images: Burt biting down on a rubber tube as his body endures spasms from electro-shock therapy; an intravenous bottle in the foreground as a dazed Burt stares into space in the background; repeated therapy sessions with the doctor. As if to connect Millicent psychically to this therapy, Aldrich intercuts shots of her crying in the night, visually linking Burt's recovery with her own. Only through separation and suffering can these two neurotic individuals transform themselves into self-actuated adults.

The resolution of the film is handled with understatement, a rare mode in Aldrich's dramas, but necessary for the positive ending not to seem forced. Millicent and Burt meet in the gardens of the sanitarium. She is intent on setting him free now that he is "recovered." The camera favors her as she nervously rattles off a speech about her intentions. He listens patiently, respectfully, but finally he speaks, asking to rejoin her, not out of gratitude or out of neurotic need, but out of genuine love.

Hush...Hush, Sweet Charlotte

Hush...Hush, Sweet Charlotte was clearly conceived as an informal sequel to What Ever Happened to Baby Jane?; but, in addition to its production problems, the development of the script refocused it somewhat. The setting is an antebellum Southern manse which does bear an uncanny resemblance to the *Baby Jane* house. More than its filmic predecessor, this house is a descendant of gloomy castles and mansions of Gothic fiction from Walpole and Mary Shelley through the Sisters Brontë and Poe. As in *Baby Jane,* the characters of *Hush...Hush, Sweet Charlotte* are drawn from Gothic fiction, types who are psychological ciphers for sundry neurotic and/or psychotic disorders. Whereas the mystery of who was responsible for Blanche's condition was subsumed within Jane's insane plotting, the mystery involving the murder of Charlotte's lover, the solution of which is only revealed in the final minutes of the film, is more central to *Hush...Hush, Sweet Charlotte.* The visual style of the film is, like *Baby Jane,* a cinematic analog for the melodramatic prose of both films' literary antecedents: moody, filled with images of evil, doom, and decay.

The mansion in which the characters of this film reside is really not simply a setting. It is as much a character as any human in the film. Like the typical sites of Gothic literature, it provides a dimly lit, compartmentalized environment within which the characters can work out their psychological destinies. Houses such as these, as Freud pointed out in his essay "The Uncanny," are primal areas, substitutes for the womb, where individuals wrestle with their basic inner conflicts.

As in most primal struggles, the figure of the Oedipal father dominates. It begins with the first jump cuts of the exterior of the mansion, where the voice of Big Sam Hollis reverberates as he berates John Mayhew, the married lover of

his daughter Charlotte, for the "theft" of his beloved child. Big Sam's incestuous rage will influence all the future actions of his daughter and his niece, Miriam, whom he has adopted as a second daughter.

This incident precipitates the mutilation and murder of John Mayhew, for which Charlotte is blamed and which leaves her a recluse as well as an object of pity and terror. Big Sam's image also looms over Charlotte's nightmare, as decidedly as

Right, Charlotte Hollis (Bette Davis) poses by her father's grave in a child's dress and pigtails.

his intimidating portrait looms over the house. In fact, in one dream they are transposed. In a high-contrast dream repetition of the formal ball seen in the prologue, during which John is murdered, Charlotte watches her lover approaching. He touches her hand and the dance begins. Soon, however, the hulking figure of her father enters. He pushes John back. Then suddenly the camera angle adjusts to reveal that Big Sam is headless and missing a hand, mutilated just like Mayhew was. Revolted by this incestuous transposition, Charlotte shoots the "phantom" father but cannot escape his psychic influence. Even Charlotte's costumes and hair style confirm her fixation on her father. She still wears pigtails and white crinoline dresses, very much like the "little girl" Big Sam adored.

Big Sam also leaves his imprint on the antagonist of the story, Miriam. She is driven to torture her cousin Charlotte with images and sounds from her past. The music Mayhew wrote becomes the theme "Hush...Hush, Sweet Charlotte," and it echoes through the house just as he played it on the piano. There are other unexplained anomalies: a cleaver, flowers, and a mutilated hand on the hardwood floor as the French doors mysteriously swing open; her lover's decapitated head rolling down the stairs; poison pen letters written by supposedly anonymous hands. Miriam tortures Charlotte not only out of greed for the inheritance Big Sam left but also out of "sibling" rivalry for the affections of the father she never truly had. Miriam tries to hide her true feelings from the other characters and from the audience with words of concern and sympathy for her cousin. But periodically her dark side emerges, as when she tells Charlotte, "I'm never going to suffer for you again!" Only Velma the servant sees through Miriam. "You're finally showing the right side of your face," she remarks, just before Miriam smashes a chair over her and brutally kicks her down the stairs.

As in *What Ever Happened to Baby Jane?* and many other, non-Gothic films, Aldrich periodically tests the boundaries between objective and subjective points of view. In this film the disturbances center on whether or not the sounds and images from Charlotte's past—the mutilated body parts, the theme played on the piano, the disembodied voice calling her name, etc.— are real or not. Initially Aldrich gives the spectator no clues. As no one else in the house seems to see or hear these occurrences, the audience is left to assume they are seeing the events from Charlotte's hysterical point of view, that is, subjectively through her eyes, the eyes of a demented recluse. Other characters may try to convince the viewer that she is not insane as when the Sheriff suggests that "she's not really sick. She just acts that way because people expect it." But the "tangible" facts contradict their claims.

Not until the dream sequence at the ball does Aldrich alter the staging to push the audience out of Charlotte's mind and into an objective posture. By using extreme high-contrast images and an halation effect around the charac-

Previous, Miriam Deering (Olivia de Havilland, left) is disturbed by the words of her Cousin Charlotte (Bette Davis).   Opposite, a middle-aged Charlotte (Bette Davis) imagines dancing with her young lover, John Mayhew (Bruce Dern), in a dream sequence.

ters' bodies, Aldrich gives the viewer the visual cues which signify something "unreal" and which consequently cast doubt on all that has been seen through Charlotte's eyes. To settle the confusion, Aldrich finally reveals the "plot": Miriam and her lover, Dr. Drew, have planted the macabre objects and created the melancholy sounds in order to drive Charlotte mad.

The ending of *Hush...Hush, Sweet Charlotte* strongly foreshadows the resolutions of two other Aldrich films, *The Legend of Lylah Clare* and *The Grissom Gang*. Like those later films, *Hush...Hush, Sweet Charlotte* disparages media exploitation. One of the most unsympathetic characters in the film is the reporter from the "true crime" magazine. Charlotte's story in the magazine is called "Crimes of Passion" and features a lurid cover with the subtitle "no head, no hand." The reporter sneaks around her house, invading Charlotte's privacy as he snaps pictures of the frightened woman. The scene is subjectified to demonstrate Charlotte's terror through a quick montage of close-ups of her screaming intercut with reverse angles of flash bulbs going off like gun shots.

Even after Charlotte has "dispatched" her tormentors in the climax of the film by toppling a gigantic urn down onto Miriam and her lover, the exploitation continues to the final minutes of the film. As the police take the now subdued Charlotte away and she learns that it was her lover's wife who actually murdered him, reporters still hound her and the town gossips create even more outrageous stories about the tortured woman. Like the growling dogs at the end of *Lylah Clare* or the crowd of reporters in *The Grissom Gang*, media relentlessly hounds its subjects, no matter their guilt or innocence. Or as the insurance investigator says, in summing up the irony of the film, "Charlotte Hollis suffered all her life for a murder she never committed."

II.

The Big Knife

Much of the invective of *The Big Knife* derives from the original Odets play. The film does add a quasi-satirical dimension in scenes such as those with Rod Steiger's blubbering, unbalanced Stanley Hoff crying to Jack Palance's reluctant movie star, Charlie Castle, "Charlie, Charlie...the pain of this moment!" But the overall effect of the portrayals is an ensemble not only of Hollywood's clichés about itself but also of prototypical Aldrich gargoyles. The unabashed theatrics, the drum rolls at dramatic moments, the wildly expressive dialogue—"You came in here and threw this mess of naked pigeons in my face!"—create the vulgarity and hysteria which are inherent to Aldrich's stylized, personal interpretation of "tinsel town."

For Charlie Castle the Hollywood dream resolves itself into an oppressive universe, at least partially of his own making. Insulated in his California ranch-style home, he is surrounded by a host of dependents, which include his trainer, Nick; his wife and son; his aging agent, Nat; and Buddy Bliss, who took the blame for Charlie in a car accident. There are also his demons, embodied by studio head Hoff, modeled physically and emotionally after Columbia's Harry Cohn, and Hoff's flunkey, Smiley Coy. But mostly Charlie is plagued by his own guilt at his lack of integrity. Aldrich's extreme angles and short lenses distort the perspectives of Charlie's world, externalizing the frenzy of his viewpoint. Charlie constantly seeks shelter, roaming around his spacious house like a hunted animal until he finds an appropriate hiding place, behind a lamp, the rear of a sofa, etc. He deludes himself even further by seeking comfort in Romantic concepts of himself. "The warrior minstrel with the forlorn hope" is what Smiley Coy mockingly calls him, although Charlie misses the sarcasm. Alternately he is the clown in his Rouault painting. "He broods," Charlie notes self-reflexively; "I've been looking at it a lot lately." Unfortunately for Charlie he is neither of these abstractions. A more accurate and incisive analysis of his character is given by the narrator whose voice the audience hears over a montage of luxurious Bel Air mansions: "Charlie Castle is a man who sold out his dreams but can't forget them."

Besides being a man who has lost his integrity, Aldrich also presents his protagonist as a weak, childlike individual. Even though his size and physique mark him as an athlete, a perception reinforced when Charlie spars with Nick and by the fight sequence from one of his movies which he screens at his home, his cowering before Hoff and his numerous bouts of self-pity mark him as a dependent personality: "All my life I've yearned for people to bring out the best in me." While discussing his contract with his agent, Charlie reacts

Opposite, two angry confrontations between Charlie Castle (Jack Palance, right) and Stanley Hoff (Rod Steiger) with very different results.

frenziedly. That frenzy is soothed by the attentions of his trainer, Nick. Charlie is left spent, as his head in low angle projects from the edge of the massage table and his agent looms in the background.

Even Charlie's wife, who knows him best and upon whom he most depends, cannot resist telling him to "grow up before it's too late." His emotional dependency is most clearly defined in his second confrontation with Hoff. This time he is accompanied by his wife, drawing strength from her visually and emotionally as she sits by his side during the psychological battle with the overbearing Hoff. He demonstrates some of the courage, to which the audience had only heard other characters refer, and refuses to go along with Hoff's nefarious plans for Dixie, a witness to Charlie's crime. As Hoff begins to rant and rave, spraying the room with saliva, Charlie rushes at him in his own rage. The terrified Hoff, his arms protecting his face, curls into a ball. In a single cut the emotional dynamics of the scene are altered. Charlie looms in the foreground, with the camera over his shoulder, while Hoff cringes in the background. Charlie Castle has found a moment of glory.

This scene in which Charlie stands up to Hoff for the first time acts as a counterbalance to his earlier meeting with the studio head, which, typical of Charlie, was filled with anxiety and self-delusion. Charlie began that first meeting resolute in his decision not to sign with Hoff for another seven years. Emotionally, Charlie is trapped in the patriarchal psychology of the old-style studio system which Hoff represents. In an even earlier sequence, Charlie's wife had asked him directly, "What do you believe in now?" That question echoed a similar query by the Hedda Hopper-like columnist to which Charlie had answered in an offhanded manner, "Health." Charlie knows that mental or emotional health as an artist and a husband is impossible until he is free of Hoff. With the threat of his wife's permanent departure hanging over his head, Charlie confronted Hoff and tried to maintain an equal footing with the studio boss. He stood while Hoff sat giving him a dominant position in the frame. His words were self-assured. And when all those present finally sat, the characters were arranged in the frame as equals: Hoff and his assistant Smiley on the left and Charlie and his agent on the right.

Notwithstanding, after Charlie told the initially agreeable Hoff about his decision not to re-sign, his confidence in himself as an artist and a man began to break. Soon Charlie was sitting as Hoff stood over and browbeat him. Charlie even turned his back to Hoff and then clutched a pillow to his stomach as if to smother some deep pain. Visually the elements of the framing shifted so that the foreground and background became constricting rather than concealing. Charlie could only take the easy way out. Forced to realize he was neither the clown nor the medieval minstrel which he imagined and that he could not es-

Opposite, Stanley Hoff (Rod Steiger, left) stands over a beaten Charlie Castle (Jack Palance), who signs a new contract while Smiley Coy (Wendell Corey) and Charlie's agent Nat Danziger (Everett Sloane, right) look on.

cape the real world, Charlie ended the scene literally on his knees and signing a contract for another seven years.

Aldrich saw Charlie's suicide as a triumph; and the dramatic context he creates reinforces this view. Charlie must either submit to Hoff's blackmail or face ruin. Presented with two unacceptable alternatives, he steps around both of them by choosing to end his life. In existential terms, it is the ultimate affirmation of control over one's own destiny. For most existential figures, life as it is provides the key to understanding self and the freedom to act. For Charlie Castle, the "movie star," only at the studio, with its connotations of fictional existences and false settings, is life real. At the studio there is visual and figurative continuity to Charlie's life. Among the painted flats and artificial daylight he is at ease. The fluid motion which follows him at eye level on the sound stage captures the sense of barriers being removed. Yet even then, there is an underlying tension in the sustained shot that follows Charlie and his rival for Marion's affections, Hank, as it moves through the sound stage and ends at the dressing room. The long take, which impends a cut or visual break at any given moment, parallels Charlie's emotional situation on the edge of a breakdown.

The final craning shot of the film after Charlie's suicide, up out of the set and into the heights of the actual sound stage on which *The Big Knife* was filmed, completes the metaphor. The Charlie who has suffered existential anguish and taken his own life is, after all, just a character in a movie. As the camera moves back and back piercing the imaginary fourth wall and ceiling of the set, it creates a sardonic afterthought: "Hollywood" life is not, figuratively or literally, a real life. It is not lived but only acted out in an empty search for stage center with darkness surrounding.

What Ever Happened to Baby Jane?

Charlie Castle's way out is suicide. Jane Hudson's is madness. Strictly speaking, *What Ever Happened to Baby Jane?* is less a film about Hollywood's mentality than about Jane's aberrant behavior, for her psychoses initiate its action. Still the film has much to say, explicitly and implicitly, about Hollywood. *What Ever Happened to Baby Jane?* introduces the component of time into the "Hollywood breakdown." Charlie Castle's nightmare is of unspecified duration. It retains the open-ended time and action, or the condensation of them, that the original had on stage. *What Ever Happened to Baby Jane?* has neither this suspended quality nor any stated temporal point of view, as for instance the structuring via a flashback from a particular character in *Sunset Boulevard.* Substituted for time scheme or specific character perspective is an overall sequential scheme, which breaks the film into acts or scenes. There are several more than a classic five, and each ends with a kind of visual curtain.

The temporal organization is rooted in the two pre-title flashbacks which constitute a rough prologue. Situating these scenes before the titles and super-imposing years (1917 and 1935 respectively) as each begins accentuates the sense of separation from the rest of the narrative. In other words, *What Ever Happened to Baby Jane?* does not begin as a period film and come forward. The viewer is not expected to see these early scenes as present time—they remain past within the context of both audience reality and film reality. Aldrich uses both genre expectation and the viewer's presumed awareness of the film's aged female stars to make these scenes flashbacks, because there are no characters or situations yet established from whose perspective to "flash back," only the assumption of contemporaneous action. The assumption that the audience makes, that Jane has caused Blanche's paralysis, depends on these scenes. They must be flashbacks—that is, representing a point of view that turns out to be in error—to permit the film's final plot twist.

Present time is broken down into standard sequences, but there are no standard referents to give it continuity or flow. Rather, within the dual points of view of Jane's obsessive madness and Blanche's captivity, time—or, more specifically, the passage of it—loses meaning. It is suspended or subsumed into the antagonistic framework of the narrative. Suspense itself is the factor which serves to accelerate the film's dynamic line, as Jane's succession of absences from the house are interposed with Blanche's attempts at escape. This creates a series of plot-frustrating anticlimaxes, which are frustrating or anticlimactic only in the sense of impeding the movement towards denouement.

The "past" which forms the prologue continues to encroach on the present in the form of Blanche's old movies on television or grotesque reenactments of her childhood routines. The narrative itself has assumed the structure of a trap. As Blanche's escape attempts end in recapture, she begins to understand that she is just part of Jane's twisted "scenario." The viewer, who is aware from the genre cues that Blanche's continued imprisonment is more likely than freedom, co-experiences her sense of confinement not only through normal empathy but also via the dynamics of plot-time.

The narrative organization of *What Ever Happened to Baby Jane?* is a closed system: the expectations of escape for Blanche and the viewer gradually diminish and change to one of death. The final irony—after the physical

Above, Jane (Bette Davis) and the unconscious Blanche (Joan Crawford).

Following pages, two prisoners: Blanche, behind iron bars, and Baby Jane, trapped in her own dementia.

and emotional restraints of the old dark house throughout the film—is the shift to the beach, which is expansive, sunlit, windswept, for the last scene. Aldrich's visual style supports and directs these closed and ironic aspects of the narrative. The extremes of angle and the foreground clutter are as always indicators of instability. Shots such as the overhead of Blanche spinning helplessly around in her wheel chair have multiple, expressive implications, from that of a bug in a jar or under a microscope to the claustrophobic sense of walls closing in or impeding her on four sides. All these readings reinforce the sensations of entrapment and desperation.

Interior lighting is not oppressively low-key. Rather the rectangles of daylight thrown on the walls of Blanche's room by the windows constantly restate the proximity of an exterior and of freedom. There are instances where the lighting scheme is markedly artificial or unnatural: the low light which intensifies the grotesquerie of Jane's "baby" make-up of white powder and rouge over wrinkled, sagging skin or the row of stage lights framed in the immediate foreground while Jane dances in low angle medium shot. In these scenes, the lighting serves to create an almost carnival atmosphere, a visual garishness appropriate to the inner workings of Jane's dementia.

Aldrich's use of depth in *What Ever Happened to Baby Jane?* does not allow the viewer to select a plane of action on which to focus. It is, on the contrary, a restrictive device. The telephone in the foreground as Blanche crawls down the stairs provides an objective or ironic view of the action. The phone seems to remain the same distance from her in lateral space while she moves vertically down the stairs. The movement is, in reality, a diagonal one, but the angle flattens it out. As the telephone is emblematic of freedom in Blanche's mind, its constant distance from her makes a statement about that freedom's inaccessibility. It is at once subjective or emanating from her mental state *and* objective or physically detached from her viewpoint. This contrasts with the singularly subjective expression of her struggle created by the use of hand-held medium close shots and wide angle lenses, which cause the frame to distort and shake with a convulsive quality. Depth provides a constant referent to the external stability outside the house.

The suspense in *What Ever Happened to Baby Jane?* derives not just from intercutting and other standard devices but also from the character constant of Baby Jane herself. Jane subconsciously knows that her frustration and repressed violence are attempts to ward off annihilation as evidenced in her plaintive query, "Whatever happened to Baby Jane Hudson?" Jane is alternately a child when she retreats into fantasy and a parent in her domination of Blanche. As usual, the angularity and constriction which Aldrich introduces into the motion picture's frames underscore the character tensions, in this case the aura of unpredictable and irrational behavior projected by Jane, and ex-

Opposite, Baby Jane Hudson (Bette Davis) practices for her comeback with the help of Edwin Flagg (Victor Buono).

ternalize their imbalanced and constricted emotional states. The garishness of the film may then represent a stylistic extreme or extravagance that also reflects those tensions and emotional states. In this sense, Jane's madness literally and figuratively controls the entire film.

Aldrich uses subtle ambiguity to sustain the plot contrivance in which Blanche is ultimately revealed to be responsible for her own injury. Obviously the scenes of the imperious Jane and long-suffering Blanche as children suggest that Blanche has been the reasonable and generous sibling all along. After the accident, there is a brief discussion between the producer and director on the studio lot that poses an uncertain question: "What do they make monsters like that for?" Is it a reference to Blanche's car or to Jane? In the end Jane's macabre make-up and Blanche's cadaverous death by attrition are apt vulgarizations, for Jane is still an infantile psychotic and Blanche is revealed to have been a vindictive melancholic. In the end the very "Gothicness" of *What Ever Happened to Baby Jane?* is entirely apt. It represents the characters' emotional thrashing against a closed narrative and underscores their psychological aberrations as well.

Above, Kim Novak as the legendary Lylah Clare.

The Legend of Lylah Clare

In *What Ever Happened to Baby Jane?* only marginally does an exterior factor contribute to or color the essentially personal process of vulgarization One instance is the dog food commercial which interrupts the telecast of one of Blanche's old movies and its silly slogan: "When your dog says 'Woof, woof.'" In *The Legend of Lylah Clare*, *The Killing of Sister George*, and *The Greatest Mother of 'Em All*, that process is defined both by and through factors which are substantially exterior.

To begin at the end, the final freeze frame of *The Legend of Lylah Clare* figuratively recapitulates the entire narrative which has preceded and contributed to it. The immediate context is another dog food commercial. It could be said that it is introduced by the same unnamed, ungracious announcer/character as in *Baby Jane*, because the same actor (Michael Fox) plays the part. Clearly for Aldrich, there was something in this actor's smirking expression that connoted crassness. In *Lylah Clare* Aldrich dissolves away from him standing in the forecourt of Grauman's Chinese Theater to a close shot of a colorfully labelled container being spun in the whirring mechanism of a kitchen can opener. The lighting is flat and placid with little contour on the white surfaces but highlights on the metal parts of the counter-top and the cabinet latches, as if the advertisement were for a household cleanser. As a young woman spoons the brown semisolid dog food into a pastel dish, a cutaway reveals a dog door, and suddenly a competitor for the contents of the dish enters. Then another and another, until the room is filled with frenzied animals. A close-up isolates the woman backing away, terrified as the barks and growls around her reach a high intensity, climbing up on the counter to escape. From out of the pack, a large mongrel with bared fangs and a glassy eye lunges forward and is frozen in mid-action. Over this freeze frame, Lylah's theme is reprised and the end credits roll.

In some respects this one shot is Aldrich's severest, most cynical statement about survival, not just in the film industry, but in the world in general. What it says is that in any ordinary American kitchen, typified by its vinyl plastic fixtures and glo-coat shine, the underlying situation is, quite literally, dog eat dog. Obviously the moment is surreal. Certainly, the viewer knows that no commercial would be like this. Or would it? The underlying causality is hinted at in the advertisement itself. It is in the mechanization, in the can opener with its amplified sound reminiscent of the ominous growl of the "great whatsit" in *Kiss Me Deadly*. It is in the full-lit sterility, in the bright, glistening surfaces under high-key television-style lighting. But what stands out texturally is the absolute undercurrent of instability and chaos. A pack of feral pets runs amuck as inexplicably as the manic crows and gulls in Hitchcock's allegory *The Birds*.

With a venal, impatient tone, the reporter covering the premiere cuts off Zarkan's soul-searching remarks about Elsa to cue the commercial hype. It is followed by a sardonic juxtaposition of the rabid freeze frame with Lylah's theme music, which associates it with the deaths of Elsa Campbell/Lylah Clare. That original death which spawned the legend, had been sentimentalized, sensationalized, bowdlerized, and fantasized in the course of the film. All these elements are now brought together in a way that can only suggest the triumph of savagery and vulgarity.

The events in the "legend" of Lylah Clare do not encourage abstraction or depersonalization, that is, the viewer is not encouraged to regard the characters as unreal. Initially, all the people and many of the incidents of the film seem to be rooted in stock formulations or clichés. What disassociates these elements from stereotype is the establishment of a "set" relationship between characters and events.[1] Lylah herself is introduced in a pre-credit slide-show, dissected in a series of voiceovers and chance photographic remnants of her life. She is, in short, a legendary figure from the first. Elsa Brinkman, the soon-to-be "reincarnation" of Lylah, seems a star-struck novice. The bed of her apartment is littered with fan magazines, and she takes the tour of the sidewalk stars on Hollywood Boulevard during the credit sequence. Bart Langner is a self-described "lousy ten-percenter." Zarkan, Lylah's director and lover, is clearly a megalomaniac, with his "experiment in precision loading" in which he has a bullet fired at his chest or his mocking reference to "a second coming." Barney Sheean is just as clearly a despot: "I make movies and as long as I'm alive, there's only one boss." His son may sardonically remark, "You're never going to die, Pop," but Barney defiantly shouts back, "You're damn right!" And so on, each figure is seemingly locked into a fully-defined generic role or, at least, into a clearly typed one.

Such characterizations are separated from their "cliché" antecedents by their placement in the narrative framework. The narrative itself is fragmented into contradictory possibilities. For example, the entire film might be classed as a reincarnation fantasy or

Left, Zarkan (Peter Finch, left) and an interviewer (Michael Fox) at Grauman's Chinese.

a murder mystery, depending upon the individual viewer's interpretation. A key is the functional interaction of the characters with that framework. Neither of the narrative options just given as examples is eliminated because it is never expositionally clear whether Elsa is rational or mad, whether she merely continues to act at being Lylah off the set or is actually "possessed" by her.

As did *The Big Knife*, *The Legend of Lylah Clare* contains moments of self-conscious parody and stylization. The flashbacks to Lylah's death are a conspicuous instance of this. Employing a matte "cameo" of a mesmerized Elsa in the corner of the frame over black and white slow motion images, Aldrich adds such facetious touches as echoing voiceovers, a babel of facetious cries and whispers by an unseen chorus and a bright red blotch airbrushed onto the frame during the stabbing. Unlike *The Big Knife*, *The Legend of Lylah Clare* is neither pure satire nor pure melodrama, but a difficult integration of real and unreal.

With this contention of elements at the core of the film, characters and events tend to lose their literal meaning. Much more elaborately than with the secondary issue of who injured Blanche in *What Ever Happened to Baby Jane?*, real emotions and real events are clouded in ambiguity. At the center is the question of Elsa's true state of mind. Does *The Legend of Lylah Clare* consist of simple roles and fictional incidents, which would be a literal reading of the "drama"? Or are there roles within roles and fiction within fiction? Are Sheean, Langner, Zarkan et al. simply stock types or specific characterizations seeking refuge in the stock role?

It seems apparent from their words and actions that Elsa and Zarkan, at least, are not simpleminded stereotypes. Incidents in the film quite often combine for greater import than they have singly, much as wholes can be greater than the sum of the parts. But, since the elements are ambiguous, such questions depend on individual responses for an objective answer. Directly stated, the expressive components of *The Legend of Lylah Clare* begin by setting up

a "standard" genre expectation, then they go to consciously "excessive" lengths to frustrate and alter those expectations.

There are many cues to this besides the obvious remark by Molly Luther to Zarkan: "You're borrowing a little heavily from

Right, controlling the spin: Zarkan (Peter Finch) and Molly Luther (Coral Browne).

Sunset Boulevard aren't you, Lewis?" It is, of course, Aldrich and his collaborators and not Zarkan who are alluding to the history of Hollywood as fact
and as legend. Lylah Clare is neither Garbo nor *Sunset Boulevard*'s Norma
Desmond but a composite of all the real and imaginary stars of the past. The
acting, the decor, the word choice in the dialogue, even the color scheme and
optical effects, all reflect a self-consciousness on the part of the filmmakers,
who know that these are components of a "Hollywood" movie, a movie both
made in Hollywood and about Hollywood which is simultaneously archetype
and parody.[2]

The effect of this split is twofold. First, a certain amount of purposeful confusion is injected into the film, which compels the viewer to reflect on the basic
question of what is real and what is false just to maintain a proper orientation.
Rather than suspending disbelief, this reflection is part of the viewer's compre-
hension of the complex narrative. Second, a consistent narrative tension
based on this complexity and uncertainty is created and sustained up to and
even beyond Lylah's second death. The question of Zarkan's fate is left open
or "suspended" by the actual ending. Rosella, Lylah's lover and confidante,
seems to be waiting at his house to kill him. But Zarkan is himself a creation,
the role of Hollywood director assumed by the magician Louis Flack, the
"real" person he was before he became Zarkan. Can he or any of the characters within characters really die? Will his magic save him from Rosella? The
audience can readily view the life and death of these characters as circumscribed. Their fates are as fixed as that of Joe Gillis, floating face down in
Norma Desmond's pool at the beginning of *Sunset Boulevard* but still somehow capable of telling his story. As his final image, eighteen years after *Sunset
Boulevard*, for a shot of a mad, grimacing Norma Desmond walking forward
into her close-up Aldrich substitutes bared fangs.

Throughout *The Legend of Lylah Clare*, the informing or emphatic images
of the film are often group shots. Within that self-contained, compositional re-

ality figures may still be as decisively detached, alienated, or thrown off balance as if they were framed in a tilted, low angle close-up. There are fewer off-angles and less foreground clutter than might be termed "usual" for an Aldrich picture in *Lylah Clare*. As with *What Ever Happened to Baby Jane?* other than eye-level angles are reserved for the unusual or Gothic moments. One example is the mockingly imperial extreme low angle as Molly Luther bangs her cane twice on the floor.

There is also less depth, with figures often arrayed in a plane perpendicular to the camera. When it is visible through depth of focus, the background reveals more brilliant colors. It is an amply lit decor that is not normal but almost cartoonish in the way that it conforms to the viewer's stereotyped expectations of a Hollywood mansion. There is a stress on paintings and fixtures that don't linger in the rear ground but seem to "come forward" affecting the action in their own specific ways. A painting of Lylah, for example, may mean one thing when framed behind Zarkan and quite another when seen next to Elsa. The visual usage also affects viewer response to Zarkan. Initially, he is just a mute image on a slide; and his formal introduction as a character is delayed until considerable empathy has already been built up with Elsa. Even then Zarkan might compete for viewer identification, but the first shot of him, an eye-level glimpse of his partially silhouetted form as he sits in a swivel chair with his back to the camera, dissuades it. That shot presents no human features to counterbalance the alienating effect of his arrogant words.

In many respects, that same shot first suggests Zarkan as the mythic or figurative center of the film. To the instantaneous visual dichotomy between Zarkan past, the man in the slides, and present, the man in the scene with Bart, is added the later revelation that he was once a magician named Louis Flack.

Top of this page, Elsa (Kim Novak) and Zarkan (Peter Finch) as a silhouette. Opposite page, Zarkan slaps Rosella (Rosella Falk) beneath paintings of Lylah and Elsa/Lylah (Kim Novak) herself at the top of the stairs.

The implications of press-agentry and deception contained in that original name and occupation may not be as perilously clear as "Elsa *Brink*man," the former trapeze artist; but it does connote transformation and involvement with illusion going back a long way.

Zarkan is both congratulated and warned about his second chance: "You're getting a chance to live a part of your life all over again" and "Lewis, be careful with this girl.... Remember, it's not everyone who gets two chances." Zarkan himself calls the events which are to follow, as he stands with his arms outstretched as if crucified, "the second coming of Lewis Zarkan." Unquestionably Zarkan's inability to change is rooted in his own quasi-deific perception of himself. When Bart chides him saying that "you think you created her, can create her again," Zarkan notes curtly that "the public will continue to believe what we tell them." From his obsession with "precision" to his occasional use of the editorial "we," Zarkan is the stereotype of a director as controlling egomaniac.

Elsa as Elsa, the reserved young woman in horned-rim glasses who is almost frightened off by the dogs at Zarkan's gate, never really challenges this conception. Her own transformation into Lylah, real or surrogate, also requires a transformational relationship with Zarkan, a movement away from *his* notion of reality to *hers*. "You're an illusion," he tells her; "Without me you don't exist. You're nothing!" She can only respond by showing Zarkan to himself, to Louis Flack. "Look, you are God," Elsa shouts defiantly, while holding up a distorting make-up mirror to his face, "and I'm created in your image." At that point, with someone else controlling or dictating, that is, distorting, the quality of his magician's illusions, Zarkan's position is severely undercut. Elsa's—Lylah's—last words before shooting the trapeze scene also directly question Zarkan's control: "All right, Lewis, we will see if I am an illusion."

Zarkan's psychopathic or, at least, neurotic fixation, is on what is or is not true and who makes it so: "We make the legends and the legend becomes truth." He "murders" Lylah a second time in order to affirm that he is still in control but only proves that he never was. As Zarkan confesses to the television audience: "You make a terrible mistake, and your consolation is the thought that you've learned something. You gather up the courage to start over and learn that you make the same mistake all over again." In this sense Zarkan's second failure, coupled with his own exaggerated *hubris* or his vision of himself with a tragic flaw, completes the cycle of his own figurative death set up sometime in the indefinite past. Zarkan magically disappears both as man and as "god" when his electronic image and voice are replaced first by the Barkwell dog food commercial and then by the cha-cha version of Lylah's theme. Vulgarized as it may be, Lylah is the legend. Zarkan was just Louis Flack in disguise.

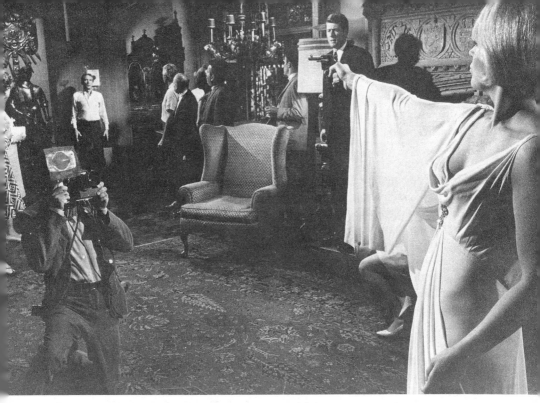

Above, an exercise in "precision loading": Elsa/Lylah (Kim Novak) takes aim at Zarkan "the Magician," while Mark Sheean (Michael Murphy) looks on. Below, Elsa and Zarkan meet young Sheean and his father, studio head Barney (Ernest Borgnine, left), for a power lunch at the Brown Derby.

The Killing of Sister George and The Greatest Mother of 'Em All

Aldrich followed *The Legend of Lylah Clare* with *The Killing of Sister George*, a film marginally about the film industry in that it focuses on a closeted lesbian who stars in a television series. Despite the many opportunities present in the narrative to underscore the vulgar and grotesque, Aldrich's adaptive style followed that of *The Big Knife* and let the characterizations speak for themselves. In *The Choirboys* the portrayal of gay men is from the perspective of the homophobic protagonists. In *The Killing of Sister George* there are no jokes about or mockery of the lesbians who are the film's protagonists.

The scene in which "George" and Alice go to a gay bar dressed as Laurel and Hardy is typical of Aldrich's staging. The couple gives their rather mediocre performance to an audience of women, some of them in male drag and others in traditional feminine apparel. They are applauded generously. When a slow dance begins, the camera pans across the faces of the couples who seem genuinely warm and affectionate, rather than lascivious or threatening. While lesbianism itself was certainly an atypical subject in 1968, the depiction is much more naturalistic than in many more recent and controversial productions such as Paul Verhoeven's *Basic Instinct*. Aldrich sees no threat to heterosexuality in George or her sisters. In his existential world view, these characters are just individuals trying "to make it through the night."

Aldrich does satirize the Hollywood way of doing things in the depiction of the pettiness and prejudice of the television industry in Great Britain. The same Hollywood hypocrisies and venalities are present: lack of artistic courage, Charlie Castle's great failing; subservience to box office returns or, in this case, ratings; betrayal which was so much a part of the emotional dynamics of the Hudson sisters in *Baby Jane* and in the Zarkan/Lylah/Elsa triad; and insincerity as earlier epitomized by Stanley Hoff.

The centerpiece of the film is the performance of Beryl Reid as June Buckridge, also known as "Sister George" after the successful television character which she created. In the opening sequence, Aldrich consciously manipulates iconic signifiers. He presents the audience with an aging, rotund, benign-looking woman with graying hair sitting at a bar and joking good-naturedly with the bartender. Her amicable nature seems to epitomize what the BBC television viewers came to love in the character of "Sister George." Then accompanied by a dramatic burst of music, George leaves the bar after an angry conversation on the phone. In a montage of shots, under the titles, she is shown walking forthrightly, even angrily, in a mannish dress suit and with a decidedly "masculine" gait, through the streets of London. Her manner now

Opposite, "Childie" (Susannah York, right) and "George" (Beryl Reid) in their Laurel and Hardy costumes chat with another couple, Leslie and her girlfriend (Eileen Page, Julie Shaw).

contrasts markedly with her initial appearance. As the audience becomes uncertain about its perception of this character, Aldrich breaks that tension in the following scene between George and her "flat mate," Alice.

The relationship between George and Alice reflects a traditional view of lesbian couples. When the audience first sees Alice, also called "Childie," she is dressed in a "baby doll" nightgown. A pan also reveals rows of children's dolls lovingly preserved along the walls. Alice's youth, innocent expressions, subservience to George—on her knees she eats George's phallic cigar as a punishment— mark her as the traditionally feminine component of the relationship. Except for such isolated bits of S & M play acting as eating the cigar, their relationship is almost mundanely normal. Like most couples, they argue over trivialities, they are jealous, particularly George who fears losing her to a younger rival, and they are genuinely affectionate as in the scene in which they don their Laurel and Hardy costumes.

What ultimately destroys their "domestic bliss" is not Alice's real or imagined indiscretions or their bickering but the entertainment industry. Throughout the film June/George goes in and out of her character, sometimes consciously, sometimes not. When June/George has tea and scones with Mrs. Croft, the TV executive who has the power to decide the fate of Sister George as a character and as a real person, June starts off the encounter playing the role of George, replete with smarmy maxims and treacly Irish accent. But by

the time Mrs. Croft has begun flirting with Alice, the rough, vulgar persona emerges as the June persona tells Alice to "shut up" and throws scones at her.

This June/George schizophrenic behavior is a variation on the one exhibited by Elsa/Lylah in *The Legend of Lylah Clare* and is reinforced by the visuals of the film. Intermittently during *The Killing of Sister George* Aldrich cuts to black-and-white footage from the soap opera in which June appears as George and creates a visual correlative for the other personality of the protagonist. From a scene in which a drunken George/June molests two nuns in the back of a cab, Aldrich cuts to a sequence from the show where Sister George tells a group of young children to pray. The underlying irony is that virtually everyone in the film calls June "George." Zarkan believed that "we make the legends, and the legends become truth"; George tells Alice about the soap opera, "It's real to millions of people, more real than you or I."

As did their rise, the downfalls of the two personas, June and George, coincide. Because of sliding ratings, the TV executives decide to "kill off" Sister George by having her hit by a truck while she is on a mission of mercy; or as Mrs. Croft tells George disingenuously, "Your death will coincide with road safety week." Totally lost in her character, George can only respond pathetically, "I've never ridden my bike unsafely!" To add insult to betrayal, Mrs. Croft offers her a part as the voice of "Clarabelle Cow, a flawed, credible cow."

The climax of the film—and the scene which earned *Sister George* its "X" rating—centers on another act of betrayal, this time by George's lover, Alice. Such a scene had (has?) an intrinsic shock value to a bourgeois audience; and Aldrich uses that impact to magnify the sense of destruction of whatever hope or ideals George had in life. The scene is lit with oblique shadows and shafts of light cutting across the characters, as if caught in a dark vortex. The camera is placed beside Alice's bed as she reclines in foreground and Mrs. Croft's towering figure, dressed in red, appears in the doorway. Both are anxious and fearful, almost hesitant. As Mrs. Croft begins, tentatively, to fondle Alice's breasts and kiss her, Alice becomes more aggressive, forcing the hand of the shocked Mrs. Croft into more intimate areas. There are repeated close-ups of Alice's face in orgasm, until a shock cut reveals the silhouette of George in the doorway of the room.

The final scene of the movie takes place on the sound stage, the location Aldrich's Hollywood characters find most comforting and "real," from Charlie Castle to Jane Hudson to Zarkan. George's initial reaction is to wander through the sound stage forlornly. When she spots a coffin, a prop for George's funeral, the camera takes her point of view and tracks into it. She lifts up the lid to find it made of balsa wood. Screaming, she thrusts it through a window while exclaiming, "Even the bloody coffin's a fake!" This act of violence precipitates an even more destructive outburst as she sets about destroying the props and equipment on the stage. Exhausted, she settles down on a

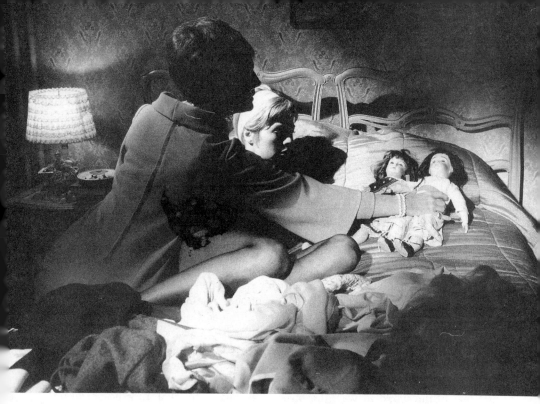

Above, a seduction strategy: Mercy Croft (Coral Browne, left) brings "Childie" (Susannah York) a new doll which she places on the bed to make a doll couple.

step and begins to "moo" like a cow. In a series of cuts, which echo the craning at the end of *The Big Knife*, the camera moves to a high angle and the screen darkens to a small square in which the broken George sits reembracing the refuge of make-believe while mooing pathetically.

What was to have been Aldrich's last Hollywood film, *The Greatest Mother of 'Em All*, would have combined the characters of Baby Jane Hudson and Lewis Zarkan in the form of Dolly Murdock, a frustrated ex-dancer, with Blanche/Lylah Clare/Elsa Brinkman in the form of her daughter Tricia, née Mary, whom Dolly makes over to be a star. Dolly's simple plan for accomplishing this is to get Tricia a job as a stripteaser, precipitate her seduction by a television producer, and extort an acting job from that person because her daughter is underage. The supporting cast includes a bisexual wife, a washed-up film director, and assorted unattractive "show-biz" types. In the manner of *Baby Jane* and *Lylah Clare* there is more straightforward vulgarization as the actor who played the dog food announcer of *What Ever Happened to Baby Jane?* and *The Legend of Lylah Clare* becomes a burlesque comic getting nowhere with his tired old gags. The "subtlest" touches are such items of decor as the red sheets and red wallpaper in the producer's bedroom.

There is also more sardonic extravagance. The director, played by Peter Finch in the Zarkan manner, suffers a heart attack just as he opens some champagne, so that when he falls to the floor the liquid which spurts from the bottle parodies orgasm as his life oozes out of him. Aldrich's twenty-minute promotional short rearranges many events in the feature script but epitomizes the cynicism that begins with the very title and ends with Tricia's suicide. As with the other Hollywood characters, Dolly Murdock suffers for her avarice and shallowness. After going to her daughter's funeral and visiting her own dying mother, Dolly's comments to the driver of a rented black limousine recap it all ironically: "You remember what I told you, there's not so much else matters in the world, so long as you love your mother."

Whatever *The Greatest Mother of 'Em All* might have been, the various scenes that were shot reveal the same distorting angles and constricting compositions of the finished films. Aldrich's style, which some dubbed sledgehammer and others merely called unconventional, retained its intensity to the end of his career. Aldrich's attitude from *The Legend of Lylah Clare* or, for that matter, from *World For Ransom* onward was equally consistent. "What matters in the world" was always subject to the mad and misguided vagaries of life and societal pressure. Whether it was within the peculiar and perverse inner structure of the Hollywood morphology or the unabashedly violent context of the world at war, the basic questions of survival and the social and moral systems remained the same.

Callahan, Trane and Erin, Morrison, Wirtz and Koertner, Massai, Hammer, O'Malley and Stribling, Charlie Castle, Zarkan, Dolly Murdock, and finally Harry Sears, they all singly or interactively confront those questions and find their own answers. As Aldrich said, in dramatizing the "struggle for self-determination, the struggle for what a character wants his life to be, [he would] look for characters who feel strongly enough about something not to be concerned with the prevailing odds, but to struggle against those odds." If Aldrich's characters must learn anything along the various paths they follow, some to salvation, others to death, it is simply, existentially, who they are. As noted earlier, Aldrich rejected the notion of "tragic destiny." Whether or not his characters come to self-knowledge, and some to despair and/or suicide as a result, did not depend on age, sex, or social standing. In *The Greatest Mother of 'Em All* the young Tricia Murdock realizes this. Before she takes her own life, she whispers, "Oh Christ, nothing's going to change." Like Charlie, there is no alternative for Tricia. In this circumstance, as Aldrich told Truffaut, "Suicide is a gesture of revolt."

In the first draft of the script by A.I. Bezzerides, there were several scenes of Dolly Murdock's life after her daughter's death as it deteriorated completely. In one scene she goes to a beach hotel to take her daughter's place as a party girl for a cheap promoter. He tells her to look in a mirror. At first Dolly sees a fantasy image of herself as a young girl; then the script reads "despite the fact

Opposite, Ann Sothern as Dolly (left) and Alexandra Hay as Tricia in the promotional short *The Greatest Mother of 'Em All*.

that Dolly is staring at herself, trying to hold on to the illusion, there emerges from the murk, the image of Dolly exactly as she is. The image is brutally cruel, brutally real." Bezzerides' draft of the screenplay ends with Dolly literally riding a merry-go-round, "endlessly searching."

Aldrich's work is full of such images, many brutally real, some also brutally cruel. There are romantics and idealists in Aldrich's world, and many of them survive. But for those who do look in the mirror, what they see is seldom pretty. When Aldrich equated his last hero, Harry Sears, to Charlie Davis in *Body and Soul*, he saw "a man struggling to redeem his self-esteem."[3] Without self-esteem, survival is empty. That is why Aldrich also asserted that "each man must fight even if he is broken." Whether it led to survival or death, the existential struggle was the path to meaning and, perhaps, to redemption.

Above, Aldrich on location shooting *Hush...Hush, Sweet Charlotte.*

Filmography

This Filmography is derived from the details published in antecedent versions, in the Master's thesis of Alain Silver and in <u>Robert Aldrich: a guide to references and resources</u> by Alain Silver and Elizabeth Ward. The latter contains the most extensive cast and crew credits which were then available. This Filmography is slightly abridged in that it omits minor cast and technical credits; but it does contain additional information on credits, production dates, and costs obtained from the Aldrich archives and other sources. The release prints are in black and white and Academy ratio unless otherwise noted with the Director of Photography's credit.

There are two major sections. The first part (1, below) encompasses the thirty feature films directed by Robert Aldrich. The second covers Aldrich's work as a Producer, Writer, Assistant Director, Director in Television, etc. and is divided into six sub-sections (2 through 7).

1. Feature Films Directed by Robert Aldrich

The Big Leaguer (1953)

Producer:	Matthew Rapf [MGM]
Screenplay:	Herbert Baker, based on a story by John McNulty and Louis Morheim
Director of Photography:	William Mellor
Art Direction:	Cedric Gibbons, Eddie Imazu
Musical Direction:	Alberto Colombo
Sound:	Douglas Shearer
Editor:	Ben Lewis

Assistant Director: Sid Sidman
Technical Advisor: John B. (Hans) Lobert
Cast: Edward G. Robinson (John "Hans" Lobert), Vera-Ellen (Christy), Jeff Richards (Abraham Polachuk), Richard Jaeckel (Bobby Bronson), William Campbell (Julie Davis), Carl Hubbell (Himself), Paul Langton (Brian McLennan), Lalo Rios (Chuy Aguilar), Bill Crandall (Tippy Mitchell), Frank Ferguson (Wally Mitchell), John McKee (Dale Alexander), Mario Siletti (Mr. Polachuk), Al Campanis, Bob Trocolor, Tony Ravis (themselves), Robert Calwell (Pomfret), Donald "Chippie" Hastings (Little Joe).

Filmed on location in Melbourne, Florida and at MGM Studios in Culver City beginning February 16, 1953.

Completed: March 4, 1953
Cost: $800,000
Distribution: Metro-Goldwyn-Mayer
Running time: 71 minutes
Released: August 19, 1953 (Los Angeles)

Synopsis

John "Hans" Lobert (Edward G. Robinson) is a former player, now the coach of the New York Giants Spring training camp for major league hopefuls in Florida. A framing device using an introductory scene of McClennan (Paul Langton), a fictional, New York sportswriter addressing the audience, permits his on-going voiceover narration as characters are introduced and the camp evaluations progress. The key rookies are third baseman Adam Polachuk (Jeff Richards), who has come to the tryouts secretly because his father (Mario Siletti) disapproves of baseball and believes him to be away at college; Bobby Bronson (Richard Jaeckel), a pitcher; wisecracking outfielder Julie Davis (William Campbell); and Lalo Rios (Chuy Aguilar), who learns English as he goes along.

Despite the encouragement of Lobert and the romantic sympathy of Lobert's niece, Christy

Left, Lobert (Edward G. Robinson) catches Polachuk (Jeff Richards) coming back to his room late.

(Vera Ellen), Polachuk's apprehension and guilt over deceiving his father causes his self-assurance to deteriorate. When McClennan writes an article about him that is reprinted in his home town paper, Polachuk's family learns of the ruse. Just as he is on the verge of abandoning baseball, Lobert arranges for his father to witness a game during which Adam's natural ability convinces Mr. Polachuk that he may have been wrong in opposing his son's interest. Davis and Rios have the talent to make the final cut; but Bronson is released by Lobert and picked up by the farm team of the arch rival Brooklyn Dodgers. Bronson pitches successfully against Lobert's squad in the exhibition game that ends the tryout season. Lobert might have kept Bronson were he not torn over dropping Tippy Mitchell (Bill Crandall), the son of a celebrated player and former teammate, from his roster. Despite concern over whether he himself will be retained by the front office for the next season, Lobert goes with his heart and does not cut the mediocre Mitchell from the squad. After seeing him play, Mitchell's father realizes that his son should give up the game and spare Lobert from having to wash him out. Mr. Polachuk learns about major league salaries and approves of Adam's playing. As the best players head for minor league clubs, Lobert and McClennan recall the events of another year.

World For Ransom (1954)

Producers:	Robert Aldrich and Bernard Tabakin [Plaza Productions/Monogram Pictures]
Associate Producer:	A. E. [Buck] Houghton, Jr.
Screenplay:	Lindsay Hardy and [uncredited] Hugo Butler
Director of Photography:	Joseph Biroc
Art Direction:	William Glasgow
Music:	Frank DeVol
Song:	"Too Soon" by Walter Samuels
Sound:	Jack Solomon
Editor:	Michael Luciano
Set Direction:	Ted Offenbacher
Production Manager:	Jake R. Berne
Assistant Director:	Nate Slott

Cast: Dan Duryea (Mike Callahan), Gene Lockhart (Alexis Pederas), Patric Knowles (Julian March), Reginald Denny (Major Bone), Nigel Bruce (Governor Coutts), Marian Carr (Frennessey), Douglas Dumbrille (Inspector McCollum), Keye Luke (Wing), Clarence Lung (Chan), Lou Nova (Guzik).

Filmed at the Motion Picture Center Studios in Hollywood in 11 days beginning April 13, 1953.

Completed:	April 26, 1953
Cost:	$100,000

Distribution: Allied Artists
Running time: 82 minutes
Released: January 27, 1954 (Los Angeles)

Synopsis

Mike Callahan (Dan Duryea) is an Irish emigré and war veteran working as a
private investigator in Singapore. He is summoned by a wartime love named
Frennessey (Marian Carr) to the nightclub where she works. There she confides to him that her husband, Julian March (Patric Knowles), may be engaged in some illegal activities and asks Callahan to disentangle him if he can.
After speaking with March and being forcibly questioned himself by a local
gangster, Callahan discovers that a black marketeer named Alexis Pederas
(Gene Lockhart) has recruited March for a scheme involving a renowned nuclear physicist, Sean O'Connor (Arthur Shields). While Callahan searches for
further information, March, impersonating a major, kidnaps O'Connor at the
airport. Pederas then sends a message to the British command that he is offering O'Connor to the highest bidder, whether Russian, Chinese, or Western.

A photographer and informant of Callahan's, who has taken a picture of
March and O'Connor driving through town, comes to Callahan with the snap-

shot; but March, aware of the incident, alerts Pederas, who has the man killed and the incriminating material planted in Callahan's room. Inspector McCollum (Douglas Dumbrille) comes to question Callahan and discovers the false clue; but Callahan escapes. After spending the night at Frennessey's, Callahan plans to slip out of town and go to a deserted jungle village where O'Connor may be hidden. He is spotted by Major Bone (Reginald Denny) of British Intelligence, who, uncertain of Callahan's role, decides to follow at a distance. In the process Bone loses immediate contact with a support force and finds himself alone with Callahan at the village. They ascertain that March and Pederas' men are indeed there with O'Connor and decide not to wait for help. Bone is wounded in the assault, but Callahan succeeds in slipping into March's bunker and holding the captors at bay with two grenades. Since O'Connor is out of the room, Callahan reacts to March's threatening gesture by throwing both charges and ducking for cover. All are killed except Callahan and O'Connor.

Callahan returns to Frennessey, having failed to save her husband but hoping to take his place. She rejects him violently, explaining that she never loved Callahan and suggests that March's platonic affection was what she wanted because men are physically repellent to her. Callahan leaves and returns to the streets of Singapore.

Apache (1954)

Producer:	Harold Hecht [Hecht-Lancaster Productions/Linden Productions]
Screenplay:	James R. Webb, based on the novel <u>Bronco Apache</u> by Paul I. Wellman
Directors of Photography:	Ernest Laszlo and [uncredited] Stanley Cortez (Technicolor;1.85:1)
Art Direction:	Nicolai Remisoff
Music:	David Raksin
Sound:	Jack Solomon
Costumes:	Norma Koch
Editorial Supervision:	Alan Crosland, Jr
Set Decorator:	Joe Kish
Make-up:	Robert J. Schiffer, Harry Maret
Production Manager:	Jack R. Berne
Assistant Directors:	Sid Sidman (1st); Robert Justman, Nate Slott (2nds)
Script Supervisor:	William Orr
Technical Consultant:	Leonard Doss
Special Effects:	Lee Zavitz, Cliff Brewer

Opposite, a lobby card from *World for Ransom*: Callahan (Dan Duryea) is cornered by Julian March (Patric Knowles, left)

Cast: Burt Lancaster (Massai), Jean Peters (Nalinle), John McIntire (Al Sieber), Charles Buchinsky [Bronson] (Hondo), John Denner (Weddle), Paul Guilfoyle (Santos), Ian MacDonald (Clagg), Walter Sande (Lt. Col. Beck), Morris Ankrum (Dawson), Monte Blue (Geronimo).

Filmed on location in New Mexico and at Keywest Studios, Hollywood, in 34 days beginning October 19, 1953.

Cost:	$1,240,000
Distribution:	United Artists
Running time:	89 minutes
Released:	June 28, 1954 (Chicago); July 21, 1954 (Los Angeles)
Original Title:	*Bronco Apache*

Synopsis

At the final surrender of Geronimo and his band, one Apache warrior, Massai (Burt Lancaster), tries to disrupt the proceedings and die gloriously in a solitary assault on the entrenched U.S. Cavalrymen. Despite the assistance of Nalinle (Jean Peters), who slips through the surrounding troops, Massai is frustrated in his attempt, captured alive, and taken off in chains. Another escape fails when Chief Scout Al Sieber (John McIntire) intercepts Nalinle's attempt to pass Massai a weapon at the railroad station where several Apaches are gathered en route to relocation in Florida under the guardianship of a corrupt Indian agent, Weddle (John Denner). During a stopover in St. Louis, Weddle is persuaded by a newspaper man to pose with his notorious prisoners for a photograph. The confusion created by the powder flash enables Massai to escape unnoticed.

After severing his handcuff chains under the train wheels, Massai wanders through metropolitan St. Louis confused and frightened by the modern sights and sounds. Stowing away on various vehicles, he reaches Oklahoma, where he unknowingly breaks into the barn of a reservation Cherokee named Dawson (Morris Ankrum). When Dawson discovers Massai, he gives him food and points out to him the merits of survival as a farmer rather than death as a warrior. Massai leaves Dawson's farm unconvinced but with a token bag of Cherokee seed corn.

On Massai's return to New Mexico, he seeks rest in the tent of Nalinle and her father Santos (Paul Guilfoyle), who is Chief in Geronimo's absence. Santos sells Massai to Hondo (Charles Buchinsky [Bronson]), an Indian cavalryman who is courting Nalinle, for liquor. Weddle and an aide reassume the duty of transporting the newly captured Massai with two renegades, but Weddle plans to fake an escape attempt by the Indians and kill them. Massai surprises Weddle first, killing the aide but sparing Weddle to deliver his "declaration of war" to the cavalry fort.

Opposite, a lobby card from *Apache* featuring Jean Peters as Nalinle.

After kidnapping Nalinle, Massai circles back to the fort, cutting telegraph wires and blowing up a wagon. He arrives in time to send an arrow into Waddle's back as he stands in the commandant's office delivering Massai's message. Massai also sets fire to the stables. Nalinle and he flee from the fort, and she eventually convinces him that she was not party to her father's treachery. They perform their own marriage ceremony and continue their flight. They are followed by Sieber and Hondo, but at the snowline the cavalrymen are forced to abandon their pursuit for the winter.

The next spring Nalinle, bearing Massai's child, is inspired by the growth of a stalk from the Cherokee corn which Massai had flung away the previous winter. She goes down to a mountain trading post for more seed. Several weeks later, Sieber visits the post while trying to pick up Massai's trail and recognizes Nalinle from the trader's description. Massai sees Sieber and his men coming up the mountain and readies himself for a last battle; Nalinle is in labor as he goes out to meet them. After storming through the soldiers' position, Massai is wounded and retreats into the tall stalks of corn he has grown from Nalinle's seed. Sieber follows him in, but as they fight hand to hand, Massai hears a baby's cry. He stands and starts back to their cabin. Sieber surmises that Massai has "just called off the war" and leaves the mountain with his men.

Vera Cruz (1954)

Producer:	James Hill [Hecht-Lancaster Productions/Flora Productions]]
Executive Producer:	Harold Hecht
Screenplay:	Roland Kibbee and James R. Webb, based on an original story by Borden Chase
Director of Photography:	Ernest Laszlo (Technicolor; SuperScope, 2:1)
Art Direction:	Al Ybarra
Music:	Hugo Friedhofer
Orchestrations:	Raul Lavista
Song:	"Vera Cruz," music by Hugo Friedhofer, lyrics by Sammy Cahn
Sound:	Manuel Topeta, Galdeno Samperio
Costumes:	Norma Koch
Editor:	Alan Crosland, Jr.
Make-up:	Robert J. Schiffer
Production Manager:	Nate Edwards
Assistant Directors:	Jack R. Berne (1st); Nate Slott (2nd)
Script Supervisor:	Meta Rebner
Special Effects:	Russell Shearman

Cast: Gary Cooper (Ben Trane), Burt Lancaster (Joe Erin), Denise Darcel (Countess Davarre), Cesar Romero (the Marquis), Sarita Montiel (Nina), George Macready (Maximilian), Ernest Borgnine (Donnegan), Morris Ankrum (Ramirez), Henry Brandon (Danette), Charles Buchinsky [Bronson] (Pittsburgh), Jack Lambert (Charlie), Jack Elam (Tex), James McCallion (Little Bit), James Seay (Abilene), Archie Savage (Ballard), Charles Horvath (Reno), Juan Garcia (Pedro).

Filmed on location in Cuernavaca, Mexico, and Churubusco Studios, Mexico City beginning March 3, 1954.

Completed:	May 12, 1954
Cost:	$1,700,000
Distribution:	United Artists
Running time:	94 minutes
Released:	January 12, 1955 (Los Angeles)

NOTE: Vera Cruz was the first motion picture released in SuperScope. This process permitted photography with normal, spherical (i.e., non-anamorphic) 35mm lenses. The vertical center portion of the negative was then used to make prints with an anamorphic 2:1 compression. These release prints, unlike 2:33:1 Cinemascope, had a square image area with a black stripe on the right edge of the same width as the optical soundtrack.

Synopsis

Joe Erin (Burt Lancaster) and Ben Trane (Gary Cooper) have both come to Mexico as hired guns. Erin, a professional killer with a band of outlaws as his associates, meets Trane, an expatriate Confederate veteran, while fleeing from local thieves. After trying and failing to take Trane's horse, Erin proposes an alliance for their mutual benefit and increased chance of survival. When they are captured by troopers, they sell their services to Maximilian (George Macready) and, after putting on a sharpshooting display during an imperial party, are assigned as bodyguards to a favorite of the court, Countess Marie Davarre (Denise Darcel).

As they escort her carriage to the coast, Trane notices from the wheel ruts that it is very heavily laden, although it has little visible cargo. Investigation discloses that the coach is filled with gold, with which the Countess has been charged to purchase more men for Maximilian's shrinking army. While Erin makes one bargain with Trane, he strikes another with the countess. His plans backfire when Nina (Sarita Montiel), a young mestizo woman who has been travelling with the column, alerts the Juaristas and enlists Trane in their cause. After Trane and Erin betray the Federal troops, they have a showdown over the gold. Trane outdraws and shoots Erin. Then he delivers the gold to Nina and her compatriots.

Below, Gary Cooper (left) and Burt Lancaster in *Vera Cruz.*

Kiss Me Deadly (1955)

Producer:	Robert Aldrich [Parklane Productions]
Executive Producer:	Victor Seville
Screenplay:	A. I. Bezzerides, based on the novel Kiss Me Deadly by Mickey Spillane
Director of Photography:	Ernest Laszlo (1.85:1)
Art Direction:	William Glasgow
Music:	Frank DeVol
Song:	"Rather Have the Blues," lyrics and music by Frank DeVol, sung by Nat "King" Cole
Sound:	Jack Solomon
Costumes:	Tom Thompson, Evelyn Carruth
Casting:	Jack Murton
Editor:	Michael Luciano
Set Decoration:	Howard Bristol
Make-up:	Robert J. Schiffer
Production Manager:	Jack R. Berne
Assistant Directors:	Robert Justman (1st); Nate Slott, Mark Sandrich, Jr. (2nds)
Script Supervisor:	Helen Gailey
Assistant to the Producer:	Robert Sherman
Special Effects:	Lee Zavitz, Cliff Brewer
Main Titles:	Joe Hernandez, Complete Film Service

Cast: Ralph Meeker (Mike Hammer), Albert Dekker (Dr. Soberin), Paul Stewart (Carl Evello), Maxine Cooper (Velda), Gaby Rodgers (Gabrielle/Lily Carver), Wesley Addy (Pat Murphy), Juano Hernandez (Eddie Yeager), Nick Dennis (Nick), Cloris Leachman (Christina), Marian Carr (Friday), Jack Lambert (Sugar), Jack Elam (Charlie Max), Jerry Zinneman (Sammy), Percy Helton (morgue attendant), Fortunio Bonanova (Carmen Trivago), Silvio Minciotti (old mover), Leigh Snowden (girl at pool), Madi Comfort (singer), Art Loggins (bartender), Robert Cornthwaite, James Seay (FBI men), Mara McAfee (nurse), James McCallian ("Super"), Jesslyn Fax (Mrs. "Super"), Mort Marshall (Ray Diker), Strother Martin (truck driver), Marjorie Bennett (manager), Robert Sherman (gas station man), Keith McConnell (Athletic Club clerk), Paul Richards (attacker), Allen Lee (William Mist), Eddie Real (side man).

Filmed on location in Los Angeles and at the Sutherland Studios in 21 days beginning November 27, 1954.

Completed:	December 23, 1954
Cost:	$410,000

Distribution: United Artists
Running time: 105 minutes
Released: May 18, 1955 (Los Angeles)

Synopsis

While returning to Los Angeles at night, private investigator Mike Hammer (Ralph Meeker) almost hits a woman who tries to flag him down. Her name is Christina (Cloris Leachman), and she tries to evade Hammer's questions about where she came from—barefoot and wearing only a trenchcoat—but eventually he learns that she has escaped from a nearby asylum. Nonetheless, he takes her through a roadblock. A few miles beyond, after a stop for gas at which she tells him that should anything happen he is to "remember me," Hammer's car is run off the road. Hammer is semi-conscious while Christina is tortured and killed. He is thrown clear when his car is pushed off a cliff.

Hammer comes to in a hospital, where his secretary Velda (Maxine Cooper) and a detective of his acquaintance, Pat (Wesley Addy), inform him that an FBI board wants to question him. Their interest and Christina's cryptic message prompt him to ignore all warnings and begin his own investigation. He follows up a number of disconnected leads, all of which point to a conspiracy against a murdered scientist named Raymondo, organized by a local gangster, Carl Evello (Paul Stewart). The conspirators attempt to buy Hammer off with a conciliatory phone call and a new sports car, from which he has his mechanic, Nick (Nick Dennis), remove two bombs. When he visits Evello's house, Evello's sister Friday (Marian Carr) tries to seduce Hammer. After subduing Evello's thugs, Hammer is asked to name his price. Hammer wants Evello to make him an offer, which angers the gangster, who implies that Hammer will regret nosing around. Hammer tracks down Christina's roommate, Lily Carver (Gaby Rogers), and hides her in his apartment. Before he can go further, Nick the mechanic is killed. After speaking to Velda, Hammer gets drunk and returns home to be abducted by Evello's men.

At the gangster's beach house he encounters Dr. Soberin (Albert Dekker), whose voice Hammer recognizes as that of Christina's killer. Overcoming the influence of pentathol administered by Soberin, Hammer overpowers Evello and ties him to the bed to be stabbed by his own man, whom Hammer then kills. He gets back to his apartment to find Carver returned but Velda missing. With Lily Carver he decodes Christina's message through a poem by Rossetti. From a morgue attendant, Hammer obtains a key which leads to a locker containing what Velda has dubbed "the great whatsit." He leaves it in the locker but goes out to find Carver gone.

At his apartment, the police are waiting; he is told that the box contains radioactive material being sought by foreign agents. When he finds the locker empty, Hammer goes to Ray Diker and follows that lead to a patient of Soberin. When he sees the doctor's name on a prescription bottle, a check of a rolodex and call to an answering service connect Soberin to the beach house. Arriving there, Hammer discovers that Lily Carver has killed Soberin to gain sole possession of the box. Carver shoots Hammer and opens the container. The radioactive material sets her on fire and begins a chain reaction. Hammer struggles through the house, finds Velda, and frees her. Together they stumble into the surf as the house explodes.

NOTE: Given "the mystery of the movie's subtly various endings,"[1] and the likelihood that the reader is familiar with *Kiss Me Deadly* from a videotape, it should be noted that two scenes, scripted as nos. 305 and 307, are missing from the end of the videotape and laser disc. These shots may also be missing from all 16mm prints of the film. The correct sequence of the ending, which is not exactly as scripted, consists of four events: (1) the house begins to explode; (2) Hammer and Velda stumble into the surf and turn to look back; (3) the house explodes into flames and the title, "The End," emerges from the center of the frame, comes forward optically, and remains superimposed over a last shot (4) of Hammer and Velda holding each other at the water's edge. Alain Silver first noted that events 2 and 4 were missing from a United Artists 16mm print when preparing the frame enlargements for his *Film Comment* article on *Kiss Me Deadly* in 1975. A close inspection of that 16mm print revealed two jump cuts combining the actual house with optical overlays and a miniature for the explosion effect. The cut is masked by the explosion; but, in fact, the lens focal length is different and the angle between the two shots of the house shifts several degrees. The last shot is also missing and the soundtrack is cut off with it. Although the sound and picture in the last shot of the house are made to fade out quickly so that the abridgement of the end title music is less apparent, the same cuts may be noted in the videotape, which implies that the two pieces may also missing from the 35mm master materials.

As we have previously noted in the Third Edition of <u>Film Noir, An Encyclopedic Reference to the American Style</u>, those shots were in the original release of the film. Some writers such as Jack Shadoian and J.P. Telotte have written on *Kiss Me Deadly* on the assumption that Mike and Velda do not stumble into the surf. Shadoian even argued that Raymond Durgnat's recollection of the ending was wrong. Robin Wood further compounded the problem by asserting that "the studio added a final shot still there in some prints showing Hammer and Velda standing amid the waves,"[2] as if to suggest Aldrich did not want the two cuts in the finished picture. In a more recent book an essayist asserts that a "gesture to the benign couple remains in some prints."[3] These shots should be in all the prints, and Aldrich never regarded them as any sort of gesture. While they had never seen a print with these scenes, Edward Arnold and Eugene Miller asked Aldrich about the ending, and he replied, "I have never seen a print without, repeat, without Hammer and Velda stumbling in the surf. That's the way it was shot, that's the way it was released; the idea being that Mike was left alive long enough to see what havoc he had caused, though certainly he and Velda were both seriously contaminated."[4] Unfortunately, the currently available commercial videos with the wrong ending are likely to remain the versions of *Kiss Me Deadly* that most people see. However, viewers of the laserdisc, which includes the theatrical trailer for *Kiss Me Deadly*, can catch a glimpse of one shot of Mike and Velda in the surf as the house explodes included in the trailer.

Below, a wounded Hammer (Ralph Meeker) and Velda (Maxine Cooper) stumble away from the beach house in the "missing" shot from *Kiss Me Deadly*.

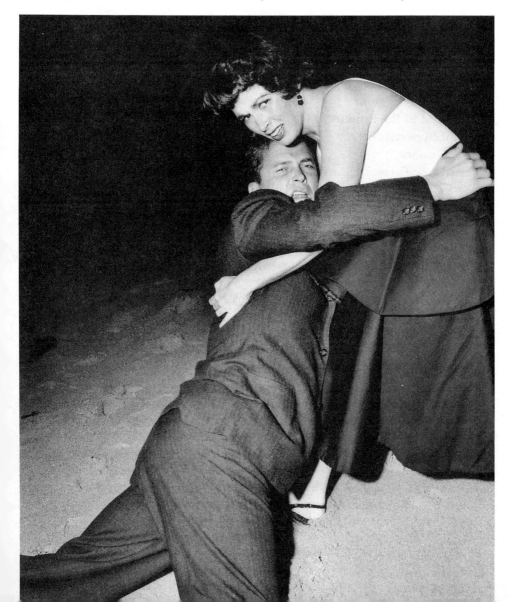

The Big Knife (1955)

Producer:	Robert Aldrich [Associates and Aldrich]
Screenplay:	James Poe, based on the play "The Big Knife" by Clifford Odets
Director of Photography:	Ernest Laszlo (1.85:1)
Art Direction:	William Glasgow
Music:	Frank DeVol
Sound:	Jack Solomon
Costumes:	Robert Richards, Evelyn Carruth
Casting:	Jack Murton
Editor:	Michael Luciano
Set Decoration:	Edward G. Boyle
Make-up:	Louis H. Hippe
Production Supervisor:	Jack R. Berne
Assistant Directors:	Nate Slott, Robert Justman,
Assistant to the Producer:	Robert Sherman
Script Supervisor:	Joe Franklin
Title Design:	Saul Bass

Cast: Jack Palance (Charlie Castle), Ida Lupino (Marion Castle), Wendell Corey (Smiley Coy), Jean Hagen (Connie Bliss), Rod Steiger (Stanley Hoff), Shelley Winters (Dixie Evans), Ilka Chase (Patty Benedict), Everett Sloane (Nat Danziger), Wesley Addy (Hank Teagle), Paul Langton (Buddy Bliss), Nick Dennis (Mickey Feeney), Bill Walker (Russell), Mike Winkelman (Billy Castle), Mel Welles (bearded man), Robert Sherman (bongo player), Strother Martin (stillman), Ralph Volke (referee), Michael Fox (announcer), Richard Boone (Narrator).

Filmed at the Sutherland Studios, Los Angeles, in 15 days beginning April 25, 1955.

Completed:	May 14, 1955
Cost:	$460,000
Distribution:	United Artists
Running time:	111 minutes
Released:	November 25, 1955 (Los Angeles)

Synopsis

Charlie Castle (Jack Palance), a former Broadway actor and current star of Hoff–Federated Pictures, does not want to renew his contract. Dissatisifed with the type of parts he has been given and his dissolute life style, he has told his agent Nat Danziger (Everett Sloane) to inform studio boss Stanley Hoff (Rod Steiger) of his decision. Additionally, Charlie's insecurity and alcoholism have estranged him from his wife Marion (Ida Lupino), to whom he hopes to be reconciled after breaking with Hoff.

Hoff appears in person and, after histrionic appeals have failed, resorts to blackmail. He threatens to expose Charlie as the drunk driver of a car which killed a child in an accident for which Buddy Bliss (Paul Langton) has taken the blame. Faced with this threat, Charlie agrees to sign. Not understanding Charlie's behavior, Marion is disappointed and distraught and refuses to return to their home. A despondent Castle has a one-night stand with Buddy Bliss's wife (Jean Hagen).

While visiting Charlie's house, Smiley Coy (Wendell Corey), Hoff's aide, confides to Charlie that he is concerned about Dixie Evans (Shelley Winters), a bit player who had been with him at the time of the accident. Smiley has a plan to take care of this problem. He tries to enlist Charlie in a plot to poison her. Charlie balks and in a confrontation with Hoff threatens to reveal that Hoff assaulted Dixie. Hoff responds by telling Castle that he will now expose him as a criminal, guilty of manslaughter.

His own past crimes and lack of integrity have pushed Charlie into a deeper depression. Even though Marion has agreed to return to him, Charlie cannot reconcile his beliefs and his life. While taking a bath he slits his wrists and dies.

Below, Charlie Castle (Jack Palance) struggles with his wife Marion (Ida Lupino).

Autumn Leaves (1956)

Producer:	William Goetz [Wm. Goetz Productions]
Screenplay:	Jack Jevne, Lewis Meltzer, and Robert Blees
Director of Photography:	Charles Lang, Jr. (1:85:1)
Art Direction:	William Glasgow
Music:	Hans Salter
Conductor:	Morris Stoloff
Song:	"Autumn Leaves," music by Joseph Kosma, original French lyrics by Jacques Prevert, English lyrics by Johnny Mercer; sung by Nat "King" Cole
Sound:	Ferot Redd, John Livadary
Costumes:	Jean Louis
Editor:	Michael Luciano
Set Decoration:	Eli Benneche
Assistant Director:	Jack R. Berne

Cast: Joan Crawford (Millicent Wetherby), Cliff Robertson (Burt Hanson), Vera Miles (Virginia), Lorne Greene (Hanson), Ruth Donnelly (Liz), Shepperd Strudwick (Dr. Couzzens), Selmer Jackson (Mr. Wetherby), Maxine Cooper (Nurse Evans), Majorie Bennett (waitress), Frank Gerstle (Mr. Ramsey), Leonard Mudie (Col. Hillyer), Maurice Manson (Dr. Masteson), Bob Hopkins (clerk).

Filmed at Columbia Studios, Los Angeles, beginning August 31, 1955.

Completed:	November 21, 1955
Cost:	$765,000
Running time:	107 minutes
Distribution:	Columbia
Released:	September 11, 1956 (Los Angeles)
Original Title:	*The Way We Are*

Synopsis

Millicent Wetherby (Joan Crawford) is an attractive middle-aged woman unable to have a fulfilling relationship with a man. She is self-employed as a manuscript typist and her only visible acquaintance is Liz (Ruth Donnelly), the manager of the court apartments where she resides. With Liz, the self-deprecating Milly analyzes her solitary life and unescorted "dates," her name for personal excursions to concerts and movies. Following a concert, she encounters a young veteran, Burt Hanson (Cliff Robertson), in a local coffee shop. His enthusiasm allows him to succeed in picking her up. He courts her vigorously and proposes marriage. Milly rejects him, ostensibly because he is too young but equally because of a sense of her own emotional vulnerability. He drops out of her life for several weeks.

When he returns, her renewed loneliness during his absence has convinced Milly to risk marriage. While living with Burt is physically and emotionally satisfying, Milly begins to notice inconsistencies both in what he tells her of his past and what he relates of his day-to-day activities. Additionally, he continues to bring her gifts which he cannot afford on his salary as a store clerk. Milly's suspicions are abruptly confirmed by a visit from Virginia Hanson (Vera Miles), who claims to be a former wife whom Burt has never mentioned to Milly. She also reveals that Burt's father, whom he has told Milly is dead, is still alive. When questioned by Milly, Burt admits that he has stolen gifts for her and lied about his past but says that he cannot remember all the circumstances which caused him to break with Virginia and his father; he only recalls returning home one day, going upstairs and inexplicably suffering a blackout. Under Milly's urging, Burt agrees to meet with his former wife and father at a local hotel, to which Milly precedes him and discovers the sexual relationship between Virginia and Burt's father (Lorne Greene). Milly attempts to care for Burt herself, but he becomes more and more uncommunicative while gradually transferring his anger to her and menacing her physically. Milly consults a psychiatrist and agrees to commit Burt, despite apprehension that a complete cure would dissipate his emotional attachment to her. She works long hours for the next several months to pay the bills for his care and finally goes to visit him prior to his release, resigned to losing him. Burt rejects her offer of freedom and convinces Milly that he wants to stay with her, not out of gratitude but genuine love.

Below, Millicent (Joan Crawford) confronts her husband's father (Lorne Greene) and ex-wife Virginia (Vera Miles, right) in *Autumn Leaves*.

Attack! (1956)

Producer:	Robert Aldrich [Associates and Aldrich]
Associate Producer:	Walter Blake
Screenplay:	James Poe, based on the play "Fragile Fox" by Norman Brooks
Director of Photography:	Joseph Biroc (1.85:1)
Art Direction:	William Glasgow
Music:	Frank DeVol
Sound:	Jack Solomon
Costumes:	Frank Beetson
Casting:	Jack Murton
Editor:	Michael Luciano
Set Decoration:	Glen L. Daniels
Make-up:	Robert J. Schiffer
Production Supervisor:	Jack R. Berne
Assistant Directors:	Robert Justman (1st); Tommy Thompson (2nd)
Script Supervisor:	William Orr
Assistant to the Producer:	Adele T. Strassfield
Technical Supervisor:	Bud Cokes
Special Effects:	David Koehler

Cast: Jack Palance (Lt. Costa), Eddie Albert (Capt. Cooney), Lee Marvin (Col. Bartlett), William Smithers (Lt. Woodruff), Robert Strauss (Pfc. Bernstein), Richard Jaeckel (Pfc. Snowden), Buddy Ebsen (Sgt. Tolliver), Jon Shepodd (Cpl. Jackson), Jimmy Goodwin (Pfc. Ricks), Strother Martin (Sgt. Ingersol), Peter Van Eyck (German officer), Steven Geray (German non-com), Louis Mercier (Frenchman), Judson Taylor (Pvt. Abramowitz), Ron McNeil (Pfc. Jones).

Filmed on location at the Albertson Ranch, Triunfo, California, and at RKO-Pathe and Universal Studios in 25 days beginning January 16, 1956.

Completed:	February 15, 1956
Cost:	$810,000
Distribution:	United Artists
Running time:	107 minutes
Released:	October 17, 1956 (Los Angeles)
Original titles:	*The Fragile Fox; Command Attack*

Synopsis

While assaulting a German bunker during World War II, nineteen men from the platoon of Lt. Joe Costa (Jack Palance) are lost. Costa holds the commander of his company, Capt. Erskine Cooney (Eddie Albert), responsible for failing to respond to his calls for assistance. After this skirmish, while the men discuss Cooney's cowardice and Costa takes out his anger at a blacksmith forge, Lt. Woodruff (William Smithers) arranges a meeting with the battalion commander, Col. Bartlett (Lee Marvin). Woodruff convinces Costa to join Bartlett, Cooney, and himself in a card game. Costa cannot resist taunting Cooney during the game, and they exchange angry words. While Cooney is sulking, Bartlett asks Costa and Woodruff not to issue a formal complaint, confessing that he must cover up for Cooney because of his father's political connections but advising them that the company will sit out the rest of the war in the rear. Costa is unconvinced but agrees not to file charges.

Bartlett fails to reckon on the Germans, who begin a counterattack that becomes the Battle of the Bulge. Cooney's company is told to hold where they are, and he sends Costa's platoon to a forward point as spotters. Before he leaves, Costa promises Cooney that if he fails to get needed support he will return to kill him, and Woodruff promises Costa that he personally will go in if needed. Costa's men advance down a hill towards the outskirts of a town. When they are met by machine gun and mortar fire, most fall back. Costa and a handful reach an outlying house. While they are watching the town, they discover two Germans, a captain (Peter Van Eyck) and a sergeant (Steven Geray), from whom they learn that heavy armor is approaching.

By the time Costa's men have eliminated a sniper in a bell tower who had them pinned down, the German tanks have arrived. Costa radios for support so that they may fall back. Claiming that he cannot commit any more men, Cooney refuses. Woodruff prepares to take his own platoon out, but Cooney orders him to remain. Infuriated by Cooney's silence and the German captain's deception, Costa pushes the enemy officer out the door to be cut down by his own forces. He and his men scramble out the back under heavy fire from the tanks. Costa is hit in the leg but stops to pick up a wounded man. By the time he has limped back up the hill carrying him on his shoulders, the man is dead.

Meanwhile, other armored units are assaulting the rest of the company in town. Cooney has lost all semblance of command and retreats to his room, where he cries hysterically. Believing Costa is dead, Woodruff goes out to organize resistance; when he returns to inform Bartlett of the situation, Cooney, fortified by alcohol, has disappeared. As Woodruff learns that three survivors from Costa's platoon are pinned in a cellar, Costa himself appears in the doorway looking for Cooney. When Costa hears that his men are trapped, he goes back to find them. Costa encounters German tanks in the street. Taking a bazooka from a fallen man, he succeeds in knocking one out; but the second machine comes forward towards Costa, pinning him in a doorway and running over his arm.

Having lost contact with Costa, Woodruff reaches the cellar where Tolliver (Buddy Ebsen), Bernstein (Robert Strauss), and Snowden (Richard Jaeckel) have taken cover. As they discuss how to get out with Bernstein, who has broken his leg, Cooney appears. Brandishing his weapon, he orders the men out into the street. While they hesitate, Costa arrives, his arm a bloody mass but his pistol leveled at Cooney. Unable to pull the trigger, he collapses and dies from loss of blood. When Cooney turns to gloat, Woodruff shoots him in the back. As relief appears, the three other men fire a round into Cooney's body and tell Woodruff to say he died from enemy fire. Woodruff is tempted by this suggestion, but when Col. Bartlett arrives and assumes Costa killed Cooney, Woodruff tells him the truth. Bartlett offers to cover it up if Woodruff will recommend Cooney for a citation. Woodruff refuses. He stands for a moment by Costa's agonized death mask and goes in to call the divisional commander.

Below, the grim red on black one sheet for *Attack!*, with the tag line: "It Rips Open the Hot Hell Behind The Glory!"

The Garment Jungle (1957)

Producer:	Harry Kleiner [Columbia]
Directors:	Vincent Sherman and [uncredited] Robert Aldrich
Screenplay:	Harry Kleiner, based on a series of articles, "Gangsters in the Dress Business," by Lester Velie
Director of Photography:	Joseph Biroc (1.85:1)
Art Direction:	Robert A. Peterson
Music:	Leith Stevens
Sound:	John Livadary
Costumes:	Jean Louis
Editor:	William Lyon
Make-up:	Clay Campbell
Assistant Director:	Irving Moore

Cast: Lee J. Cobb (Walter Mitchell), Kerwin Matthews (Alan Mitchell), Gia Scala (Theresa Renata), Richard Boone (Artie Ravidge), Valerie French (Lee Hackett), Robert Loggia (Tulio Renata), Joseph Wiseman (Tony), Adam Williams ("Ox"), Wesley Addy (Mr. Paul), Willis Bouchey (Dave Bronson), Robert Elienstein (Fred Kenner), Celia Lousky (Tulio's mother).

Filmed on location in New York and at Columbia Studios in 43 days beginning October 13, 1956.

Completed:	December 20, 1956
Cost:	$1,050,000
Distribution:	Columbia
Running time:	88 minutes
Released:	May 22, 1957 (Los Angeles)
Original title:	*The Garment Center*

NOTE: Vincent Sherman replaced Aldrich as director on December 4, 1956, 5 days before the scheduled completion of shooting and 16 days before the actual completion.

Synopsis

Korean war veteran Alan Mitchell (Kerwin Matthews) returns to New York to join his widowed father Walter Mitchell's (Lee J. Cobb) dress manufacturing business. The garment industry itself is under pressure from local unions to sign shop contracts; and Alan is suspicious that this turmoil may be connected with the death of his father's partner from a fall down an elevator shaft. Alan is somewhat alienated by his father's insistence on keeping out the union and his long-term liaison with a young buyer, Lee Hackett (Valerie French).

Eventually Alan learns that Walter has been paying protection money to a small union-busting syndicate run by Artie Ravidge (Richard Boone). Alan decides to go to the union to learn their side of the issue and, if possible, get more information about Artie Ravidge's mob. There he meets Tulio Renata (Robert Loggia) and his wife, Theresa (Gia Scala). Tulio's arguments for unionization are as emotional as Walter Mitchell's against it. Tulio appeals to Alan's liberalism, urging him to break with his father and help them organize the Mitchell employees. Alan decides to try to convince his father to unionize or, at least, break with Ravidge.

Walter, believing he can control his hired thugs, still refuses and passes on what he learns from Alan to Ravidge. The result is Tulio's brutal murder in a dark alley near his home. This radicalizes Alan, and he promises to get evidence to connect Ravidge and possibly his father with the crime. Walter himself is shocked by Ravidge's violence and implicit admission that he killed Mitchell's partner because he was pro-union. He admits his error to his son and Lee Hackett, to whom he has proposed marriage, and begins an attempt to disconnect himself from Ravidge. This only leads to his own murder at the hands of Ravidge's men.

Alan, who has already assumed some responsibility for Theresa and her child, now finds himself head of the Mitchell firm but still unable to implicate Ravidge. Freed from a promise of secrecy by Walter's death, Lee admits to Alan that she has his father's record of payoffs to Ravidge. While that material is taken to the district attorney, Alan goes to vent his anger and frustration in a physical confrontation with Ravidge. His fight is broken up by the arrival of Theresa with the police, who arrest the beaten Ravidge.

The Angry Hills (1959)

Producer:	Raymond Stross [Raymond Stross Productions]
Associate Producer:	Victor Lyndon
Screenplay:	A. I. Bezzerides, based on the novel The Angry Hills by Leon Uris, adapted for the screen by Uris.
Director of Photography:	Stephen Dade (CinemaScope)
Art Direction:	Ken Adam
Music:	Richard Bennett
Conductor:	Dock Mathieson
Sound:	A. W. Watkins
Costumes:	John Wilson-Apperson
Casting:	Lionel Grose
Editor:	Peter Tanner
Make-up:	Harold Fletcher

Production Manager: Clifton Brandon
Assistant Directors: Buddy Booth (1st); Charles Hammond (2nd)
Script Supervisor: Jane Buck

Cast: Robert Mitchum (Mike Morrison), Elisabeth Mueller (Lisa Kyriakides), Stanley Baker (Conrad Heisler), Gia Scala (Eleftheria), Theodore Bikel (Tassos), Sebastian Cabot (Chesney), Peter Illing (Leonides), Leslie Phillips (Ray Taylor), Donald Wolfit (Dr. Stergion), Marius Goring (Commander Oberg), Jackie Lane (Maria), Kieron Moore (Andreas), George Pastell (Papa Panos), Patrick Jordan (Bluey), Marita Constantiou (Cleopatra), Alec Mango (Phillibos).

Filmed on location in Greece beginning June 14, 1958.
Completed: December 10, 1958
Distribution: Metro-Goldwyn-Mayer
Running time: 105 minutes
Released: July 29, 1959

Synopsis

Mike Morrison (Robert Mitchum) is an American war correspondent trapped in Athens by a sudden German advance. Morrison's agreement with the British to acquire a list of contacts in the Greek underground and deliver it to British Intelligence puts him in jeopardy of being captured and executed as a spy. Konrad Heister (Stanley Baker), the Gestapo chief, is under intense pressure from his superiors to obtain a copy of this list, and he commissions the quisling Tassos (Theodore Bikel) to discover its whereabouts. Tassos tracks down Morrison but only succeeds in wounding him.

Morrison escapes from Athens and reaches a village of partisans, where he is cared for by Eleftheria (Gia Scala). After his recovery he joins her brother, Leonides (Peter Illing), in an abortive raid which is betrayed by a German spy posing as an escaped British soldier (Patrick Jordan). Leonides is killed and Eleftheria leads Morrison to a convent where he must hide until arrangements can be made to get him out of the country. From the convent he is taken to Lisa Kryiakides (Elisabeth Mueller), a widow and a double agent who was also Heisler's mistress. Fearing that Tassos, who has had Eleftheria tortured and killed, will soon follow the trail to her, Lisa makes hurried arrangements. A miscalculation causes Heisler to learn of her participation, and he takes her children to compel her to betray Morrison. Instead she exchanges herself for them. While she distracts Heisler, an agent named Chesney (Sebastian Cabot) kills Tassos and puts Morrison with Lisa's children on a boat leaving the country.

Ten Seconds to Hell (1959)

Producer:	Michael Carreras [Seven Arts—Hammer]
Screenplay:	Robert Aldrich and Teddi Sherman, based on the novel The Phoenix by Laurence Bachmann
Director of Photography:	Ernest Laszlo (1.85:1)
Art Direction:	Ken Adam
Music:	Kenneth V. Jones
Sound:	Henry Garlowski
Editor:	Henry Richardson
Assistant Director:	Frank Winterstein

Cast: Jack Palance (Koertner), Jeff Chandler (Wirtz), Martine Carol (Margot), Robert Cornthwaite (Loeffler), Dave Willock (Tillig), Wesley Addy (Sulke), Jimmy Goodwin (Globke), Virginia Baker (Frau Bauer), Nancy Lee (Ruth Sulke), Richard Wattis (Major Haven), Charles Nolte (doctor).

Filmed on location in Berlin and at UFA Studios in 32 days beginning February 17, 1958.

Completed:	May 10, 1958
Cost:	$1,100,000
Distribution:	United Artists
Running time:	93 minutes
Released:	September 16, 1959
Alternate Title:	In Great Britain, The Phoenix

Synopsis

Six German demolition experts, recently released from prisoner-of-war camps, are recruited by the Allies to form a bomb squad. The risks are high but the pay good, and the six men decide they will work at it for three months. To insure that those who survive will be solvent, they attach a grim rider to their pact: each man will contribute half his wages to a joint fund. At the end of the agreed period, the survivors will quit and divide the accumulated money.

The unofficial leader of the squad is Eric Koertner (Jack Palance), a former architect who has trouble retaining his idealism as he defuses bombs amidst the rubble of buildings he helped to build. His rival for command of the group, as well as his philosophical antagonist, is Karl Wirtz (Jeff Chandler). Wirtz formulated the idea of a survivor's bonus and won a moral victory over Koertner when the group adopted it. But the focus of their unstated antipathy soon shifts to Margot Hofer (Martine Carol), a widowed resident of the group's boarding house to whom both men are sexually attracted.

Although Koertner's advances towards the woman succeed, Wirtz takes solace in the fact that the men of the squad are rapidly being killed off and his belief that Koertner's idealistic despair is likely to lead to a fatal error. Ultimately, only Wirtz and Koertner remain alive. Koertner suggests that they quit now and divide the money. Wirtz refuses and uses the fact that Koertner gave his word to compel him to stay.

As the men alternate calls, luck determines who will get the dangerous bombs. Wirtz is the less fortunate, but Koertner concedes that Wirtz has been assigned a two-man bomb and, despite the fact that the agreement absolves him from responsibility, offers to help. Wirtz, however, panics. Fearing that they will both be killed, he tries to blow up Koertner with a trip wire. He fails but allows an enraged Koertner to beat him. Totally disillusioned, Koertner walks away from Wirtz. As he reaches the edge of the site, Wirtz makes a mistake and the bomb explodes.

Below, a trade advertisement for *Ten Seconds to Hell* which hoped that the explosive power of its key prop would generate a box office explosion as well.

The Last Sunset (1961)

Producer:	Eugene Frenke and Edward Lewis [Brynaprod S.A.]
Screenplay:	Dalton Trumbo, based on the novel <u>Sundown at Crazy Horse</u> by Howard Rigsby
Director of Photography:	Ernest Laszlo (Eastman Color; 1.85:1)
Art Direction:	Alexander Golitzen, Alfred Sweeney
Music:	Ernest Gold
Sound:	Waldon O. Watson, Don Cunliffe
Song:	"Pretty Little Girl in the Yellow Dress," music by Dmitri Tiomkin, lyrics by Ned Washington
Costumes:	Norma Koch
Editors:	Edward Mann(supervisor), Michael Luciano
Production Manager:	Joe Behm
Assistant Directors:	Thomas J. Connors, Jr. (1st); Nate Slott (2nd)

Cast: Kirk Douglas (Brendon O'Malley), Rock Hudson (Dana Stribling), Dorothy Malone (Belle Breckenridge), Carol Lynley (Missy Breckenridge), Joseph Cotten (John Breckenridge), Neville Brand (Frank Hobbs), Regis Toomey (Milton Wing), Adam Williams (Calverton), Jack Elam (Ed Hobbs), John Shay (Bowman), Rad Fulton (Julesberg Kid), George Trevino (Manuel), Peter Virgo (third man), Jose Torvay (Jose), Margarito de Luna (Rosario).

Filmed on location near Mexico City and Agua Caliente, Mexico, and at Universal Studios beginning May 11, 1960

Completed:	July 29, 1960
Cost:	$3,000,000
Distribution:	Universal-International
Running time:	112 minutes
Released:	June 8, 1961 (Grauman's Chinese Theater, Hollywood)
Original titles:	*Sundown at Crazy Horse; The Day of the Gun; The Hot Eye of Heaven*

Synopsis

Brendon O'Malley (Kirk Douglas), a black-suited gambler whose only sidearm is a derringer, crosses the border into Mexico to avoid arrest. He is pursued by Dana Stribling (Rock Hudson), a Texas sheriff who holds O'Malley responsible for his sister's suicide. Stribling catches up with O'Malley at the ranch of John Breckenridge (Joseph Cotten), a cattleman planning to drive his herd north to Crazy Horse in Texas for a quick sale.

Since Breckenridge is an ineffectual foreman and his ranch hands inexperienced as drovers, he has hired O'Malley as informal trail boss. Breckenridge's wife, Belle (Dorothy Malone), who as a teenager had been seduced by O'Malley, favors replacing him with the newly arrived Stribling. Breckenridge agrees to hire them both, and the drive begins with Belle and her daughter, Missy (Carol Lynley), accompanying them on the chuckwagon.

On the first stopover, Breckenridge is bullied into a barroom brawl and, despite the efforts of O'Malley and Stribling to extricate him, is shot in the back. His death leaves the two men in contention for leadership of the drive and the affections of Belle. Although they establish an informal truce and work together to overcome the hazards of bad weather and raiding Indians, Stribling makes it clear that he will try to arrest O'Malley as soon as the drive is over. Further, Belle's bitterness over her earlier abandonment by O'Malley and physical attraction to Stribling causes more friction between the two men. Missy, however, is greatly attracted to O'Malley and flirts with him constantly.

After three down-and-out drovers try to kidnap the two women, O'Malley rescues Stribling from quicksand. This action momentarily eases the tension between them, until, on the eve of crossing the river into Texas, Stribling questions O'Malley about his sister. The latter's reply, that she had been a common bar girl, leads to a fist fight which is broken up by Belle with a rifle. Her clear indication that she prefers Stribling to O'Malley causes O'Malley to succumb to the inexperienced Missy's advances.

No longer bearing rancor towards Belle, O'Malley tells her that he plans to avoid a showdown with Stribling and leave with Missy, whom he genuinely loves. Belle's revelation that he loves Missy because she is his daughter stuns him. Rather than avoid Stribling, whose plan to marry Belle has caused him to consider allowing O'Malley to escape, O'Malley challenges Stribling to meet him behind the stockyards. After saying farewell to Missy, O'Malley goes with an empty weapon to a gunfight which he could easily win and he is killed.

Right, John Breckenridge (Joseph Cotten, at left, holding the gun belt) with the rivals for his wife's affections, O'Malley (Kirk Douglas) and Stribling (Rock Hudson) in a "Hollywood" Mexican cantina. (Note: the dance hall girls in the background aren't in jail. That's just set dressing.)

What Ever Happened to Baby Jane? (1962)

Producer:	Robert Aldrich [Associates and Aldrich—Seven Arts]
Executive Producer:	Kenneth Hyman
Associate Producer:	Abe Steinberg
Screenplay:	Lukas Heller, based on the novel <u>Whatever Happened to Baby Jane?</u> by Henry Farrell, adapted by [uncredited] Harry Essex
Director of Photography:	Ernest Haller (1.85:1)
Art Direction:	William Glasgow
Music:	Frank DeVol
Song:	"I've Written a Letter to Daddy" by Henry Vincent, Henry Tobias, and Mo Jaffe
Sound:	Jack Solomon
Costumes:	Norma Koch
Casting:	Jack Murton
Choreography:	Alex Romero
Editor:	Michael Luciano
Set Decoration:	George Sawley, Ted Driscoll
Make-up:	Monte Westmore, Jack Obringer
Production Supervisor:	Jack R. Berne
Assistant Directors:	Thomas J. Connors, Jr. (1st); Harry Slott (2nd)
Script Supervisor:	Robert Gary
Script Assistant:	Adell Aldrich
Assistant to the Producer:	Walter Blake
Special Effects:	Don Steward

Cast: Bette Davis (Jane Hudson), Joan Crawford (Blanche Hudson), Victor Buono (Edwin Flagg), Marjorie Bennett (Delia Flagg), Maidie Norman (Elivra Stitt), Anna Lee (Mrs. Bates), Barbara Merrill (Liza Bates), Julie Aldred (Baby Jane), Gina Gillespie (Blanche as a child) Dave Willock (Ray Hudson), Ann Barton (Cora Hudson), Bert Freed (Producer), Wesley Addy (director), Maxine Cooper (teller), Michael Fox (announcer).

Filmed on location in Los Angeles and at Warner Bros. and the Producer's Studios beginning July 9, 1962.

Completed:	September 12, 1962
Cost:	$1,025,000 [per Aldrich documents; $825,000 in trade periodical reports]
Distribution:	Warner Bros.
Running time:	132 minutes

Released: October 31, 1962 (New York); November 7,
                                  1962 (Los Angeles)
Stock footage from *Parachute Jumper* (Director: Alfred E. Green; Warner
Bros., 1933), *Ex-Lady* (Director: Robert Florey; Warner Bros., 1933), and
Sadie McKee (Director: Clarence Brown; M.G.M., 1934).

Synopsis

In the 1920's, Baby Jane Hudson was the idol of millions, a vaudeville superstar whose childish laments and waifish dance routines supported her father,
mother, and sister, Blanche, in luxurious style. Fully aware of this, she compelled her father to spoil her shamelessly and neglect Blanche. As a adult
Blanche (Joan Crawford) succeeds in making a name for herself as an actress
in the 1930's and insists that the major studio holding her contract also find
vehicles for Jane (Bette Davis). After a director (Wesley Addy) and producer
(Bert Freed) review scenes from both sisters' latest films, they agree that Jane
has retained none of the appeal or acting ability which once sold Baby Jane
dolls by the thousands and that it would be much to the studio's advantage to
pursuade Blanche to pursue a career unencumbered by her sister.

Their plan is soon dropped, however, when Blanche is permanently para-
lyzed in an automobile accident and must abandon acting. Thirty years later,
Jane and Blanche are subsisting on insurance and meager residuals from
Blanche's days of stardom. Jane, a frustrated and garish spinster, bitterly resents having to care for her invalid sister and depending on her money for
support. Those few people who know the two women suspect that the vituperative Jane was somehow responsible for the kindly and uncomplaining
Blanche's injury. Since Jane takes Blanche's endorsed checks to the bank and
buys the household food, Blanche's only contact with the outside world is the
weekly visit of a cleaning woman, Elvira Stitt (Maidie Norman), and an occasional glance of a neighbor, Mrs. Bates (Anna Lee), from her second floor window. Blanche seldom, if ever, visits the ground floor of her house.

For years, despondency and alcoholism have caused Jane to lapse into
vivid fantasies of the past. Elvira, alarmed by suspicious actions on Jane's
part, feels compelled to warn Blanche that Jane may want to sell the house
and place Blanche in a nursing home. The fact that the house is in Blanche's
name prompts her to question Jane. To her horror, Blanche learns that Jane
does have such notions, but she receives only taunts and vague threats. To
further unbalance Blanche, Jane brings up serving trays containing the bodies
of a pet bird and a rat.

At the same time, she puts in effect her plans for a comeback. She orders
full-size versions of her Baby Jane dresses and poses with white make-up and
rouged cheeks before a full-length mirror. She also places an ad for an accom-
panist which is answered by Edwin Flagg (Victor Buono), a ne'er-do-well sup-

ported by his mother. Flagg is amazed at the spectacle of the "new" Baby Jane but goes along with her in hopes of getting a large enough advance to abandon his mother.

Listening at her door, the terrorized Blanche realizes that Jane has gained control of all Blanche's assets by expertly imitating her voice on the phone and forging her signature. When Jane goes out, Blanche desperately attempts to crawl downstairs and call her doctor. Jane returns, catches her, beats her, and drags her back upstairs, where she locks Blanche in her room. When Elvira comes to clean, Jane fires her and asks for her key. Elvira, pretending to have left the key at home, waits outside until Jane leaves for the bank and enters the house. Finding Blanche's room locked and receiving no answer to her call, Elvira forces the door. Inside, she finds Blanche gagged and tied to the bed. As Elvira struggles with the ropes, Jane returns. While Blanche watches helplessly, Jane kills Elvira with a hammer. After hiding Elvira's body in the trunk of her car, Jane dresses for Edwin Flagg's visit.

Following an argument with his mother, Flagg has gotten drunk and is brought to the door by the police, who suspect him of being a prowler. Somewhat unnerved, Jane tells them Flagg has an appointment with her. After they leave, Flagg loudly demands the advance money for his services. Hearing a

strange voice, Blanche manages to free an arm and tip over a table. Flagg, insisting on investigating the noise himself, breaks Jane's hold and rushes upstairs. Shocked at seeing the half-starved and beaten Blanche, Flagg runs away.

Fearing discovery, Jane plans to leave the house. By the following morning she has reached the beach, where she has lain Blanche in the sand and excavated a small hole. Blanche pleads for a doctor. When Jane refuses out of fear of being punished, Blanche makes a desperate confession. She admits that she was the cause of her own injury, having been at the wheel of the car attempting to run down Jane. Because of either her drunken state or trauma, Jane had obliterated the memory of this incident. Now, forced to remember, she relapses totally into her childish persona and saunters off to buy the dying Blanche an ice-cream cone. When police, alerted by Flagg, come up to question her, she tells them Blanche is down the beach. Then she notices that a crowd of bathers has gathered and begins to perform her Baby Jane act.

Sodom and Gomorrah (1963)

Producer:	Goffredo Lombardo [Titanus/Embassy, Joseph E. Levine/SN Pathé/SGC]
Executive Producer:	Maurizio Lodi-Fé
Screenplay:	Hugo Butler, assisted by Giorgio Prosperi
Directors of Photography:	Silvio Ippoliti, Mario Montuori, Cyril Knowles (EastmanColor processed by DeLuxe; 1.85:1)
Art Direction:	Ken Adam, Giovanni D'Andrea
Music:	Miklós Rózsa
Sound:	Kurt Doubrawski
Costumes:	Giancarlo Bartolini Salimbeni, Franco Antonelli
Choreography:	Archie Savage
Editor:	Peter Tanner
Set Decoration:	Gino Brosio, Emilio D'Andria
Make-up:	Euclide Santoli
Production Supervisors:	Giorgio Zambon, Giorgio Adriani, Mario Del Papa
Second Unit Director:	Oscar Rudolph
Assistant Directors:	Gus Agosti (1st); Franco Cirino, Benchekroun Larbi (2nds)
Special Effects:	Lee Zavitz, Serge Urbisaglia, Wally Veevers
Title Design:	Maurice Binder

Cast: Stewart Granger (Lot), Pier Angeli (Ildith), Stanley Baker (Astaroth), Rossana Podesta (Sheeah), Anouk Aimee (Queen Bera), Claude Mori

Opposite, Blanche (Joan Crawford) and Jane (Bette Davis) take a beach outing in *What Ever Happened to Baby Jane?*

(Maleb), Rik Battaglia (Melchoir), Giacomo Rossi-Stuart (Ishmael), Feodor
Chaliapin (Alabias), Aldo Silvani (Nacor), Enzo Fiermonte (Eber), Scilla Gabel
(Tamar), Antonio De Teffe (Captain), Gabriele Tinti (Lieutenant), Daniele
Vargas (Segur), Massimo Pietroloon (Isaac), Mitsuko Takara (Orpha), Mimma
Paimara (Arno), Alice and Ellen Kessler (dancers).

Filmed on location in Morocco and in Rome in 124 days over 11 months beginning January 23, 1961.

Completed:	June 9, 1961 (Principal Photography);
	December 14, 1961 (Supplemental
	Photography)
Cost:	$4,500,000
Distribution:	20th Century-Fox (U.S.); Titanus (Europe)
Running time:	154 minutes
Released:	January 23, 1963 (Los Angeles)
Original Title:	*The Last Days of Sodom and Gomorrah* [This
	title is used on the laser disc and video release.]

NOTE: Sergio Leone was hired to do second unit work but was fired after a
few weeks [see Biography]. He is often erroneously credited as "Co-Director."
Oscar Rudolph directed the simultaneous second unit, and Aldrich directed
many supplementary units himself.

Synopsis

In their wanderings in search of a permanent home, the Hebrews under Lot
(Stewart Granger) make a temporary camp on a plain outside the cities of
Sodom and Gomorrah. The ruler of the cities, Queen Bera (Anouk Aimee),
reacts favorably to Lot's personal appeal for permission to remain for at least
a full growing season, so that the Hebrew's supply of grain may be replen-
ished. Bera's hidden motive is fear of her nomadic neighbors, the Helamites,
who are conspiring with her brother, Astaroth (Stanley Baker), to capture her
kingdom. With Lot and his people as her de facto allies encamped between
Sodom and the Helamites' tribal land, she has additional security.

Lot is given Ildith (Pier Angeli), a former slave and personal attendant to
Bera, as a concubine. He proposes marriage to Ildith, who accepts because of
a genuine attraction to Lot and also because Bera has commissioned her to
spy on him. Ildith promises to abandon her old gods in favor of the Hebrew
Yahweh.

On their wedding day, Astaroth and the Helamites, who have been harass-
ing the Hebrews since their arrival, launch a surprise attack on the Hebrew
camp. Although the attackers are repulsed when Lot destroys a dam, flooding
the plain and drowning most of the Helamite army, Astaroth takes Sheeah
(Rosanna Podesta), one of Lot's daughters, and escapes. Since the Hebrews

have been dispossessed by the floodwaters which destroyed her enemies, Bera allows them to take refuge in her cities.

There, under the influence of the luxurious surroundings and sensual pleasure, they fall into the carnal, unproductive mode of life of the Sodomites despite Lot's admonitions. Even Lot himself is tempted until he discovers that Astaroth has reduced his daughters to concubinage and kills him. Bera must imprison Lot for killing a royal figure, although she is glad to be rid of the threat of Astaroth. Without Lot's leadership, the Hebrews fall further into pagan practice.

In Bera's dungeon, two angels appear to Lot and tell him to lead the people out of the city, as God will destroy it that very night. Lot's chains fall to pieces, and he bands together all who will listen to flee with him into the hills. At sunset, an earthquake levels the cities and fire rains from the skies, killing Bera and all her subjects. Ildith, ignoring the warning not to look back, turns around to see and is transformed into a pillar of salt.

Below, Stanley Baker in his Astaroth costume checks Aldrich's watch to see how long it is till lunch on the set of *Sodom and Gomorrah*.

4 for Texas (1963)

Producer:	Robert Aldrich [The SAM Company for Frank Sinatra, Essex Productions; Dean Martin, Claude Productions; and Associates and Aldrich]
Executive Producer:	Howard W. Koch
Associate Producer:	Walter Blake
Screenplay:	Teddi Sherman and Robert Aldrich, from an original story by Aldrich
Director of Photography:	Ernest Laszlo (Technicolor; 1.85:1)
Art Direction:	William Glasgow
Music:	Nelson Riddle
Sound:	Jack Solomon
Costumes:	Norma Koch
Casting:	Hoyt Bowers
Editor:	Michael Luciano
Set Decoration:	Raphael Bretton
Make-up:	Robert J. Schiffer
Production Manager:	Jack R. Berne
Second Unit Director:	Oscar Rudolph
Second Unit Director of Photography:	Joseph Biroc
Assistant Directors:	Thomas J. Connors, Jr. (1st); David Salven, William F. Sheean (2nds)
Script Supervisor:	Robert Gary
Script Assistant:	Adell Aldrich
Special Effects:	Sass Bedig

Cast: Frank Sinatra (Zack Thomas), Dean Martin (Joe Jarrett), Anita Ekberg (Elya Carlson), Ursula Andress (Maxine Richter), Charles Bronson (Matson), Victor Buono (Harvey Burden), Edric Connor (Prince George), Nick Dennis (Angel), Richard Jaeckel (Mancini), Mike Mazurki (Chad), Wesley Addy (Trowbridge), Jack Elam (Dobie), Marjorie Bennett (Miss Ermaline), Percy Helton (Ansel), Jack Lambert (Monk), Fritz Feld (maitre d'), Jonathan Hole (Renee), Paul Langon (Beauregard), Jesslyn Fax (the widow), The Three Stooges, Teddy Buckner and his All-Stars.

Filmed on location near Mojave, California, and at Warner Bros. Studios, Burbank, in 48 days beginning May 27, 1963.

Completed:	August 2, 1963
Cost:	$4,520,000
Distribution:	Warner Bros.

Running time: 124 minutes
Released: December 25, 1963 (Los Angeles)
Original Titles: *Two for Texas; Four for Texas*

Synopsis

Zack Thomas (Frank Sinatra) and Joe Jarrett (Dean Martin), passengers on a stagecoach for Galveston, find themselves under attack from a gang of masked riders. After driving off the bandits, Thomas makes the mistake of admitting that they were probably after his carpetbag, which contains $100,000. Jarrett relieves Thomas of the money at gunpoint. Reaching Galveston, Jarrett puts the money in the bank of a local racketeer, Harvey Burden (Victor Buono), who has partially financed Thomas's efforts to control gambling in the area.

Meanwhile, Thomas returns to the bordello run by Elya Carlson (Anita Ekberg) and makes plans to steal back his funds. Burden, hoping to eliminate both men and take over the town, sends a gunslinger named Matson (Charles Bronson) to kill Thomas, whose life is saved when Jarrett wounds the assassin. Refusing Thomas's offer to join forces, Jarrett contacts Maxine Richter (Ursula Andress), owner of a riverboat which might be converted to a gambling ship. Thomas, knowing his money has been used to refurbish the boat, plans to take it over by force. But Maxine and Elya convince the two men to join forces because they suspect Burden may move in to claim the spoils if Thomas and Jarrett fight. The womens' suspicions are confirmed when Matson and his hired guns storm the boat under Burden's orders. But they are defeated, and subsequently Burden is jailed and a double wedding takes place: Jarrett marries Maxine, Thomas weds Elya.

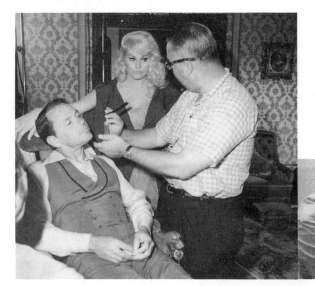

Left, given the mood on the set of *4 for Texas,* it's surprising that Frank Sinatra let Aldrich get that close to his throat, even with a prop razor, while Anita Ekberg and Mike Mazurki look on. Below, another shaving demonstration, this time on Burt Reynolds' mustache in *The Longest Yard*

Hush...Hush, Sweet Charlotte (1964)

Producer:	Robert Aldrich [Associates and Aldrich]
Associate Producer:	Walter Blake
Screenplay:	Henry Farrell and Lukas Heller, from an original story by Henry Farrell
Director of Photography:	Joseph Biroc (1.85:1)
Art Direction:	William Glasgow
Music:	Frank DeVol
Sound:	Bernard Freericks; Herman Lewis (rerecording)
Costumes:	Norma Koch
Casting:	Phil Benjamin
Editor:	Michael Luciano
Set Decoration:	Raphael Bretton
Make-up:	Bill Buell, Gene Hibbs, Jack Stone
Production Manager:	Jack R. Berne
Assistant Directors:	William McGarry, Sam Strangis (1sts); William F. Sheehan (2nd)
Script Supervisor:	Robert Gary
Script Assistant:	Adell Aldrich
Special Effects:	Percy High

Cast: Bette Davis (Charlotte Hollis), Olivia de Havilland (Miriam Deering), Joseph Cotten (Dr. Drew Bayliss), Agnes Moorehead (Velma Cruther), Cecil Kellaway (Harry Willis), Victor Buono (Big Sam Hollis), Mary Astor (Jewel Mayhew), William Campbell (Paul Marchand), Wesley Addy (Sheriff Luke Standish), Bruce Dern (John Mayhew), Frank Ferguson (editor), George Kennedy (crew boss).

Filmed on location near Baton Rouge, Louisiana, and in Los Angeles. Production began June 1, 1964 and was suspended from July 2 to July 21 and from July 29 to September 9 because of a lawsuit and restraining order against Bette Davis and the illness of Joan Crawford, who originally portrayed Miriam Deering before being replaced by Olivia de Havilland.

Completed:	November 22, 1964
Cost:	$2,265,000
Distribution:	20th Century-Fox
Running time:	133 minutes
Released:	December 24, 1964 (Los Angeles)
Original title:	*What Ever Happened to Cousin Charlotte?*

Opposite, a lobby card from *Hush...Hush, Sweet Charlotte* featuring Olivia de Havilland as Miriam and Bette Davis as Charlotte.

Synopsis

Charlotte Hollis (Bette Davis) is a recluse living with her housekeeper, Velma (Agnes Moorehead), in a decaying bayou manor. She has lived alone since the death of her father under continual taunts from local inhabitants who believe her guilty of the murder of her married lover, John Mayhew (Bruce Dern), thirty-five years before. Now Charlotte is under pressure to leave her home so that a highway can be put through. Taking advantage of the fact that her mental competence is in question, she manages to keep the road builders and local authorities at bay with a shotgun.

While the sheriff (Wesley Addy) consults with Dr. Drew Bayliss (Joseph Cotten) regarding the possibility of having Charlotte committed, her cousin, Miriam Deering (Olivia de Havilland), returns after living for some years abroad. The impoverished Miriam renews an old affair with Bayliss and, at Charlotte's invitation, moves into the Hollis house as informal custodian. Charlotte's mental condition deteriorates as she begins to hear music from the dance at which Mayhew was killed and to have visions.

Velma suspects that Miriam and Bayliss are responsible for these occurrences and that they hope to drive Charlotte truly mad and obtain legal control of her assets. She confides in Harry Willis (Cecil Kellaway), an insurance investigator

20th Century-Fox presents
An Associates and Aldrich
Company Production

Starring **BETTE DAVIS   OLIVIA de HAVILLAND**
JOSEPH COTTEN
CO-STARRING
HUSH...HUSH, SWEET CHARLOTTE   AGNES   CECIL   WILLIAM Screen Play VICTOR   Also Starring MARY / ROBERT   HENRY   LUKAS   From a Henry
                                    MOOREHEAD · KELLAWAY · CAMPBELL   BUONO · ASTOR Produced and / FARRELL ... HELLER ... FARRELL
                                                                                      Directed by ALDRICH Screenplay by

who has reopened the file on John Mayhew, but before Velma can acquire any evidence, she falls to her death. Left under Miriam's influence, Charlotte becomes convinced of Bayliss' malevolence and shoots him with a gun Miriam has given her. After the two women have left the the body out in the bayou, Charlotte tries to retreat to her room, but Bayliss, unhurt by the blank load in the gun, reappears. Caked with mud and swamp grass, this "ghost" drives Charlotte over the brink of madness. Later in the garden, as Miriam reveals that she has been blackmailing Jewel Mayhew (Mary Astor) who, she saw killing her husband, she and Bayliss discuss their plans for Charlotte's money. Charlotte overhears them from her balcony and topples over a stone urn, crushing them both. The following day, as Charlotte is removed to an asylum by the sheriff, the town women gossip about the death of Jewel Mayhew Willis appears and presents her with Jewel's (Mary Astor) confession to her husband's murder.

The Flight of the Phoenix (1966)

Producer:	Robert Aldrich [Associates and Aldrich]
Associate Producer:	Walter Blake
Screenplay:	Lukas Heller, based on the novel The Flight of the Phoenix by Elleston Trevor
Director of Photography:	Joseph Biroc (DeLuxe Color; 1.85:1)
Art Direction:	William Glasgow
Music:	Frank DeVol
Song:	"Senza Fine," music and Italian lyrics by Gino Paoli, English lyrics by Alec Wilder; sung by Connie Francis
Costumes:	Norma Koch
Editor:	Michael Luciano
Set Decoration:	Lucien Hafley
Make-up:	Ben Nye, Jack Stone, William Turner
Production Manager:	Jack R. Berne
2nd Unit Director:	Oscar Rudolph
Aerial Sequences:	Paul Mantz
Assistant Directors:	William F. Sheehan (1st); Clifford Coleman, Alan Callow (2nds)
Script Supervisors:	Robert Gary; Adell Aldrich Bravos
Title Design:	Don Niehaus

Cast: James Stewart (Frank Towns), Richard Attenborough (Lew Moran), Peter Finch (Captain Harris), Hardy Kruger (Heinrich Dorfmann), Ernest Borgnine (Trucker Cobb), Ian Bannen (Crow), Ronald Fraser (Sgt. Watson), Christian Marquand (Dr. Renaud), Dan Duryea (Standish), George Kennedy (Bellamy), Gabriele Tinti (Gabriele), Alex Montoya (Carolos), Peter Bravos (Tasso), William Aldrich (Bill), Barrie Chase (Farida).

Filmed on location near Yuma, Arizona, and Pilot Knob, California, and at 20th Century-Fox Studios, Los Angeles, beginning April 26, 1965.

Completed:	August 13, 1965
Cost:	$3,800,000
Distribution:	20th Century-Fox
Running time:	148 minutes
Released:	January 20, 1966 (London) [First shown in Los Angeles for one week only beginning December 15, 1965 to qualify for Academy Award consideration.]

Opposite, Aldrich talks to Richard Attenborough (lower right) on location for *The Flight of the Phoenix* while, from left, Hardy Kruger, Ian Bannen, Walter Blake, and James Stewart look on.

Synopsis

A twin-engine plane carrying several oil-rig workers and British soldiers from a remote desert station for a few weeks' leave is caught in a sandstorm, loses power, and crashes. The survivors find themselves in uncharted desert, without radio contact or any bearing with which rescuers might be guided. After much discussion, the reality of their situation sinks in, and Frank Towns (James Stewart), the pilot, accepts the offer of Captain Harris (Peter Finch) to set off on foot with as many supplies as can be spared in search of an outpost. Harris is to be accompanied by Sgt. Watson (Ronald Fraser), who believes the captain is marching to certain death and feigns a leg injury in order to remain behind.

The captain sets off and is secretly followed that night by one of the oil workers, Trucker Cobb (Ernest Borgnine), who had offered to go along but was ordered to stay behind due to his recent nervous breakdown while working. The next morning, Towns feels compelled to find Cobb and reluctantly leaves the group in charge of his navigator, Lew Moran (Richard Attenborough), whom he suspects caused their plight by being drunk and failing to check a weather report before departure. Towns finds Cobb dead of heat stroke and returns to the plane after a day.

While they are awaiting the results of Harris' trek, Heinrich Dorfmann (Hardy Kruger), a passenger who claims to be an aircraft designer, shows Towns some plans he has drawn up for constructing a single-engine plane from the existing wreckage. Towns dismisses it as impossibly farfetched; but when Harris stumbles back into camp after having marched in a wide circle, Towns is under pressure to come up with a plan. As supplies run low, the men discover a small group of bedouins camped beyond a nearby knoll. Fearful that they may be bandits, they are reluctant to approach them en masse. Harris volunteers to walk around and approach them from the other side. Watson, no longer able to claim injury, mutinously refuses to go along, so Dr. Renaud (Christian Marquand) replaces him.

The following morning, the bedouins have departed, leaving Harris and the doctor with their throats cut. Desperately, Towns agrees to Dorfmann's scheme. It is only after many days of exhausting labor, when the "Phoenix" is almost ready, that Towns inadvertently learns that Dorfmann is a designer of model airplanes. Convinced that a plane designed by a "toymaker" will never get off the ground, Towns nevertheless agrees to complete work. The following morning the engine turns over, and with the men clinging to the wings, the "Phoenix" takes off. Circling to the west with limited fuel, Towns spots a pumping station with its own oasis and sets the plane down.

The Dirty Dozen (1967)

Producer:	Kenneth Hyman [MKH Productions]
Associate Producer:	Raymond Anzarut
Screenplay:	Nunnally Johnson and Lukas Heller, based on the novel <u>The Dirty Dozen</u> by E. M. Nathanson
Director of Photography:	Edward Scaife (Metrocolor; Metroscope, 1.75:1)
Art Direction:	W.E. Hutchinson
Music:	Frank DeVol
Songs:	"The Bramble Bush," music by Frank DeVol, lyrics by Mack David; "Einsam,"music by Frank DeVol, lyrics by Sibylle Siegfried
Sound	Claude Hitchcock; Franklin Milton (rerecording)
Costumes:	Elsa Fennell
Editor:	Michael Luciano
Set Decoration:	John Jarvis
Production Manager:	Julian MacKintosh
Make-up:	Ernest Gasser, Walter Schneiderman
Assistant Directors:	Bert Batt (1st); Dusty Symonds (2nd)
Script Supervisor:	Angela Allen
Technical Advisor:	Richard Williamson
Special Effects:	Cliff Richardson
Title Design:	Walter Blake

Cast: Lee Marvin (Major Reisman), Ernest Borgnine (Gen. Worden), Charles Bronson (Joseph Wladislaw), Richard Jaeckel (Sgt. Bowren), John Cassavettes (Victor Franko), Jim Brown (Robert Jefferson), George Kennedy (Maj. Max Ambruster), Trini Lopez (Pedro Jiminez), Ralph Meeker (Capt. Stuart Kinder), Robert Ryan (Col. Everett Dasher Breed), Telly Savalas (Archer Maggott), Donald Sutherland (Vernon Pickey), Clint Walker (Samson Posey), Robert Webber (Gen. Denton), Tom Bushy (Vladek), Ben Carruthers (Gilpin), Stuart Cooper (Lever), Robert Phillips (Morgan), Colin Maitland (Sawyer), Al Mancini (Bravos), George Roubicek (Gardner), Thick Wilson (Worden's aide), Dora Reisser (German girl).

Filmed on location near Chenies, England, and at M.G.M. Studios, London, in sixteen weeks beginning April 25, 1966.

Completed:	October 13, 1966
Cost:	$5,400,000
Distribution:	Metro-Goidwyn-Mayer
Running time:	149 minutes
Released:	June 28, 1967 (Hollywood Paramount Theater)

NOTE: The Roadshow engagements were in 70mm with six-track Stereophonic sound. *The Dirty Dozen* was the first motion picture photographed in spherical 35mm to have 70mm release prints. The same Metroscope process with a 1.75:1 ratio was used on *Too Late the Hero*.

Synopsis

A few months before the planned invasion of Europe, Major Reisman (Lee Marvin) is summoned before a special board of Army officers. After the board reprimanding Reisman for his unconventional behavior and repeated violations of accepted army procedures, General Worden (Ernest Borgnine) offers him an opportunity to remove the black marks from his service record. He is to lead a commando group in a raid behind enemy lines and, since the odds are against anyone returning, Reisman must use "volunteers" from the prisoners on death row in the Army stockade. It is clear that this assignment is not optional for Reisman.

Reisman goes to interview his recruits and moves from cell to cell making the same proposition to each man: hard work preparing for an extremely perilous mission, little chance of returning alive, and no promise of clemency for those who survive. One by one, Franko (John Cassavetes), the petty gangster; Jefferson (Jim Brown), the angry black man; Posey (Clint Walker), the mentally deficient giant; Maggott (Telly Savalas), the sexual psychopath; Wladislaw (Charles Bronson), the railroaded noncom; and seven others are blackmailed, cajoled, or lured into volunteering.

As their training begins at an isolated camp, guarded by Sgt. Bowren (Richard Jaeckel) and an elite group of M.P.'s, Reisman makes it clear that they will work as a group or not work at all. Although most face the alternative of capital punishment, individuals continue to be unresponsive. Reisman has a particular method to bring each man into line: he humiliates Jiminez (Trini Lopez), beats Posey in hand-to-hand combat, and threatens to abandon Maggott to a "headshrinker." Captain Kinder (Ralph Meeker), who gives them all psychological exams, is appalled by the results. He offers to intervene for Reisman and allow him to weed out the worst misfits. Reisman, who by now has accepted the challenge to his own leadership ability, refuses.

As the men begin to break under Reismam's persistent tactics, the Major accepts General Worden's suggestion that his unusual unit to take part in upcoming war games in which Reisman's major antagonist is the pompous Colonel Everett Dasher Breed (Robert Ryan), head of an elite corps of paratroopers. Reisman had previously humiliated Breed by taking his unshaven, ragtag squad on a tour of Breed's camp and having one of them, Pinkley (Donald Sutherland), pass as an incognito general and review the men. During the games, Reisman's "Dirty Dozen" (so named because they refused to shave or bathe when Reisman cut their hot water privileges) easily move through "enemy" lines with a variety of illegal ruses and capture Breed's entire command post.

As the group returns triumphantly to their compound for a graduation dinner, Reisman proffers a special reward for their performance: a busload of prostitutes imported from London. The next morning, their camp is raided by Breed and his men. Aided by a maverick M.P. of Bowren's group, Breed disarms the guards and prepares to interrogate the "Dozen" on their mission. Reisman eludes capture, arms himself, and calls Breed's bluff.

The following night the men parachute out over France. Their objective is a heavily guarded chateau maintained by the German high command for the rest and recreation of its officers. Jiminez is lost in the jump, so Maggott must replace him in the strike group. While Reisman and Wladislaw, who speaks German, enter the castle impersonating Wehrmacht officers, Franco and Maggott grapple their way to the second floor. When one of the German women comes up searching for her lover, Maggott's psychotic mysogyny is set off. He loses control and stabs her, which alerts those below, who flee towards a heavily armored bomb shelter. Reisman and Wladislaw manage to disengage themselves at the last minute, but the cellar door is secured against them. Their only possible counter is to barricade the enemy in.

Outside, while Posey and Sawyer (Colin Maitland) guard the crossroads, the rest of the unit is under fire from chateau guards. As his men begin to fall, Reisman orders high explosives stuffed down the ventilators of the cellar bunker. The explosives are dowsed with gasoline and followed by grenades, which sends the entire structure up in flames. Reisman and his remaining men escape in a commandeered armored vehicle. The only known survivors of the raid are Reisman, Wladislaw, and Bowren. Visiting their hospital room back in England, General Worden reveals that the men have been given posthumous pardons. Reisman is unimpressed—he just goes on squeezing a rubber ball with his injured arm.

Left, the exploding chateau in
The Dirty Dozen.

The Legend of Lylah Clare (1968)

Producer:	Robert Aldrich [Associates and Aldrich]
Associate Producer:	Walter Blake
Screenplay:	Hugo Butler and Jean Rouverol, based on a teleplay by Robert Thom and Edward DeBlasio
Director of Photography:	Joseph Biroc (Metrocolor; 1.85:1)
Art Direction:	George W. Davis, William Glasgow
Music:	Frank DeVol
Song:	"Lylah," music by Frank DeVol, lyrics and vocal by Sibylle Siegfried
Sound:	Philip N. Mitchell; Franklin Milton (rerecording)
Costumes:	Renie [Conley]
Casting:	Lee Traver
Editor:	Michael Luciano
Set Decoration:	Henry Grace, Keogh Gleason
Make-up:	William Tuttle, Robert J. Schiffer
Stunt Coordinator:	John Indrisano
Production Manager:	George Tobin
Assistant Directors:	Clifford Coleman (1st); Dennis Donnelly, Daisy Gerber (2nds)
Script Supervisor:	Adell [Aldrich] Bravos
Assistant to the Producer:	William Aldrich
Executive Assistant:	Peter Nelson
Special Effects:	Al Burks
Special Photography:	Richard Avedon, Pier Luigi
Dog Food Commercial:	Norman Tobak, The Petersen Company

Cast: Kim Novak (Lylah Clare/Elsa Brinkmann/Elsa Campbell), Peter Finch (Lewis Zarkan/Louis Flack), Ernest Borgnine (Barney Sheean), Milton Selzer (Bart Langner), Rosella Falk (Rosella), Gabriele Tinti (Paolo), Coral Browne (Molly Luther), Valentina Cortese (Countess Bozo Bedoni), Jean Carroll (Becky Langner), Michael Murphy (Mark Peter Sheean), Lee Meriwether (girl), James Lanphier (legman), Robert Ellenstein (Mike), Nick Dennis (Nick), Dave Willock (D.P.), Peter Bravos (butler), Ellen Corby (script clerk), Michael Fox (premiere M.C.), Hal Maguire (second legman), Queenie Smith (hairdresser), Sidney Skolsky (columnist), Mel and Barbara Ann Markweister (aerialists), Dan Borzage (clown), William Aldrich (assistant M.C.).

Filmed on location in Los Angeles and at M.G.M. Studios in Culver City in 60 days beginning July 12, 1967.

Completed:	November 16, 1967
Cost:	$3,490,000

Distribution: Metro-Goldwyn-Mayer
Running time: 130 minutes
Released: August 21, 1968 (Grauman's Chinese Theater,
                           Hollywood)

NOTE: The original television production, *The Lylah Clare Story*, directed by Franklin Schaffner and starring Tuesday Weld aired as a *The Dupont Show of the Week* on May 19, 1963 on NBC.

Synopsis

Bart Langner (Milton Selzer) has discovered a young woman named Elsa Brinkmann (Kim Novak) who bears a striking resemblance to the former Hollywood star Lylah Clare. Langner and his sister, Becky (Jean Carroll), show Elsa a slide collection of Lylah and her director-husband, Lewis Zarkan (Peter Finch), in an effort to convince her that she would be ideal for a filmed biography of the late star. Unknown to either of them, Elsa is already obsessed with Lylah and stardom; her hotel room is filled with cheap picture books and fan magazines concerning Lylah. Nonetheless, something about the prospect frightens her.

The following morning Langner visits Zarkan to coax him out of retirement and into joining him on the project. Zarkan is skeptical. Why is Langner, a "lousy ten percenter," so anxious to produce a motion picture? Langner confesses that he is dying of cancer and wants to accomplish something significant before the end. He hopes to persuade Zarkan's former studio boss, Barney Sheean (Ernest Borgnine), to finance the picture. Zarkan is unmoved but, partially because of the goading of his housekeeper, Rosella (Rosella Falk), agrees to meet Elsa. When Elsa is late for the important dinner, Zarkan's impatience turns to savage sarcasm over dessert and coffee.

Finally, when Elsa does arrive, Zarkan wants to keep her waiting, but Langner rushes out and Rosella follows. Both former intimates of Lylah Clare are struck by Elsa's physical resemblance to the dead actress. Under Zarkan's insistence, Rosella relates the first flashback version of Lylah's death for Elsa's benefit: pursued home by a young man, shortly after her marriage to Zarkan, Lylah succeeded in killing her attacker but fell to her death, a victim of acrophobia. When Zarkan begins to insult Elsa, she snaps back at him a perfect imitation of Lylah's German-accented voice.

The following day, Langner goes to Sheean with his proposition. When Sheean is dubious, Langner points out that the television value of all of Lylah's old pictures would be greatly enhanced by a successful biography. Sheean agrees to let his designer, Bozo Bedoni (Valentina Cortese), produce some copies of Lylah's old gowns for a press conference but makes no other commitments. He does send his son, Peter (Michael Murphy), to observe the conference.

After days of arduous rehearsal of possible questions, various cosmetic preparations, and a change of name, Zarkan invites the press to his home for an unveiling of Elsa Campbell. Among those in attendance is the crippled gossip columnist, Molly Luther (Coral Browne). The conference goes well until Molly begins her questions, ruthless probes of Elsa's personal life. Assuming the Lylah persona, Elsa launches a verbal attack of her own, until Molly leaves in a huff, pausing only to cast a menacing glance at Barney Sheean, who has arrived late.

Ignoring the fact that his bargaining position may be compromised, Zarkan takes Lylah to dinner at the Brown Derby, where Sheean also happens to be dining. Struck by the first sight of Elsa, Sheean's interest is rekindled; but he uses Luther's antagonism to try to get a better deal. Only Langner's arrival with a preview copy of a *Life* magazine that features Elsa's photo on the cover prevents Zarkan from compromising. The deal is made, but Elsa, who has been ignored all evening, is angered when Zarkan toasts Lylah and not her. She storms off with Sheean's son.

When Elsa returns to Zarkan's house for her things, he confronts her. Attempting to hurt him, she breaks into Lylah's former room which he keeps locked. There she discovers torn bedclothes and slashed furniture, just as Lylah left them. Moved by this evidence of Zarkan's devotion, she allows him to seduce her. Zarkan relates a second version of Lylah's death: she had brought the young man with her to irritate him. After the man fell, Zarkan could not grab Lylah in time to save her from falling also.

As production on the film begins, a weary Elsa comes more under Rosella's influence. A drug addict and former lover of Lylah, Rosella makes Elsa dependent on various pills. As the shooting progresses, the Lylah persona seldom manifests itself; but when it comes to the final sequence, the stabbing of Lylah's assailant, Elsa cannot bring herself to play the scene. Zarkan feigns satisfaction with what he has and ends principal photography. Only after viewing a rough cut does Zarkan reveal his plan for a new ending: Lylah will die in a fall rehearsing for a trapeze film. When Langner protests that this is false and tries to assert himself as producer, Zarkan tells him that the negative of the first ending has mysteriously burned. Elsa, however, sits silently through this discussion and leaves without committing herself.

When Zarkan has reassembled his crew to shoot the added scenes, Elsa is entertaining Zarkan's gardener in her dressing room. Sheean visits the set to remind Zarkan of his promise to finish in six months or forfeit his editing rights. Zarkan goes into Elsa's dressing room to insist that the day's shooting begin immediately and finds that Elsa has lapsed totally into the Lylah persona and knows things about his relationship to Lylah which had never been revealed. Overhearing these revelations, Rosella is somewhat unnerved. Knowing that Zarkan is unpredictable, she threatens to punish him if harm comes to Elsa.

Meanwhile, Elsa, a former circus performer, has decided to do the trapeze work herself. Over protests from some of the crew, Zarkan and Sheean agree to let her. She performs two jumps, but when Zarkan directs her to look down at the camera, a third flashback passes through her mind. In it, Lylah's assailant is revealed to be a woman and Zarkan forces Lylah to look down, causing her to fall from the stairs. Then, from the trapeze, Elsa/Lylah looks down at Zarkan; she becomes dizzy and falls. She is catapulted off the edge of the net and breaks her neck. Zarkan orders the others to play out the scene as Lylah dies.

At the premiere of Zarkan's film, various industry people are interviewed concerning Elsa's death. Zarkan, realizing his error, is barely coherent. Rosella, watching on television in Zarkan's home, has loaded one of his guns. As she waits for Zarkan, a dog food commercial is run: a housewife sets out a dish so tempting it brings a horde of terrorizing mongrels through the doggie-door, forcing her to flee.

Below, Aldrich directs Kim Novak in a scene from a Dietrich-like "Lylah Clare" picture.

The Killing of Sister George (1968)

Producer:	Robert Aldrich [Associates and Aldrich/Palomar Pictures International]
Associate Producer:	Walter Blake
Screenplay:	Lukas Heller, based on the play "The Killing of Sister George" by Frank Marcus
Director of Photography:	Joseph Biroc (Metrocolor; 1.85:1)
Lighting Cameraman:	Brian West [London]
Art Direction:	William Glasgow
Music:	Gerald Fried
Sound:	Dick Church [U.S.]; Robin Gregory [London]
Costumes:	Renie [Conley]
Editor:	Michael Luciano
Production Supervisor:	George Tobin
Production Manager:	David Bennett [London]
Set Decoration:	John Brown
Make-up:	William Turner
Assistant Directors:	Eddie Saeta (UPM/1st); Daisy Gerber (2nd) [U.S.]; Dennis Robertson (1st); Richard Gill, Chips Fairlie (2nds) [London]
Script Supervisor:	Adell [Aldrich] Bravos
Assistant to the Producer:	William Aldrich

Cast: Beryl Reid (June Buckridge/"Sister George"), Susannah York (Alice "Childie" McNaught), Coral Browne (Mercy Croft), Ronald Fraser (Leo Lockhart), Patricia Medina (Betty Thaxter), Hugh Paddick (Freddie), Cyril Delevanti (Ted Baker), Sivi Aberg (Diana), William Beckley (floor manager), Elaine Church (Marlene), Brendan Dillon (Bert Turner), Mike Freeman (Noel), Maggie Paige (maid), Jack Raine (deputy commissioner), Dolly Taylor (tea lady), Meier Tzelniker (Mr. Katz), Cicely Walper (Mrs. Coote), Jack Adams (Byron Webster), Rosalie Williams (Mildred) Eileen Page (Leslie), Julie Shaw (girlfriend).

Filmed on location in London and at the Aldrich Studios, Los Angeles, in 66 days beginning June 10, 1968.

Completed:	October 10, 1968
Cost:	$2,555,000
Distribution:	ABC Palomar International
Running time:	138 minutes
Released:	December 12, 1968 (Fox Theater, Hollywood)
MPAA Rating:	X

Synopsis

June Buckridge (Beryl Reid) is a middle-aged actress who portrays a nurse named "Sister George" in a very successful English television soap opera. June is an alcoholic and insecure about her part, and repeated brushes with fellow cast members and BBC management lead her to suspect that they may plan to write her out of the show. Following a particularly argumentative rehearsal, June stops at a local bar and then attempts to take over a cab carrying two nuns. The nuns, horrified at June's behavior and recognizing her as "Sister George," complain to their superiors.

While June is wallowing in self-pity and abusing her dependent "roommate" and lover, Alice "Childie" McNaught (Susannah York), the Church authorities complain to the network about June's vulgar attack on the nuns. Mrs. Mercy Croft (Coral Browne), a BBC executive, is sent to extract an apology from June. After witnessing June's life-style, Mrs. Croft informs June that "Sister George's" audience appeal is shrinking and that cast changes may be required to bolster the show.

Despondent, June drinks more heavily than ever and seeks commiseration from Betty Thaxter (Patricia Medina), a prostitute living next door. Ultimately, June receives a script in which "Sister George" suffers only a mild illness and quickly recovers. Dressed as Laurel and Hardy, she and Childie celebrate at a local gay bar and even ask Mrs. Croft to join them. Surprisingly, Mrs. Croft accepts. Undismayed by the exclusively lesbian clientele of the bar, Mrs. Croft completely deflates June's exuberance by revealing a new script decision: "Sister George" is to be struck by a truck and killed in the next episode.

June staggers away and out of the bar, leaving Childie with Mrs. Croft. After the filming of "Sister George's death," June is given a farewell party and offered a job on a new animated production as the voice of "Clarabelle Cow." Insulted by the proposition, June vehemently refuses. Arriving home to seek solace, June discovers that Mrs. Croft has seduced Childie. After a final argument with June, Childie decides to pack up and move in with the attentive Mrs. Croft. Abandoned by all, June goes back to the sound stage searching for traces of her former success. Enraged at having everything taken from her, she slashes the studio sets, wrecking as much as she can before becoming exhausted. Sitting on a bench in the darkened stage, she realizes what she must do and begins to practice "Clarabelle Cow's" somber "moos."

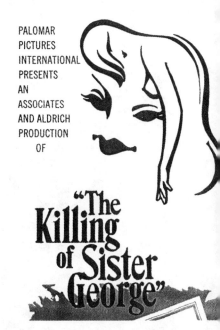

PALOMAR PICTURES INTERNATIONAL PRESENTS AN ASSOCIATES AND ALDRICH PRODUCTION OF

"The Killing of Sister George"

Above right, the provocative graphic for the original release of *The Killing of Sister George*.

Too Late the Hero (1970)

Producer:	Robert Aldrich [Associates and Aldrich—ABC Palomar]
Associate Producer:	Walter Blake
Screenplay:	Robert Aldrich and Lukas Heller, from an original story by Robert Aldrich and Robert Sherman
Director of Photography:	Joseph Biroc (Metrocolor; Metroscope, 1.75:1)
Art Direction:	James Vance
Music:	Gerald Fried
Sound:	Dick Church; Frank Milton (rerecording)
Costumes:	Charles James
Casting:	Lynn Stalmaster
Editors:	Michael Luciano; Albert Nalpas (montage)
Set Decoration:	John Brown
Make-up:	William Turner, Jack Stone
Production Supervisors:	Fred Ahern; Vicente Nayve [Philippines]
2nd Unit Director:	Oscar Rudolph
2nd Unit Photography:	Nonoog Rasca
Assistant Directors:	Grayson Rogers (1st); Malcolm Harding (2nd)
Script Supervisor:	Ken Gilbert
Assistant to the Producer:	William Aldrich
Technical Advisors:	Capt. Robert Lefever, Takashi Ohashi
Special Effects:	Henry Millar, Jr., Lee Vasque
Title Design:	Richard Kuhn

Cast: Michael Caine (Pvt. Tosh Hearne), Cliff Robertson (Lt. jg. Sam Lawson), Henry Fonda (Capt. John G. Nolan), Ian Bannen (Pvt. Thornton), Harry Andrews (Lt. Col. Thompson), Denholm Elliott (Capt. Hornsby), Ronald Fraser (Pvt. Campbell), Lance Percival (Cpl. McLean), Percy Herbert (Sgt. Johnstons), Michael J. Parsons (Pvt. Rafferty), Harvey Jason (Signalman Scott), William Beckley (Pvt. Currie), Don Knight (Pvt. Connally), Sean MacDuff (Pvt. Rogers), Martin Dorsey (Pvt. Griffiths), Roger Newman (Pvt. Riddle), Ken Takakura (Major Yamaguchi), Sam Kydd (Sergeant-Major), Patrick Jordon (soldier).

Filmed on location near Subic Bay in the Philippines and at the Aldrich Studios, Los Angeles, in 92 days beginning January 15, 1969.

Completed:	June 27, 1969
Cost:	$6,250,000
Distribution:	Cinerama Releasing Corporation
Running time:	133 minutes

Opposite, Aldrich stages a fight scene between Ronald Fraser and Michael Caine, while Ian Bannen (top left) and Denholm Elliott (top right) look on.

Released: May 20, 1970 (Egyptian Theater, Hollywood)
MPAA rating: GP [Certificate X in Great Britain]
Alternate Title: For television, *Suicide Run*

NOTE: The Roadshow engagements were in 70mm with six-track Stereophonic sound.

Synopsis

Lt. Lawson (Cliff Robertson), a code expert with the American forces in the Pacific, is summoned by his commander, Capt. Nolan (Henry Fonda). Although Lawson is scheduled for stateside leave, Nolan has an assignment for him: liaison officer with a British unit about to raid a Japanese outpost. Lawson attempts to refuse the mission, but Nolan makes it clear that he has no options.

Lawson arrives at the British-held southern tip of a remote island and discovers a small, irregular unit under the command of Col. Thompson (Harry Andrews). Thompson confirms the details given him by Nolan: Lawson will accompany a patrol into the Japanese-held, northern portion of the island to knock out their ship-watch outpost. Lawson will use his knowledge of Japanese codes to send fake messages and misdirect the enemy fleet. The fifteen-man detachment is led by Capt. Hornsby (Denholm Elliott). Lawson soon learns that the British soldiers' lack of respect for their field commander stems from their knowledge of his inability to lead. Yet despite the fact that Hornsby lets them fall into an ambush in which several men are killed, the raiders manage to reach the Japanese radio transmitter.

Lawson and Pvt. Hearne (Michael Caine) suspect that the guards have been alerted to their presence in the area. Nonetheless, when infiltration at night fails, Hornsby storms the radio shack. Hearne and Lawson hang back, refusing to expose themselves unnecessarily. Hornsby, without Lawson to send messages, elects to destroy the radio but is killed by Japanese troops. The remnants of the patrol fall back, trailed by the Japanese and their portable loudspeaker system, over which Major Yamaguchi (Ken Takakura) exhorts them to surrender.

Finally, three of the weary and hungry Britishers decide to surrender, despite Hearne's and Lawson's warnings that they will be executed. As the messages from the loudspeaker continue, Hearne and Lawson trace the wires back to the microphone. Not realizing that Yamaguchi has kept his promise to spare the other men, they kill him and resume their flight. At last, they reach a no-man's-land between the Japanese and British perimeters. Encouraged by the onlooking British, they take off across the open stretch but come under machine-gun and rifle fire. A few yards short of the objective, one man is hit and falls. Only when he reaches the British camp does Hearne look back and realize Lawson has been killed.

The Grissom Gang (1971)

Producer:	Robert Aldrich [Associates and Aldrich—ABC Pictures]
Associate Producer:	Walter Blake
Screenplay:	Leon Griffiths, based on the novel <u>No Orchids for Miss Blandish</u> by James Hadley Chase
Director of Photography:	Joseph Biroc (Metrocolor; 1.85:1)
Art Direction:	James Vance
Music:	Gerald Fried
Songs:	"I Can't Give You Anything but Love, Baby," lyrics by Dorothy Fields, music by Jimmy McHugh, sung by Rudy Vallee; "I Surrender, Dear," music by Harry Harris, lyrics by Gordon Clifford
Sound:	Dick Church; Harry W. Tetrick (rerecording)
Costumes:	Norma Koch
Casting:	Lynn Stalmaster
Choreography:	Alex Romero
Film Editors:	Michael Luciano; Frank Urioste (associate)
Set Decoration:	John W. Brown
Make-up:	William Turner
Production Supervisor:	Fred Ahern
2nd Unit Director:	Leon Chooluck
Assistant Directors:	Malcolm Harding (1st); William Morrison (2nd)
Script Supervisor:	Robert Gary
Assistant to the Producer:	William Aldrich
Special Effects	Henry Millar, Jr.
Title Design:	Don Record

Cast: Kim Darby (Barbara Blandish), Scott Wilson (Slim Grissom), Tony Musante (Eddie Hagen), Robert Lansing (Dave Fenner), Irene Dailey (Ma Grissom), Connie Stevens (Anna Borg), Wesley Addy (John P. Blandish), Joey Faye (Woppy), Don Keefer (Doc), Dotts Johnson (Johnny Hutchins), Mort Narshall (Heinie), Michael Baselon (Connor), Ralph Waite (Mace), Hal Baylor (Chief McLaine), Matt Clark (Bailey), Alvin Hammer (Sam), Dave Willock (Rocky), Alex Wilson (Jerry McGowen), Elliott Street (gas station boy), John Steadman (old man), Raymond Guth (farmer).

Filmed on location near Sutter Creek and Modesto, California, and at the Aldrich Studios, Los Angeles, in 64 days beginning July 6, 1970.

Completed:	November 13, 1970
Cost:	$3,000,000

Distribution: Cinerama Releasing Corporation
Running time: 128 minutes
Released: May 28, 1971 (Pix Theater, Hollywood)
MPAA Rating: R [Certificate X in Great Britain]

Synopsis

Three petty Kansas City gangsters, Joe Bailey (Matt Clark), Frank Connor (Michael Baselon), and Sam (Alvin Hammer), plan the kidnapping of a local heiress, Barbara Blandish (Kim Darby). After she and her boyfriend, Jerry (Alex Wilson), a football player, have an argument and start home from a roadhouse, their car is run off the road. Jerry tries to resist the three assailants and is killed. Barbara is then taken to a run-down farmhouse owned by an ex-fighter named Johnny Hutchins (Dotts Johnson). Acting on a tip, the farmhouse is visited the next day by members of the Grissom Gang, led by Slim Grissom (Scott Wilson). They confront Bailey, a former associate, with their knowledge. In a brief but violent skirmish, the three original kidnappers are killed. Hutchins is spared, and Blandish is taken to the Grissom farmhouse. She remains there while the gang, run by "Ma" (Irene Dailey), waits for a response to its ransom demand.

Barbara's father, John P. Blandish (Wesley Addy), raises and pays one million dollars to recover his daughter. The gang members cover their traces; they murder a street photographer who knew of the original abduction, and Eddie Hagen (Tony Musante) seduces Connor's former girlfriend, Anna Borg (Connie Stevens). Slim, who is inexperienced with women, translates his sexual attraction to Barbara into what he believes is love. Ma Grissom had planned to kill Barbara after receiving the ransom money; but Slim will not hear of it. Trying to make the most of a bad situation, Ma beats Barbara and tells her that she will be spared if she initiates Slim sexually. Barbara is repulsed by Slim's childish infatuation; but when Slim realizes that he is in control of the situation, he forces her to submit to him.

With the ransom money the gang purchases a nightclub. In an ornately furnished room in the back, Slim installs himself with Barbara. Thinking Slim will eventually tire of her, Ma permits this. After several months have passed without the police finding a trace of his daughter or his money, Blandish hires Dave Fenner (Robert Lansing), a private investigator. Following a hunch that the three missing gangsters may have been involved, Fenner seeks interviews with their contacts. Posing as a talent agent, Fenner tricks Anna Borg into revealing what she knew of Connor's participation.

Hagen visits Anna and recognizes Fenner, who is about to leave. Fenner clubs Hagen with his briefcase and escapes. When Anna suddenly realizes Hagen's involvement in the kidnapping, he shoots her. As Fenner goes to Hutchins and is questioning him, Slim and the gang are alerted by Hagen and surround the Hutchins' place. As police, notified by Fenner, approach the house the gang blows it up. Hutchins is killed but Fenner survives. Hagen, realizing that he will be blamed for not eliminating Anna sooner, takes Barbara and returns to the abandoned Grissom farm. Slim pursues them there; and just as Eddie is about to rape Barbara, Slim stabs him.

Returning to the club with Barbara, Slim finds it under siege and flees. The police kill Ma and the other gang members inside. In the aftermath they discover Slim and Barbara's room. Disgusted by this evidence of his daughter's liaison with a criminal, Blandish loses interest in her return. The following morning Slim and Barbara are tracked down to a barn in a nearby farm. As the police surround them, Slim confesses his love for Barbara, which she reciprocates. Taking his gun, Slim goes out to be shot down. As Barbara is taken away by Fenner, reporters crowd around, asking about her relationship to the dead gangster. Her father shuns her, and she rides off silently in Fenner's car.

Below, Aldrich clowns with Joey Faye on the set of *The Grissom Gang*, possibly reflecting on the status of his deal with ABC.

Ulzana's Raid (1972)

Producer:	Carter de Haven [De Haven—Aldrich]
Associate Producer/Screenplay:	Alan Sharp
Director of Photography:	Joseph Biroc (Technicolor; 1.85:1)
Music:	Frank DeVol
Art Direction:	James Vance
Sound:	Walden O. Watson; James Alexander
Costumes:	Glenn Wright
Editor:	Michael Luciano
Set Decoration:	John McCarthy
Make-up:	Mike Moschella, Tony Lloyd
Production Manager:	Ernest B. Wehmeyer
2nd Unit Director:	Oscar Rudolph
Assistant Director:	Malcolm Harding
Script Supervisor:	Robert Gary
Special Effects:	Sass Bedig, Jack Fagard

Cast: Burt Lancaster (McIntosh), Bruce Davidson (Lt. Garnett DeBuin), Richard Jaeckel (the sergeant), Jorge Luke (Ke-ni-tay), Joaquin Martinez (Ulzana), Lloyd Bochner (Captain Gates), Douglass Watson (Major Wainwright), Karl Swenson (Rukeyser), Dran Hamilton (Mrs. Riordan), John Pearce (corporal), Aimee Eccles (McIntosh's Indian woman), Gladys Holland (Mrs. Rukeyser), Richard Bull (Ginsford), Margaret Fairchild (Mrs. Ginsford), Otto Reichow (Steegmeyer), Dean Smith (Trooper Horowitz), John McKee (company clerk), Nick Cravat, Ted Markland, R.L. Armstrong, Hal Maguire, Richard Farnsworth, Chuck Courtney, Larry Randles, Walter Scott (troopers), Hal Baylor (Curtis), Ross Loney (rider).

Filmed on location near Nogales, Arizona, and Las Vegas, Nevada, in 48 days beginning January 18, 1972.

Completed:	March 11, 1972
Cost:	$2,400,000
Distribution:	Universal
Running Time:	103 minutes
Released:	October 18, 1972 (Chicago); November 22, 1972 (Los Angeles)
MPAA Rating:	R [Certificate X in Great Britain]

Synopsis

As the troopers at a cavalry fort in Arizona play a Sunday game of baseball, an outrider brings word that a party of ten Indians has left the nearby reservation of Chiracahua Apache. When a group dispatched to question the reservation dwellers brings back word that the war party follows Ulzana (Joaquin Martinez), a charismatic leader whose avowed mission is to terrorize all white settlers in his homeland, the commandant assembles a troop to pursue them. Over the objections of his chief scout, McIntosh (Burt Lancaster), the troop is placed under the command of a newly commissioned and totally inexperienced officer, Lt. Garnett DeBuin (Bruce Davidson). DeBuin, who is still under the moral influence of his father, a fundamentalist minister, disapproves of his scouts, both the rough talking McIntosh, who "lives in sin" with an Indian woman, and the "savage" Ke-ni-tay (Jorge Luke).

Despite his scouts' warnings, DeBuin's avowed purpose is to deal with Ulzana in a civilized manner. Various riders have been sent out to warn the local farmers of the threat and to escort those who wish to come back to the safety of the fort. The detachment of searchers comes across a family on their first day of tracking; a husband and wife murdered, a trooper mutilated after he had taken his own life, but the son spared to live with the trauma of witnessing the massacre. Another settler is found buried up to his neck in front of his smouldering home. Unable to understand the motivation for such atrocities, DeBuin questions Ke-ni-tay on the Apache mentality. The only explanation the scout offers is that Ulzana seeks psychic power and hopes to acquire it from the souls of his victims.

As the pursuit continues, Ke-ni-tay recognizes a ruse of the renegades. Most have abandoned their horses, leaving one or two riders changing mounts every few hours to exhaust the cavalry's horses in following a false trail. McIntosh and Ke-ni-tay ride off in opposite directions at right angles to the cavalry column, planning to intercept the riders as they double back. At dawn, McIntosh spots the Indians; he gives chase and, although his own horse is shot, kills one of the riders and wounds the other. When the troopers arrive, McIntosh informs them that he has killed Ulzana's son. After dark, the soldiers mutilate the body in retaliation for their comrade, which greatly disturbs DeBuin. He also orders a reluctant sergeant (Richard Jaeckel) to pursue the wounded Apache.

The following day, the pursuers reach another gutted ranch; but here the Indians have left alive the rancher's wife, raped and scarred. The sergeant returns, having lost another man in killing the wounded Indian. McIntosh surmises that Ulzana's tactic is to force them to divide and send the crazed woman back to the fort with an escort, which he can attack to replace his lost horses. At McIntosh's suggestion they do divide—McIntosh, the sergeant and five others start back, hoping to lure Ulzana out and hold him until DeBuin can arrive. Ke-ni-tay remains with DeBuin and quickly realizes that Ulzana has posted a lookout to make sure the main force does not double back. While he goes up into the foothills to kill him, DeBuin waits.

Meanwhile, McIntosh reaches a narrow pass. Although he knows the Apaches are probably above, the group rides on. As they come under fire, a flash from the fieldglasses of Ulzana's lookout confuses DeBuin. Thinking it a signal from Ke-ni-tay, he starts back. The ferocity of Ulzana's attack is too much for McIntosh. The troopers try to hide behind their horses, but they bolt away. Ulzana's lookout, who is racing to warn his leader, is caught and killed by Ke-ni-tay; but DeBuin still arrives too late. He finds McIntosh, mortally wounded, protecting the woman, and all the others dead. Ke-ni-tay, coming down from the mountain, never pauses but continues after Ulzana. While the soldiers account for the rest of the Apaches, Ke-ni-tay runs down the renegade leader and brings the body back to DeBuin, who orders it burned over pro-tests that the head should be taken back to verify his death. At McIntosh's in-sistence, DeBuin and his remaining men ride off, leaving him behind to die alone.

Below, Burt Lancaster and Richard Jaeckel share a mount in *Ulzana's Raid*.

The Emperor of the North Pole (1973)

Producer:	Stanley Hough [Inter-Hemisphere Productions]
Executive Producer:	Kenneth Hyman
Screenplay:	Christopher Knopf
Director of Photography:	Joseph Biroc (DeLuxe Color; Panavision, 1:85:1)
Art Direction:	Jack Martin Smith
Music:	Frank DeVol
Song:	"A Man and a Train," lyrics by Hal David, music by Frank DeVol; sung by Marty Robbins
Sound:	Dick Overton; Theodore Soderberg (rerecording)
Costumes:	Ed Wynigear
Casting:	Jack Baur
Film Editors:	Michael Luciano; Roland Gross, Frank Capacchione (associates)
Set Decoration:	Raphael Bretton
Make-up:	William Turner
Production Manager:	Saul Wurtzel
2nd Unit Director:	Michael D. Moore
Assistant Directors:	Malcolm Harding (1st); Barry Steinberg, Larry Powell (2nds)
Script Supervisor:	Howard Hohler
Special Effects:	Henry Millar, Jr.
Title Design:	Walter Blake

Cast: Lee Marvin (A No. 1), Ernest Borgnine (Shack), Keith Carradine (Cigaret), Charles Tyner (Cracker), Malcolm Atterbury (Hogger), Simon Oakland (policeman), Harry Caesar (Coaly), Hal Baylor (yard man), Matt Clark (yardlet), Elisha Cook (Gray Cat), Joe di Reda (Dinger), Liam Dunn (Smile), Diana Dye (Prudence), Robert Foulk (conductor), James Goodwin (Fakir), Ray Guth (Preacher), Sid Haig (Grease Tail), Karl Lucas (Pokey Stiff), Edward McNally (yard clerk), John Steadman (Stew Bum), Vic Tayback (yard man), Dave Willock (Groundhog), Ralph Montgomery (Alkee Stiff), Don Blackman (Old Shine), Hal Jon Norman (Pegleg), Harry Hickox (Elder), Danny Big Black (Hobo), Wayne Sutherlin (Gink), Ben Hoffman (Halfy), Forrest Wood (station agent), Joe Hayworth (Ash Eater), Jack Collins (dispatcher), Richard Doughly (the Cub), James Kingsley (machinist), George McFadden (Prairie Special engineer), Ben Dobbins (mechanic).

Filmed on location near Cottage Grove, Oregon, and at 20th Century-Fox Studios in 74 days beginning July 11, 1972.

Completed:	October 5, 1972
Cost:	$3,800,000
Distribution:	20th Century-Fox
Running time:	118 minutes [126 minutes before general release]
Released:	May 23, 1973 (New York); June 29, 1973 (Los Angeles)
MPAA Rating:	PG

NOTE: This film was originally released in New York under the title *The Emperor of the North Pole*, but was changed to *Emperor of the North* for the Los Angeles and subsequent runs.

Synopsis

In the early years of the depression, Freight Number 19 runs through the Northwest and acquires a reputation among hoboes as an "unrideable" train. Its brutal guard, "Shack" (Ernest Borgnine), carries a small hammer clipped to his belt and has killed several hoboes without compunction. On this particular day a solitary 'bo named "A No. 1" (Lee Marvin) has hopped No. 19 from a trestle overpass. As he settles in, unaware that Shack has already hurled one hobo from the train and is stalking others, another man runs up alongside and jumps into A No. 1's car.

"Cigaret" (Keith Carradine) quickly establishes himself as a boaster; his lack of skill in boarding has caused him to be spotted by Shack, who stands above them, amused by their discussion. Unimpressed by Cigaret, A No. 1 returns to his own thoughts. Shack slams and locks the freight car door, planning to deal with them both in the Willamette yard. Unable to force the door open, Cigaret's bravado evaporates, and he begins to panic. A No. 1 admits that their position looks bad but saves his energy.

As they approach the yard, he piles up some straw by the wall of the car and sets it afire. Above them, Shack realizes what is happening and instructs the engineer to hurry into the yard. As soon as the flames have charred and weakened the wall, A No. 1 kicks out a portion and jumps through, tumbling out of the train at the edge of the yard. Cigaret hesitates too long; by the time he jumps, the train has entered the yard, and he is captured. The yard crew realize that a brash greenhorn like Cigaret could not have accomplished the fiery escape from Shack's clutches, and they question him regarding A No. 1. Since most of the yard men have had run-ins with Shack, they wonder if a 'bo has finally materialized who could tarnish Shack's reputation for perfect runs. The yard men establish a betting pool and send one of their number to the hobo jungle to challenge A No. 1. While they continue to discuss the possibilities of A No. 1's attempt, Cigaret takes advantage of their inattention to escape.

Opposite, ad art before the title change on *Emperor of the North Pole*.

Only one man can be...

EMPEROR OF THE NORTH POLE

Lee Marvin & Ernest Borgnine
meet in the fight of the century.

20th Century-Fox Presents

LEE MARVIN · ERNEST BORGNINE · KEITH CARRADINE in "EMPEROR OF THE NORTH POLE
Co-starring CHARLES TYNER · MALCOLM ATTERBURY · HARRY CAESAR · SIMON OAKLAND
Produced by STAN HOUGH · Directed by ROBERT ALDRICH · A KENNETH HYMAN PRODUCTION
Written by CHRISTOPHER KNOPF · Music by FRANK DeVOL · "A Man And A Train" Sung by BILL
MEDLEY · Lyrics by HAL DAVID / Music by FRANK DeVOL · COLOR BY DE LUXE®

20th
CENTURY
FOX

Arriving at the hobo jungle, Cigaret discovers that A No. 1 has been awarded a hero's welcome by the assembly of bums, who have voted him "The Emperor of the North Pole." Cigaret wastes no time in claiming half of A No. 1's empire, but the bums are as capable as the yard men of recognizing a greenhorn and ignore his protests. After an indecisive morning in which he wanders around dodging police and even getting baptized, A No. 1 decides to accept the yard men's challenge. Shack, aware of the contest, decides to take the No. 19 out of the yard at high speed, but the hoboes break open a switch, sending the freight train into a siding and allowing A No. 1 to clamber aboard.

As he prepares his tactics for survival, A No. 1 discovers that Cigaret has also jumped the train. Meanwhile, Shack, infuriated at having his train side-tracked, wastes no time in stopping it to search, forcing the bums to take cover in the surrounding brush. When the No. 19 starts up again, Shack spots them and prevents them from climbing on. As Cigaret mocks him, A No. 1 demonstrates that he is not yet ready to quit. He greases the track to slow down an oncoming express and rides it right back to where the No. 19 has pulled into a siding to allow it to pass. Shack realizes that he is not dealing with any ordinary roadbum, when he again spots A No. 1 aboard his train. He threatens to corner the unarmed hoboes with his deadly hammer, but A No. 1 slams on the emergency brake, enabling both men to leap off.

Shack watches from above a boxcar while a defeated A No. 1 catches his breath on the side of the hill and tells Cigaret he has had enough. Sensing a chance to seize A No. 1's meaningless empire, Cigaret scrambles up the hill and gets back on the No. 19. After a moment's pause, in which Shack's attention is diverted to Cigaret, A No. 1 wearily follows. It takes Shack little time to corner the inexperienced Cigaret on a flatcar at the rear of the train and begin to beat him savagely.

Reluctantly, A No. 1 interrupts and, after a desperate struggle, wrenches away Shack's weapon and pummels him, finally throwing the semiconscious guard off the flatcar. As Cigaret starts to bluster about "their" victory, A No. 1 pushes him off the train also, yelling back that he doesn't have the right attitude to call himself a hobo.

Left, Burt Reynolds reads over Aldrich's shoulder before rehearsing the football sequences in *The Longest Yard*.

The Longest Yard (1974)

Producer:	Albert S. Ruddy
Associate Producer:	Alan P. Horowitz
Screenplay:	Tracy Kennan Wynn, from a story by Albert S. Ruddy
Director of Photography:	Joseph Biroc (Technicolor; 1.85:1)
Production Design:	James S. Vance
Music:	Frank DeVol
Songs:	Lynyrd Skynyrd's "Saturday Night Special" written by Ronnie Van Zant and Edward Calhoun King; "Teach Me To Cheat," sung by Judy Kester; "Roadside Roses," sung by Jack Barlow; "Paramount on Parade," by Janis and King; "Born Free," by Barry and Black; "You Got to be a Football Hero," by Sherman, Lewis and Fields, performed by the Soul Touchers Band and Chorus
Sound:	Fred Faust; John Wilkinson (rerecording)
Costumes:	Charles James
Casting:	Joyce Selznick
Film Editors:	Michael Luciano; Frank Capacchione, Allan Jacobs, George Hively (football sequences); Steve Orfanos (montage)
Set Decoration:	Raphael Bretton
Make-up:	Tom Ellingwood, Guy Del Russo
Production Manager:	Russ Saunders
2nd Unit Director/Stunt Coordinator:	Hal Needham
2nd Unit Photography:	Cliff Poland
Assistant Directors:	Clifford Coleman (1st); Ron Wright (2nd)
Script Supervisor:	Alvin Greenman
Assistant to the Producer:	Bettye McCartt
Technical Advisor:	Patrick Studstill
Special Effects:	Thol Ogden Simonson
Title Design:	Walter Blake

Cast: Burt Reynolds (Paul Crewe), Eddie Albert (Warden Hazen), Ed Lauter (Captain Knauer), Harry Caesar (Granville), Ray Nitschke (Bogdanski), Mike Henry (Rassmeusen), Joe Kapp (Walking Boss), John Steadman (Pop), Bernadette Peters (Warden's secretary), Michael Conrad (Nate Scarboro), James Hampton (Caretaker), Anitra Ford (Melissa), Pepper Martin (shop steward),

Ernie Wheelwright, Jr. (Spooner), Tony Cacciotti (Rotka), Richard Kiel (Samson), Pervis Atkins (Mawabe), Dino Washington (Mason), Charles Tyner (linger), Mort Marshall (assistant warden), Robert Tessier (Schokner), Michael Fox (announcer), Joe Dorsey (bartender), Chuck Hayward (trooper 1), Alfie Wise (trooper 2), Dr. Gus Carlucci (team doctor), Jack Rockwell (trainer), Sonny Shroyer (Tannen), Ray Ogden (Schmidt), Don Ferguson (referee), Tony Reese (Levitt), Steve Wilder (J.J.), George Jones (Big George), Wilbur Gillan (Big Wilbur), Wilson Warren (Buttercup), Joe Jackson (Little Joe).

Filmed on location in and around Georgia State Prison, Reidsville, Georgia; Beverly Hills, California; and at Paramount Studios in 62 days beginning October 4, 1973.

Completed: December 18, 1973.

Cost: $2,900,000

Distribution: Paramount (U.S.); CIC-American (Great Britain)

Running time: 121 minutes (U.S.); 122 minutes (Great Britain)

Released: August 21, 1974 (Loew's State, Orpheum, New York City)

MPAA Rating: R [Certificate X in Great Britain]

Alternate Title: In Great Britain, *The Mean Machine*

Synopsis

Former professional football star Paul Crewe (Burt Reynolds) violently severs his relationship with a Palm Beach heiress (Anitra Ford). He slaps her around then steals her car and eludes the police, whom she summons to arrest him. After a high-speed chase through the central city, Crewe finally pushes the battered vehicle into the river. When two policemen come to question him in a nearby bar, he provokes them into a fight. For auto theft and resisting arrest, Crewe is sentenced to a year at hard labor in Citrus State Prison.

Arriving at the prison, Crewe finds that his reputation has preceded him. Many inmates are openly contemptuous of an athletic superstar who ruined his career by shaving points. Warden Hazen (Eddie Albert), however, feels no compunction about asking Crewe to help his semiprofessional team of guardsmen win a national championship. Opposed to this idea is Captain Knauer (Ed Lauter), coach and quarterback of the team, who warns Crewe with his fists not to accept Hazen's offer. Crewe's compliance with Knauer's threat angers Hazen, who sends Crewe to work on the swamp reclamation detail shackled to a rebellious black prisoner, Granville (Harry Caesar). Crewe tries to keep a low profile while on the chain gang, but he is taunted constantly by guards and fellow inmates, particularly the trustee, Unger (Charles Tyner), one of Hazen's informants. Only "Caretaker" (Jim Hampton) and "Pop" (John Steadman), a lifer who lost all hope of parole when he struck Hazen, are in any way friendly.

When Crewe is finally goaded into a fight, the guards urge the men to hurt each other severely. But Crewe redirects his violence at Knauer and, as a result, is sent to solitary. In order to escape the "box," Crewe tells Hazen he has reconsidered his offer. After watching the guards in practice, he suggests that what they need is a tune-up game. Hazen likes the idea and orders Crewe to organize a team of prisoners for just such a purpose.

Reluctantly, with Caretaker as his assistant, Crewe begins putting a team together. The first volunteer is Nate Scarboro (Michael Conrad), an aging former pro. Caretaker acquires prison records to suggest both the likeliest players and the guards' weaknesses. After convincing the largest and meanest white inmates to participate, Crewe appeals to Granville to help recruit the best black athletes. Under the enticement of being able to hit the guards where it hurts, they ultimately accept assignments. Unger, spying for Hazen, badgers Crewe to become assistant coach without success. Meanwhile, Caretaker arranges a tryst between Crewe and Hazen's secretary (Bernadette Peters) in exchange for a film of the guards in action and plaster casts and drugs from the dispensary. He even plans for new team uniforms. The rejected Unger takes revenge by booby trapping the light bulb in Crewe's cell; but it is Caretaker, coming to get something for Crewe, who is burned to death when the bulb explodes.

Saddened by Caretaker's death, the prisoners' view of the game as an opportunity to even the score for years of abuse is strengthened. They stun the guards just by taking the field in black uniforms labelled "Mean Machine." In the first two quarters, the Mean Machine also surprises the guards by its ability. Although they make mistakes which allow the guards to score, the prisoners make offensive moves which keep the score close at half time and defensively injure several of the guards.

Dismayed by his team's poor showing, Hazen calls Crewe to the shower room between periods. While Capt. Knauer earnestly chews out his men in the next room, Hazen fixes the game by telling Crewe he has a confession from Unger which implicates Crewe in Caretaker's death. Hazen threatens to use this information against him unless Crewe throws the game by twenty-one points. Frightened by the prospect of life imprisonment for murder, Crewe's play in the third quarter is a succession of poor passes and fumbles, which allows the guardsmen to get a three-touchdown lead. Unknown to Crewe and contrary to their deal, Hazen lets Knauer encourage the guards to give the inmates all the physical abuse they can deliver. With Granville hurt and the team aware that he is throwing the game, Crewe takes himself out.

While he watches the prisoners being brutalized, Crewe catches Pop's look of disapproval and remembers Pop's avowal that hurting Hazen was worth a life term. Crewe returns to the field and is hit hard several times when Mean Machine blockers abandon him. When he does manage to gain ground, his men are convinced Crewe has decided to play to win. Finally, it is the last play of the game, with the inmates' line of scrimmage on the guards' one-yard line. As Crewe rolls out on an option, he spots a hole and plows his way through, scoring a comeback upset at the gun.

At first Hazen is too stunned to speak; then as Crewe walks back alone towards the end zone, Hazen tells Capt. Knauer that Crewe is trying to escape and must be shot. Knauer grabs a rifle and takes aim but hesitates out of new-found respect for Crewe and ignores Hazen's enraged orders to fire. When Crewe bends down to pick up the game ball and heads back, both men make evident their disgust with Hazen; and Crewe goes into the showers uncertain of his fate.

Hustle (1975)

Producer:	Robert Aldrich [RoBurt Productions/Paramount in association with Churchill Service Company]
Executive Producer:	Burt Reynolds
Associate Producer:	William Aldrich
Screenplay:	Steve Shagan
Director of Photography:	Joseph Biroc (Eastmancolor; 1.85:1)
Art Direction:	Hilyard Brown
Music:	Frank DeVol
Songs:	"Yesterday When I Was Young," by Charles Aznavour, English lyrics by Herbert Kretzmer, sung by Charles Aznavour; "So Rare," lyrics by Jack Sharpe, music by Jerry Herst; "A Man and a Woman," by Francis Lai; "Mission Impossible," music by Lalo Schifrin; "Begin the Beguine," by Cole Porter
Sound:	Jack Solomon; John Wilkinson (rerecording)
Costumes:	Oscar Rodriguez, Betsy Cox
Casting:	Jack Baur
Film Editor:	Michael Luciano
Set Decoration:	Raphael Bretton
Make-up:	Tom Ellingwood
Production Supervisor:	Eddie Saeta
Assistant Directors:	Malcolm Harding (1st); Phil Ball (2nd)
Script Supervisor:	Adell Aldrich
Assistant to the Producer:	Walter Blake
Special Effects:	Henry Millar, Jr.

Cast: Burt Reynolds (Lt. Phil Gaines), Catherine Deneuve (Nicole Britton), Ben Johnson (Marty Hollinger), Paul Winfield (Sgt. Louis Belgrave), Eileen Brennan (Paula Hollinger), Eddie Albert (Leo Sellers), Ernest Borgnine (Santoro), Jack Carter (Herbie Dalitz), Sharon Kelly (Gloria Hollinger), James Hampton (bus driver), David Spielberg (Bellamy), Catherine Bach (Peggy Summers), Chuck Hayward (morgue attendant), David Estridge (albino), Peter Brandon (minister), Naomi Stevens (woman hostage), Med Flory (albino-beating cop), Steve Shaw (cop in elevator), Dino Washington (cop in elevator), Anthony Eldridge (laugher), John Duke Russo (man in phone booth), Don Billett (cop in t-shirt), Hal Baylor (police captain), Nancy Bonniwell (girl in airport bar), Don "Red" Barry (airport bartender), Karl Lukas (Charley), Gene Chronopoulos (bartender), Patrice Rohmer (Linda, a dancer), Alvin Hammer (liquor store clerk), Dave Willock (liquor store clerk),

Queenie Smith, Marilyn Moe (customers), Robert Englund (hold-up man), George Memoli (foot fetish man), Fred Willard (interrogator), Thad Geer (second hold-up man), Kelly Wilder (Nancy Gaines).

Filmed on location in Los Angeles, Pasadena and Marina del Rey, California in 47 days beginning November 20, 1974.

Completed:	January 31, 1975
Cost:	$3,050,000
Distribution:	Paramount (U.S.), CIC-American (Great Britain)
Running time:	120 minutes (U.S.); 118 minutes (Great Britain)
Released:	December 25, 1975 (multiple run, Los Angeles)
MPAA Rating:	R [Certificate X in Great Britain]
Original titles:	*All the Other Angels; City of the Angels; Home Free*

Synopsis

When a bus full of children on a beach outing discovers the body of a young woman (Sharon Kelly) in the surf, Lt. Phil Gaines' (Burt Reynolds) morning off from the Los Angeles Police Tactical squad is interrupted. He leaves the house he shares with French-born Nicole Britton (Catherine Deneuve) troubled by personal problems. Nicole, who came to the U.S. as a highly paid call girl, continues to practice her profession part time because Gaines, apprehensive after divorcing an unfaithful wife, will not make an unqualified emotional commitment to her. Gaines leaves knowing she resents the occasions when his job spoils their time together and may unconsciously retaliate by "turning a trick."

Gaines and his partner, Sgt. Louis Belgrave (Paul Winfield), establish that the girl may be Gloria Hollinger, a reported runaway of some years earlier; they summon her parents, Marty and Paula Hollinger (Ben Johnson and Eileen Brennan), to the morgue for identification of the corpse. At the sight of Gloria's unclad body unceremoniously rolled out from a cold drawer, Hellinger attacks Gaines and abuses him verbally for not even covering the body. Gaines acknowledges that it was callous of them but feels compelled to tell Hollinger that Gloria most likely died of a self-induced drug overdose following attendance at a party. The detectives also know she was a frequent performer at sex parties and in stag reels.

As Paula Hollinger tries to console her husband in their daughter's long unused room, Gaines goes home and discovers Nicole in an erotic phone conversation with a client. Gaines disconnects the phone and tries once again to express his feelings to Nicole. The following morning, Gaines and Belgrave are called before Chief John Santoro (Ernest Borgnine) and questioned about Hollinger's allegation to the district attorney that the police are covering up his daughter's murder. Gaines assures him it was suicide; and Belgrave's desire to keep the case open is thwarted. Outside, Gaines does agree to follow up on a photograph found in the dead girl's possession, but his ambivalence about the case is increased by Hollinger's belligerence and his accusations of a cover-up.

Somewhat mollified by Paula Hollinger's thanks and her admission that her husband has not been the same since his wartime experiences, Gaines decides to follow up on the photograph. Before he can begin, he receives a call that a man whom Gaines had once arrested and was institutionalized has been released, killed two women, and taken another hostage in a garment workshop, where he now is demanding to see Gaines. By the time Gaines and Belgrave reach the scene, Gaines is almost out of control in his indignation over a system of justice which not only brushes aside Marty Hollinger because he is, as Santoro says, "nobody," but which also lets a psychopath go free.

Arriving at the garment workshop, Gaines crosses police barricades to join the psychopath on the top floor. Knowing that Gaines will be killed if he exchanges himself for the hostage, Belgrave jumps through a skylight and shoots the psychopath. Gaines sees the man is not dead and puts a bullet in his head to insure that he will never be let loose again. The results of enlarging the Hollinger girl's photograph disclose her standing next to her roommate, Peggy Summers (Catherine Bach), and a prominent attorney named Leo Sellers (Eddie Albert). Even as Gaines is pondering whether to harass Sellers, who is not only a powerful figure but is responsible for bringing Nicole to Los Angeles, she is spending the afternoon on Seller's yacht.

While there, Nicole watches Sellers make a call from a public telephone, not knowing that the connection is with a city in the Midwest and that he is listening to the sound of an explosion signaling the death of a union leader. After the call, Sellers returns to Nicole, unaware that he has made the call on a phone coincidentally tapped by narcotics officers. While Hollinger, following up on information given him by Gloria's roommate, goes to a nightclub where his daughter once worked as an exotic dancer, the Tactical Squad is given the tape of Sellers' telephone call and Gaines recognizes the voice.

After being confronted with the call, Sellers, although he knows the tapes could not convict him of any crime, admits that the Hollinger girl frequented his parties, including one the night before she died. Gaines accepts Sellers' story, which suggests the motive for her suicide was simply fatigue with her dissolute life-style. Sellers also tells Gaines that Nicole was with him when he made the call. This provokes a violent argument when Gaines returns home, which leads to his striking Nicole, then to a tearful reconciliation.

The following morning Gaines is dismayed to learn from Paula Hollinger that Marty has been beaten up by employees of the nightclub where he went to ask questions. Although he is sufficiently outraged to visit the club himself and physically abuse the M.C. (Jack Carter), Gaines confides to Belgrave that if Hollinger follows the trail to Sellers he may be more seriously hurt. After he learns from Hollinger's wife that her infidelity was one of the causes of Gloria's estrangement and that, ironically, she was not even Marty's child, Gaines begins to see too many depressing parallels with his own past. He convinces Belgrave that they must disillusion Hollinger by showing him a stag reel, acquired from Sellers, featuring his daughter. Yet this makes Hollinger even more determined to find the person responsible for Gloria's death.

When Gaines and Belgrave learn from Paula that Hollinger has beaten Peggy Summers to learn Sellers' name, they race to Sellers' home only to discover Hollinger has already murdered him. Even as he lectures Hollinger, Gaines tampers with evidence to make it look as if Hollinger acted in self-defense. Shooting the stupefied Hollinger in the arm perfects the alibi, at which point Belgrave realizes that Gaines may well have engineered the entire thing out of jealousy over Nicole. Still, he goes along with Gaines. Exorcised of the ghosts of his past, Gaines calls Nicole and proposes that they go to San Francisco and rediscover each other. On his way to the airport, he stops at a liquor store, stumbles into a robbery, and is killed. Belgrave appears at the airport to break the news to Nicole.

Opposite, a lobby card from *Hustle* featuring Catherine Deneuve as Nicole and Burt Reynolds as Gaines.

Twilight's Last Gleaming (1977)

Producer:	Merv Adelson [Lorimar Productions in association with Bavaria Atelier presenting a Geria GmbH Production]
Executive Producer:	Helmut Jedele
Screenplay:	Ronald M. Cohen and Edward Huebsch and [uncredited] Tom Mankiewicz, based on the novel Viper Three by Walter Wager
Director of Photography:	Robert Hauser (Technicolor; 1.85:1)
Production Design:	Rolf Zehetbauer
Music:	Jerry Goldsmith; "My Country 'Tis of Thee," sung by Billy Preston
Sound:	James Willis; John Wilkinson (rerecording)
Costumes:	Tom Dawson
Film Editor:	Michael Luciano
Art Direction:	Werner Achmann
Make-up:	Georg Jauss, Hans Peter Knoepfle
Production Supervisor:	Henry Sokal
Production Executive for Lorimar:	Harry Sherman
Production Executive for Geria:	Lutz Hengst
Production Associate for Aldrich:	Walter Blake
Assistant Directors:	Wolfgang Glattes (1st); Peter Eitzert (2nd)
Script Supervisor:	Alvin Greenman
Technical Advisor:	H. Andrew Erwin
Special Effects:	Henry Millar, Jr.
Title Design:	Walter Blake

Cast: Burt Lancaster (Lawrence Dell), Richard Widmark (General Martin MacKenzie), Charles Durning (President David T. Stevens), Melvyn Douglas (Zachariah Guthrie), Paul Winfield (Powell), Burt Young (Garvas), Joseph Cotten (Arthur Renfrew), Roscoe Lee Browne (James Forrest), Gerald S. O'Loughlin (General Michael O'Rourke), Richard Jaeckel (Captain Towne), Vera Miles (Victoria Stevens), William Marshall (William Klinger), Charles Aidman (Colonel Bernstein), Leif Erickson (Ralph Whittaker), Charles McGraw (General Crane), Morgan Paull (Lieutenant Cannellis), Simon Scott (Phil Spencer), William Smith (Hoxey), Bill Walker (Willard).

Filmed on location near Munich, West Germany in 65 days beginning February 16, 1976.

Completed:	May 14, 1976
Cost:	$6,200,000
Distribution:	Allied Artists
Running time:	143 minutes
Released:	February 9, 1977 (multiple run, Los Angeles)
MPAA rating:	R
Original titles:	*Viper Three; Silo III*

Synopsis

It is Sunday, November 16, 1981. While President David Stevens (Charles Durning) shaves and prepares to receive a former teacher, four men—Dell (Burt Lancaster), Powell (Paul Winfield), Garvas (Burt Young), and Hoxie (William Smithers)—ambush an Air Force truck on a country road. They dispatch the occupants, take their uniforms, and drive towards a nearby Titan missile installation. On a road in Colorado, SAC General MacKenzie (Richard Widmark) is driven to work and pays no attention to the radio news broadcast about four escaped convicts. At the White House, James Forrest (Roscoe Lee Browne) asks the President not to extradite a political assassin. Stevens refuses; his military aide General O'Rourke (Gerald O'Loughlin) arrives as Forrest leaves and tries to change Stevens' mood with light banter.

At the missile base, the convicts pass the questioning of the security guards. Mindful of the television monitors mounted on a central bunker, they stall their truck between two gates and overpower the guards as they try to push it clear. Dell enters the bunker to cover the remaining guard. When Hoxie enters and shoots him, Dell turns and kills Hoxie. Using Dell's unexplained knowledge of the installation, the three remaining convicts complete their descent to the missile control center located 400 feet underground. Posing as the relief team which they have ambushed, Dell and Garvas trick the two launch technicians into opening the massive steel door to the control center. As the convicts burst in, one of the technicians, Captain Towne (Richard Jaeckel), recognizes Dell as a fellow Vietnam War prisoner; but it is too late to sound an alarm, and he is overpowered. Towne also knows that Dell is a former Air Force general and co-designer of the missile installation, a man convicted on dubious murder charges after threatening to reveal secrets about U.S. military operations in Vietnam.

With his technical knowledge, Dell activates the supposedly fail-safe, impeding features in the launch console. He finishes and announces that he has taken control of the site. While General MacKenzie's beeper summons him from a church service, Dell pleads for Towne's assistance. Because Hoxie, who had the knowledge to open a wall safe in the control center, has been killed, Dell must have the combination to obtain the keys inside it; and only those keys turned simultaneously can begin the actual launch of the missiles.

Towne tells Dell that he is deceiving himself if he thinks that he can beat the system, and he refuses to help. Garvas then tortures the other technician and gets the combination.

When MacKenzie reaches the SAC command center and telephones Dell, the former general delivers his ultimatum: a personal line to the President or the missiles will be fired. MacKenzie, one of the men responsible for Dell's disgrace, verifies through an electronic check that Dell has fully activated the console. Although he still doubts that Dell has the keys, MacKenzie reluctantly picks up his direct line to the White House. Stevens receives the call in the company of O'Rourke and Defense Secretary Guthrie (Melvyn Douglas); then O'Rourke quickly summons other key cabinet members and joint chiefs. In the presence of these advisers, a somewhat incredulous Stevens contacts Dell and hears his demands: ten million dollars, a plane to a neutral country, Presidential publication of National Security Council document 9759, and Stevens himself as hostage.

After Stevens has stalled for time to read the document, which the majority of his advisers believe should not be published, and found Dell adamant on that point despite a counter offer of twenty million dollars, the joint decision is to permit MacKenzie to attack the installation. A number of armored personnel carriers deploy in plain view of the television scanners as a diversionary tactic, so that a helicopter may lower a four-man squad onto the one blind spot directly over the bunker. While Dell opens the silo doors and demands the APC's stop where they are, two men carrying a tactical nuclear weapon climb down the cables in the elevator shaft.

As they prepare to arm the bomb just outside the control room door, one of them slips and falls against it, triggering an alarm. Before the convicts can react, the technicians burst through the locked door of their quarters. They are subdued, but Garvas is killed. Enraged at MacKenzie's attempt, Dell and Powell turn the keys, and three missiles rise up out of their silos. MacKenzie asks for permission to detonate the bomb; but Stevens refuses, and the men are withdrawn. O'Rourke convinces Stevens that only by agreeing to the terms and becoming a hostage can he lure Dell out of the control center, where he is now virtually invulnerable and obviously capable of launching the missiles.

Despite his misgivings, Stevens leaves for the installation; but first he secures the promise of Secretary Guthrie that, should Stevens be killed, Guthrie will make public document 9759. MacKenzie deploys snipers in the abandoned APC'S, as Stevens goes down alone to meet Dell. Powell has convinced Dell that even the President's life will be sacrificed before the document is published and that there is little chance of success. But when Dell decides to launch the missiles, Powell refuses to turn the other key; he prefers that small chance to none. Stevens tries to reassure the two convicts that there is no trap awaiting them. Nonetheless they make their way cautiously up to the bunker, and once outside they stand on either side of Stevens and spin around to avoid presenting themselves as clear targets.

When the three men are halfway to the Presidential plane, the snipers open fire, killing Dell and Powell but also fatally wounding Stevens. O'Rourke reaches him first, and Stevens has him call Guthrie over. Before he dies, Stevens reminds Guthrie of his promise; and, with O'Rourke cradling the President's body, the Defense Secretary is left to ponder whether he will fulfill his promise to the dead man.

In his last films Aldrich used split screen extensively. Below, clockwise from top left: Charles Durning; central command; Burt Lancaster; Richard Widmark in *Twilight's Last Gleaming*.

The Choirboys (1977)

Producers:	Merv Adelson, Lee Rich [Lorimar—P.A.C. Cinematografica]
Executive Producers:	Pietro Bregni, Mario Bregni, Mark Damon
Associate Producer:	William Aldrich
Screenplay:	Christopher Knopf and Joseph Wambaugh [uncredited], based on the novel by Wambaugh
Director of Photography:	Joseph Biroc (Metrocolor [processing]/Technicolor [prints]; 1.85:1)
Art Direction:	Bill Kenney; Sid Tinglof (set design)
Music:	Frank DeVol
Sound:	James Contreras; Bill McGaughey (rerecording)
Costumes:	Tom Dawson, Yvonne Kubis
Casting:	Jack Baur
Film Editor:	Maury Weintrobe
Set Decoration:	Raphael Bretton
Make-up:	Tom Ellingwood
Production Manager:	Eddie Saeta
Assistant Directors:	Malcolm Harding (1st); Cheryl Downey (2nd)
Script Supervisor:	Adell Aldrich
Assistant to the Producer:	Walter Blake
Special Effects:	Henry Millar, Jr.

Cast: Charles Durning ("Spermwhale" Whalen), Louis Gosset, Jr. (Calvin Motts), Perry King (Baxter Slate), Burt Young (Sgt. Dominic Scuzzi), Randy Quaid ("Whaddayamean" Dean Proust), Clyde Kusatsu (Francis Tanaguchi), Stephen Macht (Spencer Van Moot), Tim Mcintire (Roscoe Rules), Chuck Sacci (Cheech Sartino), Don Stroud (Sam Lyles), James Woods (Harold Bloomguard), Charles Haid (Nick Yanov), Robert Webber (Deputy Chief Riggs), George DiCenzo (Lt. Grimsley), Vic Tayback (Sgt. Pete Zoony), Barbara Rhoades ("No Balls" Hadley), Phyllis Davis (Foxy/Gina), Blair Brown (Kimberly Lyles), Jeanie Bell (Fanny Forbes), Michele Carey (Ora Lee Tingle), Joe Capp (hod carrier), Jim Davis (Drobeck), Jack DeLeon (Luther Quigley), David Spielberg (Lt. Finque), Michael Wills (Blaney), Susan Batson (Sabrina), Claire Brennen (Carolina Moon), Gene Chronopoulos (card player).

Filmed on location in Los Angeles and at M.G.M. Studios, Culver City in 55 days beginning March 28, 1977.

Completed:	June 20, 1977
Cost:	$6,500,000
Distribution:	Universal
Running time:	119 Minutes

Released: December 23, 1977 (Los Angeles)
MPAA Rating: R [Certificate X in Great Britain]

Synopsis

In Vietnam in 1969, two American soldiers, Lyles (Don Stroud) and Bloomguard (James Woods), conceal themselves a cave. As the enemy throws
flames into the cave, Lyles has a traumatic moment in which he imagines that
he cannot breathe. In 1975 the police night watch reports for roll call at the
Fairfax precinct house. Sgt. Yanov (Charles Haid) checks off various patrol
teams: including the oldest man, Whalen (Charles Durning), and his partner,
Slate (Perry King). Others include Van Moot (Stephen Macht) and Sartino
(Chuck Sacci); Lyles and Bloomguard (James Woods); Motts (Lou Gosset)
and Tanaguchi (Clyde Kusatsu); Rules (Tim McIntire) and Proust (Randy
Quaid). When the watch commander, Lt. Grimsley (George DiCenzo), appears, Whalen takes the opportunity to air several gripes. Grimsley replies with
a threat to bust Whalen before his upcoming completion of twenty years' service and full retirement eligibility. Yanov concludes by inviting the men to
"choir practice" at his home that evening.

In the narrow parking lot, the men back out a dozen patrol cars simultaneously, which infuriates the ineffectual Grimsley. At "choir practice," a noisy post-
watch party at which the men concentrate on drinking and playing cards,
Whalen gropes at a policewoman in the pool, and she storms away to dress and
leave. While she is sitting on a glass-top table combing her hair, a drunken Sartino crawls in and begins to kiss the glass beneath her, until she discovers him
and becomes hysterical.

The following night, Rules and Proust receive a call concerning a woman
perched on a roof ledge. When the reach the scene, Proust recommends waiting for the sergeant, but Rules, a rascist, insists on talking to the African-American woman. When Rules tells her to go ahead and jump, she does. When the
sergeant does arrive, Rules claims that they were unable to reach the roof in
time to speak with her.

While Grimsley is eating at a coffee shop, a woman enters and engages him
in small talk. Then she leads him back to a motel where Whalen and Slate are
staked out. They burst in on Grimsley's interlude. Grimsley realizes that he has
been set up but tacitly agrees to stop riding Whalen.

The following afternoon when the alternate watch commander, Lt. Finque
(David Spielberg), opens his locker, he is attacked by a duck that has been
placed inside. He is forced to appear at roll call with his face bruised and ban-
daged. As patrol begins, Slate and Whalen stop at a local striptease club,
where Slate introduces Whalen to Foxy (Phyllis Davis), one of the performers.
Afterwards Whalen advises Slate not to get involved with that sort of woman;
but Slate confesses a compulsion to do just that.

The next choir practice is at MacArthur Park. Rules has fallen asleep drunk, and Tanaguchi shows the others how he has lured a duck out of the lake and up to Rules' body with breadcrumbs. He has also opened Rules' fly and closed it again on the duck's head. The animal's thrashing finally rouses Rules, who jumps up screaming and falls into the lake. The others then take his pants and leave him handcuffed to a tree. A gay man who is walking his poodle finds Rules but is scared off by his shouting. When the others return to release him, Rules pulls out a gun and begins shooting, until Whalen knocks him down.

At the following watch, Bloomguard, Lyles, and Slate report to Vice Sgt. Scuzzi (Burt Young) for temporary assignment. While Bloomguard gets picked up by two prostitutes, Lyles and Slate stake out a department store men's room. Rules, who has been summoned to arrest a shoplifter, comes in unknowingly to use the men's room. When Zoony comes in shortly afterwards, he initiates an impromptu prank by making sexual advances towards Rules. This ends in a brawl. While Lyles and Slate are separating Zoony and Rules, Bloomguard is chasing the two women down a residential street, as they shout "Rape!" Scuzzi is somewhat disenchanted with his new charges, so the next day he sends all three to stake out an apartment believed to be used by a highly-paid prostitute specializing in "bondage." Slate thinks that the form of the woman in the window is familiar but does not discuss it further with his companions. Meanwhile, Zoony brings in a young man who has solicited him in the park. After encouraging him to get counseling, Scuzzi lets him go.

Later that evening, Rules and Proust answer a call in a low-rent building where African-American and Chicano laborers are fighting. Rules antagonizes each man in turn with racial slurs, until both turn on the policemen and beat them. The following afternoon, roll call is held outside so that the precinct Captain and a Deputy Chief can issue the monthly citation for outstanding service to Rules. Despite the catcalls which accompany Rules' acceptance, Deputy Chief Riggs (Robert Webber) praises his aggressiveness and encourages the other men to do likewise.

Lyles and Bloomguard return to regular patrol, and Lyles drives by the apartment which they had previously staked out. When they see signs of activity, they decide to stage their own raid. The woman turns out to be Foxy; and while Bloomguard holds her in the outer room, Lyles discovers that the customer tied up in her torture chamber is Slate. Lyles frees Slate but is too disturbed to agree to meet him later and discuss his behavior. The next day's roll call begins with Yanov's announcement that Slate has been found dead by his own hand. Whalen, who had previously been told by Finque to take down a picture of another suicide from a display of officers killed in the line of duty, gets up and leaves. Lyles soon follows.

That evening's choir practice has become a wake by the time Rules arrives in the precinct's paddy wagon. He tells the others that he has learned that Slate's body was covered with whip marks but is prevented from elaborating when Lyles lunges at him. Bloomguard deduces what happened the previous night but can't persuade Lyles to stop consuming alcohol and pills. Eventually Lyles staggers semiconsciously into the back of the paddy wagon, where the others have already deposited a drowsy Van Moot. Rules finds them there and latches the door. When he is unable to get out, Lyles imagines that he is back in the Vietnamese cave and unable to breath.

The young man whom Scuzzi had freed and who has returned to the park hears Lyles' shouts and goes to open the door. The frenzied Lyles draws his gun and shoots the young man. When the others arrive and are unable to resuscitate him, they decide to concoct a story to cover up the killing. Riggs suspects that Bloomguard's story is a fabrication but is unable to get anything from Lyles, who has been committed. Grimsley, who now works for Riggs, suggests that he bring in Whalen alone and interrogate him personally. When Riggs gives Whalen the alternatives of immunity or dismissal from the force without his pension, Whalen agrees to name everyone involved.

After he has taken his retirement and gone north to operate a fishing boat, Whalen receives a letter from Motts containing a newspaper clipping which reveals that Riggs has merely perpetuated the cover-up and given all the men six-month suspensions. Whalen returns and threatens to go to the press with the real story. Riggs relents, and all the choirboys are reinstated.

Below, the "Dirty Ten": the cops in *The Choirboys*.

The Frisco Kid **(1979)**

Producer:	Mace Neufeld
Executive Producer:	Howard W. Koch, Jr.
Associate Producer:	Melvin Dellar
Screenplay:	Michael Elias, Frank Shaw
Director of Photography:	Robert B. Hauser (Technicolor; 1.85:1)
Production Design:	Terence Marsh
Music:	Frank DeVol
Sound:	Jack Solomon; Arthur Plantadosi, Les Fresholtz, Walter Goss (rerecording)
Costumes:	Dennis Fill
Choreography:	Alex Romero
Film Editors:	Maury Winetrobe, Irving Rosenblum, Jack Horger
Set Decoration:	Marvin March
Make-up:	William Turner, Giannina Bush
Stunt Coordinators:	Chuck Hayward; Mickey Gilbert
Production Manager:	Edward Teets
Assistant Directors:	Mel Dellar (1st); Peter Bergquist (2nd)
Script Supervisor:	Doris Grau
Technical Advisors:	George American Horse; Rabbis Steven Robbins and Meyer Heller
Special Effects:	Henry Millar. Jr.
Title Design:	Walter Blake

Cast: Gene Wilder (Rabbi Avram Belinski), Harrison Ford (Tommy Lillard), Val Bisoglio (Chief Gray Cloud), George Ralph DiCenzo (Darryl Diggs), William Smith (Matt Diggs), Ramon Bieri (Jones), Leo Fuchs (Chief Rabbi), Penny Peyser (Rosalie), Jack Somack (Bender), Walter Janowitz (old Amish man), Beege Barkett (Sarah Mindl), Clyde Kusatsu (Ping), Shay Duffin (O'Leary), Joe Kapp (Monterano), Allen Rich (Bialik), Henry Rowland, Richard Dunham (Amish men), Cliff Fellow (Mr. Daniels), Vincent Schiavelli (Brother Bruno), Ian Wolfe (Father Joseph), John Steadman (booking agent), Steffen Zacharias (Rosensheine), Eda Reiss Merin (Mrs. Bender), John Bleifer (first rabbi), Kenny and Warren Selko (the boy), Leo Fuchs (head rabbi), Ben Kahlon, Michael Elias, Rolfe Sedan, Rusty Blitz, Sam Nudell, Gabriel Curtis, Larry Gelman, Zachary Berger, Martin Garner (rabbis), Paul Smith (Mishkin), Carol Helvey (young woman), Brad Neufeld (Julius), Bret Briggs, Brad Briggs, Chip Frye (Amish boys), Linda Stearns (mother), Heidi Stearns (Jane), Steve Levine (conductor), Jacques Hampton, Roy Kaye (fishermen), Catherine Chase (woman on train), June Constable (Amish woman), George Barrows (ticket seller), Gloria Hayes (Indian woman), Alex Romero (old man), Robert Padilia (medicine man).

Filmed on location in Rio Rico, Arizona; Greeley, Colorado; and Jenner, California and at the Burbank Studios [Warner Bros.] in 59 days beginning October 30, 1978.

Completed:	January 20, 1979
Cost:	$9,200,000
Distribution:	Warner Bros.
Running Time:	122 minutes.
Release date:	July 6, 1979 (New York)
MPAA Rating:	PG
Original title:	*No Knife*

NOTE: Aldrich replaced director Dick Richards during pre-production on September 1, 1978.

Synopsis

In 1850 the head of a Polish rabbinical school selects one of his poorest pupils, Avram Belinski (Gene Wilder), to emigrate to San Francisco and establish a congregation among Jewish "Forty-niners." The leader of that community, Samuel Bender (Jack Somack), has even offered the hand of his elder daughter in marriage.

At a farewell gathering, Belinski is entrusted with an antique Torah for the new temple. Belinski lands in Philadelphia and learns that the ship he was to take around the Horn has already sailed. Having been told by the head rabbi that San Francisco was situated close to New York, Avram hires a wagon to take him north. The owners of the wagon, Darryl and Matt Diggs (George Di Cenzo and William Smith) and their fellow traveler Jones (Raymond Bieri) transport Avram just outside Philadelphia where they rob and beat him.

Shaken by the loss of his funds and a silver plate that had been attached to the Torah, Avram wanders over the unfamiliar countryside and stumbles onto an Amish settlement. The Amish dress is so similar to his own that Belinski assumes he has somehow found an immigrant Jewish enclave. He faints when he sees a Christian bible in one man's pocket. The Amish give Avram train fare to Akron, Ohio.

In a pullman men's room, Avram first crosses paths with Tommy Lillard (Harrison Ford), a thief. While Avram is in the toilet, Lillard robs the other passengers. When Belinski emerges, he suddenly realizes that it is the Sabbath eve and he is forbidden to ride by Jewish law, so he gets off the train. To acquire money to finish his journey, the rabbi takes a job working on the railroad. He proves so inept at hammering ties that he is demoted before he can earn enough to purchase his own covered wagon. He buys a horse instead.

Above, Indians with a sense of religious irony prepare to crucify Rabbi Avram Belinski (Gene Wilder)

As he rides around aimlessly, Avram reencounters Tommy Lillard. The outlaw is amused by the spectacle of Avram alone on the prairie, cursing in Yiddish, and going the wrong way. On a whim, he agrees to put the rabbi back on the proper trail. After traversing the plains, Lillard recommends that they hole up for the winter. Belinski refuses to delay his trip any longer, and Lillard reluctantly helps him cross the snow-bound Rocky Mountains. When they finally reach a town, Lillard decides to replenish his funds. He asks Avram to hold the horses while he goes into a bank. He returns with a bundle of stolen money, and before Avram can protest they are galloping out of town.

The next day, the rabbi refuses to compromise his scruples about riding on the Sabbath even to elude a posse. Avram mounts up as the sun sets, and the two men evade the posse but fall into the hands of Indians. They are about to be tortured, when Avram's chanted Hebrew prayer catches the attention of Chief Gray Cloud (Val Bisoglio). He is so intrigued by Avram's religious scruples and courage during a "purification by fire" that he frees him hoping he will pray to his God for rain. While Avram is explaining that his God does not produce rain on demand, there is a cloudburst. Despite Lillard's warning Avram dances with the tribe and eats some hallucinogenic victuals. He awakens in a monastery, where Lillard has taken him to recuperate.

When the two men reach the next town, Avram wires back his share of the bank money, which infuriates Lillard. While he goes in search of a brothel, Belinski wanders into the local saloon and spots his assailants from Pennsylvania at a gaming table. Outraged, Avram tears the silver Torah plate from around the neck of Matt Diggs. The Diggs brothers and Mr. Jones beat Avram until Lillard appears and intervenes. Under the threat of Lillard's gun, Avram's money is returned. The following morning, Belinski and Lillard reach the Pacific Ocean. As they celebrate the completion of their trek by plunging in, the Diggs brothers and Jones surprise them. When Matt Diggs contemptuously kicks the Torah into a campfire, Avram dives in frenziedly to save it. This distraction allows Lillard to grab his gun. He kills Jones and wounds Matt but is shot himself by Darryl Diggs. Darryl is out of ammunition, and Avram picks up Jones' gun but doesn't shoot until Darryl tries to get his brother's revolver. Avram kills him.

The next day, Avram, dressed in Lillard's clothes, attempts to deposit the Torah inconspicuously at the home of Samuel Bender. When he is surprised by Bender's younger daughter, Rosalie (Penny Peyser), Avram claims to be a cowboy from Texas delivering the book for "a rabbi" and hurries off. When he rejoins Lillard at a local cafe, Belinski confesses to having lost his faith and apologizes for momentarily placing the Torah above Lillard's life in importance. While Lillard argues with him, Bender and part of his congregation arrive and convince Avram to assume his post. Bender's daughter loves someone else, but he offers the hand of Rosalie instead. Already smitten from the earlier meeting, Avram gladly accepts.

The Jewish community's celebration is interrupted by the reappearance of Matt Diggs, who has cold-cocked Tommy. Avram refuses the gunfight, and sidesteps Diggs' physical attack. Tommy has come to his senses and stops Diggs from getting his gun. Avram tells Diggs to get out of town. At the wedding to Rosalie, Avram is struck by the magnitude of all that has happened to him in America, now culminating in his unexpected wedding with a bank robber serving as his best man.

...All the Marbles (1981)

Producer:	William Aldrich [MGM/Aldrich Co.]
Associate Producers:	Walter Blake, Eddie Saeta
Screenplay:	Mel Frohman
Director of Photography:	Joseph Biroc (Metrocolor; 1.85:1)
Production Design:	Carl Anderson
Music:	Frank DeVol with arias by Mozart, Leoncavallo, Verdi
Sound:	Richard Church; Michael Kohut, Jay Harding, Frank Reale (rerecording)
Costumes:	Bob Mackie
Casting:	Reuben Cannon
Choreography:	Kathryn Doby
Film Editors:	Irving C. Rosenblum, Richard Lane

Art Director:	Beala Neel
Make-up:	William Turner
Stunt Coordinator:	Mickey Gilbert
Production Manager:	Eddie Saeta
2nd Unit Director:	Adell Aldrich
2nd Unit Photography:	William Burch
Assistant Directors:	Tom McCrory, Chuck Myers (1sts); Robert Shue, Paul Moen (2nds)
Script Supervisor:	Grace Wilson
Technical Advisor:	Mildred Burke
Special Effects:	Dennis Dion
Title Design:	Walter Blake

Cast Peter Falk (Harry), Vicki Frederick (Iris), Laurene Landon (Molly), Burt Young (Eddie Cisco), Tracy Reed (Diane), Ursuline Bryant-King (June), Claudette Nevins (Solly), Richard Jaeckel (Reno referee), John Hancock (Big John Stanley), Lenny Montana (Jerome), Charlie Dell (Merle Le Fevre), Chick Hearn (himself), Cliff Emmich (obese promoter), Clyde Kusatsu (Clyde Yamashito), Joe Greene (Himself), Marlene Petrilli (Akron wrestler #1), Karen McCay (Akron wrestler #2), John Terry (Akron doctor), Alvin Hammer (Geisha doctor), Angela Aames (Louise), Stanley Brock (Myron), Susan Mechsner (Creature #1), Leslie Henderson (Creature #2), Taemi Hagiwara (Geisha #1), Aijumi Hori (Geisha #2), Faith Minton (Big Mama).

Filmed on location in Youngstown, Ohio; Las Vegas, Nevada; and MGM Studios, Culver City beginning November 14, 1980.

Completed:	February 24, 1981
Cost:	$9,300,000
Distribution:	MGM/UA.
Running Time:	112 minutes.
Released:	October 16, 1981 in Los Angeles.
MPAA Rating:	R
Alternate Titles:	*...And All the Marbles*; later released as *The California Dolls*

Synopsis

Harry Sears (Peter Falk) is the opera-loving, money-hustling manager-trainer of the California Dolls, female tag-team wrestlers in search of fame, fortune, and respect. Iris (Vicki Frederick), the worldlier of the two, had an affair with Harry at some time in the past; but now the relationship between them is purely professional. Molly (Laurene Landon), the naive one, is addicted to pain pills.

Together the trio travels the the backwoods and mill towns of Ohio and Illinois trying to break into the big-time ranks of women's professional wrestling. Harry uses his wits and occasionally a baseball bat to extricate them from difficult situations. The Dolls perform in the face of such indignities as brutal crowds, dingy arenas, and even mud wrestling at a county fair. For Iris the mud wrestling episode is almost the breaking point. She angrily confronts Harry over it but ends up in his arms as he comforts her. Eventually the Dolls do manage to build up a reputation through repeated victories.

After losing to their arch rivals, the Toledo Tigers, in Chicago but gaining nationwide recognition in the process, Harry manages to swing a major bout in Reno. The promoter is, however, Eddie Cisco (Burt Young) who hates Harry for refusing to knuckle under to him. Iris sleeps with Eddie to guarantee the match. When Harry finds out about it he strikes Iris. Later Harry bets Eddie that his Dolls will win the bout.

In Reno Harry orchestrates a spectacle for the bout by paying off the audience, staging sing-a-longs, and renting outrageous costumes for the Dolls. Molly also breaks her drug habit in Reno. The Dolls win the hard-fought match against the Toledo Tigers, and Harry wins his bet with Eddie. The trio has made a grab for "all the marbles" and come up champions.

Left, Molly (Laurene Landon) grabs a Toledo Tiger by the tail.

METRO-GOLDWYN-MAYER
PRESENTS

AN ALDRICH COMPANY PRODUCTION

"....ALL THE MARBLES"

PETER FALK

VICKI FREDERICK LAURENE LANDON AND BURT YOUNG

WRITTEN BY **MEL FROHMAN** PRODUCED BY **WILLIAM ALDRICH**

DIRECTED BY **ROBERT ALDRICH**

THIS SUMMER'S NO-HOLDS-BARRED-FREE-FOR-ALL-FOR-FUN!

MGM motion pictures are distributed in the United States, and Canada by United Artists, and throughout the rest of the world by Cinema International Corporation.

© 1981 Metro-Goldwyn-Mayer Film Co.

2. Short Film Directed by Robert Aldrich

The Greatest Mother of 'Em All (1969)

Producer:	Robert Aldrich [Associates and Aldrich]
Associate Producer:	Walter Blake
Screenplay:	A. I. Bezzerides and Leon Griffiths
Director of Photography:	Joseph Biroc (EastmanColor; 1.85:1)
Art Direction:	James Powell Vance
Song:	"Good Morning, Starshine," music by Galt MacDermot, lyrics by James Rado
Sound:	Dick Church
Choreography:	Alex Romero
Costumes:	Charles James
Editors:	Frank Urioste; Albert Nalpas (montage)
Make-up:	William Turner
Production Supervisor:	George Tobin
Exterior Scenes Director:	Tom Buchanan

Exterior Photography: Verne Carlson
Assistant Director: Daisy Gerber
Script Supervisor: Adell Aldrich Bravos
Assistant to the Producer: William Aldrich

Cast: Peter Finch (Sean Howard), Ann Sothern (Dolly Murdock), Alexandra Hay (Tricia Murdock), Kate Woodville (Eva Frazer), Barry Russo (Gene Frazer), Peter Hooten (Jack), Michael Fox (night club comic), Clark Gordon (Collinson), Angela Carter (night club waitress).

Filmed at the Aldrich Studios, Los Angeles, beginning July 28, 1969.

Completed: August 8, 1969
Cost: $140,000
Running time: 20 minutes
Alternate Title: *The Big Love*

NOTE: Aldrich produced this promotional reel in an attempt to raise production financing for a full-length film. The original script by A. I. Bezzerides is dated February 3, 1965. The revised version, which is summarized below, is credited to Bezzerides and Leon Griffiths and dated May 19, 1969.

Synopsis

Dolly Murdock, a middle-aged, grass widow and frustrated actress, is married to a travelling toy salesman, Harv, who is seldom home. Dolly is struggling to keep up payments for her mother's care in a rest home and, at the same time, promote her own daughter's show business career. Although Tricia Murdock is only fifteen, Dolly has her working as an exotic dancer at a local nightclub, hoping that she will be discovered.

One night, Gene Frazer, a television producer, visits the club and invites Tricia to his home for a nightcap. His seduction of Tricia is interrupted by the arrival of his wife, Eva, whose bisexuality leads her to join them in bed. Tricia, somewhat dazed by this encounter, is deposited at her doorstep and given five hundred dollars by Frazer's chauffeur.

Dolly, after a display of indignation, goes to Frazer's ofices and threatens to charge him with statutory rape. Frazer agrees to "do something" for Tricia's career, beginning with an invitation to a party. That afternoon, while Tricia has gone to the beach to meet with a boyfriend named Jack, Harv Murdock returns after a six-month absence. Inadvertently, he takes some prospective clients to a nightclub and is outraged to discover that his daughter is one of the performers. While Harv goes backstage to create a commotion, Dolly whisks Tricia out and takes her to Frazer's party.

On arrival, they encounter Sean Howard, a washed-up feature director reduced to doing hack work for Frazer. After overwhelming Howard with compliments, Dolly systematically touts Tricia's ability to all the guests, much to the dismay of the Frazers. Howard takes Tricia in tow and, when Frazer draws

Opposite, echoes of *Lylah Clare*: Alexandra Hay as Tricia and Peter Finch as washed-up director Sean Howard in *The Greatest Mother of 'Em All.*

him away, mocks the producer's proposed series in front of her. Infuriated, Frazer tells him he has just lost the job. Howard leaves with Tricia, and a vituperative Frazer tells a gossip columnist that Tricia is underage.

Dolly returns home to find Harv waiting, and a heated argument ensues. Tricia returns home in the middle of it and runs to her room followed by Harv, who locks Dolly out. While they talk, Tricia asks Harv why she shouldn't be beautiful and triggers a brief sexual response from her father. Shocked by the incident, Harv abandons Tricia to Dolly and leaves the next morning. As Dolly drives Tricia to Howard's home in the afternoon, she encourages her to solidify her relationship with him. Tricia willingly complies; but after Howard completes what he believes is his seduction of her, his press agent arrives to show him an item in a trade paper linking him to a juvenile. Howard tells him it is too late for denials; he goes up to find Tricia watching a cartoon show and is overcome by her guilelessness.

Soon the tryst between Howard and Tricia is an item in the scandal magazines, and while Dolly plots to reap financial benefit through blackmail, Howard has other ideas and "abducts" Tricia. Dolly chases his sports car in her own battered vehicle, which ends up out of commission on a canyon road. She goes to the police, but they do not take her seriously. At Howard's mountain chalet, Tricia has accepted his proposal of marriage but, as he opens a bottle of champagne, Howard collapses and dies from a heart attack.

At the funeral, Dolly tries to focus media attention on Tricia's plight and talent, much to the exasperation of the mourners. When Tricia goes to the beach with Jack to try to clear her head of recent events, Dolly tries to sell her diary, detailing her liaison with Howard. That fails, but Tricia arrives home to find a nightclub owner who wants her to dance at a club in the valley. Tricia screams at him to get out and then finds her diary on a table. Realizing her mother's

latest scheme, Tricia slaps Dolly and initiates a vicious fight, which ends when Tricia secures the diary and leaves the unconscious Dolly on the floor. Dolly is roused by a visit from Eva Frazer, inviting Tricia to come over to their house again, alone. Dolly takes this news up to Tricia with hopes that Frazer may still put her in a television show. The following morning Dolly finds Tricia dead of an overdose of sleeping pills. After the funeral, and accompanied by Jack, Dolly visits her mother at the rest home and finds her almost catatonic.

The promotional film includes several scenes shot from the Bezzerides and Griffiths revised script but edited in different sequence, as follows:

1. Tricia's (Alexandra Hay) striptease, coached by Dolly (Ann Southern) and observed by both Frazer (Barry Russo) and Sean Howard (Peter Finch).

2. A scene [shot by second unit] of Tricia in a park with Jack (Peter Hooten).

3. Tricia's visit to Frazer's home.

4. Tricia meeting again with Jack.

5. Tricia watching cartoons in Howard's bed.

6. The confrontation between Dolly and Howard.

7. Howard's proposal of marriage and subsequent death while at the mountain chalet.

8. Dolly and Collinson (Clark Gordon), owner of the valley nightclub, meeting Tricia.

9. Frazer's seduction of Tricia and the intrusion and participation of Eva (Kate Woodville), ending with a freeze-frame of an anguished Tricia.

3. Feature Films Produced by Robert Aldrich

The Ride Back (1957)

Directors:	Allen H. Miner and [uncredited] Oscar Rudolph
Producer:	William Conrad [Associates and Aldrich]
Executive Producer:	Robert Aldrich
Associate Producer:	Walter Blake
Screenplay:	Anthony Ellis
Director of Photography:	Joseph Biroc (1.85:1, printed with a Sepia tint)
Art Direction:	William Glasgow
Music:	Frank DeVol
Song:	"The Ride Back," by Frank DeVol, sung by Eddie Albert
Sound:	Joseph L. Edmonson
Editor:	Michael Luciano
Assistant Director	Jack R. Berne

Cast: Anthony Quinn (Kallen), William Conrad (Hamish), George Trevino (border guard), Lita Milan (Elena), Victor Millan (Padre), Ellen Hope Monroe (the girl), Joe Dominguez (Luis), Joe Towers (boy)

Filmed on location in Northern Mexico beginning September 21, 1956.

Completed:	October 12, 1956
Distribution:	United Artists
Running time:	79 minutes
Released:	May 1, 1957
Alternate Title:	*The Way Back*

NOTE: Oscar Rudolph directed 10 days of added scenes, retakes, and stunts after replacing Allen Miner.

Synopsis

A small border town is shaken by the arrival of Hamish (William Conrad), a U.S. marshall, seeking a man. A local priest (Victor Millan) tells Hamish he is concerned about the moral influence of a self-exile named Kallen (Anthony Quinn) on his parishioners, particularly Elena (Lita Milan), who lives with Kallen. Despite his lack of authority, Hamish arrests Kallen and prepares to take him back across the border to Mexico. On the first leg of the journey they are pursued by Elena, who attacks Hamish and tries to free Kallen. When she fails, Kallen tries to appeal to Hamish's sympathy, but the marshall is unrelenting. After they cross the border, Hamish and Kallen discover a farmhouse burned by a raiding party of Indians; the only survivors are two young children. Taking the children with them, the men continue on until attacked by

Opposite, Hamish (William Conrad) arrests Kallen (Anthony Quinn) at the urging of the local priest (Victor Millan) and despite the protests of Elena (Lita Milan).

members of the same raiding party. With Kallen's aid, Hamish beats them off, although he is wounded in the process. Kallen takes him to the outskirts of town and is willing to accompany him in; but Hamish, convinced of Kallen's reform, tells him to return to his home.

What Ever Happened to Aunt Alice? (1969)

Directors:	Lee H. Katzin and [uncredited] Bernard Girard
Producer:	Robert Aldrich [Associates and Aldrich—ABC-Palomar]
Executive Producer:	Peter Nelson
Screenplay:	Theodore Apstein, based on the novel The Forbidden Garden by Ursula Curtiss
Director of Photography:	Joseph Biroc (Metrocolor; 1.85:1)
Art Direction:	William Glasgow
Music:	Gerald Fried
Sound:	Dick Church
Costumes:	Renie [Conley]
Casting:	Lynn Stalmaster
Editor:	Michael Luciano (supervising); Frank Urioste
Set Decoration:	John Brown
Make-up:	William Turner
Production Supervisor:	Fred Ahern
Unit Manager:	Eddie Saeta
Assistant Director:	Daisy Gerber
Script Supervisor:	Richard Chaffee

Cast: Geraldine Page (Mrs. Marrable), Ruth Gordon (Mrs. Dimmock), Rosemary Forsyth (Harriet Vaughn), Robert Fuller (Mike Darrah), Mildred Dunnock (Miss Tinsley), Joan Harrington (Julia Lawson), Peter Brandon (George Lawson), Michael Barbara (Jim Vaughn), Peter Bonerz (Mr. Bentley), Richard Angarola (Sheriff Armijo), Claire Kelly (Elva), Valerie Allen (Dotty), Martin Garralaga (Juan), Jack Bannon (Olin), Seth Riggs (Warren), Lou Kane (telephone man).

Filmed on location near Tuscon, Arizona, and at the Aldrich Studios, Los Angeles, beginning October 23, 1968.

Completed:	January 5, 1969
Cost:	$1,690,000
Distribution:	Cinerama Releasing Corporation
Running time:	101 minutes
Released:	August 20, 1969
MPAA Rating:	M

Opposite, echoes of *Baby Jane*: Geraldine Page and Ruth Gordon in *What Ever Happened to Aunt Alice?*

NOTE: Bernard Girard resigned as director after four weeks of filming on November 25, 1968 because of a production dispute. Lee Katzin replaced him on November 27, 1968 and completed the picture.

Synopsis

Mrs. Claire Marrable (Geraldine Page) murders her husband for his money, only to discover that his estate consists of a solitary stamp album. Nevertheless, she is determined to acquire substantial means for her retirement and so moves to a small desert community in Arizona where she hires a succession of rich but lonely women as companion/housekeepers. After she gains each one's confidence and fortune she murders them, burying them in her garden. Ultimately she hires Alice Dimmock (Ruth Gordon), who is investigating the death of Mrs. Marrable's previous victim, Miss Tinsley (Mildred Dunnock). Alice is assisted by her nephew, Mike Darrah (Robert Fuller), and Mrs. Marrable's next-door neighbors, the Vaughns (Rosemary Forsyth and Michael Barbers). Just as they begin to substantiate their suspicions, Mrs. Marrable discovers Alice's ruse and, after beating her unconscious, places her in a car and pushes it into a lake. Then Mrs. Marrable attempts to silence the Vaughns by setting their home on fire. But the Vaughns are rescued, and Mrs. Marrable awakens the next morning to discover that her victims have been exhumed and that her husband's stamp album was worth $100,000.

4. Feature Film as Screenwriter

The Gamma People (1955)

Producer:	John Gossage
Director:	John Gilling
Screenplay:	John Gilling and John Gossage from an original story by Louis Pollock and [uncredited] Robert Aldrich
Director of Photography:	Ted Moore
Production Designer:	John Box
Music:	George Melachrino
Editor:	Jack Slade, Alan Orbiston

Cast: Paul Douglas (Mike Wilson), Eva Bartok (Paula Wendt), Leslie Philips (Howard Meade), Michael Caradici (Hugo), Walter Rilla (Boronski), Martin Miller (Lockner).

NOTE: Aldrich wrote the original story for actor John Garfield and producer Irving Allen in 1950. When Garfield was "graylisted" the project as shelved until Gossage and Gilling acquired it. Aldrich sued over disputed rights and credits and reached a settlement.

Distribution:	Columbia (U.S.)
Release Date	September 12, 1956
Running Time	76 minutes

5. Productions as Assistant Director and Assistant Producer

As Second Assistant Director (all for RKO Studios)

1942   **Joan of Paris**
Directed by Robert Stevenson.
The Big Street
Directed by Irving Reis.
The Falcon Takes Over
Directed by Irving Reis.

1943   **Bombardier**
Directed by Richard Wallace.
Behind the Rising Sun
Directed by Edward Dmytryk.
A Lady Takes a Chance
Directed by William A. Seiter.

Adventures of a Rookie
Directed by Leslie Goodwins.

1944   **Rookies in Burma**
Directed by Leslie Goodwins.
Gangway for Tomorrow
Directed by John H. Auer.

NOTE: Aldrich recalled working on perhaps a dozen other projects as Second Assistant Director, in particular "a lot of Westerns," probably a series of adaptations from the novels of Zane Grey.

As First Assistant Director

Shorts.

From 1943 to 1945 Aldrich worked on two-reel comedies at RKO: the "Mr. Average Man" series starring Edgar Kennedy and the Leon Errol series for director Leslie Goodwins. Aldrich also assisted Jules Dassin on the "Music Master" series: *The Trio: Rubinstein, Heifetz, and Piatigorsky* (1952).

From late 1945 to 1948, Aldrich worked for Enterprise Studios as a unit production manager, studio manager, assistant screenwriter, and first assistant director on several United Artists features. Aldrich worked during the initial pre-production on *Teresa* with director Fred Zinnemann but, when the production was postposed in 1948, went over to work at MGM. Aldrich has been incorrectly credited elsewhere as First A.D. on *On Our Merry Way* (1948, first assistant director, Joseph Depew) and *Red Light* (1949, first assistant director, Mel Dellar).

Features.

1945   **The Southerner** (United Artists)
Directed by Jean Renoir.

1946   **The Story of G.I. Joe** (United Artists)
Directed by William Wellman.
Pardon My Past (Columbia)
Directed by Leslie Fenton.
The Strange Love of Martha Ivers (Paramount)
Directed by Lewis Milestone. [Aldrich replaced Richard McWhorter after three-fourths of the filming had been completed]

1947   **The Private Affairs of Bel-Ami** (United Artists)
Directed by Albert Lewin.
Body and Soul (United Artists)

Directed by Robert Rossen.

1948   ***Arch of Triumph*** (United Artists)
          Directed by Lewis Milestone.
          So This Is New York (United Artists)
          Directed by Richard Fleischer.
          No Minor Vices (Metro-Goldwyn-Mayer)
          Directed by Lewis Milestone.

1949   ***Force of Evil*** (Warner Bros.)
          Directed by Abraham Polonsky.
          Caught (MGM/Enterprise)
          On Added Scenes Directed by John Berry [uncredited; Aldrich
          was also uncredited]
          The Red Pony (Republic)
          Directed by Lewis Milestone.
          A Kiss for Corliss (United Artists)
          Directed by Richard Wallace.

1950   ***The White Tower*** (R.K.O.)
          Directed by Ted Tetzlaff.

1951   ***The Prowler*** (Universal)
          Directed by Joseph Losey.
          M (Columbia)
          Directed by Joseph Losey.
          Of Men and Music (20th Century-Fox)
          Directed by Irving Reis.
          First Assitant Directors: Aldrich and Joseph Boyle.
          New Mexico (United Artists)
          Directed by Irving Reis.

1952   ***Abbott and Costello Meet Captain Kidd*** (Warner Bros.)
          Directed by Charles Lamont.
          Limelight (United Artists)
          Directed by Charles Chaplin.

As Production Supervisor

1951   ***When I Grow Up*** (Eagle-Lion)
          Directed by Michael Kanin.
          Produced by Sam Spiegel.

As Assistant to the Producer

1951   ***Ten Tall Men*** (Columbia)
            Directed by William Goldbeck.
            Produced by Harold Hecht.

1952   ***The First Time*** (Columbia)
            Directed by Frank Tashlin.
            Produced by Harold Hecht.

6. Feature Film as Actor

1951   ***The Big Night*** (United Artists)
            Produced by Philip A. Waxman.
            Directed by Joseph Losey.
            Starring John Drew Barrymore (George La Main), Preston Foster
            (Andy La Main), Joan Loring (Marion Rostina), Howard St. John
            (Al Judge), Howland Chamberlin (Flanagan), Dorothy
            Comingore (Julie Rostina). Aldrich had a bit part as a Ringside
            Fight Fan.

7. Television Work as Director

1952-53. **The Doctor** (*The Visitor* in syndication) (Procter & Gamble for
NBC-TV). A total of forty-four episodes aired from August 12, 1952 through
June 28, 1953. Aldrich directed seventeen episodes, three from his own
scripts, of this half-hour, filmed anthology format series in which the title character introduced dramas based on medical problems. It was produced in New
York on three-day-per-episode shooting schedules. Producer: Marion Parsonnet. Cast: Warner Anderson (the Doctor).

China Smith *(The Affairs of China Smith)* (Bernard Prockter Productions for
Syndication). This was a half-hour, filmed adventure series. Six episodes were
filmed in Mexico, but pressure from American unions, partcularly the American Federation of Radio and Television Artists, persuaded the producer to return to the U.S. Other episodes were shot in Los Angeles and San Francisco.
Aldrich directed four episodes which were shot on a three shows per six-day
week schedule. [Note: the series resumed in 1954-55 as *The New Adventures
of China Smith*.] Producer: Bernard Tabakin. Associate Producer: Buck
Houghton. Cast: Dan Duryea (China Smith), Douglas Dumbrille (Inspector
Hobson), Myrna Dell ("Empress" Shira).

1953. *The Schlitz Playhouse (Playhouse of the Stars)* (Meridian Pictures for CBS-TV). This series began as a live hour anthology but switched to a half-hour filmed format beginning June, 1952 with production at the Samuel Goldwyn Studios. Series Executive Producer: William Self. Aldrich directed one episode:

The Pussyfootin' Rocks

Producer	Edward Lewis
Teleplay:	Luther Davis
Director of Photography:	Manuel Gomez Urquiza
Music:	Johnny Mercer
Production Supervisor:	Oscar Dancigers

Cast: Joan Blondell (Calamity Jane), Buddy Edsen, Kathleen Freeman (The Ripplehissian Gang), Irene Dunne (Host).

Air Date:	November 21, 1953
Running Time:	22 minutes

1953 *Four Star Playhouse* (Four Star Productions/Official Films for CBS-TV). [Note: re-issued as *NBC's Best In Mystery* and *Singer Playhouse*.] This series was a half-hour filmed anthology alternating between four stars (Dick Powell, Charles Boyer, David Niven, and Ida Lupino) with production at RKO-Pathe Studios. Series Executive Producer: Don W. Sharpe. Associate Producer: Warren Lewis. Aldrich directed five episodes, three with Dick Powell; two with Charles Boyer:

The Squeeze

Producer	Dick Powell
Teleplay:	Blake Edwards
Director of Photography:	George E. Diskant
Art Director:	Ralph Berger
Production Supervisor:	Ruby Rosenberg
Assistant Director:	Bruce Fowler
Editor:	Samuel Beetley

Cast: Dick Powell (Willy Dante), Joan Camden (Susan), Herb Vigran (Monte), Regis Toomey (Lt. Waldo), Richard Jaeckel (Stan), Mario Siletti (Deras), Karl Lukas (Ernie).

Air Date:	October 1, 1953
Running Time:	22 minutes

The Witness

Producer:	Dick Powell
Teleplay:	Seeleg Lester, Merwin Gerard
Director of Photography:	George Diskant
Art Director:	Duncan Cramer
Editor:	Samuel Beetley
Production Supervisor:	Lloyd Richards
Assistant Director:	Bruce Fowler

Cast: Dick Powell (Mike Donegan), James Millican (D.A.), Charles Buchinsky [Bronson] (Frank Dana), Marian Carr (Alice Blair Dana), Strother Martin (Ted Blair), Robert Sherman (Philip Baedeker), Walter Sande (Peterson), Charles Evans (Judge), Nick Dennis (Nick).

Air Date:	October 22, 1953
Running Time:	22 minutes

The Hard Way

Producer:	Dick Powell
Teleplay:	Blake Edwards
Director of Photography:	George Diskant
Art Director:	Ralph Berger
Production Supervisor:	Ruby Rosenberg
Assistant Director:	Bruce Fowler
Editor:	Samuel Beetley

Cast: Dick Powell (Willy Dante), Robert Osterloh (Stan the Stickman), Regis Toomey (Lt. Waldo), Herb Vigran (Monte), Elizabeth Fraser (Janice Howl), Jack Elam (Vick), Lennie Bremen (Tino).

Air Date:	November 19, 1953
Running Time:	22 minutes

The Gift

Producer:	Charles Boyer
Teleplay:	John and Gwen Bagni
Story	Amory Hare
Director of Photography:	George Diskant
Art Director:	Duncan Cramer
Editor:	Samuel Beetley
Production Supervisor:	Lloyd Richards
Assistant Director:	Bruce Fowler

Cast: Charles Boyer (Carl Baxter), Maureen O'Sullivan (Minna Baxter), George Lennox (Dan Tobin), Joan Camden (Mrs. Mitchell), Amy Doran (Salvation Army woman), Eddie Firestone (young father), Virginia Christine (clerk), Lennie Bremend (Bartender), Gene Hardy (man from Virginia).

Air Date:	December 24, 1953
Running Time:	22 minutes

The Bad Streak

Producer:	Charles Boyer
Teleplay:	John and Gwen Bagni
Director of Photography:	George Diskant
Art Director:	Duncan Cramer
Editor:	Samuel Beetley
Production Supervisor:	Lloyd Richards
Assistant Director:	Bruce Fowler

Cast: Charles Boyer (Barry Reneck), Virginia Grey (Angela), Robert R. Arthur (David), Esther Dale (Mrs. Weston), John Hoyt (Bentridge), Horace McMahon (Chick), Manuel Paris (croupier).

Air Date:	January 14, 1954
Running Time:	22 minutes

1959 *Hotel de Paree* *(The Sundance Kid)* (CBS-TV). Series Executive Producer: William Self. Aldrich directed the pilot episode which was shot in April, 1959.

Producer:	Julian Claman
Teleplay:	Sam Rolfe
Director of Photography:	Joe Biroc
Art Direction:	William Glasgow
Editor:	Jack Ogilvie
Music:	Dimitri Tiomkin
Production Supervisor:	Dewey Starkey
UPM/Assistant Director:	Jack R. Berne

Cast: Earl Holliman (the Sundance Kid), Judi Meredith (Monique Devereax), Jeanette Nolan (Tante Annette Devereaux), Strother Martin (Aaron Donager), Theodore Bikel (Carmoody), Jack Elam (Flute).

Air Date:	October 2, 1959
Running Time:	22 minutes

1959 **Adventures in Paradise** (ABC-TV). An hour, filmed adventure series based on a concept developed by Martin Manulis and James A. Michener. Series Executive Producer: Martin Manulis. Associate Producer: Peter Nelson. Aldrich directed the pilot (*The Black Pearl*, production no. 3501) on a ten-day schedule in May, 1959, which was aired as the second episode of the series. He also directed a series episode (no. 3504) on a seven-day schedule.

The Black Pearl

Producer:	Richard Goldstone [20th Century-Fox]
Teleplay:	James A. Michener, Thelma Schnee
Director of Photography:	Maury Gertsman
Art Direction:	Ben Hayne
Sound:	W.D. Flick
Casting:	Robert Walker
Editor:	Tom Scott
Assistant Directors:	Jack R. Berne (1st); Edward Haldeman (2nd)
Script Supervisor:	Doris Grau

Cast: Gardner McKay (Adam Troy), Patricia Medina (Mme. Celeste Soulange), Anthony Steel (Charles Remley), Kurt Kasznar (Wagner), Lon Chaney, Jr. (One Arm), Abraham Sofaer (Timaui), Weaver Levy (Oliver), Hal Baylor (Thompson), Freddie Letuli (Tangi), Clifford Botelha (boy).

Air Date:	October 12, 1959
Running Time:	47 minutes

Safari at Sea

Producer:	Richard Goldstone [20th Century-Fox]
Teleplay:	James A. Michener, Bill Barrett

Cast: Gardner McKay (Adam Troy), John Ericson (Jeff Hazen), Diana Lynn (Nicole Hazen), Weaver Levy (Oliver Kee), Anthony Eustrel (doctor), Genevieve Aumont (girl in bar).

Air Date:	November 16, 1959
Running Time:	47 minutes

Key art from key films in Aldrich's career, derived from such diverse sources as Mickey Spillane and the Bible. Opposite, Aldrich reclines on the set of *Sodom and Gomorrah*.

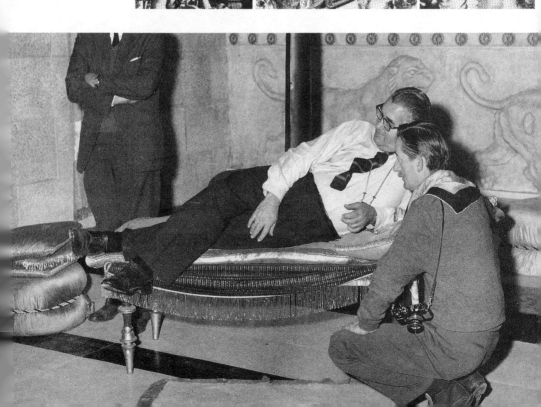

"...The men of Sodom were wicked and sinners before the Lord exceedingly..." —GENESIS, XIII, 13

Above, Aldrich about to receive an award from the French Cinematheque presented by French Consul J.F. Roux (right), who listens to Ernest Borgnine.

Projects, Honors, and Awards

C'est la goddam vie! The funeral is Friday.[1]

There are two sections in this chapter which detail (1) those various Projects which Aldrich had in development at some point in his career and some of which were subsequently made by others and (2) Honors and Awards accorded to Aldrich and/or his films both during his lifetime and after his death.

As is typical of producers and directors in the film industry, Aldrich was constantly optioning and developing material for possible production. Throughout his career, as an individual, in partnership with others, or as head of Associates and Aldrich and its successor companies, Aldrich had many projects in various phases of development at the same time. The Association (later Alliance) of Motion Picture and Television Producers maintains a title registration service, which Aldrich used for many scripts and story ideas. The date of registration is used as the reference for the start of development, although some projects such as *The Sheltering Sky* or *Kinderspiel* were in development for over twenty years up to Aldrich's death.

1. Feature Projects

1951 An untitled project based on the life of evangelist Aimee Semple McPherson from a story by Herman Mankiewicz to be directed by Joseph Losey.

1954 *My Gun Is Quick*: second adaptation of a Spillane novel produced by Victor Seville (Parklane Productions) originally to be filmed by Aldrich. Ultimately filmed in 1956 and directed by George White.

1955 *Kinderspiel*: the original project by J.B. Harding concerned a "children's revolt" in New England over the existence of nuclear weapons. It was to be produced by Columbia and directed by Aldrich but was shelved after the dispute with the studio over *The Garment Jungle*. Aldrich tried to resurrect this project in the 1980s with a new script by Lukas Heller, set in Germany near a NATO base. He was awaiting word on financing when he died.

Candidate for President: a revised script by Teddi Sherman from an original by Aldrich and Don Weis to be produced by Associates and Aldrich with another director on a $250,000 to $300,000 budget. Shelved.

Machine for Chuparosa: a romantic adventure of a man and his daughter who plan to purchase a fantastic machine in Mexico City. Aldrich traveled to Paris to the set of *The Hunchback of Notre Dame [Notre Dame de Paris]* to try to sign Anthony Quinn and Gina Lollobrigida but failed.

Pot Luck for Pomeroy or *Pot Luck with Pomeroy*: a comedy by Robert Russell, Ben Starr, and Herbert Baker set in Britain about rival British and American generals who are both vying to hire a topnotch cook to be made on a $700,000 budget. United Artists partially underwrote the development, which included three new writers in 1956. After briefly considering Frank Tashlin to direct, Aldrich later sent it to Billy Wilder who gave him the last word in 1959: "Dear Bob: No wonder you can't hypothecate this picture. It's a real dog. Bury it. Regards, B.W."[2] The rights reverted to United Artists in 1964.

Tyranny or *Tyranny for Texas*: an original screenplay by A.I. Bezzerides about the problems of the Mexican majority in Texas during the time it was an independent country. Shelved, although Aldrich used portions of it in *4 for Texas*.

Until Proven Guilty: the story of a teacher unjustly accused of raping a 14-year-old student based on the play, "Storm in the Sun," by Fern Mosk and Anne Taylor. This project was developed for Columbia with draft scripts by Lewis Meltzer and Oscar Millard, and Aldrich approached Olivia de Havilland about starring. Columbia rejected the script as too controversial and rescinded their contract with Aldrich in early March for "failure to revise the screenplay in accordance with our suggestion and...work cooperatively."[3] Aldrich quickly sued and settled when Columbia agreed to pay all costs, but the project was never revived.

1956 *Masterminds*: from a teleplay by Robert Condon adapted by Teddi Sherman. Oscar Rudolph was to direct this story set in New York about a young English lord and his servant who capture a mobster. Alternate title: *Two If By Sea*.

Monkey Doll: option on a play by Jack Rosenstein about a glamourous society writer who is unfulfilled romantically.

Now We Know: from a story by John O'Hara, scenario by Halsted Welles and intended to star Richard Widmark and Katharine Hepburn for United Artists on a budget of $800,000. Announced as still planned in 1964 then shelved.

3:10 to Yuma: a project which Aldrich developed with David Heilweil by commissioning a script by Halsted Welles from a story by Elmore Leonard. United Artists would have funded it on a limited budget like *The Ride Back*; but it was sold to Columbia for $30,000 and given up by Aldrich after his dispute with Columbia. Subsequently produced by Heilweil and directed by Delmer Daves for Columbia.

Which Way'd They Go: a pilot TV script by Aldrich and Don Weis, a kind of *Bugsy Malone* meets *Blazing Saddles* which cast child actors in a Western parody. Dropped after rejection by CBS as too much of "a one-joke idea."[4]

1957 *The Snipe Hunt*: a script by John Kneubuhl about a psychopathic killer who hides out in boy's camp as a counselor, which Aldrich acquired in a package deal with William Conrad, who had developed the property to produce and star in and for Bernard Kowalski to direct. Aldrich got backing from United Artists for a budget up to $600,000, of which a third was for the two leads, and made a series of offers to actors ranging from Orson Welles, Tony Franciosa, and Tony Randall to James Cagney, Gene Kelly, and Edward G. Robinson.

The Undefeated: a script by David Chantler based on a novel by I.A.R. Wylie. Developed with Hammer Films then sold to them because Aldrich considered it to be anti-French.

Unfinished Safari: a screenplay by Hugo Mozo from a story by Aldrich, about three escaped convicts and an anthropologist and his wife who discover a lost African city ruled by Leelo, "a white goddess."

1959 *The Angry Odyssey*: a story by Aldrich and Robert Sherman later scripted by Lukas Heller about a young North American who opens a restaurant/bar on an undeveloped Greek island which inspires hostility from the locals. After *The Dirty Dozen*, it was scheduled to be filmed in Greece in 1967 starring John Cassavetes as part of a two-picture deal with *Lylah Clare*. MGM returned the rights after Associates and Aldrich signed a multi-picture deal with ABC-Palomar, and it became one of the projects in the revised ABC deal. After a script polish by Leon Griffiths, Lee Katzin was hired to direct the picture in 1969. When John Cassavetes would not agree to star in the picture for the amount ABC wanted, the project was dropped from the ABC slate. Alternate title: *Angry Island Odyssey*.

The Ferrari Story: a story by Aldrich and Don Weis, loosely based on Lucky Luciano, about a gangster who aided the Allies in the invasion of Sicily.

Scripted by Hugo Butler and set to be co-produced with the Italian company, Galatea. After disputes with the owner of the rights to the Lucky Luciano story, Galatea dropped out, claiming breach of contract over lack of clear title.

Grand Illusion: Aldrich tried to acquire the English-language remake rights to Jean Renoir's film but was turned down by Renoir.

Magdelen: Aldrich briefly optioned from the Hearst Corporation Adela Rogers St. John's novel, <u>Magdelen '49</u>, about a prostitute whose faith is restored by an ex-GI mental patient who thinks he is the son of God.

Pursuit of Happiness: a treatment by Errol John from a story by Jack Wagner about the conflict between two revolutionaries, a Lumumba-type and a moderate, in Pariland, a mythical African nation throwing off colonial rule. Packaged for overseas production with *Cross of Iron* in 1960.

Taras Bulba: a script by David Chantler from the novel by Nikolai Gogol, sold by Aldrich after his work overseas. Aldrich commissioned numerous screenplay drafts on this project, but despaired of making it outside of Eastern Europe because of the tremendous cost of shooting in the U.S. or another Western country. Aldrich pointedly did not want Yul Brynner to play Taras, but after the project was eventually purchased by Harold Hecht, it was directed by J. Lee Thompson and starred Brynner and Tony Curtis.

The Tsar's Bride or *The Czar's Bride*: a Sixteenth Century romance written by Aldrich and Robert Sherman about Dimitri, the Polish pretender to the Russian throne. A second draft script was written in 1964 by Eddie Harper [Huebsch]. The project was dropped and revived several times but eventually abandoned because he found it unfeasible to produce in the Soviet Union and felt it was impossible to film it in another location. Alternate Titles in 1966: *Dimitri* or *Dimitri and Marina*.

1960 *Cross of Iron* or *Das Eiserne Kreuze*: a script by Lukas Heller expanded from his half-hour teleplay about German POWs in England produced by the BBC in 1961. In a deal with the German company, CCC, Aldrich was to direct both English and German-language (by Peter Berg) feature versions for Executive Producer Arthur Brauner on a $1 million budget. After disputes and a lawsuit over the project, Aldrich tried to package it again in 1963 for Oscar Rudolph to direct on a $1.5 million budget with John Mills, Curt Jurgens, and Peter Van Eyck. Shelved after that attempt. [NOTE: Not related to the Sam Peckinpah film of the same name.]

Tutti Frutti: a story by Jack Wagner.

1963 *Brouhaha* or *Sheik of Araby*: a British comic play by George Tabori, adapted by Ian Hunter and Hugo Butler, to star Peter Sellers as a bungling sultan. Aldrich committed $50,000 to script development, but after postponement because of production overrun on *Hush...Hush, Sweet Charlotte* and loss of acting commitment from Vittorio Gassman, the project was shelved.

Genghis Khan's Bicycle: a comic play by Refik Erduran about emigres set in Istanbul and adapted into a musical comedy by Gene Lerner. Dropped in 1965 after the release of *America, America* and several adventure films shot in Istanbul.

Mr. Man: a proposed television series based on a one-hour script by Lukas Heller from a story by Aldrich about a comic private investigator. Planned to star Victor Buono, Marjorie Bennett, and Eva Six and to be produced by Associates and Aldrich. Dropped when network backing was not obtained.

The Sacco-Vanzetti Story or *This Agony, This Triumph* or *Agony and Triumph*: an option on a teleplay by Reginald Rose which aired on NBC to be made into a feature starring Marcello Mastroianni on a $950,000 budget.

The Snow Queen: option on a teleplay by Robert Thom and Edward de Blasio.

The Strong Are Lonely: a concept by Aldrich based on a play, "Das Heilige Experiment," by Fritz Hockwaelder about an Indian of mixed parentage caught up in the conflict between Spanish colonists and Jesuit missionaries. Dropped after a six-month option.

1964 *Paper Eagle*: announced after Aldrich optioned the novel in progress by Anthony Ellis. Shelved.

The Sheltering Sky: based on the novel by Paul Bowles, adapted by Jean Rouverol and Hugo Butler. Richard Zanuck signed Aldrich to direct this script for Fox on a $2.8 million budget. The project was shelved. Bernardo Bertolucci eventually directed an adaptation produced by William Aldrich in 1990.

There Really Was a Gold Mine: planned as a semi-sequel to *Vera Cruz* to be produced by Aldrich. Shelved.

Vengeance Is Mine: a retitled adaptation by Aldrich and A.I. Bezzerides of *The Ferrari Story*.

1965 *...All the Way to the Bank*: a script by Jean Rouverol and Hugo Butler from a teleplay, *Home, Sweet Home*, by Eric Bercovici and Jud Taylor, originally produced for *The Chrysler Theater*, about two retired safe-crackers who steal money from a mob boss's safe deposit box to benefit an old folk's home. Aldrich tried to package the project with John Wayne or James Stewart for Richard Zanuck at Fox which invested $7,500 in the rights purchase. As noted in the Biography, when it fell through, he accepted MGM's offer to direct *The Dirty Dozen*. Alternate titles: *The Old Men's Story, The Benevolent Banditi*.

Nightmare: a concept by Larry Cohen for one-hour, suspense televison series about a man who has ESP experiences while sleeping. Lukas Heller wrote the pilot script to be produced by Associates and Aldrich and 20th Century-Fox for ABC. Dropped by network. Alternate titles: *I Wake Up Screaming* and *The Sleeper*.

Monte Walsh or *Sunset Trail* [new working title in 1966]: a script by Lukas Heller from a novel by Jack Schaffer. Originally scheduled to be shot for Fox, which invested $50,000 in the script, after *The Dirty Dozen*. It was postponed when the two picture deal with MGM for *The Legend of Lylah Clare* and *Angry Odyssey* was negotiated. It was also part of the ABC deal. Schaffer's novel and Heller's script were subsequently purchased from Associates and Aldrich for $150,000 by National General/Cinema Center Films in 1968 and a film adaptation starring Lee Marvin was directed by William Fraker and released in 1969.

1966 *Wolf from the Door*: a comic script by Robert Sherman based on a novel by Rupert Croft-Cooke about a struggling American in Paris who writes a risqué novel to make some money and earns literary accolades.

1967 *The Crowded Bed*: a comic novel by Henry Sackerman and a script by Theodore J. Flicker, who was to direct an Associates and Aldrich production for ABC-Palomar on a $2.7 million budget, about a *ménage à trois*. ABC would not approve the script in 1968 and the project was shelved after the termination of the ABC contract in 1971.

The Plaza: Aldrich first tried to develop this as a television series modeled on the "FOUR STAR concept...a tremendously successful anthology series in which the stars were owners of the production company, as well as artistic participants."[5] In 1969, Associates and Aldrich optioned Eve Brown's non-fiction book The Plaza: the Life And Times of the Famous Hotel to be produced as a fictionalized feature on a $3.25 million budget. Aldrich's first draft script from his story with Edward Harper {Huebsch] and Robert Sherman was rewritten by Gore Vidal in 1971. After *The Grissom Gang* and the end of the ABC deal, Aldrich and CMA tried to package it at MGM, United Artists, and elsewhere but failed. After an attempt to revive the script in 1976 as *The Beverly Wilshire*, it was shelved.

Rage of Honor: a script by Denne Bart Petticlerc about an old cowboy alienated by the industrial development in Northern California in 1929 to be produced on a $3 million budget. Aldrich approached James Stewart, John Wayne, and even Clint Eastwood (who was in his thirties at the time) about the lead. For the woman's role, Aldrich asked Ruth Gordon to get the script to Katharine Hepburn who wrote back: "I can't think of a single thing to say about that script which would not be insulting to it—especially to you—Good God—Blood and pomposity—Rotten police and butchered horse—You're hard up?"[6] Rights sold December, 1971. Alternate Title: *The Woods Are Burning*.

Rebellion: a script by Theodore Apstein from his and Aldrich's adaptation of a novel, West of Appomattox, by Nelson and Shirley Wolford set in Mexico after the American Civil War and similar to *Vera Cruz* in that it focuses on American mercenaries in the conflict between French forces and Juaristas. To be produced on a $5.5 million budget under the amended deal with ABC-Palomar but shelved when disputes over completed and planned projects cut short the ABC commitment. Alternate title: *Revolution*.

1968 *Coffee, Tea, or Me*: a humorous book about airline stewardesses by Trudy Baker [JoAnn Blaisdell de Cancino] and Rachel Jones [Melva Hicks] originally adapted by Donald Bain. Aldrich optioned the property, commissioned a script by Ben Starr, and made it part of the amended agreement with ABC-Palomar on a $2.7 million budget. Shelved after that deal was terminated. The project was ultimately produced by others as a Movie-of-the-Week in 1973.

Mame: Aldrich believed he had an agreement with ABC to produce and direct the film version of the stage musical and threatened to sue before letting the matter drop: "it appears that it will be necessary for me to take legal action against ABC and probably against Warners/Seven Arts since they induced ABC to breach the MAME agreement."[7]

1969 *Billy Two Hats*: an original screenplay by Alan Sharp, ultimately sold to Norman Jewison, and directed by Ted Kotcheff as *The Lady and the Outlaw*.

An untitled *Danish Youth Movie*: a story by Aldrich about a disenchanted, liberal couple who emigrate to Denmark. It was planned for an inexpensive European production on a $500,000 budget.

The Doubtful Disappearance of Deborah Danvers: a story by Aldrich about a young, upper-class English woman who runs off to the Philippines with an immigrant Italian man. It was planned to star unknown actors cast during test sessions in London and Rome and to be produced on a $950,000 budget.

The Love Council: a 19th Century play by Oscar Panizza optioned after a 1968 revival in Paris and planned for production in Europe on a $2.25 million budget.

The Movement: a novel by Norman Garbo centered on 24 hours of a student protest at a Midwestern university to be produced on a $3 million budget.

What Ever Happened to Dear Elva?: script by Theodore Apstein based on the novel Goodbye, Aunt Elva by Elizabeth Fenwick, about a woman and son who force a neighbor to impersonate their murder victim. Also known as *Goodbye, Dear Daisy*. Shelved after the end of the ABC deal.

1970 *The Human Condition*: a treatment by Robert Sherman about the moral conflicts of Japanese, English, and American characters in occupied Burma during World War II. Development title: *Philippine WW II Jap*.

Television Projects considered in the packaging discussions with ABC and the William Morris Agency included: *The Assassins*, a treatment by Reginald Rose; *The Devil's Whisper*, a suspense novel by Lee Borden; *Never Step On a Dream*, a mystery novel by Winifred Wolf; *The Room Upstairs*, a Gothic romance by Mildred Davis; and an outline for a *What Ever Happened To...* series by Theodore Apstein.[8]

1972 *All the Marbles*: a script based on a story idea by Aldrich, Robert Sherman, Edward Harper [Huebsch], and William Aldrich, about three disillusioned, about-to-retire non-coms who smuggle pearls out of Vietnam during the last days of the U.S. involvement. Planned to star Lee Marvin on a $3.9 million budget.

Film of Memory: based a novel by Maurice Droun optioned briefly from MGM and to be scripted by Christopher Knopf for a $2,350,000 co-production with Carlo Ponti to star his wife, Sophia Loren. After several months of negotiation, it was dropped when Aldrich was "unable to find ANYONE who shares my considerable excitement about the potential..."[9] Eventually directed by Vincente Minnelli and starring Liza Minnelli and Ingrid Bergman.

Kill the Dutchman: a script by Leon Griffiths based on a novel by Paul Sann about the assassination of gangster "Dutch" Schultz. The film was to be produced and directed by Aldrich for MCA-Universal but dropped after proposed star George C. Scott made too many creative demands and Aldrich "even offered the producership of the epic (title only) to Al 'Godfather' Ruddy if he could secure the services of James Caan but apparently this has bombed out as well."[10]

Time Off: a script by Dennis Shryack and Michael Butler about two disillusioned hard-hats who drive to Mexico and start up a *ménage à trois* when they pickup a French woman in Las Vegas. Originally to star Burt Reynolds and Brigitte Bardot then, in 1974, Reynolds, Robert Redford, and Mireille Mathieu. Alternate title: *Two Weeks with Pay*.

1973 *The Yakuza*: screenplay by Paul Schrader and Robert Towne. Aldrich was engaged by Warner Bros. to direct this film for $200,000 plus points, but was replaced by Sydney Pollock. After disagreements with Paul Schrader over the script, Aldrich's choice for the lead, Lee Marvin, would not accept Warners' offer. When Robert Mitchum was cast he had director approval but, after a long meeting with Aldrich, turned him down.

Charlie Casbah: a comic script by Robert Aldrich about a small-time hoodlum deported to Algeria during World War II.

1974 *Dracula*: adapted from Bram Stoker's novel, abandoned by Aldrich after the release of the parodies *Young Frankenstein* and *Andy Warhol's Dracula*.

1975 *Seven Day Soldiers*: adapted by Lukas Heller from Tony Kendrick's novel, a story reminiscent of *All the Way to the Bank* about robbers who siphon off money from the Swiss account of a Latin American dictator, to have been produced and directed by Aldrich for First Artists, but dropped because Aldrich's Lorimar deal tied up his services.

Stand On It: based on a novel by William Neely and Robert K. Ottum to star Burt Reynolds. Aldrich tried to interest Lorimar in a Lukas Heller adaptation in 1976. Eventually it was directed by Hal Needham and Reynolds in 1983 as *Stroker Ace* from a script by Needham and Hugh Wilson.

1977 *Memoirs of Hecate County*: a screenplay by Wendell Mayes based on the series of autobiographical sketches by Edmund Wilson. Aldrich hoped to produce and direct it starring Robert Redford but after "bringing to Merv [Adelson]'s attention the Wendell Mayes script,"[11] the property was left with Lorimar.

The Day That I Die: a screenplay by Abraham Polonsky adapted from the novel by P.F. Kluge about Micronesia during World War II. Aldrich planned to produce and direct.

Someone Is Killing the Great Chefs of Europe: a screenplay by Peter Stone from the comic mystery novel by Nan and Ivan Lyons which was eventually produced as *Who Is Killing the Great Chefs of Europe?* by William Aldrich for The Aldrich Company and Lorimar while Aldrich was at work on *The Choirboys*. It was directed by Ted Kotcheff.

Bruno Bonelli: an original screenplay by Frank Perelli to be directed by Adell Aldrich for the Aldrich Company.

1978 *The Sophie Tucker Story*: a musical project based on the life of the singer.

The Queen of the Rebels: based on a story by Ugo Betti about a prostitute who becomes queen of a country in revolution.

1979 *Arctic Rampage*: After preparing the production, Aldrich had numerous disagreements with producer Albert Ruddy and was replaced by Peter Hunt before shooting began. Original title: *War at Rat River*. Release title: *Death Hunt* (1981).

Sudden Death: a football project to be produced by Mace Neufeld for Orion and Warner Bros. that was postposed when Aldrich accepted *The Frisco Kid* and then abandoned by Warners.

1980 *Man on Fire* Aldrich was to direct from an original by A.J. Quinnell. Paul Heller and Ronald Neame were to produce for Aldrich's company.

Twin: a script by Lukas Heller, a mystery to co-star Peter O'Toole and Cheryl Ladd.

For Export Only: an undated script by Aldrich which recycled *The Ferrari Story* and *Vengeance Is Mine* as comedy, concerning a group of gangsters deported to Italy in the 1960s and their various illegal enterprises there.

The Heart is an Auctioneer, an undated drama by Aldrich, probably from the early 60s, about three Americans in France, a wealthy couple and the wife's lover, who all perish during an Alpine climb.

J.J.,T. or *Joe Jadek, Texan* an undated movie-of-the-week script by Teddi Sherman based on a story by Aldrich which recycles the "Joe Jarrett" segments of *4 for Texas*.

Other titles registered by Aldrich include: **1956** *Jungle Princess*; **1957** *The Ambassadors, The Commentator, [The] Left Bank*; **1959** *Infinity*; **1960** *Room of Dark*; **1965** *...As a Snowball in the Sun* or *Snowball in the Sun*; **1966** *Make Love, Not War*; **1967** *Flower Power, Rum Runners, Bootleggers, Three for Kiwitt.*[12]

Other projects reported optioned or developed by Aldrich: **1957**, *Hank Johnson* and *H for Heroin*; **1958**, *The Catalyst* by Ronald Duncan and/or A.I. Bezzerides; **1960**, *Optimist Under the Elms* by Hugo Butler; **1964**, *Cycle Boots* and *Doll Monsters*;[13] and undated, *Dial Tone* by Keats Leigh and *Noble House* by James Clavell.[14]

2. Honors, Awards, Nominations, and Citations

1946 and **1951** Vice-president of the Screen Directors Guild, which became the Directors Guild of America in 1960.

1947-48 President (i.e. Chairman) of the Assistant Directors Council of the Screen Directors Guild.

1955 *The Big Knife*: Silver Lion Award from the 16th Venice Film Festival.

1956 *Attack!*: Italian Film Critics' award for best film and screening at the 17th Venice Film Festival.

Autumn Leaves: Silver Bear Award for Best Direction from the 6th Berlin Film Festival

Champion Director 1954-55 Award based on U.S. box office returns from the Motion Picture Herald

1957 *Attack!*: Citation as Best North American Director of 1956 from the Cantaclaro Festival in Caracas, Venezuela

1958 U.S. representative on the Judge's Panel at the Brussels Film Festival

1959 Chairman of the Judges' Jury at the Berlin Film Festival

1960 Member of the Jury at the Cork Film Festival

1962 *What Ever Happened to Baby Jane?*: screened at the Cannes Festival.

What Ever Happened to Baby Jane?: One Academy Award for Norma Koch for Best Black-and-White Costume Design. Four nominations for Best Actress, Bette Davis; Best Supporting Actor, Victor Buono; Best Black-and White Cinematography, Ernest Haller; and Best Achievement in Sound, Jack Solomon.

1963 *Hush...Hush, Sweet Charlotte*: Seven Academy Award nominations for Best Supporting Actress, Agnes Moorehead; Best Cinematography, Joseph Biroc; Best Art Direction and Set Decoration, Black-and-White, William Glasgow, Raphael Bretton; Best Costume Design, Black-and-White, Norma Koch; Best Film Editing, Michael Luciano; Best Music Score, Frank DeVol; and Best Song, "Hush...Hush, Sweet Charlotte."

1965 *The Flight of the Phoenix*: Two Academy Award Nominations for Best Supporting Actor, Ian Bannen and Best Editing, Michael Luciano.

1967 *The Dirty Dozen*: Director of the Year Award from the National Association of Theater Owners

The Dirty Dozen: One Academy Award to John Poyner for Best Sound Effects. Three nominations for Best Supporting Actor, John Cassavetes; Best Editing, Michael Luciano; and Best Sound: MGM Sound Dept.

Retrospective of Aldrich's work at the San Francisco Film Festival in October.

1968 January 3 is named "Aldrich Studios Day" by the City of Los Angeles.

1973 Silver Medal awarded by Cinémathèque Française in conjunction with a retrospective of Aldrich's work.

The Emperor of the North Pole: screened at the 23rd Berlin Film Festival.

1973-74 Vice-president of the Directors Guild of America

1975-79 President of the Directors Guild of America

1978 Retrospective of Aldrich's work at the National Film Theater, London, sponsored by the British Film Institute.

1983 Short retrospective (ten films) at the La Rochelle Film Festival.

1984 The Directors Guild of America creates the annual Robert B. Aldrich Award for extraordinary service to the Guild and its membership.

"All of Aldrich," a complete retrospective of Aldrich's feature work as director at the University of California, Los Angeles, co-sponsored by the DGA and the U.C.L.A. Film Archives.

1994 A retrospective of Aldrich's work at the Film Society of Lincoln Center, New York.

A retrospective of Aldrich's work at the 14th Annual Film Festival of Amiens and the Cinémathèque Française, Paris.

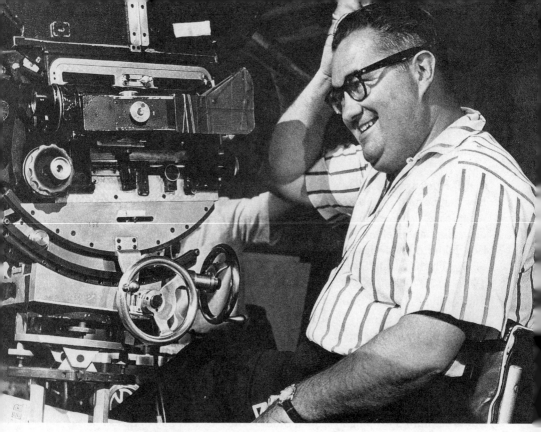

Above, Aldrich directs *The Big Knife* in 1955. Below, twenty-three years later, Aldrich on location with *The Frisco Kid*.

Appendix:

Interview with Robert Aldrich

The following interview conducted by Alain Silver was commissioned by *Film Comment* Magazine in November, 1970 and recorded on the afternoon of December 21, 1970 in Robert Aldrich's office at the then Aldrich Studios, 201 North Occidental Boulevard, Los Angeles, California. Aldrich was then in the process of supervising editing of *The Grissom Gang*. Also present during the interview was Jerry Pam, Aldrich's press agent. This text was edited from a transcription of approximately one hour and forty-five minutes of recorded time and includes a substantial amount of material which was omitted from the version published in *Film Comment* (Spring, 1972) for reasons of length. Also incorporated here are some remarks and observations made by Aldrich during an informal half-hour conversation after the tape recorder was turned off.

Silver: I want to ask about your tie, which you drape around your neck the same way Barney Sheean does in *The Legend of Lylah Clare*.

Aldrich: That's a dull joke actually. When I first came out here I used to be reasonably athletic, enough to stay in shape. Then came a time in the 50s that I put on forty pounds, and I just didn't have the time or the money to get a brand new wardrobe. So it became expeditious not to button my shirt, simply because I couldn't. By the time I had enough money to buy new shirts, it had become a habit. I don't know but you hang on to those idiosyncrasies. So I gave it to Ernie Borgnine—Barney Sheean was a poor man's Harry Cohn.

Silver: No tape decks arrayed behind the desk?

Aldrich: We thought about it, but it doesn't work. It only worked with Cohn.

Silver: I was originally planning to start with the standard line about your early career as production clerk and assistant director or "How to build a small studio empire in thirty years…"

Aldrich: Well, thanks for the small empire. But if I were starting out today, I'd marry some producer's daughter or illegitimate cousin—the only way to start in this business is at the top.

Silver: Well, then how did you get that first job directing a feature?

Aldrich: Mayer before his decline, before he was overthrown by Dore Schary, had wanted to put the sons of the guys who helped him form Metro into production work; and they had this thing called the "Sons of the Pioneers." That was really the name of it. Matt Rapf was one of them. Arthur Loew was one. Three or four guys whose fathers had been helpful in first forming Metro. Under Schary they made seven or eight pictures. I had been at Enterprise [Studios], and Herbert Baker, who had written one of the pictures for [Stanley] Kramer [*So This is New York*] was doing a baseball picture with Matt Rapf. And Herbie told him, "There's a very bright guy in town who's done a lot of productions; he's doing television now in New York. You should get this guy. He's a very good athlete. He knows athletes." Well, there was nobody there [in this unit at MGM] who really had any production experience. So they were looking for "bright young guys" who'd been on the firing line for a while, someone they thought they could give an opportunity to and who knew what he was doing, because they didn't. So we made that picture with Eddie Robinson in what is now Cape Kennedy in sixteen, seventeen days, out of nowhere. The world wasn't waiting for that picture. It was a picture about the New York Giants and Metro had the foresight to open it in Brooklyn; so you can't have expected it to do very well.

So nothing much came out of it; and I did some more television and *World for Ransom*. Hecht and Lancaster saw *World for Ransom* and liked it; and out of that, not out of *The Big Leaguer* came *Apache*. On the strength of *World for Ransom*, I got *Apache*. I had worked for Hecht-Lancaster before, under a different relationship. They made two pictures, *Ten Tall Men* and a Frank Tashlin picture [*The First Time*] on which I was associate producer or assistant to the producer or something. We had an argument over the credit on those films; but we had a pretty good relationship.

Silver: When did the problem with the ending come up?

Aldrich: The problem started with the [Paul I.] Wellman novel. [Joe] Losey had wanted to buy it and couldn't. I had wanted to buy it myself but couldn't afford it. In the novel, Massai hears his son being born, suspects that it may be a trap, but goes in anyway; and they kill him. That's the inevitable conclusion of the story, that he be killed. The internal relationships between [Jean] Peters as Nalinle and Lancaster as Massai, between Massai and the Army, Massai and the other Apaches, they're all built on the inevitability of his death. Of course, United Artists and Hecht became apprehensive of that so-called downbeat ending. I made noise but they didn't hear me. Burt held out for a week or so; but they finally convinced him. Well, United Artists is the money and Burt is the talent, so then you go through the steps, but you know they're going to use the happy ending.

Silver: The last shot, from the helicopter, moving back, which anticipates the ending of *The Big Knife*, was that planned for Massai's death? Didn't you shoot both versions?

Aldrich: He was shot coming out of the corn field, but we merely went through the motions on that. I'm not sure that the other ending would have cut together. We never assembled it, because we knew from the day we shot the two endings, we'd be stuck with the happy one. It was an economic decision.

Silver: I think it was Truffaut who suggested that *The Big Knife*'s economic failure was because it was too moral at a time when psychology was in vogue. Your pictures seem to be as much about survival as about morality.

Aldrich: Well, you usually have set of principles that you try to identify with the "good guys"; and a set of values of which you disapprove that identify the "bad guys." I seldom did but in that Truffaut piece, I think I referred to my father, who saw only one of my pictures before he died, and that was *The Big Knife*. So the explanation of its failure is simple. My father was man of considerable means and reasonably intelligent but very old school. When he saw the picture, he asked, "Tell me one thing. Am I to understand that his [Castle's] choice was to take or not take $5,000 a week?" I said, "Yes." "Well then, you'll never have a successful picture." I asked, "Why not?" "Because there is no choice." That may seem to demean my father's sophistication; but it doesn't really. He saw something that [Clifford] Odets and me and Jim Poe and Charlie Castle, we never saw.

Silver: Did any of your family or school background in economics relate in any way to those early jobs, to breaking in?

Aldrich: It had some bearing. I broke in when they were making filmed television in New York. They really didn't know how to make filmed television there; they just didn't have a clue. All they were paying directors was scale. Who the hell wanted to go live in New York and work for scale? Only guys who had never directed or couldn't get a shot. Walter Blake, who is now associate producer on most of my pictures, convinced these people who were doing the Camay soap shows that I was a genius waiting behind a rock out here. I had been assistant director on a Chaplin picture [*Limelight*], so he told them that I had directed Chaplin. Nobody directs Chaplin except Chaplin, but these guys didn't know the difference. So I went back to New York and did, I don't know, thirty or forty shows.

Silver: It was kind of a fluke then?

Aldrich: Luck, luck...

Silver: And those few months in New York established you more than all the assistantships and other production work?

Aldrich: They couldn't care less. That opened the door enough for the first step inside. But otherwise it's no different that if any sergeant in the world tells a captain, "I can do the lieutenant's job." Nobody's going to believe you. All those years they don't mean as much as you might think they mean. They mean that much in terms of personal gratification, but if you're in a very tough league with a lot of rookie players, it doesn't make that much difference that you can run or punt or pass as well as the next guy. The guy calling the signals, they'll give him a tryout. But your experience or knowledge don't really have much to do that with that "trial period." And waiting out that period is always tough. Someone once said that lasting power is the most important power. Especially in this business. Staying at the plate or staying at the table, staying in the game, is the essential. You can't allow yourself to get passed over or pushed aside. Very, very talented people got pushed aside and remained unused. That's the problem: staying at the table.

Silver: You seem to have a fair share of luck "at the table"?

Aldrich: An old joke. Because there are so many of those talented people, if you must make a choice between luck and talent, you have to opt for luck. It's nice to have some of both, or a lot of both; but if you can't, luck is the answer. Nowhere else more so than in this business. The right place, the right time, the right script, all the right auspices—they made the difference to directors, writers, actors.

Silver: Is it really necessary nowadays to act as your own producer in order to remain a director?

Aldrich: Well, yes, you lessen the enemy. Then you only have the distributor to fight. There's always a problem whether it's a producer or a financing company, when someone wants to intrude into your sphere; but it is considerably lessened if you don't have a separate producer. One discovers that during any kind of "growth" in this industry. Growth is a pompous word; but we do shut our eyes to thievery—at what level do we participate? Do we endorse it? Probably we're all guilty of that at some time.

Silver: But has money or unwillingness to "shut your eyes" ever really hampered you?

Aldrich: I think I made three very good movies, *The Big Knife, Attack!,* and *Kiss Me Deadly.* I worked almost for nothing, economically, on those movies. They got caught up in the system and were not profitable pictures. Things that you hoped would explode out of good movies didn't quite happen. And I came back to this country, after having made some dogs in Europe to cash in on what I thought would see me through another period of trials namely my considerable ownership in these former projects. They cost so little that I thought they had to have a large equity! TV sales, at least. I found that I had almost no equity, or at best nominal. I think my fifty percent in those three pictures was $35,000; not each but altogether, of which I had to pay a large part to my producer representative who watched the store. So you end up with $20,000 for half of three pictures; and you begin to understand, you have a graphic lesson in what the ground rules are. And they are: you don't get yours, they get theirs. You have to divide up. [When it's] between you and them or [between] you and you, you become cynical in terms of what preference to give survival and what preference to give material that might make a fine film which nobody or very few would go to see. That was the break. When I came back from working in Europe in '58, I really started to work on the theory of how to stay at the table. I realized that, just by the law of averages, if you're careful in choosing projects and settling costs, your taste and knowledge will, out of every six or seven pictures, produce one that makes a good deal of profitable return for everybody. I also realized that, for all the critical acclaim, *The Big Knife* and *Attack!* and *Kiss Me Deadly* could not keep me in the ball game. I added a few disasters of my own after that.

Silver: *Kiss Me Deadly* wasn't always one of your favorites.

Aldrich: People have always said that. What I thought, it happened quite often with French critics, particularly when Truffaut and Chabrol and all those guys were at *Cahiers*, was that they read many, many things into *Kiss Me Deadly*. I appreciated their enthusiasm, but I just couldn't take a bow for it. Because *Kiss Me Deadly*, at its depth, had to do with the McCarthy Era, the end justifying the means, and the kind of materialistic society that paid off in choice rewards, sometimes money, sometimes girls, sometimes other things.

Left, Aldrich rides a prop German tank on the set of *Attack!*.

But it wasn't as profound as many of the French thought it was. I did like it; it did everything I hoped it would do and more. I think I did a good job on it, that everybody connected with it did a good job; but it isn't that deep a piece of piercing philosophy as the French thought it was.

Silver: You've called *Kiss Me Deadly* an anti-McCarthy picture. Although Stanley Hoff is a composite of Mayer and Cohn, whom we've already mentioned, the McCarthy figure seems more physically present in *The Big Knife*. When Danziger raises his arm in a kind of neo-Fascist salute, "Hail, Columbia," both meanings are there.

Aldrich: Well, of course, he [Hoff] is McCarthy. But I'm terribly ambivalent about the Hoff character. When we made *The Big Knife*, Harry Cohn and Jack Warner were still in full flower, and Mayer was only recently fallen. Nobody had seen the abyss. We'd had twenty years of petty dictators running the industry during which time everybody worked and everybody got paid, maybe not enough, but they weren't on relief. Seventeen years later you wonder if the industry is really more healthy in terms of creativity. Are we making more or better pictures without that central control? But when everybody worked under those guys, they hated them. So we took the drum roll from Nuremberg and put it under the Hoff character's entrances and exits. But, you know, you can have a certain fondness for the way Cohn and Mayer got things done. Cohn took a while to realize that I did *The Big Knife*. Halfway through the "honeymoon" period when I was signed with Columbia, he asked me, "Did you do *The Big Knife*?" I said, "Yes." "You son of a bitch. If I'd known that you never would have been here." The Hoff crying came from Mayer, who is reported to have been able to cry at the drop of an option. But the big rebuff that Odets suffered was at the hands of Columbia, so there was more of Cohn in the original play than there was of Mayer.

Silver: What made you use those long takes in *The Big Knife* and also in *World for Ransom* and *Kiss Me Deadly*?

Aldrich: It has a direct relation to economy and personnel. Ernie Laszlo is a very good cameraman, but his trademark isn't speed. That was a problem. *The Big Knife* was made in 16 days, and *Kiss Me Deadly* was made in 22 days. If you elect to go with a cameraman that's not very, very fast, you have to, up front, make the decision that you are not going to get the kind of cutting coverage you'd normally like to have. You have to sacrifice setups and hope the performances are good enough, because they're cast in concrete. On *Attack!*, made in the same period, I wanted Joe Biroc, who is almost twice as fast. That gives you an opportunity to work with a one-camera system, which I used until the time I came back from Italy, and still get twice as much coverage. So the selection of the cameraman sets a good deal of the style of the picture. You have a five or six page sequence which needs to be lighted once,

Opposite page, Aldrich possibly discussing a "modified Rushmore" with Cinematographer Joe Biroc on the set of *The Flight of the Phoenix*.

and it'll take three to five times longer to light it for six or seven close-ups or cutaways. So you did it in a master.

Silver: You have some recurring framing concepts. For example, you may place characters in close shot foreground, frame left, and frame right will be another figure visible in depth of focus, with perhaps a lamp or some other object further restricting the space. You started doing that in television and you do it, for instance, in both *The Big Knife* and *The Angry Hills*. Those are several years apart, with different cameramen in different countries, and yet strikingly similar in visual conception. How much time and detail you put into planning your shots, how precisely do you know what you want in advance of shooting?

Aldrich: You have—I think "style" is a pompous word—but you have a certain way of doing things. Ordinarily, when you block out the scenes you have in mind the kind of composition that would lend itself to what you want to say in that sequence. With quick lenses, you can stage in depth, you can pose something in the foreground and build up enough to hold something else in the background. I never use Panavision lenses because the staging will fall off to such a degree that you'll have to let somebody go [out of focus], either keep the guy in front sharp and forget the guy in back or dial back and forth which is always disconcerting. When we block the scenes, we have those four ugly faces in South Dakota: the modified "Rushmore," the medium "Rushmore," and the Big "Rushmore." A big Rushmore puts a guy right up in the foreground with somebody back there. They're just "trade names" that I use with Biroc mostly, because we've been together so long.

Some scenes lend themselves to that kind of framing; but you'll find with a certain kind of dialogue scene, it's just not possible to do that. You look for

ways, but it's not always there. And you can't bend a scene to fit the camera; it just doesn't work that way.

Silver: Why do you use all that foreground clutter?

Aldrich: Well, [Lewis] Milestone used to tell young hopefuls that there wasn't enough real interest in any frame to justify attention any longer than necessary. If you could find something to block off the concentration of the audience towards the point in the frame that interests you, if you could throw garbage in front of the camera to block off the rest of the apartment or the rest of the desert, [you might] possibly enhance the shot. You'll see Losey do it, and [Jules] Dassin do it, in terms of trying to limit the area of concentration. You can only do so much, so that the audience doesn't become aware. A lot of framing is done for that reason. That isn't always the motivating [factor], but it really is better than over-the-shoulder when you want to get rid of the rest of the room and just concentrate on what somebody is answering.

Silver: Are those the kind of shots that you block out in your mind ahead of time or put on your "worksheet"?

Aldrich: When you're through blocking a scene, at the end of a rehearsal, you know pretty much where the master angle's going to be, what kind of coverage you're going to have, and in most cases, where the camera's going to be. Now, what you don't know and what the bane of your existence is are the little things that you're going to add. When you're through with rehearsal, in theory, the script clerk should be able to give you a pretty close timing; yet it's always off by an hour. An hour because, when you actually do the scene, you add a second here or a second there, an extra bit of business here, two extra lines there. By the end of the picture you've put on sixty minutes. Now perhaps those sixty minutes will prove better or more important than sixty minutes that were in the picture originally. Probably not, but let's say twenty of those will stay and another forty will go. So, yes, you know pretty well where the camera's going to be when the time comes, but you may frequently alter or append to your original conception.

Silver: Do you actually change lines or add lines, before or during shooting, to any great extent?

Aldrich: Well, I don't think the script is holy. We change lines all the time to make it work. I like to work very closely with the writer in the first place. I wrote the original on the Sinatra picture [*4 for Texas*]; you could change that over and over and it was still a disaster. I did the original on *Too Late the Hero*, and Lukas Heller made it a much better script. There is no frozen reverence towards what's written. That's not to say that the writer didn't conceive of a proper line in the first place. He just wasn't privy to the pressures of the moment that might bring out a better line. I'm a great friend of [John] Cassavetes—some actors are critical of the "rigidity" of my concept, others are uncomfortable with the way John does his pictures. Everybody does it differently. I say to the actors, "Look, if you're uncomfortable with the line, come up with one that you are comfortable with that says the same thing." We try it once or twice. If it works, we keep it. If it doesn't, we throw it out. It's as simple as that.

Silver: You said once that you had a weakness for "flowery dialogue."

Aldrich: Well, look at *The Big Knife*. At the time, I thought that kind of theatrical flavoring was extraordinary. I'm afraid neither Jim Poe nor I were tough enough in editing some of Odets' phrases as we should have been. Both Poe and I—I did the first pass on *The Big Knife*—were more in awe of Odets than we should have been; but he was giant then. He was not only a giant but his style was a fad. But when Poe did *Attack!* right after that, we tried to keep the exaggerated or larger-than-life kind of attitude, in terms of speech pattern, out of it. I did two or three pictures with Hugo Butler, and he'd just go wild. I consider him a fine writer. Lukas Heller, with whom I've made four or five pictures, is more refined than Odets, a little larger-than-life, theatrical maybe, but flowery isn't the word. There's a lot less of that kind of dialogue in *The Grissom Gang*.

Silver: "Take a chance, Mr. Callahan. Love is a white bird, yet you cannot buy her."

Aldrich: *World for Ransom*. That's Butler. He wrote that script. Funny thing. There are optimists in this society, not many left, who thought that some day those guys would get postmortem credit for their work. So he wrote *World for Ransom*, and I put my name on it to try and get him the credit. And it went into arbitration with the Writer's Guild, and another guy [Lindsay Hardy] got total screen credit on it. It was a joke. He [Hardy] no more wrote that script than walk on water. Butler made that total screenplay.

Silver: Did you have any trouble with the Marian Carr character, the overtones of lesbianism?

Aldrich: We had more trouble with Madi Comfort handling the mike in *Kiss Me Deadly* than we did with that. We thought we would get in trouble with half the things in *World for Ransom*. Nobody ever questioned them; nobody seemed aware of it. We made that picture in ten days, ten and a half days. We ran out of money and went back to do some Eversharp [razorblade] commercials to get enough to finish it.

Silver: Was it envisioned as a kind of spinoff, to capitalize on the popularity of *China Smith*?

Aldrich: We had a break in the *China Smiths*—I did quite a few of them. We had about four weeks off, and we told [Bernard] Tabakin, who was producing the series, that if he could come up with a script, we would all donate our services. I guess that's literally what we did.

Silver: And you called Butler an optimist. How was it that you could be associated with him, Joe Losey, Chaplin, Jules Dassin, Abraham Polonsky—a significant number of blacklistees—and come out unscathed?

Aldrich: Well, you know, that's not a new question. I always answer that I was either too dumb or too young to be a Communist. If I had worked with Ring Lardner or Losey or [Robert] Rossen or Polonsky or Butler or [Dalton] Trumbo or any of those guys, who were five or ten years older than I was, earlier than I did, a kind of hero worship might have made it necessary for me to be a member of the party. But by the time I got into close contact with them, the heat was already on. They were already in trouble or about to be— the handwriting was on the wall. They weren't looking for recruits. It wasn't as much a matter of converting anybody anymore as a matter of personal survival, of who was going to Mexico, who was going to Paris, who was going to England. When I was assistant for a lot of them, they were on the verge of trouble. They were [like Dassin], making Music Master shorts for Piatagorsky and Rubenstein and Heifitz, just to get enough money to skip the country. I got served but nobody ever picked up the subpoena, and I was never called to testify. Just fortunate.

Silver: Other young directors who broke in around the same time and didn't get blacklisted, like Nicholas Ray or Sam Fuller, they haven't worked as steadily as you have either.

Aldrich: They are both very talented guys; and Nick had some major success. I think Nick got caught up in political problems, and that hurt his employability. If a guy is in a gray area, politically or socially, all he needs is one disaster to move him into a black area. Then people will say he's unemployable. Fuller is something else. He has great energy and a great eye, and a good batting average, too, which people forget if you get one or two dogs in a row. I think Sam is a gifted guy, but he has a tendency to tell people to shove it up their ass, which is the proper and correct thing to do at times, but it doesn't make getting the next assignment any easier.

Silver: What was the cause of your difficulties with Columbia on *The Garment Jungle*?

Aldrich: Very simple. Harry Kleiner had written a very, very good script, tough as nails. I had an across-the-room relationship with Cohn: he wanted me to come there; I didn't want to come there. He had certain projects; I didn't like them. But he offered me this script, and I said fine and went to New York to start shooting. A strange thing happened at the start. A girl I had known in New York, just a friend of a friend, called my wife to go out to lunch; and she told her, "I don't think Bob should make *Garment Jungle* until he gets it cleared." "What do you mean cleared?" She said, "Bob'll know what I mean. I can set up dinner with 'a guy'." My wife told me this story; and

I couldn't believe it, because this "guy" was Frank Costello's right hand man. So I called Cohn and he said, "That's bull shit. We've got this cleared and there's no problem." But when I went to dinner the next night with this "guy" who was very proper, very polite, terribly solicitous, he told me again, "Bob, don't make this picture. It hasn't been cleared. We'd like you to make it, no reason you shouldn't, but Mr. Cohn knows this has to be cleared." So I left for California the morning after, and I reported this to Cohn. Finally, after some hectic calls to Las Vegas, they discovered [that] a copy of the script had never been sent to be cleared. They ironed it out. But Cohn's little oversight could have caused trouble. As time went on, Cohn became more and more apprehensive about the project. And Lee Cobb was impossible. He had just come off a big triumph in "[Death of a] Salesman," he didn't want to be a rough father. He didn't want to have people dislike him. And it was necessary for him to be a tough, miserable son of a bitch, not a good guy. So every day someone or other would want me to soften the script. Then I got very sick on a Thursday night; I had the flu. Five o'clock Friday afternoon, [my agent] Ingo Preminger came up to see me and announced, "I don't know how to tell you this, but you're fired." I said, "You've got to be kidding." But I called up [Samuel] Briskin, and he wouldn't talk to me. I called up Cohn, and he wouldn't talk to me, so I figured I was fired.

Silver: What was your contractual arrangement with them that caused you to be out of work for some time?

Aldrich: Nothing. I didn't breech the contract, so they had to pay it out. They paid me and I sat home and I couldn't get a job. Now that year was over, and I could not get a job. It goes back to staying at the table. William Faulkner's the only guy I know who could go away to the back marshes of Mississippi and they'd never know the difference; he was so quiet and concealed. Anybody that stays away for a while, voluntarily or involuntarily, risks never coming back. Then somebody brought me *The Phoenix [Ten Seconds to Hell]*. I figured I might as well get out of town, so I rewrote it much to its detriment and went to Germany. I stayed [in Europe] to make *The Angry Hills* for Raymond Stross. He understood that Metro was buying film by the yard then, and Mitchum was reasonably hot. So they thought that as long as it was an hour and a half with Mitchum and some Greek scenery, it would work. Obviously, it didn't,

Silver: It was cut to that length after your cut, wasn't it?

Aldrich: Yeah. That's when they really do the old-fashioned thing. You asked me about producers. Well, the Strosses of this world just hang back there and let you work your ass of, till you're all through, and then say, "Fine. Good-bye. Thank you, very much." Your director's cut or two previews don't mean a thing. Despite whatever promises about length or final cut they made to you, they take it back then and do what they were going to do in the first place.

Silver: It makes that end title rather ironic, "Finis. A Raymond Stross Production."

Aldrich: [laughs] It certainly does.

Silver: That whole question of final cut brings to mind that scene from *Lylah Clare*, the Sheean/Zarkan negotiation at the Brown Derby. I suppose part of the irony of that scene is that for all the past problems with producers, you have often filled both roles, Sheean's and Zarkan's, producer and director.

Aldrich: The irony, it seems to me, is that the system, at best, just doesn't work. Sure a producer has to be judicious about handing one or three or five million dollars to someone; but once it's done he should have enough confidence in himself, in his own choice, to back that guy. You don't have to make him a full partner, but at least support his decisions or don't go into it. In any case, are they qualified by being close enough to that material to make a judgment about cutting, six months, a year, or a year and a half later? Let's say a rough cut runs four hours, and the director has taken that four hours down to two. Now along comes a producer who says, "Take another twenty minutes out of it." How the hell does he know what's going on, that there isn't something more valuable than the next twenty minutes in the two hours you've already taken out. John Cassavetes had me look at his new picture [*Minnie and Moskowitz*] when it was three hours long. I liked it, but my comment was "they'll cut it." To whom are you as a director going to turn the picture over to cut? Why shouldn't Cassavetes have final word over that picture?

It's not a new moan and groan. I can rattle off twenty pictures, mine included, that would be helped enormously if they were cut. But to whom are you going to entrust that task? We are in that position now with the picture that we're making ABC. Marty Baum, who up until a year ago was an agent, runs ABC. Has he, in that year, learned all there is to know about cutting? And yet I know that, when I turn the picture in, the distributor [ABC] will make changes. That doesn't make my life happy or worry-free. Because it's like having a professional who's designed a car discover that somebody's gardener is going to come along and change the position of the front wheels.

Silver: Some years after the fact, are you still dissatisfied with *The Legend of Lylah Clare?*

Aldrich: I think it has a number of flaws. I was about to bum rap Kim Novak, when we were talking about this the other day, and I realized that would be pretty unfair. Because people forget that Novak can act. I really didn't do her justice. But there are some stars whose motion picture image is so large, so firmly and deeply rooted in the public mind, that an audience comes to a movie with a preconception about that person. And that preconception makes

Opposite page, Aldrich directs George Kennedy and Kim Novak, in a scene that would require her to act like Garbo portraying Anna Christie with a German accent.

"reality," or any kind of myth that's contrary to that preconceived reality, impossible. To make this picture work, to make Lylah work, you had to be carried along into that myth. And we didn't accomplish that. Now, you know, you can blame it on a lot of things. but I'm the producer and I'm the director. I'm responsible for not communicating to that audience. *I* just didn't do it.

Silver: Perhaps the reason I'm asking about *Lylah Clare* is that I've always had the feeling it was particularly close to you as a project. You are sitting there now with a prop painting of Lylah from the movie hanging on the wall behind you.

Aldrich: Yes, I always thought that picture would work. With the exception of a change of leading ladies, I'd make the same picture, tomorrow, again. Of course, it still wouldn't make money.

Silver: Is your disappointment in it mainly financial then?

Aldrich: No. My disappointment with it is believability. I think Kim did a very good job, but she's very angry with me. I used a German voice for her during the German period, because nobody can speak with that kind of accent, they really can't. So I brought over a German actress of some repute and worked for a long time to get it done well. Of course, she was furious because, quite properly, her ego tells her that she does a good German accent. It may be good; but it's not good enough. Things like that make the difference. So audiences never believed that picture, and that's why it didn't work. You find people who like bits of it—Peter Finch or the Italian women or Borgnine—and then you'll find some who took the whole concept as an affront.

Silver: You can't help but see in it, I think, a reflection of that vulgarization which Hollywood has subjected people to. That freeze-frame at the end—the bared fangs—is genuinely savage, more savage than the whole of *The Big*

Knife and perhaps more "antisocial" or "antiestablishment" in its implications than anything in *The Dirty Dozen* for all its controversy.

Aldrich: That ending was pretty good. But you can't get too many people to agree with that, I'd agree with you. With *The Dozen* two things happened. One, Heller and I stumbled onto the dissatisfaction, particularly on the part of the younger public, with the establishment. I'd like to say we anticipated that kind of success; but we didn't really. If you read the book, however, that kind of antiauthoritarian attitudes, that point of view, isn't there; and Heller did an excellent screenplay. So we got on a wave that we never knew was coming; not a wave, a tidal wave. But we didn't see it forming.

Silver: And you made a lot of money.

Aldrich: Oh, Christ! One of the sad rewards of this business is that when money comes in that fast, some of it has to stick. Somebody has to pay you.

Silver: What about the problems with *The Killing of Sister George*? Did you see them coming? Would that even be a problem, an "X" rating, if you made it today?

Aldrich: Well, I'd have to suggest that you rephrase your question. "Is that an 'X' today?" depends on who you make it for. If you made it for Metro, Mr. Valenti and his hatchet men would go and say that it was a family picture, you'd probably get a "G" for it. If you made it as an independent, it would probably still be an "X." They might consider it for an "R" or "GP," for a minute.

Silver: Is it just that you had the bad fortune of being one of the first to arrive at the ratings board—after all that pre-publicity—before they realized that if all the pictures like *Sister George* were "X's" that they would end up with too many on their hands?

Aldrich: A number of things happened. It's tiresome to think about them; not because this question isn't welcome, but because I didn't know who to fight. You know that we tried to get ABC to join us in a suit against the [Los Angeles] *Times*, in a suit against KMPC [a Los Angeles radio station], but they wouldn't. So we went ahead and sued the *Times* anyway, by ourselves; and we asked the Federal Communications Commission to revoke the license of KMPC, which they didn't do. Two years have gone by, and you find Valenti battling the press up in San Francisco and paraphrasing word for word our indictment about censorship of movies, which is a little ludicrous. But the big problem was that the majors never believed they could make profitable "X" pictures. They jumped to the conclusion that "X" was a dirty letter. Once *Midnight Cowboy* came out and was very profitable and won awards, they wanted to take the "dirty" label off. So they drew up a whole new bill of particulars. Everything that was made by a major studio for a cost of at least X amount of dollars suddenly had some redeeming, "artful" feature and became

an "R." I guess we're the only business in the world that has retroactive legis-
lation of that sort. But we had finished production on *Sister George* before
those abc's of the "X's" were out. People think that Preminger changed the
Code. That's bull shit. The Code was changed on narcotics when Fox bought
Hatful of Rain. It was changed on profanity when Warners made *Virginia
Woolf* and didn't care. It was changed on sex when Metro won that re-rating
on *Ryan's Daughter*. The majors, the fellows in the club, they pay the dues
and they prescribe the rules. Eventually, ABC behaved a lot better over *Sister
George*'s rating than they did about economic issues.

Silver: In that economic context, how about an old project such as *Too Late
the Hero*, which you've said had been lying around in a drawer for a decade
and which quite a few people had probably pegged—correctly as it turned
out—as a loser, how does it still come to be made?

Aldrich: When you've had a big, big success, people who should know better
lose their perspective about your infallibility. Right away it's "Let's make another one!" Let's go back and buy the first novel of some guy who, ten novels
later, wrote a hit. That's ludicrous. You may have better projects, but you
can't sell better projects, you really can't. ABC wanted another *Dirty Dozen*.
The only other "Dirty Dozen" I had in the drawer was one I wrote in 1959
with Bob Sherman. So we pulled out *Too Late the Hero*, and they thought it
was sensational. So did Metro. But at Metro they wanted a budget of nine million seven [hundred thousand] to make it, which was too high. Well, we'd had
Lylah Clare in the store for a couple of years, and Metro was in a buying
mood, so I said, "What about something like *The Big Knife*?" And we made
Lylah Clare. Now I think we have some extraordinarily good, fresh projects.
But *Hero* was less than successful, so now all our properties are scrutinized at
a whole other level. It can get terribly sad, but it's true that your opinion is
only as good as your last picture.

Silver: You've got *The Grissom Gang* roughly assembled now. Are you satisfied with it at this stage?

Aldrich: I think it's a good picture. It's a personal story, but yet it has quite a
bit of violence. Still, I think it's quite sentimental.

Silver: How did you come to pick Scott Wilson for the picture?

Aldrich: It was like a play-off in the National League. The system is that we
had a nomination, then ABC had one, then we had one, then they had one,
until we had exhausted a series of three each. We had a notion of who they
wanted and who they didn't. I'd seen Scott Wilson in several pictures and
liked him; and of all those that ABC would be likely to nominate, he was the
least objectionable. So we played the cards; we nominated someone that we
knew they did not like to knock off someone that they really wanted. And
again it was really luck. He is much better than the actor we originally wanted

for the picture. But if ABC had put him out of sequence, nominated him in another position, we'd have ended up with somebody else. He would have been knocked off. *The Grissom Gang* may or may not make money. It's not a commercially oriented picture. It won't make money for us because it's cross-collateralized back against our lawsuit with ABC.

We had a big western called *Rebellion*. It was at the very heart of our law-suit with them. It was *Vera Cruz* with balls, energy, and real sex. They approved the project. They had a major commitment; and we came up with a budget of seven million dollars. Now, I don't blame them for not wanting to make the picture for seven million. I do blame them for not honoring their contracts for not trying to find a way out, a compromise solution. We spent a lot of time preparing that picture. Seven million was too big a risk for them to take on that material, from their position. And yet I think just as many people will go broke trying to make *Easy Rider* sequels, for a little money, as went broke trying to follow up *Sound of Music*. That's studio management. As with *Greatest Mother* or *Too Late the Hero*, you have to be terribly careful about not making a picture that will be affected by a change in the audience's frame-work of acceptance between the time you start and the time you finish. That's an enormous problem. Whatever you say today risks strongly going out of date in the fifteen month time-lag between the start of shooting and release.

Silver: So you make *The Grissom Gang*, a 30s picture.

Aldrich: That has something to do with it. Yes.

Silver: How does this affect future projects. Does this mean it's time for *Genghis Khan's Bicycle*?

Aldrich: [laughs] We lost the rights to that. I think it's being made into a musical.

Silver: *Vengeance is Mine*, the gangster script with Bezzerides?

Aldrich: He and I were paid by a couple of Italians who have been suing us ever since, so I guess that's out, too. That was the story of a mythical [Lucky] Luciano set in Sicily during World War II. The projects we have on the fire at the moment, in order of likelihood, are *Rage of Honor; What Ever Happened to Dear Daisy?; Coffee, Tea, or Me; Billy Two Hats; The Crowded Bed;* some-thing tentatively called *The Plaza*.

Silver: You've hung on to some projects for a long time and gotten quite passionate about them. You said in an old interview, "Taras Bulba is me." How did you feel when it ended up sold to Yul Brynner, the one actor you didn't want?

Aldrich: You know I sold it to another guy. That's when I came back from England with no money at all, when the tax guys put a sign up on my house to sell it. That's when I cashed in those three pictures I mentioned earlier to United Artists for twenty grand. We had no money. I had breakfast most

Opposite, Aldrich directs Robert Lansing and Kim Darby in a scene cut from the final version of *The Grissom Gang*, Barbara Blandish's suicide.

mornings about 6:30 at a restaurant nobody knew was open in the morning; but this guy, Joe Kaufman, came in there two or three mornings in a row. I should have been smart enough to know that this bum would never get up at 6:30 in the morning for nothing. The third morning, he asked me, "What did you ever do with that script, *Taras Bulba*?" I said, "I still have it." Then he asked, " You want to sell it?"; and I said, "Sure." "How much do you want for it?" I said, "I'll tell you what I've got into it: $61,491." It was some odd number like that, which I happened to know exactly. "How do you know that?" Well, the tax guy had been adding up all my assets to see what they were worth, and that's what he was counting for this picture. "Would you sell it for that?" I needed money, so "Sure!" The next day, he was there saying, "I've got the money. I'll give you an advance check for $15,000." This was fascinating. We had a buyer and a seller, four lawyers, *and* a tax guy. We drew up a contract in which he had to pay me $15,000 then pay the government the balance in installments, so I sold *Taras Bulba* to him. It was quarterly payments, and three months later a second check came to me to endorse over to the government; and it was signed by Harold Hecht. Joe bought it for him or sold it to him.

Silver: Maybe he read that interview. [laughter] What ever happened to *The Greatest Mother of 'Em All?*

Aldrich: We made that mini-movie with Peter Finch, Alexandra Hay, and Ann Sothern just at the time that everybody was getting very sanctimonious about sex pictures. It's a half-hour movie, like a long trailer, and I think it's pretty good. But nobody wanted this thing about a broken-down Hollywood director who found a sixteen-year-old girl and shacked up with her and had a heart attack, etc. We spent $90,000 getting it mounted to show people what it was all about, which I thought was an ingenious piece of showmanship; but nobody else agreed with me. I also think that it was very stupid timing. If I had been bright enough, I would have realized that the cycle had passed. Whereas

a year before that picture would have sold like hot cakes. So no more war pictures and no more "Hollywood" pictures for a while. I'm a sucker for them. I can't find any and I'm trying not to look. *Greatest Mother* was in the original ABC package. The turnaround on it, because of the ABC advance, would cost us a fortune. Without numbers that make sense, we'll probably let it drown.

Silver: What is *Rage of Honor* about?

Aldrich: It's another period picture, about an aging cowboy set in Northern California in 1929. It's collision between two eras, between his attitude and mores and the industrial progress of a small town. I think it's the best script we have.

Silver: Any cast in mind?

Aldrich: Well, anybody that reads it says John Wayne; and I've got to admit that Wayne could be marvelous. But I think the guy should be Joel McCrea. I don't know if McCrea is bankable or if he'd come out of retirement. Right now nothing is bankable, so you don't have to ask that question?

We'll probably change the title on *Aunt Alice*. As a matter of fact, I went to New York last week to give it to Helen Hayes, and we did change the title. I know she's not about to play in *that* kind of melodrama. They're fun, and they've always been profitable, but it's tough getting that kind of picture made today.

Coffee, Tea, or Me is from the pocket book about "stewardi." Not a single person likes our screenplay except me. Everybody says the book is great, the idea is great, but the script stinks. I don't agree. What we've done is taken the Doris Day formula and flipped it. We've got a virgin who's doing everything she can to get laid, because all the other stewardesses are swingers and having a great time; but she can't. No matter what happens, something always stops her. I respect these other opinions and start thinking, "Jesus Christ, I must be wrong." Then I take it home and read it again and I laugh myself to death, I think it's hysterical. So nobody likes it except me.

Billy Two Hats is a Western, a kind of small, personal, simple statement Western. A lot smaller in concept and budget than *Rebellion* was.

Silver: Your production budgets have never seemed inflated, yet you got criticized for making *The Dirty Dozen* and not contributing to Bobby Seale's defense fund.

Aldrich: And I noticed in the trade papers yesterday that something like 81 directors, 45 writers, and 78 composers condemn the industry for not freeing Angela Davis. These people don't think there's any gray area about the justice involved. I know that sounds conservative, but I don't mean to be. If I weren't wearing both hats, I'd like to make a picture that would free Angela Davis. But I don't want the producer part of me to lose so much money that he can't make the next one.

Selected Bibliography

This Selected Bibliography is based on the extensive listings in <u>Robert Aldrich, a guide to references and resources</u>. It has been updated to include material published since that book appeared. It has also been abridged by removing most of the short newspaper and trade periodical pieces that chronicled Aldrich's projects and other professional endeavors and reviews of individual films. Annotations are given only when on pieces by Aldrich or when the subject matter is not clear from the title.

Books:

Arnold, Edwin T. and Miller, Eugene L. <u>The Films and Career of Robert Aldrich</u>. Knoxville, Tennessee: University of Tennessee Press, 1986.

Cohen-Solal, Annie. <u>Sartre, a Life</u>. New York: Pantheon Books, 1987.

Combs, Richard, ed. <u>Robert Aldrich</u>. London: British Film Institute, 1978.

Coursodon, Jean Pierre. <u>American Directors</u>. Volume II. New York: McGraw-Hill, 1983. Pages 1-11.

Flynn, Thomas R. <u>Sartre and Marxist Existentialism</u>. Chicago: University of Chicago Press, 1984.

Gallafent, Edward. Essay on *Kiss Me Deadly* in <u>The Book of Film Noir</u>. Ian Cameron, ed. New York: Continuum, 1993.

Higham, Charles. <u>The Celluloid Muse: Hollywood Directors Speak</u>. London: Angus and Robertson Ltd., 1969. Pages 21-40. [Interview; Filmography, page 255.]

Lowry, Ed. Essay in <u>International Dictionary of Films and Filmmakers, Volume II</u>. New York: Perigee, 1984. Pages 7-9.

Mahéo, Michel. Robert Aldrich. Paris: Rivages, 1987.

Micha, René. Robert Aldrich. Brussels: Club du Livre de Cinéma, 1957.

Parish, James Robert and Pitts, Michael R. with Gregory Mank. Hollywood on Hollywood. Metuchen, New Jersey: Scarecrow Press, 1978.

Piton, Jean-Pierre. Robert Aldrich. Paris: Edilig, 1985.

Sadoul, Georges. Dictionnaire des Cineastes. Paris: Editions de Seuil, 1965. p. 8-9.

Sarris Andrew. The American Cinema: Directors and Directions, 1929-1968. New York: E.P. Dutton and Company, 1968. p. 64-65.

_____. Confessions of a Cultist. New York: Simon and Schuster, 1971.

Shadouin, Jack. Dreams and Dead Ends. Cambridge, Massachusetts: MIT Press, 1977. Pages 265-284. [Chapter on Kiss Me Deadly.]

Sherman, Eric, ed. Directing the Film: Film Directors on Their Art. Boston: Little, Brown, 1976.

Silver, Alain and Ward, Elizabeth. Robert Aldrich, a guide to references and resources. Boston: G.K. Hall, 1979.

Tavernier, Bertrand and Coursodon, Jean-Pierre. 50 Years of American Cinema. Paris: Editions Nathan, 1991. Pages 241-243.

Telotte, J.P. Voices in the Dark: The Narrative Patterns of Film Noir. Urbana and Chicago: University of Illinois Press, 1989. Pages 198-215. [Chapter on Kiss Me Deadly.]

Wilson, Colin. The Outsider. New York: Delta, 1956.

Periodicals:

Aldrich, Robert. "American Report." Cahiers du Cinéma, Nos. 150-151 (December, 1964), pages 24-25. [Response to five questions from Cahiers about current projects and working problems.]

_____. "Can You Ask a Business To Lose Money?" New York Herald Tribune, August 25, 1965, page 31. [Questions lack of alternative funding sources for unusual films.]

_____. "The Care and Feeding of Baby Jane." New York Times, November 4, 1962. [On preproduction and shooting problems with Whatever Happened to Baby Jane?.]

_____. "Mes Deboires en Europe." Cahiers du Cinéma, No. 107 (May, 1960), pages 2-6. [Translation of Films and Filming pieces on the difficulties of studio work in the United States and freelance work overseas.]

_____. "Director's Formula for a Happy Cast." Los Angeles Times, February 7, 1966, pages 13, 29. [On The Dirty Dozen and working with actors.]

_____. "Filmmaking in an Era of New Liberality." Los Angeles *Times*, December 15, 1968. [On *The Killing of Sister George.*]

_____. "The High Price of Independence." *Films and Filming*, Volume 4, No. 9 (June, 1958), pages 7, 35. [On the difficulties of studio work in the United States and freelance work overseas.]

_____. "Hollywood...Still an Empty Tomb." *Cinema*, Volume 1, No. 6 (May-June, 1965), pages 4-6, 28. [Discussion of the "Hollywood" movie and the emphasis on commercial success.]

_____. "Impressions of Russia." *Action*, Volume 6, No. 4 (July-August, 1971), pages 7-10. [On a visit to Russia through a program organized by the Directors Guild.]

_____. "Learning from My Mistakes." *Films and Filming*, Volume 6, No. 9 (June, 1960), pages 2-6. [On production problems with *Ten Seconds to Hell* and *The Angry Hills.*]

_____. "The New Audience." [Unpublished: on the change in what an audience expects from a filmmaker.]

_____. "Sex and Violence Justified." *America*, No. 92 (May, 1955). [Discussion of controversial elements in *Kiss Me Deadly.*]

_____. "TV Techniques In Feature Filmmaking." *TV Review*, No. 2739 (March 31, 1960), pages 3, 10. [How to shoot features quickly.]

_____. "What Ever Happened to American Movies?" *Sight and Sound*, Volume XXXIII, No. 1 (Winter, 1963-64), pages 21-22. [On his plans to cross-collateralize comercial ventures with less popular "art" films.]

_____. "What Ever Happened to the Majors?" [Unpublished: on the loss of vitality at the major studios because of high overhead and wasteful methods.]

_____. "Why I Bought My Own Studio." *Action*, Volume 4, No. 1 (January-February, 1969), pages 7-10. [Economic reasons for buying his own facility.]

Aldrich, Robert and Bertolucci, Bernando. "Dialogue." *Action*, Volume 9, No. 2 (March-April, 1974), pages 23-25. [Transcript of a conversation on censorship.]

Anon. "Aldrich's ABC Slate Doubled to 8 Films." *Daily Variety*, January 28, 1969, page 1.

_____. "Bob Aldrich to Make 4 Pix for Palomar." *Daily Variety*, October 3, 1967, pages 1, 11.

_____. "'Czar Beats A Committee,' Sez Aldrich Who Yens 'Scope'." *Variety*, June 21, 1967, pages 7, 28. [On upcoming deal with unnamed distributor, acting as your own producer, and the studio "czar" system as preferable to the "committee" system.]

_____. "No Middle-aged Hitchcock." *Variety*, January 20, 1963. [After finishing *Hush...Hush, Sweet Charlotte*, Aldrich wants a change from suspense melodramas.]

_____. "Robert Aldrich 1918-1983." Directors Guild of America *News*, Volume 8, No. 1 (January, 1984), pages 1-3. [Short career piece and excerpts from memorial service.]

Avrech, R. "Lookback: *Ulzana's Raid*." *Millimeter*, June, 1975, page 41.

Beaupre, Lee. "Bob Aldrich: Candid Maverick." *Variety*, June 21, 1973, page 24. [Discusses upcoming *Emperor*, removal from *The Yakuza*, and the failure of ABC pictures.]

Bitsch, Charles. "Bio-filmography de Robert Aldrich." *Cahiers du Cinéma* (November, 1956), No. 64, pages 59-60.

Bitsch, Charles and Tavernier, Bertrand. "La Fonction de Producer." *Cahiers du Cinéma*, Nos. 150-151 (December, 1964), pages 78-84. [Interview about Aldrich's experiences in Europe.]

Blevins, Winfred. "A Fine New Studio on a Fine Old Site." Los Angeles *Herald Examiner*, August 14, 1968.

Borde, Raymond. "Un Cinéaste Non-conformiste: Robert Aldrich." *Les Temps Modernes*, No. 24 (May, 1956), pages 1681-1696. [Career article from a Marxist/Existentialist perspective.]

Brion, Patrick; Mahéo, Michel; Rabourdin, Dominique; Simsolo, Noël. "Dossier—auteur Robert Aldrich." *Cinema 84*, No. 302 (February, 1984). [Interview.]

Byrne, Bridget. "Robert Aldrich: 'I'm a Better Director Than People Think I Am.'" Los Angeles *Herald Examiner*, October 11, 1970. [Discusses legal problems with ABC and *The Grissom Gang*.]

Byron, Stuart. "'I Can't Get Jimmy Carter to See My Movie,' Robert Aldrich Talks." *Film Comment*, Volume 13, No. 2, (March-April, 1977), pages 46-52. [Interview.]

Calendo, John. "Robert Aldrich Says Life Is Worth Living..." *Andy Warhol's Interview*. August, 1973, pages 29-33. [Interview.]

Cates, Gilbert. "Robert Aldrich 1918-1983." Directors Guild of America *News*, Volume 8, No. 1 (January, 1984), pages 1-2. [Transcript of speech.]

Cameron, Ian and Shivas, Mark. "Interview and Filmography." *Movie*, No. 8. pages 8-11.

Chabrol, Claude. "Evolution du Film Policier." *Cahiers du Cinéma*, Nos. 54 (December, 1955), pages 27-33.

_____. "Directed By:" *Cahiers du Cinema*, Nos. 150-151 (December, 1964), pages 113-114.

Champlin, Charles. "Aldrich Weighs Hollywood's Future." Los Angeles *Times*, August 24, 1969.

_____. "Aldrich's Safari in Mogul Country." Los Angeles *Times Calendar*, August 25, 1974, pages 1, 37-39.

_____. "Aldrich: He Spreads the Credits Around." Los Angeles *Times Calendar*, June 26, 1977, pages 1, 13, 45.

Combs, Richard. "Worlds Apart: Aldrich Since The Dirty Dozen." *Sight and Sound*, Volume 45, No. 2 (Spring, 1976), pages 112-115.

_____. "Aldrich's Twilight." *Sight and Sound*, Volume 46, No. 3 (Summer, 1977), pages 186-187.

Derry, Charles. "The Horror of Personality." *Cinefantastique*, Volume 3, No. 4 (Fall, 1974), page 15-19. [Interview and article.]

Durgnat, Raymond. "The Apotheosis of Va-va-voom." *Motion*, Volume 1, No, 3 (Spring, 1962), pages 30-34.

Duval, Bruno. "Aldrich le Rebelle." *Image et Son*, No. 306 (May, 1976), pages 25-44. [Career analysis.]

Eyles, Allen. "The Private War of Robert Aldrich." *Films and Filming*, Volume 13, No. 12 (September, 1967), pages 4-9. [Based on an interview about *The Dirty Dozen*.]

Eyquem, Oliver. "Bio-filmographie de Robert Aldrich." *Positif*, No. 182 (June, 1976), pages 18-24.

Fagin, Steve. "Robert Aldrich."*Film Reader*,1, 1975, pages 70-72, 119. [Brief career analysis and filmography.]

Fenin, George. "Interview with Robert Aldrich." *Film Culture*, Volume 2, No. 4 [#10.] (July-August, 1956), pages 8-9.

Flynn, Hazel. "Aldrich Wants To Make Dream Film." Hollywood *Citizen News*, October 31, 1963.

Gazano, Robert and Casso, Manuel. "L'homme d'Aldrich." *Cinéma*, No. 258 (June, 1980), pages 20-33.

Grant, Lee. "Songs of Discord from 'The Choirboys'." Los Angeles *Times*, December 7, 1977 [Details Joseph Wambaugh's dissatisfaction with Aldrich's adaptation of his novel The Choirboys.]

Greenburg Joel. "Interview with Robert Aldrich." *Sight and Sound*, Volume 37, No. 1 (Winter, 1968-69), pages 8-13.

Harwood, Jim. "WG Demands 'Jurisdictional Piracy,' So Says the Directors Guild, Adding That It Will Strike If Producers Accede to Scribes." *Daily Variety*, January 20, 1977, page 1.

Head, Anne. "Aldrich's long term dream project." *Screen International*, July 9, 1983. [Update on *Kinderspiel*.]

Henstell, Bruce and Silke, James, eds. *Dialogue on Film, No. 2, Robert Aldrich*, 1972. [Abridged transcript of a seminar with Aldrich on *The Dirty Dozen* and directing methods held November 2, 1971 at the American Film Institute Center for Advanced Film Studies, Beverly Hills. Complete transcript is available at the Feldman Library at the Center.]

Higham, Charles. "Robert Aldrich."*Action*, Volume 9, No. 6 (November-December, 1974), pages 16-21. [Interview.]

Hoberman, J. "The Great Whatzit." *The Village Voice*, March 15, 1994, page 43.

Holden, Stephen. "A Brash Outsider Inside Hollywood." New York Times, Match 11, 1994. pages C1, C16.

Jarvie Ian. "Hysteria and Authoritarianism in the Films of Robert Aldrich," Film Culture, No. 22 (Summer, 1961), pages 95-111.

Krueger, Eric. "Robert Aldrich's Attack!." Journal of Popular Film, Volume 2, No.3 (Spring, 1973), pages 262-276.

Legrand, Gérard. "Robert Aldrich et l'incomplétude du nihilism." Positif, No. 182 (June, 1956).

Levin, Gerry. "DGA Comes Out Swinging on New Contract Demands." Hollywood Reporter, May 19, 1977, page 1.

Loynd, Ray. "Director Robert Aldrich: Emperor of an Empty Studio." Los Angeles Herald Examiner, July 1, 1973, pages D1, D6.

Mann, Roderick. "Robert Aldrich—No More Mr. Nice Guy." Los Angeles Times Calendar, October 11, 1981, page 25.

Masson, Alain. "L'incroyable Aldrich." Positif, No. 275 (January, 1984).

Mayersberg, Paul. "Robert Aldrich," Movie, No. 8 (April, 1963), pages 4-5. [Interview and article.]

McBride, Joe. "DGA's Threats and Olive Branches—Guild Prez Aldrich Unveils Preliminary Positions for AMPTP." Daily Variety, May 19, 1977.

McCarthy, Todd. "Robert Aldrich, Director, Producer, Dies in Hollywood at 65." Daily Variety, December 7, 1983, pages 1, 22.

McGilligan, Pat. "Aldrich: Movies' Battling Director." Boston Globe, June 19, 1977.

Mills, Bart. "Last Gleaming of Admiral X—Overlay of a Crackup." Los Angeles Times Calendar,June 6, 1976, page 36. [Based on interview with Aldrich about Twilight's Last Gleaming.]

Moullet, Luc. "Le Poete et le Geometre." Cahiers du Cinéma, No. 101 (November, 1959), pages 53-54. [Article on Ten Seconds to Hell.]

Murphy, A.D. "Bob Aldrich's Dream Deal." Daily Variety, January 4, 1968, pages 1, 10.

Murphy, A.D. and Setlowe, Rick. "Aldrich Plots Film Combine." Daily Variety, July 10, 1970, page 1, 14.

Musco, Don. "Aldrich Dedicates New Lot for His Own, Rental Pictures." Hollywood Reporter, August 12, 1968, page 4.

Odets, Clifford. "In Praise of a Maturing Industry." New York Times, November 6, 1955. [Discusses The Big Knife and Aldrich.]

Ornstein, Bill. "Associates and Aldrich Co. Hopes To Make 4-6 Pictures Per Year." Hollywood Reporter, April 24, 1967, page 1.

Powers, James. "Dialogue on Film: Robert Aldrich." American Film, No. 4 (November, 1978), pages 51-62. [Abridged version of A.F.I. seminar.]

Rabourdin, D., ed. "Robert Aldrich," *Cinéma*, No. 302 (February, 1984), pages 15-37.

Reid, John Howard, ed. "George Addison interviews Robert Aldrich." *Film Index* (Australia), No. 6.

Ringel, Harry. "Robert Aldrich: the Director as Phoenix." *Take One*, (September, 1974). [Career article.]

_____. "Up to Date with Robert Aldrich." *Sight and Sound*, Volume 43, No. 3 (Summer, 1974), pages 166-169. [Interview.]

Rivette, Jacques. "On Revolution." *Cahiers du Cinéma*, No. 54 (Christmas, 1955), p. 18.

Robinson, George. "Three by Aldrich." *The Velvet Light Trap*, No. 11 (Winter, 1974), pages 46-49. [Analysis of *Attack!*, *The Big Knife*, *Kiss Me Deadly*.]

Sarris, Andrew. "Whatever Happened to Bobby Aldrich?" *The Village Voice*, October 28, 1981, page 49. [Review of *...All the Marbles* and career evaluation.]

Sauvage, Pierre. "Aldrich Interview." *Movie*, No. 23 (Winter, 1976-1977), pages 50-64. [Interview.]

_____. "Entretien avec Robert Aldrich." *Positif*, No. 182 (June, 1976), pages 8-17. [Translation of *Movie* Interview.]

Sequin, Louis. "Racket dans la Couture." *Positif*, No. 29 (July, 1957), page 43. [Article on *The Garment Jungle*.]

Setlowe, Rick. "Bob Aldrich and Dick Lester Have Differing Views of War Films." *Daily Variety*, October 24, 1967, page 6.

_____. "'Grissom Gang' 4th And Probably Last Film Aldrich Will Make For ABC." *Daily Variety*, June 4, 1970, pages 1, 10.

Sharp, Alan. "White Man Unforks Tongue for Ulzana." Los Angeles *Times*, May 14, 1972.

Silver, Alain. "Mr. Film Noir Stays at the Table." *Film Comment*, Volume 8, No. 1 (Spring, 1972), pages 14-23. [Interview and Bio-filmography.]

_____. "*Kiss Me Deadly*: Evidence of A Style." *Film Comment*, Volume 11, No. 2 (March/April, 1975), pages 24-30.

Simon, John. "The Star Spangled Boner." *New York*, February 14, 1977. [Review of *Twilight's Last Gleaming* and career evaluation.]

Steritt, David. "Films." Los Angeles *Herald-Examiner California Living*, May 30, 1976, pages 4-5. [Brief Interview.]

Tailleur, Roger. "Avènement du Cinema Américain." *Positif*, (May 16, 1956), pages 11-24.

Telotte, J.P. "Talk and Trouble, *Kiss Me Deadly*'s Deadly Discourse." *Journal of Popular Film*, No.2, 1985, pages 69-79.

Thomas, Kevin. "Major Independent: Touch of Film Past at Studio Dedication." Los Angeles *Times*, August 12, 1968.

Truffaut, François. "Interview with Robert Aldrich." *Cahiers du Cinéma*, No. 64 (November, 1956), pages 2-11.

_____. "Interview with Robert Aldrich." *Cahiers du Cinéma*, No. 82 (April, 1958), pages 4-10.

Tusher, William. "Aldrich Challenges Valenti." *Film and Television Daily*, December 18, 1968, pages 1, 9. [Concerning the "X" Rating given *The Killing of Sister George* by the MPPA.]

_____. "Aldrich versus the System." *Film and Television Daily*, February 4, 1969, pages 1, 6. [On lawsuits over *The Killing of Sister George*.]

_____. "'Twilight's' and Controversy: They Wanted It and Got It."*Daily Variety*, January 20, 1977, page 1. [Discusses the political controversy over *Twilight's Last Gleaming*.]

Vernon, Scott. "Aldrich: Blunt, Successful." Los Angeles *Herald Examiner*, July 12, 1970.

Wilmington, Michael. "Goodbye to Slam-Bang Robert Aldrich." *L.A. Weekly*, December 23-29, 1983, pages 45-46.

Windaler, Robert. "Interview with Robert Aldrich." New York *Times*, September 3, 1967.

Notes

Biography

1. Pierre Sauvage, "Aldrich Interview." *Movie*, Winter, 1976-1977, p. 56. [NOTE: The quotes are from Pierre Sauvage's typescript transcription of the interview and may vary slightly from the referenced published version.]

2. Letter from Aldrich to attorney Lee Steiner dated December 5, 1966.

3. Appendix, p. 345. [NOTE: An edited version of this interview appeared as "Mr. Film Noir Stays at the Table," *Film Comment*, Spring, 1972. This particular quote was part of the excised material. Pages references are to the longer version reproduced as an Appendix in this book.]

4. Letter from Aldrich to studio head Harry Cohn dated August 15, 1957.

5. Sauvage, p. 56.

6. Ray Loynd, "Director Robert Aldrich: Emperor of an Empty Studio, " Los Angeles *Herald Examiner*, July 1, 1973, p. D6.

7. Unpublished typescript of an interview with Aldrich conducted some time in 1967 for the use of Jerry Pam, Aldrich's publicist, p. 23.

8. Sauvage, p. 56.

9. Charles Higham, "Robert Aldrich," *Action*, November-December, 1974, p. 18

10. Gil Cates speaking at the Directors Guild memorial tribute to Robert Aldrich on December 7, 1983.

11. Edwin T. Arnold and Eugene L. Miller, The Films and Career of Robert Aldrich, Knoxville, Tennessee: University of Tennessee Press, 1986, p. 7.

12. Loynd, p. D6.

13. Pam, p. 24.

14. Ibid, p. 25.

15. Aldrich speaking at DGA Milestone tribute in August, 1979, quoted by Gil Cates at DGA Aldrich tribute.

16. Pam, p. 24.

17. Michel Ciment, Conversations with Losey, London and New York: Methuen, 1985, p. 124

18. Ciment, p, 123

19. Appendix, p. 343.

20. Higham, p. 18 and, identifying Clarence Brown by name, Loynd, p. D6

21. Ciment, p. 125.

22. Appendix, p. 352.

23. Ciment, p. 124

24. Norman Lloyd, Stages: of Life in Theatre, Film and Television, Limelight: New York, 1993, p. 130.

25. Appendix, p. 345.

26. Ibid, p. 344.

27. Idem

28. Ibid, p. 351.

29. Tape recording of a discussion between Burt Reynolds and Aldrich at a Directors Guild seminar, 1977.

30. Telephone conversation between Bernard Tabakin and Alain Silver, June 13, 1994.

31. Letter from Aldrich to playwright Clifford Odets dated May 3, 1953.

32. Higham, p. 18.

33. Robert Windaler, Burt Lancaster, New York: St Martin's, 1984, p. 79.

34. Joel Greenburg, "Interview with Robert Aldrich." *Sight and Sound*, Winter, 1968-69, p. 9.

35. Robert Aldrich, "Director's Formula for a Happy Cast." *Los Angeles Times*, February 7, 1966, p. 13.

36. Pam, pp. 10-11.

37. Sauvage, p. 58.

38. Idem

39. Appendix, p. 358.

40. Higham, p. 19.

41. Raymond Borde and Étienne Chaumeton, Panorama du Film Noir Américain, Paris: Éditions de Minuit, 1983, p. 277.

42. Appendix, p. 347.

43. Pam, p. 20

44. Appendix, p. 346.

45. Pam, p. 2.

46. Addison, p. 2,

47. Clifford Odets, "In Praise of a Maturing Industry," *New York Times*, November 6, 1955.

48. Higham, p. 19.

49. Appendix, p. 352.

50. Pam, p. 31.

51. United Artists memorandum from Arthur Krim to Seymour Peyser, cc: to Aldrich, dated June 10, 1957.

52. Idem

53. William R. Meyer, Warner Brothers Directors, New York: Arlington, 1978, p. 294.

54. Columbia Inter Office Communication from Harry Kleiner to Aldrich dated November 19, 1956.

55. Undated, unaddressed, and unattributed draft memorandum in Aldrich's file on *The Garment Center*.

56. Greenburg, p. 10.

57. Letter from Aldrich to Leon Stein, head of the New York garment workers union, dated July 10, 1957.

58. Letter from Aldrich to Harry Cohn dated August 15, 1957 .

59. Letter from Harry Cohn to Aldrich dated August 16, 1957

60. Associates and Aldrich had sued over Columbia's refusal to pay for the script costs on *Until Proven Guilty* in March, 1957 which was settled a month later. [See **Projects** section.]

61. Letter from Max Youngstein, United Artists Vice-president, to Aldrich dated August 25, 1958.

62. Robert Aldrich, "Learning from My Mistakes." *Films and Filming*, Volume 6, No. 9 (June, 1960), p. 5.

63. Appendix, p. 353.

64. Ibid, p. 349.

65. These articles overlapped somewhat in content and appeared in foriegn periodicals, the British *Films and Filming* and the French *Cahiers du Cinema*. See the Bibliography for full details.

66. Appendix, p. 359.

67. Sauvage, p. 56.

68. Letter from Aldrich quoted in Kirk Douglas, The Ragman's Son, New York: Simon & Schuster, 1988, p. 330.

69. Sauvage, p.

70. John Calendo, "Robert Aldrich Says Life Is Worth Living..." *Andy Warhol's Interview*, August, 1973, p. 33.

71. Sauvage, p. 59.

72. Ibid, p. 60.

73. Roderick Mann, "Robert Aldrich—No More Mr. Nice Guy." *Los Angeles Times Calendar*, October 11, 1981, p. 25.

74. Richard Combs, ed. <u>Robert Aldrich</u>, London: British Film Institute, 1978, p. 44.

75. Idem

76. Charles Champlin, "Aldrich: He Spreads the Credits Around." *Los Angeles Times Calendar*, June 26, 1977, p. 13.

77. Sauvage, p. 59.

78. Anon., *Hollywood Citizen-News*, June 17, 1965.

79. Robert Aldrich, "The Care and Feeding of Baby Jane." *New York Times*, November 4, 1962.

80. Letter from Aldrich to screenwriter Lukas Heller dated May 26, 1961.

81. Aldrich, "Care and Feeding."

82. Many of the facts and figures in this book are taken from the internal reports and memoranda of the Associates and Aldrich and others which were kept in Aldrich's personal files. Some, such as the "A&A CO., INC. STATISTICAL DATA - Film Distribution" report which contains the grosses and percentages cited for *What Ever Happened to Baby Jane?* and other pictures and appears to have been prepared sometime in 1965, are undated.

83. Aldrich memorandum to attorney I.N. Prinzmetal detailing the "Sinatra Breach" dated May 31, 1963.

84. The Associates and Aldrich "Literary Property Status Report" of May 18, 1963 lists nine features and one television series (none of which were ever produced) and their accumulated costs to date.

85. Randall Riese, <u>All About Bette</u>, Chicago: Contemporary, 1993, p. 237.

86. Pam, p. 33.

87. The STATISTICAL DATA report indicates a "Ratio of Gross to Negative Cost" for 1.6 to 1 for *Charlotte* and 4.6 to 1 for *Baby Jane*.

88. Hazel Flynn, "Aldrich Wants To Make Dream Film." *Hollywood Citizen News*, October 31, 1963.

89. Anon., "No Middle-aged Hitchcock," *Variety*, January 20, 1963.

90. Robert Aldrich, "Can You Ask a Business To Lose Money," *New York Herald Tribune*, August 25, 1965, p. 31.

91. Idem

92. Appendix. p. 356.

93. Letter from Aldrich to John Wayne dated October 5, 1965.

94. Letter from Aldrich to French film critic Raymond Borde dated March 10, 1956.

95. Bill Ornstein, "Associates and Aldrich Co. Hopes To Make 4-6 Pictures Per Year." *Hollywood Reporter*, April 24, 1967, p. 1.

96. Anon., "Bob Aldrich to Make 4 Pix for Palomar," *Daily Variety*, October 3, 1967, p. 11.

97. A.D. Murphy, "Bob Aldrich's Dream Deal," *Daily Variety*, January 4, 1968, p. 1.

98. Ibid, p. 10.

99. Appendix, p. 347.

100. Anon., "Aldrich Planning Distribution," *Hollywood Reporter*, December 19, 1963, p. 1; and Anon., "Full Slate," *New York Times*, November 3, 1963.

101. Anon., "Aldrich Plans Eight Films to Cost $14 Million," *Boxoffice*, November 4, 1964; and Anon., "Aldrich Has Over $250,000 Invested in Three Films," *Boxoffice*, November 14, 1964

102. Ornstein, p. 1.

103. Associates and Aldrich Inter-Office Memorandum from Gene Metcalf to Aldrich dated October 17, 1966.

104. Bruce Henstell and James Silke, eds., *Dialogue on Film, No. 2, Robert Aldrich*, 1972, p. 15.

105. Sauvage, p. 61.

106. Henstell and Silke, p. 15.

107. Appendix, p. 355.

108. Ibid, p. 356.

109. Idem

110. Anon., "Aldrich's ABC Slate Doubled to 8 Films," *Daily Variety*, January 28, 1969, p. 1.

111. Appendix, p. 357.

112. Letter from ABC to Associates and Aldrich dated April 29, 1969.

113. Appendix, p. 357.

114. Harry Ringel, "Up to Date with Robert Aldrich," *Sight and Sound*, Summer, 1974, p. 167.

115. Lee Beaupre, "ABC Films Result: 30 of 36 in Red: Total Loss $47 Mil," *Daily Variety*, May 31, 1973, p. 3

116. Army Archerd, "Just for Variety," *Daily Variety*, May 21, 1969, p. 2.

117 Rick Setlowe, "'Grissom Gang' 4th And Probably Last Film Aldrich Will Make For ABC," *Daily Variety*, June 4, 1970, p. 1.

118. Appendix, p. 358.

119. Cross-complaint by ABC Pictures Corp. filed against Associates and Aldrich with the Superior Court of the State of California for the County of Los Angeles, No, 966160, January 6, 1970, p. 10.

120. Appendix, p. 359.

121. Idem

122. Form S-1 Registration Statement for Geneve Productions Sierra Enterprises, p. 4.

123. William Morris Agency Inter-Office Correspondence from Rowland Perkins to Saw Weisbord dated July 15, 1970.

124. Letter from Richard Zanuck, then Senior Executive Vice President at Warner Bros., to Aldrich dated August 2, 1971.

125. Letter from Aldrich to Peter Crouch dated June 16, 1971.

126. Pam, p. 7.

127. Anon., "Marvin Set for 'Emperor'," Los Angeles Herald-Examiner, February 23, 1972, p. B-10.

128. Marshall Fine, Bloody Sam, The Life and Films of Sam Peckinpah, New York: Donald I. Fine, 1991, p. 223.

129. Ringel, p. 169.

130. Telephone conversation between Paul Schrader and Alain Silver, May 18, 1994.

131. Stuart Byron, "'I Can't Get Jimmy Carter to See My Movie' Robert Aldrich Talks," Film Comment, March-April, 1977, p. 50.

132. Idem

133. Lee Beaupre, "Aldrich Philosophizes On Biz Where You're 'Only As Good As You Last Pic'," Daily Variety, June 21, 1973, p. 3

134. Idem

135. Letter from Aldrich to John Calley at Warner Bros. dated June 27, 1974.

136. Idem

137. Loynd, p. D1.

138. Anon., "Aldrich Studios Sold to Video Cassette," Daily Variety, July 3, 1973.

139. Dialogue on Film, p. 19.

140. Letter from Aldrich to screenwriter Leon Griffiths dated Septmber 7, 1973.

141. Pam. p. 27.

142. Higham, p. 20.

143. Sauvage, typescript p. 51 [cut from version published in Movie]

144. Byron, p. 47.

145. Letter from Aldrich to attorney Eric Weissmann dated August 24, 1976.

146. Memorandum entitled "A Not So Brief Brief Concerning Some of the Reasons Why Lorimar Must Pay Aldrich Additional Compensation Now" dated August 5, 1976, p. 1.

147. Ibid, p. 7.

148. Letter from Aldrich to George Chasin dated August 24, 1976.

149. Adelson quoted in an Aldrich Company Inter-Office Memorandum from William Aldrich to Robert Aldrich dated October 5, 1976.

150. Champlin, p. 13.

151. Draft of a letter from Aldrich to Al Ruddy undated but written in October, 1975, pp. 2-3.

152. Anon., "Allied Pumping $3.5 Mil into 'Gleaming' Hype," Daily Variety, January 20, 1977, p. 34.

153. Aldrich/Reynolds seminar.

154. Champlin, p. 13.

155. Idem

156. Anon., "Bob Aldrich Says 'Twilight's' Went Through Seven Scripts On Way To Final Version," Daily Variety, January 20, 1977, p. 34.

157. Pat McGilligan, "Aldrich: Movies' Battling Director" *Boston Globe*, June 19, 1977.

158. Combs, p. 42.

159. Ibid, p. 43.

160. Anon., "Aldrich Elected DGA President, Succeeds Wise," *The Hollywood Reporter*, July 1, 1975, p. 7.

161. Army Archerd, "Just for Variety," *Daily Variety*, June 15, 1977, p. 3.

162. Adele Field, ed., DGA Directory of Members 94, Los Angeles: Directors Guild of America, 1994, p. 18.

163. Byron, p. 49.

164. Tabakin telephone conversation, June 13, 1994.

165. Unpublished DGA Oral History of Joe Youngerman interviewed by David Shepard and Ira Skutch.

166. Letter from attorney Aldrich to attorney Eric Weissmann dated November 2, 1979.

167. Letter from Martin Baum [as Aldrich's agent and not president of ABC Palomar] to Aldrich dated May 21, 1979.

168. Unmailed letter from Aldrich to Eric Weissmann dated October 18, 1979.

169. Weissmann letter, November 2, 1979.

170. Jim Harwood, "Failure To Inform Director Aldrich of 'Arctic' Costs Ruddy and Chow 45G," *Daily Variety*, April 18, 1980, p. 1.

171. Letter from Aldrich to Eric Weissmann dated August 24, 1976. 172. Mann, p. 25.

173. Idem

174. Appendix, p. 360.

175. Jeffrey Wells, "Peter Falk & Robert Aldrich Tell It Straight," *The Film Journal*, October 19, 1981, p. 10.

176. Flynn.

177. Anne Head, "Aldrich's long term dream project." *Screen International*, July 9, 1983.

178. Idem

179. Mann, p. 25.

180. Anon., "'Czar Beats A Committee,' Sez Aldrich Who Yens 'Scope'." *Variety*, June 21, 1967, p. 7.

181. Letter from Aldrich to Ted Soderberg at 20th Century-Fox dated May 4, 1973.

182. This and following observations by her are taken from a conversation with Adell Aldrich, September 21, 1994.

183. Letter from Aldrich to Losey quoted in David Caute, Joseph Losey, A Revenge on Life, New York: Oxford University Press, 1994, p. 384.

184. Arnold and Miller, p. 164.

185. Sauvage, p. 64.

186. Raymond Borde, "Un Cinéaste Non-conformiste: Robert Aldrich." *Le Temps Moderne*, May, 1956, p. 1684.

187. Sauvage, p. 64.

188. Telephone conversation between Jerry Pam and Alain Silver, December 7, 1994.

189. Sauvage, p. 64

190. Wells, p. 10.

191. Pam conversation.

192. Charles Champlin, "Aldrich's Safari in Mogul Country," *Los Angeles Times*, August 25, 1974, p. 38.

Introduction

1. Bridget Byrne, "Robert Aldrich: 'I'm a Better Director Than People Think I Am'." The Los Angeles *Herald-Examiner*, October 11, 1970,

2. David Steritt, "Films." Los Angeles *Herald-Examiner California Living*, May 30, 1976, p. 4.

3. René Micha, <u>Robert Aldrich</u>, Brussels: Club du Livre de Cinéma, 1957, p. 1.

4. Letter from Raymond Borde to Aldrich dated only February, 1956, p. 1.

5. Champlin, "Mogul Country," p. 1.

6. Paul Schrader, "notes on *film noir*," *Film Comment*, Spring, 1972, p. 12.

7. Andrew Sarris, <u>The American Cinema</u>, New York: E.P. Dutton, 1968, p. 84.

8. Andrew Sarris, "What Ever Happened to Bobby Aldrich?" [Review of *All the Marbles*], *The Village Voice*, October 28, 1981.

9. Robin Wood, "Creativity and Evaluation: two *film noirs* of the '50's," *CineAction!*, No. 20/21, November, 1990. p. 19.

10. Sarris, <u>American Cinema</u>, p. 85.

11. Minty Glinch, <u>Burt Lancaster</u>, New York: Stein & Day, 1984. p. 49.

12. Wood, p. 20.

13. Sarris, <u>American Cinema</u>, p. 84.

14. Wood, p. 17.

15. Ibid, p. 9.

16. Borde, *Le Temps Moderne*, p. 1688.

17. Mike Davis, <u>City of Quartz</u>, New York: Vintage, 1992, p. 37.

18. Sauvage, p. 55.

19. Robert Aldrich, "What Ever Happened to the Major Studios." [Unpublished article written for *Esquire* Magazine]

20. Fletcher Knebel, "Hollywood: Broke—And Getting Rich," *Look* Magazine, November 30, 1970, p. 46.

21. Letter from Aldrich to Vincent Canby dated August 22, 1974.

22. Steritt, p. 4.

23. Ringel, p. 168.

24. Abraham Polonsky at the DGA Aldrich memorial.

Chapter One

1. Obviously, *The Big Leaguer* as Aldrich's feature debut would literally contain the first of his heroes. The point here is that *World For Ransom* is not only the first directorial assignment which Aldrich chose for himself but one on which he extensively rewrote the script. It was also his debut as producer (with Bernard Tabakin) and his initial teaming as a feature director with a number of those technicians who were to become regular collaborators: Joseph Biroc, photographer; William Glasgow, art director; Frank DeVol, composer; and Michael Luciano, editor.

2. Cf. Appendix, p. 350: "Milestone used to tell young hopefuls.... "

3. François Truffaut, "Interview with Robert Aldrich," *Cahiers du Cinéma*, No. 64 (November, 1956), p. 10.

Chapter Two

1. Ringel, p. 168.

2. In the original ending of *The Grissom Gang*, which Aldrich discarded after the previews, Barbara jumped from Fenner's car to drown herself in a lake. Fenner chose not to prevent her.

Chapter Three

1. It is interesting to note that the title of one of Aldrich's last, unrealized projects was the football story, *Sudden Death*.

2. Raymond Durgnat, "Paint it Black: the Family Tree of *Film Noir*," *Cinema* (U.K.), Nos. 6/7, 1970, p. 50.

3. Some contemporary commentators believed the interracial cooperation in *The Longest Yard* mirrored an aspect of the prison rebellion at Attica in 1971. *The Longest Yard*'s sympathetic treatment of the convicts may well have been Aldrich's response to the event and the act of sending in troops by his cousin, Governor Nelson Rockefeller, which Aldrich publicly decried.

Chapter Five

1. Borde and Chaumeton, p. 277.

2. A more detailed analysis of elements of style in *Kiss Me Deadly* with four dozen frame enlargements from the picture appeared in *Film Comment* (March-April, 1975). A revised and expanded version appears in Film Noir Reader (Limelight Editions, 1995).

Chapter Six

1. The term "set" here is used to designate a literal product of the sum of two parts or subsets which in dramatic terms is not merely additive but dynamic. In other words, 1 plus 1 equals 11 not 2. *The Legend of Lylah Clare* is not unique in Aldrich's work in this regard, but it offers some of the clearest examples.

2. Aldrich wrote about the portraits, most of which are only visible in the background of scenes set in the mansion, that "the paintings themselves have to be unique, genuine, authentic, and terribly, carefully done in terms of costume and composition so they look like a real integral part of the fabric of the 'once upon a time' life of Lylah and Zarkan." [Memorandum from Aldrich to Max Arnow dated March 16, 1967.] Aldrich contracted Richard Avedon to shoot the stills of Novak open which the paintings were based. [Deal Memorandum with Avedon dated May 5, 1967.]

3. Mann, p. 25.

Filmography

1. J. Hoberman, "The Great Whatzit," *The Village Voice*, March 15, 1994, p. 43.

2. Wood, p. 20.

3. Edward Gallefent, "*Kiss Me Deadly*" in The Book of Film Noir, New York: Continuum, 1993, p. 246.

4. Arnold and Miller, p. 245.

Projects

1. Letters from Aldrich to David Picker at United Artists dated June 5, 1973 (1st Sentence) and to Billy Wilder dated August 19, 1959 (2nd sentence).

2. Letter from B[en].B. Kahane of Columbia to Associates and Aldrich dated March 4, 1957.

3. Letter from director Billy Wilder to Aldrich dated August 17, 1959.

4. Letter from Harry Ackerman of CBS to Aldrich dated April 11, 1956.

5. From a television series proposal without author credit dated January 20, 1967.

6. Letter from actor Katharine Hepburn to Aldrich dated September 16, 1969.

7. Letter from Aldrich to Martin Baum [as his agent] dated March 13, 1968.

8. Draft of a "TV Sudmissions Letter" in a memorandum from Peter Nelson to Aldrich dated August 27, 1970.

9. Letter from Aldrich to Mr. and Mrs. Carlo Ponti dated January 29, 1973.

10. Letter to Leon Griffiths, September 7, 1973.

11. William Aldrich memorandum to Aldrich, October 7, 1976, p. 2.

12. Report of "Titles Registered in Behalf of the Associates and Aldrich Co., Inc. as of September 14, 1967."

13. Gene Metcalf memoranda, October 17, 1966 and June 6, 1967.

14. Arnold and Miller, pp. 229-230.

Index

As in the text, film titles are indicated in italics; novels and long-form non-fiction are in bold face. Additional detail is provided in parenthetical annotations. In the case of persons with more than one occupation, the most appropriate are listed.

Page numbers in italics indicate illustrations. Scene stills and advertising art are indexed as illustrations under each film's title; production stills of Aldrich and others at work are only indexed according to the persons in the photograph. References to entries in the Filmography, Projects, and/or Interview sections appear after the semi-colon. The pure data in the Filmography is not indexed. Only the films themselves, their alternate or original titles, illustrations, and special notes are indexed.